Economy and Society

Economy and Society: Overviews in Economic Sociology

Edited by
Alberto Martinelli and
Neil J. Smelser

SAGE Publications
London • Newbury Park • New Delhi

First published 1990

SAGE Publications Ltd
6 Bonhill Street
London EC2A 4PU

SAGE Publications Inc
2455 Teller Road
Newbury Park, California 91320

SAGE Publications India Pvt Ltd
32, M-Block Market
Greater Kailash – I
New Delhi 110 048

British Library Cataloguing in Publication Data

Economy and society: overviews in econommic sociology. –
(Sage studies in international sociology, v. 41)
1. Economics. Social aspects
I. Martinelli, Alberto II. Smelser, Neil J. (Neil Joseph)
1930–
330

ISBN 0-8039-8416-2
ISBN 0-8039-8417-0 pbk

Library of Congress catalog card number 90-52900

Filmset by Mayhew Typesetting, Bristol, Great Britain
Printed in Great Britain by J. W. Arrowsmith Ltd., Bristol

Contents

Preface

This volume, while the responsibility of the editors and authors, is in many respects a product of the Research Committee of Economy and Society of the International Sociological Association. Both of us were among the founders of that Committee, and both of us have served as Chair during the past ten years. We would like to think of the book as an expression of the mission, work and future of that Committee.

The idea for a kind of state-of-the-art volume occurred to us about the time of the World Congress of the ISA in Mexico in 1982. We discussed it among colleagues at that time, and received a generally positive response. As is almost always the case with international projects, the gestation, planning, commitment, writing, defaulting, substituting, delaying, editing and negotiating process took many years. We would not boast that we have set a record for in-embryo existence, but we have come close. It is for others to evaluate this book, but we are satisfied that its final appearance will help to consolidate the growing tradition of international research on problems of economy and society, and to contribute modestly to the quality of that tradition.

We would like to thank many for their co-operation and assistance. Our first debt is to the authors, for both their performance and their forbearance. We thank the Publications Committee of the ISA for making it an official Association publication; Stephen Barr of Sage Publications for his positive reception of the manuscript and his intelligence and sensibility in negotiating its publication; and Christine Egan, assistant to Neil Smelser, who facilitated everything with her attention to the mountains of correspondence and processing of multiple manuscripts.

Alberto Martinelli, University of Milan
Neil J. Smelser, University of California, Berkeley

About the Authors

Arnaldo Bagnasco is Professor of Urban Sociology at the University of Turin, Italy. He is the author of many works in economic sociology and is editor of *L'altra metà dell'economia. La ricerca internazionale sull'economia informale* (1985).

Johannes Berger is Professor of Sociology at the University of Mannheim, Germany. His recent publications include *Selbstverwaltete Betriebe in der Marktwirtschaft* (with Volker Domeyer and Maria Funder, 1988) and *Kleinbetriebe im wirtschaftlichen Wandel* (with Volker Domeyer and Maria Funder, 1990).

Volker Bornschier is Professor of Sociology at the University of Zurich and President of the World Society Foundation. He has published numerous articles on economic sociology, on social change and on world system analysis, and is the author or editor of ten books, the most recent of which is *Westliche Gesellschaft im Wandel* (1988).

Gary Gereffi is Associate Professor in the Sociology Department at Duke University. He is the author of *The Pharmaceutical Industry and Dependency in the Third World* (1983) and co-editor (with Donald Wyman) of *Manufacturing Miracles: Paths of Industrialization in Latin America and East Asia* (1990).

A.H. Halsey is Professor at Nuffield College, Oxford. His recent publications include *British Social Trends Since 1900* (1988) and *English Cultural Socialism from Thomas More to R.H. Tawney* (with Norman Dennis, 1988).

Andrzej K. Koźmiński is Chair of the Management and Organization Department at Warsaw University and is visiting professor at the Anderson Graduate School of Management at UCLA. He has published several scholarly articles in leading academic journals.

Alberto Martinelli is Dean of the Faculty of Political Sciences at the University of Milan and Professor of Sociology and Political Science. Among his publications are *Università e società negli Stati Uniti* (1978) *The New International Economy* (with H. Makler and N.J. Smelser, 1983) and *Economia e società* (1986).

Michio Morishima is a former Sir John Hicks Professor of Economics at the London School of Economics. His recent publications include *Ricardo's Economics* (1989), *The Economics of Industrial Society* (1985) and *Why has Japan 'Succeeded'?* (1982).

Ayşe Öncü is Professor and Chair at the Department of Sociology in Bogaziçi University, Istanbul. Her publications in English include articles in leading academic journals and chapters in collected volumes. Her current research is on 'Macro-politics of Deregulation and Micro-politics of Banks in Turkey'.

Neil J. Smelser is a University Professor of Sociology at the University of California, Berkeley. Among his publications are *Economy and Society* (with Talcott Parsons, 1956), *Social Change in the Industrial Revolution*

(1959), *The Sociology of Economic Life* (1962, 1974) and *Handbook of Sociology* (1988).

Hanspeter Stamm is undertaking research for his PhD in economic sociology at the University of Zurich. He has published, as part of a team, on international financing, external public debt and multilateral rescheduling arrangements.

Richard Swedberg is Associate Professor in the Department of Sociology at the University of Stockholm. He is the author of *Economic Sociology: Past and Present* (1987), *Economics and Sociology: Redefining their Boundaries* (1990) and *Joseph A. Schumpeter: His Life and Work* (1991). He is currently preparing a study of the EC.

1

ECONOMIC SOCIOLOGY: HISTORICAL THREADS AND ANALYTIC ISSUES

Alberto Martinelli and Neil J. Smelser

Throughout its history sociology has shown a tendency to be complex and diversified in content, without notable consensus with respect to its paradigmatic organization, and permeable at its boundaries. At the same time certain themes have continued to arise and rearise, thus lending a continuity to the discipline. Among these themes are inequality and stratification, social integration, the nature of community, the nature of society, and societal development. Central among these recurrent themes is the relationship between economy and society. Few classical sociologists failed to give this motif a central place in their theories, and it continues to be the focus of a vital concentration of research and debate in contemporary times. That focus is also notable because it has occupied a place for economists as well, though in many cases their thought about this relationship has taken the form of implicit assumptions rather than explicit analysis. We divide our introduction to this state-of-the-art collection of essays on economy and society into two parts: a review of some classical theoretical formulations at the macroscopic level and a statement of some central analytic issues in economic sociology.

Part I: Major Formulations of Economy–Society Relations

Modern Capitalism and Classical Political Economy

As the second part of this introduction will indicate, it is possible to treat the relations between economy and society in analytic terms, without special reference to distinctive historical eras or types of society. In its historical origins, however, the economy and society is closely linked with the rise of industrial society and with its attendant, largely middle-class democratic revolutions beginning in the second half of the eighteenth century. Its rise as a distinctive preoccupation of social thinkers can be understood as conditioned by two basic developments associated with those revolutionary changes: (1) the growing differentiation of economic structures from social structures and relations — for example the differentiation between economy and state in the early, laissez-faire stages of capitalistic development, the dissociation of kinship from economic production under the factory system. This separation permitted the development of a culturally separated field of economics, with sociology and its sub-branches emerging and consolidating later; (2) the problem of social order (integration) as this preoccupied the emerging social commentators and social scientists; in particular, the potential for capitalist economic structures and processes to generate inequalities and injustices, disrupt community life, and to foster social instability became the foci of attention. In these senses the study of economy and society arose from those intellectual attempts, modelled after the scientific mode of enquiry, to grasp the fundamentals of modern capitalist society.

The rise of the relevant modern social sciences, then, represents a kind of double differentiation: first, the differentiation of distinct social structures (economic production, banking, markets and distribution structure, urban structure, modern kinship structure) from one another, thus making them more visible and accessible to study; and second the differentiation of the social-scientific mode of enquiry from existing philosophical, religious and historical thought, carrying forward some of the themes of that thought but simultaneously emulating the logical-experimental methods as these had developed in the natural sciences.

The starting point of our illustrative historical account is classical political economy, the first coherent and systematic attempt to understand economic and social relations in a modern scientific sense. Adam Smith's political economy is based on the postulate of *homo oeconomicus*: a simplified set of assumptions about human action, seen as the result of the behaviour of isolated individuals, each pursuing his or her own interests and making free and rational choices after having calculated the prospective costs and benefits. (The economic actor is thus an 'exceptional statistician', as Arrow ironically defined him later.)

On the basis of a further set of assumptions and calculations, Smith came to regard the equilibrium of the market and social order as the spontaneous outcomes of the profit-maximizing activities of individuals.[1] The market dynamics by which this result was attained followed from Smith's special solution of humanity's relation to the natural environment and to each other as flowing from maximizing behaviour in satisfying their wants and in choosing the means to satisfy them. The attendant processes were presented as the natural laws of economics, applicable not only to early capitalist society but presumably over a wide historical and comparative sweep.

The first creative simplification of classical economics, then, was the simplification of human psychology by adopting the view of people as instrumental, rational, maximizing materialists. While this simplification excluded most of the rest of psychological nature, an argument might still be made for it on theoretical and methodological grounds as necessary for creating an analytical model for scientific analysis.[2] (It was a 'model' in a second sense, for it contained a set of idealized criteria for evaluating the correctness or incorrectness of existing economic arrangements and for guiding social policy.) There was a second creative simplification, too. By focusing more or less exclusively on economic motivation, behaviour and interaction, other features of social action and social structure were left out of sight or reduced: the dynamics of culture were frozen into fixed tastes and preferences; collective action was expressed as an aggregation of individual actions, without an internal social dynamic; the polity was represented passively, with little attention to the processes of political conflict and negotiation leading to policies; and aspects of personal interchange other than the economic were left out of account. In its classical formulation, in short, the classical solution was as near as might be imagined to a pure economic solution; it is difficult to say much about economy *and* society within the confines of such an extreme formulation, because so many aspects of that relationship were resolved by simplifying assumptions.

The unreality and the evident limited applicability — limited, that is, to a certain model of capitalist society — has been addressed and in some ways overcome by developments along two lines: first, economists themselves have altered the specific assumptions of the classical school and extended its applicability, as we will illustrate later. Second, as time went on, the social sciences — dealing directly with those parts of the society that the economists had simplified — began to develop, and take the form of major social science disciplines we know at present, mainly as sociology, anthropology, and political science, but more specific bodies of knowledge as well, such as demography, information science and organization theory.

The rise of the other social sciences — and here we have sociology most in mind — was also conditioned in large part by the conditions of early industrial capitalism.[3] As indicated, the social changes initiated by the commercial and industrial revolutions involved a series of differentiations that produced new institutions — the modern family, the urban community, new agencies of social control such as the police — that became more clearly visible as objects of study. In addition, the urban and industrial changes produced a whole new range of social problems — crime, addictions, broken families, poverty — which demanded explanation and amelioration. But above all, the pace of change, the instabilities, the strains and contradictions of the economic revolution led to the erosion if not destruction of many traditional integrative institutions, such as the monarchy, the church, the local community, the artisan guilds, and the extended peasant family; much of the agenda of the emerging new social sciences was thus concerned with the problems of integration, or the problem of 'how is society (or social order) possible?'

Those social scientists working on the edges of the already developed economic sciences adopted a range of strategies in relation to them. Pareto, for example, took economic explanations as more or less adequate to analyse one kind of social action, and invented other constructs (for example 'derivations', 'residues') to deal with other aspects of reality (Pareto, 1935); Weber took the mentality of modern society ('rational calculation') as a phenomenon to be explained, and laid out the ideal-type institutional conditions under which it was possible (Weber, 1947); and Marx and Polanyi (1944), while addressing some of the problems of classical economics directly, looked outward and raised questions about phenomena (for example, class conflict, group hegemony, political instability) that were outside the analytic realm of classical political economy.

Whatever the historical origins of the rise of economics and sociology as separate disciplines, their emergence as such poses three sets of questions: first, what are the *formal* relations between them with respect to logical structure, types of hypotheses, explanatory models, and so on? second, what are the distinctive ranges of empirical data each calls into question and generates findings about? and third, how can the substantive findings of one modify the parametric assumptions of the other and vice versa?

In the remainder of Part I we will consider the thought of several general theories in the tradition of economic sociology — Karl Marx, Max Weber, Joseph Schumpeter, Karl Polanyi, and Talcott Parsons and Neil Smelser — each of whom attempted to work out alternative and more comprehensive frameworks for the study of economy and society than those generated by the classical political economists.[4] Each attempted to address issues associated with the three questions posed in the last paragraph, though with varying degrees of completeness.

Karl Marx. In his own programme, Marx had in mind neither revising classical political economy from within nor forming a new social science completely distinct from it; he was aiming to generate no less than a new theory of society. While he incorporated most of Ricardo's theoretical insights, he 'historicized' them by regarding the 'natural laws' of political economy as relevant only to a specific phase of a world-historical evolutionary process, the phase of bourgeois capitalism. The larger set of laws within which political economy (and other forms of knowledge specific to other economic phases) is the definite sequence of historical phases through which human society passes. Each phase has its own dominant modes of production and distribution, and its own set of principles of functioning. The other item on Marx's agenda, of course, was the idea of revolution, which referred both to the mechanism of transition from one phase of economic development to another, and to the purposes to which his own knowledge was to be put in the revolutionary destruction of capitalism.

Marx's conception of the relations between economy and society parallels his distinction between two pairs of key concepts in his theory: productive forces vs. social relations of production and structure vs. superstructure. His most succinct statement of the former is the following: 'in the social production of their existence men enter into necessary relations, independent of their will, which correspond to a given stage of development of productive forces' (Marx, 1913). By this assumption Marx replaced the classical economists' assumption of free and rational choice with a more deterministic one: forces rooted in the mode of production impose themselves upon individuals. The real, or structural basis of society is the complex of productive forces (machines, labour, technical knowledge) and the corresponding social forces (property rights, authority, class relations). Resting on this structure is the superstructure, constituted by legal and political institutions and by culture, and determined by and expressing the material conditions inherent in the structure.

Marx's theory of social change — which replaces the naturalistic materialism of classical economics — is rooted in a process of dialectical materialism. This conception regards society as never static but as totalities in the making. The engine of change is contradictions between the structural and the superstructural forces. The fundamental type of contradiction — analysed most completely with reference to capitalist society — is the changing division of labour, which generates inequalities, as well as asymmetries of power and class conflict. Applying the method of dialectical materialism means identifying the primary contradiction of vital ruptures in society, including the forces that are rising to negate the existing relations. Marx regards the crucial contradictions in the dialectical process as material, not cultural. This is what is meant by the famous dictum that Marx turned Hegel upside down; to regard real, economically based class interests and conflicts, not ideas, as the driving force of civilization.

Capitalism is like all other phases of history in that it contains the germs of its own destruction. But in capitalism the process is particularly accelerated:

> The bourgeoisie cannot exist without continuously transforming the means of production, hence the relations of production, hence the whole of social relations. . . . The continuous revolutionizing of production, the unceasing shaking of all social conditions, the eternal uncertainty and movement distinguish the bourgeois epoch from all previous ones. . . . Everything which is solid melts into the air. . . . (Marx and Engels, 1964: 7)

The basis for this dynamism — and the resulting precariousness and ephemerality — of capitalism is found in the mechanisms that propel it forward. It is driven by an intense competition between firms in the market, which makes for an accelerating process of improvement of the bases of productivity, mainly by the application of superior technology to the means of production. This process of improving technology, moreover, is simultaneously a means of exploiting the labouring class further through an accumulation of greater surplus value; as such it intensifies the inequality of owners and workers, and increases the conflict between them. Through this complex process involving competition, the intensification of contradictions, the concentration of capital, the falling rate of profit, overproduction, and recurrent crises, capitalism speeds toward self-destruction. This is realized through the process of increasing worker class consciousness and ultimately worker revolution, which serves to destroy the capitalist system and replace it with a communal mode of production.

In developing this theory Marx widened the scope of the economy as it is found in other versions of social theory — as a system more or less isolated from society as in classical economics, or as one cognate system among many as found in some functionalist theories. For Marx, the forces emanating from the economy radiate throughout society and continuously transform it through the generation of contradictions. (This view of economy and society as found in Marx is a more accurate rendition, we believe, than a static 'reductionist' or 'deterministic' reading.) Taking classical political economy as a starting point, Marx expanded its horizons in two directions: first, instead of taking its basic character as a given, he developed a theory of social change that gave an explanation for its historical appearance; and second, at the other 'end' of the economic consequences, he regarded some of the consequences which the economists regarded as the 'end of the line' (for example distribution of the shares of income) and treated them as a phenomenon (a class system) with an entire dynamic (class conflict) and outcome of its own.

To look at this matter of widening the scope of the economy in yet another way: like the political economists, Marx took as his starting point the analysis of exchange relations. But instead of taking these as given, he moved 'behind' them, as it were, and attempted to account for them not in terms of their internal laws (supply and demand) but in terms of the double significance of human labour as a good and as a source of economic value. This formulation is, of course, the labour theory of value associated with Marxian economics. And while this theory has generated the greatest storm of criticism and debate as to its verifiability and its validity, it stands — from our special perspective here — as a broadening of the classical economists' vision of economy and society.

In addition to its status as an economic theory, Marx's work has a sociological core. This core is his focus on social classes as the actors in the dynamics of social change. In the first instance, of course, classes are 'deduced' from the economic categories of labour, surplus value, wage and profit. But above and beyond this Marx develops a theory of the process by which class groups become more than social categories (*Klasse für sich*). While the dynamics of the dialectic posit a certain inevitability in this transformation, there is at the same time a conception of agency in the theory. Geographical concentration and proximity in the work place, processes of communication and the development of common consciousness, the appearance of leaders, and their fashioning of an organized collectivity — these are the mechanisms by which a class comes to form its own purpose and destiny. This view of a sociological process that develops within a framework generally determined by economic relations and forces also strikes us as a sounder rendition of Marxist theory than of static determinism.

The evolving history of capitalist societies has indicated that Marx's sociology of class formation and class action is more complex than he foretold, and for that reason the fate of capitalism as a whole has differed, too. His view of an industrially based proletariat has been complicated by the rise of armies of service workers and the barriers to class consciousness and class action that accompany this development. In some cases, too, the very instruments that would be regarded as arms of the proletarian struggle — unions, parties, and so on — have proved historically to be bases for integrating workers into the system and dulling the revolutionary impulse. The development of other institutions as capitalism moves forward — specifically, extensions of the democratic franchise and the development of systems to safeguard the security and welfare of workers — have had the same kind of effect. Yet, different as these outcomes are to what Marx originally envisioned, they stand in one sense as proof of the strength of those underlying forces of economy and class that shaped them. For these reasons, Marx's theory must be regarded as one of the fundamental contributions to the analysis of the relationship of economy and society, because it reintroduced the economy into the social system, identified some of the major contradictions of industrial capitalism, and laid the groundwork for a sociology of classes and class action.

Max Weber. Many historical commentators have tended to stress the differences between Marx and Weber, especially in relation to Weber's sometimes antagonistic dialogue with Marx on the relative importance of material and cultural factors in history. Genuine as this difference is, it is equally important to point out their affinities. First, both succeeded in widening the view of the relations between economy and society from that of the classical economists. Second, they both 'historicized' capitalism through their historical and comparative studies. Third, they took as contingent rather than fixed the relationship between economic and social forces — Marx regarding that relationship as dialectical and Weber as mutually conditioning. And finally, both stressed the intrinsically contradictory and conflictual character of all social systems, including above all that of rational bourgeois capitalism.

But to return to the differences. Marx's main avenue for understanding the capitalist mode was to root it in a general theory of historical development, of which it was the most advanced form. Marx strove to understand the anatomy of capitalism, in short, through the laws of its evolution. By contrast, Weber selected certain aspects of capitalism, identified certain correlations, congruences and conditional relations between those aspects, and attempted to verify these by drawing comparison with non-capitalist societies — without, however, attempting to formulate a general theory of change of philosophy of history. It is true that Weber had a number of very recurrent preoccupations, especially to discover the key to the character of western rationalism and to focus on the relations between fundamental religious beliefs and economic structures and processes; but even in these efforts Weber focused on certain central relationships and did not develop — indeed, remained hostile to — a fully-fledged model of explanation or historical evolution.

In addition to this cautious — relative to Marx — methodology of explanation, Weber was more reluctant to establish a definite link between scientific (theoretical-empirical) analysis and moral conclusions. For Marx, the moral necessity for the downfall of the capitalist (or any other) system was as clear as — indeed, derived from — its historical necessity. Weber was aware that scientific findings had moral implications, but these were not derived. Furthermore, his rigorous distinction between value judgements and factual judgements reveals this same sense of contingency. This probably explains why Weber holds more fascination than Marx for those engaged in complex comparative scholarship and why Marx holds more fascination for leaders of mass social movements and for 'intellectuals' in general.

A third difference between the two theories is that while Marx focuses clearly on the functioning of the capitalist system (profit, innovation, competition and accumulation), Weber attends more closely to questions of the genesis of capitalism. Marx's theory of primitive capital accumulation as the transition to modern society is not a thorough historical study but a reconstruction of the processes of capital formation and the liberation of labour from serfdom and corporate ties. Weber's focus, on the other hand, is more precisely on the historical conditions underlying its genesis (as well as its failure to appear) and is grounded in the most thorough scholarship on religion and other causal factors.

A fourth difference concerns the substantive relations between economy and society. Weber virtually reverses Marx's emphasis in places. He takes the same economic phenomena — free wage labour and profit-making — and analyses them in terms of cultural and motivational significance. Both are related to the phenomenon of rationality, which helps explain the rise of capital accumulation and the structuring of labour. However, Weber does not totally reject Marx's emphasis on material relations and conflictual class relations; what he does reject is Marx's monolithic formulations, arguing that economic interests are only one factor, existing side by side with ideal interests and the struggle for domination.

Weber's substantive writings are enormously varied, ranging from the early writings on commercial law and ancient economic history to the first sociological works on the transformations of agrarian relations and the psycho-physics of industrial work; from the methodological essays to the great comparative studies of religions and from the systematic analysis of the relationship between economic and social action to the late lectures on economic history. Running through all of them is the preoccupation with the nature of rationality in general and the nature of modern capitalism and western rationalism in particular.

Similarly, his explorations of the relations between economy and society are wide-ranging in content, dealing with the relations between capitalism and bureaucracy, the relations between economic class and other forms of stratification, the link between market freedom and the growth of cities, and the tension between formal and substantive rationality in economic action. But the most important thread in these writings is the link between religious ethics, economic mentality and economic action, which is also central to the understanding of rationalism and capitalism in the West.

For Weber, modern capitalism is a great complex of interrelated institutions, including the market economy, business corporations, free and voluntary labour, public credit, a stock exchange, and so on. Each institution has its own history and its own relations with other institutions. However, for Weber, especially in his essay on the Protestant Ethic but also in his more general comparative religious studies, this complex of institutions is tied together by a common mentality, the spirit of capitalism, which is in turn related to the ascetic ethic of Calvinism and Puritanism.

To review the essentials of Weber's argument, both the capitalist entrepreneur and to some degree the individual wage earner are distinguished from their historical predecessors in traditional economies by virtue of their rational and systematic pursuit of economic gain, reliance on calculation measured in relation to this economic criterion, the extension of trust through credit, and the subordination of consumption in the interests of accumulation. These are the elements of the rational economic actor's *Zweckrationalität*, by which he establishes a systematic relationship between preferred goals and the best means to reach them.

In his famous and controversial thesis, Weber argued that the advent of ascetic Protestantism provided an especially fruitful breeding ground for the mentality of economic rationality. Rational action becomes possible when human beings postulate a natural reality free from magical and ritual elements and a religious faith posited on the absolute transcendence of God. While many of the elements of ascetic Protestantism are found in Jewish monotheism, with its rational prophecies, and the early

Christian tradition, the Reformation, especially in its Calvinist manifestation, brought these elements to fruition. In this religion humanity stands alone before God, without the mediation of rites and ceremonies of repentance and absolution; the sacred is not immediately apparent as it is in primitive religions, and salvation is not possible through sacraments, as in Catholicism. Rather, each individual's state of grace is determined ('predestined') by God's inexorable choice. Defined as such, the problem of salvation is a painful one. Each person must consider himself or herself as chosen and reject doubt as the work of the devil; lack of self-confidence in this is seen as a sign of insufficient faith. The critical link in Weber's reasoning is that unceasing, planned, methodical work and the rational organization of life are seen as 'evidence' of this self-confidence and, ultimately, the possession of grace. When this viewpoint is applied to profane economic activity, it is translated into the notion of worldly success, because of its evidence of planning and self-control. By this complex formula Weber arrives at the final irony: that material success is a sign of ascetic realization.

In developing this case, Weber shunned deterministic claims and put forth no case that he was building a general theory. He was, first, aware that socioeconomic conditions, such as the formation of medieval cities with a socially cohesive urban middle class and a universalistic ethic of trade, had influenced the religious movements of the Reformation. And, like Marx, he was aware of the legitimizing functions of beliefs in the arena of class relations. Finally, Weber considered the Protestant Ethic as only one — though a central one — of the phenomena which contributed to the rise of rationalism in western civilization, others being the development of experimental science, rational law and rational government administration.

The specific investigations into Protestantism and capitalism are embedded in an ambitious range of comparative studies in Weber's work. They are best seen as a part of the great works on the economic ethics of the major world religions, published between 1916 and 1919 in the *Archiv für Sozialwissenschaft*. From these studies it is seen that the specific western relationship between Protestantism and capitalism is only a single instance of the relationship between the origins of an economic mentality and the specific contents of religious beliefs.

In his comparative studies of religion and in the remainder of his last work, the incomplete *Wirtschaft und Gesellschaft*, Weber dealt with the problem of modern capitalism and western rationalism in two ways: in the sociology of religion, the problem is dealt with directly, as Weber explored the linkage of the religions of classical China and India and ancient Palestine in terms directly comparable to his studies of the modern west. In his theoretical work on economy and society he dealt with the problem more indirectly, as a systematic analysis of the typical relations between forms of economic life and modes of social organization, such as communities and organizations. His systematic exploration of multiple possibilities of relationships — often specifying their positive or negative implications for capitalist development — supplies a larger theoretical base for a sociological understanding of the unique historical phenomenon of rational bourgeois capitalism.

The methodological device by which Weber analysed the relations between economy and society — and a myriad other relations as well — was the ideal type. By this device Weber was able to construct generic concepts (bureaucracy, patrimonialism, pietism and so on) which were built in large part on inductions from historical study but at the same time were represented in such a way as to move a distance away from historical particularism and thus to permit statements of sociological relationships of a fairly general order. Another methodological distinction Weber pressed was that between the interpretive understanding of historical phenomena (*Verstehen*), and the establishment of causal relations between them, which he regarded as two separate but essential features of investigation and verification in his scholarly programme. Weber's particular formulations relating to the use of ideal types and the role of understanding in investigation have been criticized extensively, but the social scientific issues they attempt to solve continue to be unavoidable.

Joseph Schumpeter. Whereas both Marx and Weber declined to work within the traditions of classical political economy, each relativizing it and attempting to account for its subject matter in the context of a larger scheme, Schumpeter worked mainly within that scheme, especially in his work on business cycles and the impact of entrepreneurial innovation. He did not attempt to substitute a different general theory of social relations for economic theory, but in his work used categories and insights from cognate disciplines, mainly sociology but to a lesser extent political science and psychology. In common with both Marx and Weber, however, Schumpeter was concerned with the understanding of the particular historical reality of capitalism as an economic system, and in integrating historical knowledge with theoretical constructions. From the standpoint of theoretical ambition, Schumpeter stood midway between the other two: he was more convinced than Weber of the feasibility of general, systematic theory and made an effort to synthesize ingredients from the various social science disciplines to this end; but he did not attempt, as did Marx, to construct a general evolutionary theory of economy and society or a philosophy of history.

The sociological element occupied a large place in Schumpeter's work, mainly as a complement to the basic economic core. As he spelled out his view in the introduction to *The History of Economic Analysis* (1954), economic analysis has the task of studying how people behave at a given time and what effects derive from their behaviour, whereas economic sociology has the task of studying why they happen to behave in the larger institutional context in which economic activity is implicated. This stress appears implicitly in his frankly economic works on economic development and business cycles, but brought it directly into view in his great sociological works on capitalism, socialism and democracy and on social classes and imperialism.

Schumpeter's sociology interacts with his economics in at least three ways. First, in the development of key analytical concepts such as the entrepreneur, he utilized sociological and historical insights to make his portrayal of that agent more realistic and convincing. Second, in his attempt to transform the basic assumptions of economic theory — such as the rationality of the economic actor and the attainment of economic equilibrium — into workable research questions, he called upon insights and formulations from sociology and the other social sciences. Third, he was always prepared to invoke non-economic, predominantly sociological variables at any moment when economic analysis did not seem to yield an adequate account of matters; for example, in his analyses of the crises of capitalism he goes beyond the study of economic cycles and raises questions of its social-political contradictions. We will illustrate Schumpeter's methodological openness to sociology in relation to three topics in his work: the role of entrepreneurship, innovation and leadership in his theory of economic development; the relationship between the entrepreneurial function and the formation of bourgeois classes; and the question of economic stability and social instability in capitalism.

The entrepreneurial function is the key element in Schumpeter's theory of development. He defined it as innovation — the introduction of a new combination of the factors of production (and labour) which, when combined with credit, breaks into the static equilibrium of the circular flow of economic life and raises it to a new level. The entrepreneur changes the conditions of supply, combines existing resources in new ways, and thereby sets up a new production feature. Weber stressed the revolutionary character of the entrepreneur (and sometimes held it in the same kind of awe as Marx held the revolutionary proletariat). But even though it is sometimes personified, Schumpeter regarded the entrepreneur mainly as a function: it does not imply the requisite of property, is not based on the assumption of risk, and does not require belonging to a business organization. But it remains the case that the entrepreneurial function is clearly and dynamically set aside from the activities of the everyday businessman.

To demonstrate the entrepreneur's exceptional qualities and role, Schumpeter drew on a range of sociological and psychological insights. Entrepreneurship, he argued, calls for a certain type of personality and conduct, which differs from the rational conduct of the economic man. The entrepreneur is a bold leader, willing to break through ordinary constraints; this sets him off from the routine manager. Leadership, moreover, involves the capacity to think the new, to grasp the essential, to set the incidental aside, to act quickly, to understand by intuition. The entrepreneur acts through his will and personal authority; he must be willing to forgo the criticisms that always arise when new and innovative behaviour is regarded as deviant and dangerous. While having some elements in common with religious and military leaders of the past, the entrepreneur is, however, less heroic. He is a leader in a rational and anti-heroic civilization, and as a result does not excite the charismatic feelings and collective enthusiasm of those who make or defend whole civilizations. The entrepreneur operates in a more limited sphere, and occupies a more precarious place in society.

Entrepreneurship as a specific historical phenomenon, Schumpeter realized, rests on the premiss of the differentiation of a distinct economic sphere separate from others. In previous epochs the entrepreneurial function was fused with others in the actions of political, religious and social leaders. Entrepreneurship and the entrepreneur is the form — the ideal type, if you will — of leadership that appears specifically and historically in capitalism. Given the importance of innovation and competition in that kind of economy — as Marx correctly stressed — the entrepreneur is a particularly appropriate and even essential phenomenon for capitalist dynamism.

Schumpeter also dealt with the psychology of entrepreneurship. Entrepreneurial conduct involves a mix of rational and emotional elements. On the one hand, it is rational in that it calls for a great measure of forecasting and planning. On the other hand, it is not narrowly utilitarian because it rests on an autonomous drive to achieve and create for its own sake, and also rests on a dream on the part of the entrepreneur to establish, ultimately, a family dynasty. The entrepreneur takes advantage of rationally based components of his environment, such as money, science and individual freedom, and he orients his conduct to rational values, but that is not the end of the story. Entrepreneurial innovation is basically a creative act, and deviant from the bourgeois culture which defines rationality from the narrower viewpoint of calculating to one's short-term advantage. The 'rationality' of the entrepreneur has an element of profit and gain, but in addition is based on the desire and capacity to think of the new and original and to act on those thoughts. In this formulation Schumpeter deviates from the assumptions of both neoclassical economists and the thought of scholars like Weber, Pareto, Sombart and Tönnies, all of whom, in different ways, tended to equate utilitarian rationality with capitalism.

With respect to the question of the relationship between entrepreneurship and social classes, Schumpeter actually developed a unique view of social stratification. For him, the class structure is the hierarchical order of families. Individuals belong to classes independently of their own wills. The fundamental factor which explains the mobility of families within classes is the same as that which explains mobility from one class to another: the capacity to adapt to the needs set by the social environment of a specific historical epoch, and to demonstrate those abilities necessary for a leadership role. Social classes change slowly over time, like hotels, occupied by different populations. To illustrate this view of stratification, Schumpeter developed a statement of the relations between functions and rank in the rise and decline of the German aristocracy and in the historical phenomenon of patrimonialism.

The performance of socially important functions is the core element of classes because it generates social prestige and consolidates society into ranks. Once established, moreover, the social prestige system tends to acquire a life of its own — the life of social rewards, gratifications, influence and deference — and often survives long after its functional base has eroded. The status of the upper classes in society, and of the leading families in those classes, is consolidated through the solidarity ties between their members and the transmission of social privileges from one generation to another. In capitalist society as such, the bourgeoisie is the leading class because they have performed the innovating and leadership functions in the economy and because they acquire, consolidate and transfer prestige, power and wealth to future generations. At the same time, this process helps explain the decline of the bourgeoisie as well, as the entrepreneurial function tends to fade and bourgeois institutions such as private property and contract are weakened.

Schumpeter's theory of class is fundamentally different from that of Marx, who ties it to the structure of production itself. It also differs from the theory of elites as propounded by Mosca and Pareto, based as it is on the performance of socially important functions rather than the protection of power positions in society. Schumpeter's theory has a more functionalist flavour. At the same time, it differs from classical functionalist formulations because it regards the class system at a given time as a mix between socially relevant and important roles on the one hand and the preservation of an inherited class legacy on the other.

To turn to the third illustration, Schumpeter also developed a theory of the crisis of capitalism, which is also a basically sociological theory. While recognizing the importance of economic effects such as the stifling of competition under conditions of large firms and monopoly capitalism, and while recognizing that phenomena such as the Great Depression of the 1930s serve to dramatize the economic failures, Schumpeter's theory of the crisis of capitalism relies more on 'non-economic' considerations, particularly his theory of classes.

There are two ways in which Schumpeter's theories of development and economic cycles impinge on his theory of crisis in capitalism. In the first instance, the development of monopoly capitalism — capital concentration and giant firms — does not impinge directly on the capitalist system, but does so indirectly by its erosion of the institution of private property and its weakening of the role of the innovating entrepreneur. Second, late capitalism tends to generate a deep social crisis, involving the decline of the central institution of the bourgeois family, the destruction of intermediate and protective strata and the worsening social climate that is due to the corrosive critique by intellectuals of bourgeois values and capitalist institutions. The failure of capitalism is not an economic failure. As Schumpeter himself puts it:

> the actual prospective performance of the capitalist system is such as to negative [*sic*] the idea of its breaking down under the weight of economic failure, but its very success undermines the social institutions which protect it, and 'inevitably' creates conditions in which it will not be able to live and which strongly point to socialism as the heir apparent. (1950: 61)

That Schumpeter's prediction has not materialized, and that capitalism has proved more resilient than he — and Marx, for different reasons — predicted, prompts us to seek for those aspects of his analysis of the end of capitalism which are not convincing.

Let us turn to the first component of the crisis of capitalism, the progressive decay of the entrepreneurial function by virtue of the routinization of innovation in large organizations, thus rendering the entrepreneurial function superfluous and undermining the bourgeois basis for continued dominance. As Schumpeter dramatically put it, 'the forerunners of Socialism were not the intellectuals and political activists who preached it, but the Vanderbilts, the Carnegies and the Rockefellers' (1950: 134). In addition, there is the melting down of key institutions of property and contract. The limitation of Schumpeter's view in this regard is due largely to his belief that the competitive economy of the individual, innovative entrepreneur is the only brand of capitalism. In reality, capitalism has proved compatible with the existence of very large firms and with state intervention and control of the economy. It might also be questioned whether the destruction of 'protective social strata' is also a liability for capitalism. Schumpeter argued, for example, that the alliance of the British bourgeoisie with surviving aristocratic elements added to its vitality, because of the key role it played in the political role of government. That view has been challenged, for example by Barrington Moore, Jr (1966) who argued that the alliance between the bourgeoisie and the traditional estates is an obstacle, rather than a facilitating condition, for capitalist development.

Schumpeter also argued that in later capitalist development the intellectuals played a leading role in discrediting its values and institutions. He asserted that capitalism tends to breed social unrest because it simultaneously holds out the hope for growth and improvement and at the same time generates a high level of personal insecurity. The expression of the resulting dissatisfaction is facilitated, furthermore, by the existence of political freedom and tolerance of dissent, another hallmark of bourgeois capitalism. In this context the role played by an expanded group of economically unemployed and politically dissatisfied intellectuals can be decisive. Sound in some respects, this argument also overestimates the 'unemployment' of intellectuals in advanced capitalist societies — particularly with their expanded university systems — and underestimates the stabilizing influence of political tolerance in complex and diversified societies.

The final component of Schumpeter's view is the deterioration of the bourgeois family and household. This process is traced to the diffusion of utilitarian values and to the spread of patterns of consumption that undermine its exclusivity of status symbolization and household maintenance. Once again, Schumpeter's assertions appear to be overdrawn, and to underestimate the adaptability of institutions and groups in capitalist society. To a large degree it is still the case that marriage ties, family solidarity and cultural affinities generated by common experience in educational institutions continue to operate in various ways in different countries to sustain the bourgeoisie as a class with a leading if not an altogether dominant role (Bottomore and Brym: 1989).

Schumpeter's view of capitalist crises bears some affinities to Marx's conception of capitalist breakdown and Weber's conception of bureaucratization and the routinization of charisma as hallmarks of late capitalism. There are important differences, however. Whereas Marx identified the contradictions of capital accumulation — that is to say, the success of capitalism — as the root cause of crisis, Schumpeter looked to the obsolescence of the entrepreneurial function and the decay of capitalist institutions. And while Weber's views of social change envision a variety of escapes from the 'iron cage' of capitalism through the renaissance of old values and the rise of new charismatic prophets, Schumpeter foresaw, fairly straightforwardly, the inevitable decline of capitalism.

Karl Polanyi. Like the others we have discussed, Polanyi developed a view of the economic that is broader than the alternative posed by the tradition of political economy. His central thesis is that the economy is 'embedded' in the larger society (thus establishing his partial affinity with the views of the American institutional economists, Veblen, Commons and Mitchell). Polanyi's work is less widely known and cited in the literature on economy and society than those we have already considered, but all the same he offers an articulate critique of the paradigm of political economy, as well as contributing to the understanding of the interplay of economic and social phenomena, the analysis of economic institutions, and the understanding of the mechanisms and contradictory tendencies in industrial capitalism.

Polanyi argued that the relation of economy and society varies over time, but as a general rule the latter has priority and control over the former. In the broad historical and comparative sweep, the economy is immersed in social relations and economic agents do not act to maximize their material interests but rather to safeguard their social positions, status pretences and social advantages. Modern capitalism is 'exceptional' in this regard, because the economy is subordinated to social relations less than in most societies. In fact, Polanyi regarded market and industrial capitalism as resulting from a process by which the economy has freed itself from societal controls and subordinated all other aspects of social life to its needs. So pervasive has been this process that students of modern industrial society have tended to forge its exceptionalism — its unique place in human history — and to think of it instead, and mistakenly, as manifesting universal, general laws.

In all his works, Polanyi was preoccupied with three central issues: the market economy and its contradictions; the self-regulating market as the fundamental institution; and the limitations of the claims to universal validity of the paradigm of classical and neoclassical economic theory. These themes are all seen in his first and best-known book, *The Great Transformation* (1944), which was a great and ambitious attempt to trace the origins and causes of 'nineteenth-century civilization' (i.e., modern industrial capitalism) and its collapse in the twentieth century. The collapse, Polanyi argued, was visible in the crisis of most of the international institutions of capitalism, such as the gold standard and international finance, the balance of power, constitutional democratic government, the balance of power among the great powers and, above all, the self-regulating market.

Polanyi's central thesis in that book is that the self-regulating market was the great institutional mechanism of economic regulation in capitalism, but that it could not exist for long 'without annulling the human and natural substance of society' (1944: 3), physically destroying humanity and transforming the environment into a desert. The economy, structured on the basis of the self-regulating market, radically separated itself from other social institutions and constrained the rest of society to function according to its laws, in the meantime transforming land and labour into 'fictitious commodities'. The defensive strategies that the economy attempted — such as regulating the market from the political centre — themselves generated further contradictions. Much of Polanyi's critique, in fact, is based on the analysis of what he called the 'double movement' stemming from the attempt to control the intractable conflicts between the market economy and society, seeking to permit the coexistence of the free, self-regulating market with its integration by means of controls on the exchange of labour, capital and natural resources.

Polanyi 'tested' this central and perhaps oversimple thesis by drawing on historical materials from the period of the early industrial revolution in Britain and from the twentieth-century period of international instability. For the earlier period Polanyi analysed not only the market forces but also a number of social policies, including social and labour legislation, union strategies, tariff policies, and central bank activities. Throughout the work, moreover, Polanyi augmented his analysis by a running critique of the philosophical and theoretical principles of utilitarianism and classical economics, against which he juxtaposed his own alternative conception of the economy as an institutional process. Finally, Polanyi included a line of analysis which was more distinctly sociological, namely how to maintain a requisite degree of social solidarity in an individualistic society dominated by utilitarian values. That question has not been answered to this date, we believe, as the large, modern welfare states continue to struggle with the inexorable tensions between economic efficiency and market freedom on the one side and social regulation and social rights on the other.

Having presented this brief summary of Polanyi's thesis and its defence, it remains to note a few points of criticism. First, because of his view of the embeddedness of the economy in other institutions, Polanyi implicitly adopted a fundamentally organic view of society, emphasizing above all the structural context of almost all social action and social policies. One consequence of this organic or holistic view of society is to underplay the independent historical significance of classes, their interests and their activities as independent sources of understanding the march of capitalism, as well as its subsequent crises. Second, Polanyi seems to view capitalism in such 'exceptionalist' terms that he treats its rise almost as the artificial result of exogenous factors, rather than as developing from any internal dynamic of its own. In this connection, it may be an irony that Polanyi, so polemically at odds with the economists' alleged attempts to treat the laws of the capitalist economy as universal, committed the opposite error of regarding capitalist society as such a deviation from the norm that he produces too particularist a view of that economic system.

Central to Polanyi's critique of economic theory is his notion of the 'economicist fallacy'. He identified two distinct features of economic life: the 'substantive' aspect, which defines the institutionalized relations between humans and their social and natural environments and aims at satisfying human needs; and the 'formal' aspect, which rests on the notions of a choice between alternatives and a scarcity of means, and on the idea of a logical relationship between means and ends. The 'economicist fallacy' is mistaking the second aspect for the whole of economic life. That fallacy has arisen in tandem with the rise of the formal market economies with their supply–demand relations since the eighteenth century, which was mistaken by the economists as being natural and universal. Moreover, the 'laws' that economists have generated are not human laws, because they fail to take into account the human context of economic activity. According to Polanyi, Marx was moving in the right direction when he took up the social relations of production and their dynamics, but because he remained so much within the Ricardian world-view of the economy, he did not move far enough. Polanyi and his colleagues, moreover, took as their task the demonstration of the institutional modes of regulating economic activity other than the market.

Polanyi's general point about the limited validity of the model of rational economic action echoes the points made among scholars in the German historical school, Weber, Pareto, and the American institutional economists. The debate continues to this day, as we will indicate later. Those who stress the non-universality of economic assumptions are no doubt correct. But Polanyi's strict division of economic activity into its 'substantive' and 'formal' aspects seems likely to suggest that formal economic analysis is some kind of historical freak, that it is useless in studying economies other than that of liberal capitalism in a limited historical period. One of the unfortunate features of Polanyi's position, if pressed, is that it would seem to discourage the development of general economic theory and, indeed, to discourage systematic comparative analysis between rational bourgeois capitalism and other systems, because they differ so fundamentally from each other.

On the more constructive side, Polanyi and his associates developed an almost 'physical' view of economic activity, meant to contrast with the market-money-exchange model of formal economists. Economic activity is a constant movement of people, material means, capital and technical knowledge around the society. Economic activity does, after all, require the mobilization of resources and the distribution of product. The key questions that Polanyi and his associates wanted to ask are: in what kind of institutional realities is this process embedded, and, accordingly, what kinds of principles govern the flow of economic goods through the society? If the questions are phrased in that manner, then non-economic institutions, such as religion and government, become paramount in the analysis.

Based on their own anthropological researches, Polanyi and his associates formulated a typology of three principles of economic integration: reciprocity, redistribution and exchange. Each type entails different forms of distribution in space: reciprocity indicates correlated transactions between symmetrical groups (for example, gift exchanges); redistribution indicates appropriative transactions to and from a 'centre' (for example, administratively organized distribution of food, philanthropy); and exchange refers to transactions between 'hands' in a market system (purchase and sale). A corollary of this classification is that in societies which possess those kinds of structural groupings (for example, symmetrically organized kinship), the mode of economic transfer will be shaped accordingly.

A number of critical questions can be raised about his typology. In the first instance, it may be incomplete; it does not seem to cover, for example, political mobilization of economic goods and services for collective action (such as the conduct of war). Second, the typology is a basically static, classificatory scheme with no sense of the principles of economic dynamics or the transformation from one system to another. An example of attempting to make exchange more dynamic is found in the work of the transaction-cost economists, who argue that when costs exceed benefits when exchanging in a market-money-price system, alternative modes of exchange and distribution will be devised (as in the case of the rise of informal bartering, and in administered distribution of public goods). Third, because of his own scholarly agenda, Polanyi probably overestimated the disruptive and disintegrative aspects of the market principle, and underestimated the negative possibilities of the other (for example, one-sided exploitation in a reciprocative system and arbitrary despotism and autocratic centralism in a redistributive system). Despite these shortcomings, Polanyi's general critique seems valid, and he offered some helpful guidelines for moving in the direction of developing a comparative economics that takes institutional context into explicit account.

Talcott Parsons and Neil Smelser. Perceiving a decades-long lull in systematic activity such as that of Marshall, Weber and Pareto to combine economy and society, Parsons and Smelser turned their hands to this effort in the mid–1950s. Parsons had made earlier forays on this score in his early work on German writers on capitalism and in his synthetic work, *The Structure of Social Action* (1937). But the enterprise of Parsons and Smelser twenty years later took place in a new intellectual context and, accordingly, their work is set apart from that of their predecessors in several important respects.

First, *Economy and Society* was one phase in Parsons's

ambitious programme to create a general theory of action, including a theory of society. In *Economy and Society* (1956), Parsons and Smelser did not espouse a general evolutionary theory or develop a philosophy of history (as did Marx), did not undertake a vast, comparative study of cultures and institutions (as did Weber), and did not attempt to develop a historically specific theory of capitalist dynamics and contradictions (as did Schumpeter and Polanyi). Their plan was to lay out, in the most abstract analytic terms, the major exigencies that confront societies, to catalogue the major types of differentiated subsystems that are oriented toward meeting these exigencies, and to identify the major relations between the subsystems. The special relations between economy and society were to be spelled out in the context of this enterprise. In addition to these items on their agenda, Parsons and Smelser were impelled to lay out the main similarities and differences between economic theory and other types of theory in the social sciences, and to try to synthesize them.

Second, Parsons and Smelser were working within an explicitly functionalist framework, as this theoretical framework had evolved in the first half of the century. The relevant ingredients of this approach included the biologically derived notion of the contribution of social activities to societal functions, a notion of interdependence of different roles and institutions, and a notion of equilibrium and equilibrating processes. Taken together, this meant that Parsons and Smelser were working with a causal imagery of functional independence, and this set them apart from their predecessors, who stressed other kinds of relation, such as materialist determination, elective affinity, and domination. In addition, Parsons and Smelser paid less attention to system-specific contradictions than did the other theorists we have considered.

Third, and also in contrast to their predecessors, Parsons and Smelser accepted a great many of the categories and relations of formal economic theory — the factors of production, supply and demand, theories of credit and money, and equilibrium solutions — as legitimate theoretical frameworks and, in certain respects, as models of social science theorizing. They viewed economic theory, however, as a special case of a more general theory. They argued that economic structures and processes constituted the parametric constraints for other bodies of theoretical and empirical investigation, and vice versa. They did not attempt to 'relativize' them in the same ways that Marx, Weber and Polanyi did, even though they were aware of the comparative limitations of the market economy model (1956: 80–3).

Central to the case presented by Parsons and Smelser is the idea that the economy is one of several societal *subsystems*, to which it bears special relationships of mutual dependence. What are these subsystems?

(a) Latent pattern-maintenance and system-management (L). Every society has a system of values and beliefs that operate as legitimizing and sustaining arrangements for its major institutions and as structured motivational patterns for its members. Part of the institutionalized energy of society goes towards the maintenance of the consistency and integrity of these values and to providing outlets for the 'tensions' that arise in connection with conformity with them. Institutions that specialize in this 'latency' function are religion, science, the family and education.

(b) Goal-attainment (G). This function refers to the ways in which the society establishes specific goals — legitimized by the dominant values — and mobilizes the population to attain these goals. Parsons and Smelser identified this subsystem as society's 'polity', which was constituted mainly but not exclusively by the institution of government, the main mobilizing agency in society.

(c) Adaptation (A). The legitimized and institutionalized goals — for example, warfare, maximization of the aesthetic, economic productivity — are not realized automatically, and the society has to devote some of its energies to providing generalized facilities — a reservoir of societal means. It is this adaptive function around which the economy is structured.

(d) Integration (I). While the L function deals mainly with the function of legitimation, all social life entails a great deal of individual and group conflict, and a certain level of its institutionalized arrangements are devoted to handling this and promoting social solidarity. The main institutional complexes involved here are the legal system, the 'peacekeeping' aspects of the state, and the differential allocation of facilities and rewards and the maintenance of a system of stratification.

Parsons and Smelser developed this scheme in many directions, but in this summary we will identify only the major ways in which economics and society impinge on one another in their theory.

The most important relationship between the subsystems of

society is that of exchange. The other subsystems are responsible for generating the major resources (factors of production) for the economy, which in turn supplies them with its own output. The exchange between the latency system (in this case, households) and the economy is motivated labour which is exchanged, ultimately, for consumer goods and services for the economic sustenance of the household and its style of life. Mediating this exchange is the medium of money, which takes the form of wage payments for labour and prices for goods and services. Parsons and Smelser developed a comprehensive catalogue of exchanges regarding land, capital and organization (entrepreneurship) as well, each with corresponding societal subsystems. They also developed a theory of generalized social media — wealth, power, influence and value commitments — corresponding to the four major subsystems and providing the mechanisms that facilitate the exchanges between them.

A second relationship is that the other subsystems determine in large part the value of the parameters of economic activity. For example, with respect to 'tastes', Parsons and Smelser criticized the traditional view of these as individual and 'given'. They argued that tastes are not only shaped by community interaction, but that they are structured by the exigencies and activities of other subsystems. Similarly, Parsons and Smelser developed a critique of simplified assumptions such as indifference curves or the marginal propensity to consume, giving instances of ways in which family exigencies and cultural values structure these and other functions, which in turn give shape to economic activity.

Third, non-economic forces structure economic exchange through the institutionalization of normative systems such as contract, property and law, and thus build into these exchanges certain 'non-economic' factors into markets. They developed an account of the market for professional services, for example, showing how it deviated from classical exchange notions developed by economists, by virtue of special value and normative commitments associated with professional roles. On the basis of this line of analysis they laid out an elaborated set of criteria for classifying different kinds of imperfection in economic markets.

Finally, Parsons and Smelser developed the germs of a theory of economic growth, phrased more in terms of institutional structuring than according to the usual economic criteria such as gross national product. They developed a model of economic change, in which pressure from cultural values and from environmental forces combine to yield a sense of dissatisfaction with economic forces. By a complicated, multi-stage process, the economic and other agents adapt by developing a more differentiated structure for the execution of economic activity. As a current example, they chose the phenomenon of the differentiation of ownership and control in American corporations. Their model of economic change draws from Adam Smith's notion of the division of labour as the source of economic efficiency, Durkheim's theory of functional differentiation, and Weber's conceptualization of cultural values as providing legitimizing criteria for economic change. Towards the end of the volume Parsons and Smelser generalized this model of change, and gave a general sketch of the development of modern western capitalism as a series of crucial differentiations of the economy from kinship, ascribed stratification systems, and traditionalist political organization. This was as close as they came to developing a general account of industrial capitalism, and on this score they contrast with the other theorists whom we have considered.

As our sketch shows, Parsons and Smelser were addressing a line of theoretical issues very different from the others reviewed, so that in some respect their theory stands in an orthogonal relationship to them. Their work has been criticized by Polanyi, Arensberg and Pearson (1957) as not regarding economic life as sufficiently embedded in institutional life, and thus committing some of the same errors as did the classical economists. Parsons and Smelser's formulation has also been criticized for its abstractness and its failure to generate specific hypotheses and explanations about specific historical societies, and has been subjected to the general range of criticism directed towards functionalism regarding its neglect of domination, conflict and change. Different and critically opposed to other theories as it is, however, it shares with them a preoccupation with the strengths and limitations of the fundamental agenda laid down by classical economics.

Part II: The Problematics of Economic Sociology

At this point our discourse shifts from the historical to the analytic mode. Part of our interest in the 'state of the art' of economy and society is to lay out the main questions — or problematics, if you will — of that area, conceived as a more or less articulated sub-discipline of research. We present this as the editors' judgements about research themes and priorities, not as an exhaustive review of the literature of economic sociology (though we will select references to certain works in theory and empirical research) nor as a statement which we claim would have universal consensus among those working in the area of economy and society in different nations and regions of the world.

The Idea of the Economic Actor

Any discussion of the character of economic life must include, if not begin with, the psychological substratum of that life — that is, the motivation of the economic actor. The main intellectual heritage to be cited in this connection is that of English utilitarianism (Halévy, 1928) as formulated in the works of the classical writers of political economy, taken over in modified form in Marxian materialism, refined in neoclassical analysis, and both modified and extended in contemporary economic and social thought. This version of rationality has proved one of the most pervasive intellectual forces in the history of social thought in the past two and a half centuries (Dumont, 1977).

In the simplest form, the classical economic version of economic rationality is based on the assumption that the individual actor will behave in such a way as to maximize his or her material well-being, or utility, in economic transactions. An additional assumption is that both buyers and sellers will possess full knowledge of the availability and prices of products, job opportunities, and other market conditions. These first two assumptions are linked by a third, a postulate of rationality, whereby it is assumed that buyers and sellers, possessing preferences and full information, will act rationally on the basis of these. They will not make errors, they will not forget what they know, and they will not act irrationally (that is, on bases counter to their interests and information).

This model of general rational behaviour is framed in the context of certain further assumptions about the interaction of buyer and seller. It is assumed that they will meet in a peaceful setting in which it is understood that neither will engage in transactions other than economic exchange (for example coercion, violence); that certain institutional arrangements (such as property laws, a state that will maintain social order) will guarantee the integrity of this peace and protect it from disruption; that neither economic agent has power over the other or over the price of the product exchange; that each will make offers on the basis of his or her own preferences (supply schedule and demand schedule), and that on this basis an equilibrium price point will be reached. It is assumed, finally, that the exchange will not be negotiated (haggled over) in such a way as to make for a deviation from the more or less automatic intersection of the schedules of each.

This classical model has been subjected to the greatest variety of modifications over time; indeed, it might be argued that one of the major sources of innovation in economic thought is found in tracing the implications of such modifications. A non-exhaustive list of these modifications would include: the refinement of the notion of rationality by the invention and elaboration of indifference curves in neoclassical economics; modifications of economic preferences under conditions when seller or buyer controls the conditions of price or supply, i.e., imperfect competition (Robinson, 1948; Chamberlain, 1948); alterations in economic behaviour when information is not complete (Stigler, 1961); relaxations of the principle of maximization, for example in the notions of 'bounded rationality' and 'satisficing' (Simon, 1957); changes in the terms of rationality when the good in question is public, not private (Harden, 1968), including the problem of the 'free rider' (Olson, 1968); modification of the principles of economic rationality as institutional conditions are varied (North, 1987); extension of the idea of economic rationality to traditionally non-economic settings such as voting behaviour (Downs, 1957); participation in social movements (Oberschall, 1973), decisions to marry and bear children (Becker, 1981); and the formulation of rationality as a general feature of social life (Becker, 1976; Coleman, 1990).

By the same token, the idea of rationality has been subjected to a diversity of lines of fundamental criticism. Among these are that economic rationality (rational accounting) is realizable only under certain institutional and historical conditions (Weber, 1947); that it is only one of the great range of orientations of social and political life (Pareto, 1935); that its utilitarian underpinnings are invalid accounts of human conduct in institutional life (Durkheim, 1948); that economic rationality is an institutionalized value, not a general psychological propensity (Parsons, 1954); that economic rationality is a specifically western, market-based phenomenon, and does not apply to societies bound by traditionalist values (Firth, 1971; Polanyi et al., 1957); that utilitarian thinking undermines the moral dimension of the human condition (Etzioni, 1988).

It seems to us that the most appropriate task for the economic sociologist is not to continue the by now stale debates over the fundamental place of rationality, non-rationality and irrationality in human life; the merits and demerits of economic imperialism, and the like. It seems more fruitful to take economic rationality as a variable feature in human institutional life, and to devote research to understanding and explaining that variation. With respect to the firm (whether in a free-market or administered economy), it should be asked under what conditions more or less unfettered calculations based on costs and benefits are possible, and what other kinds of considerations — for example jurisdictional demands on the part of officers and departments within a firm and other adjudication; political influences from regulating agencies or party apparatus — influence and divert such calculations. With respect to the household (this, not the individual, is the calculating and decision-making unit in many lines of economic analysis), how do considerations of sharing and equity between family members, exigencies associated with the life cycle, and other aspects of the family's 'communal' rationality (Weber, 1947) act as sources of family 'tastes' and as the source of other types of calculation other than cost–benefit? (We will mention family and other determinants of the rationality of the labourer later.)

More generally, the political-economic scene in the contemporary world does not seem to be one in which individuals, firms and nations work on the basis of economic rationality and the maximization of efficiency (technological and economic competition between nations notwithstanding), but that most major decisions are made on the basis of a complicated process of confrontation, conflict, dialogue and political compromise between different *kinds* of rationalities (economic rationality, the rationality of military preparedness and national security; of environmental protection and preservation; of cultural integrity and territoriality of racial/ethnic groups, and so on). That is to say, the main bases of action and public policy are accommodative and synthetic, not the deliberate actions taken in the name of a set of programmed tastes; in that sense the political and integrative can be said to have displaced the economic and the central organizing basis of contemporary societies.

The Ideas of Exchange and the Market

Exchange as the typical mode of economic activity is a natural outgrowth of the conception of economic rationality. The phenomenon of exchange is based on the minimal assumptions that different goods and services have different kinds of utility and that individuals will seek to realize these through barter, trade, and buying and selling (Smith, 1937). In classical economic theory the market as macroeconomic phenomenon was little more than a numerical aggregation of the thousands of microeconomic exchanges that constitute the economic behaviour of individual trading partners interacting with one another. A further assumption of the classical economists was that according to the laws of economics all exchanges would 'clear' freely and the market would always be in equilibrium in accordance with the dominating principles of marginal utility, marginal costs and marginal return.

Like the phenomenon of economic motivation, the ideas of exchange and the market have undergone modification and elaboration in economic and other social scientific thought. Types of exchange other than the free market have been identified, including exchange based on the norm of reciprocal obligation (Mauss, 1954); status and authority reinforcement (Malinowski, 1922; Sahlins, 1972); and redistribution, charity and philanthropy (Polanyi et al., 1957; Boulding, 1973). The classical model of market equilibrium — which did not envision disequilibria — has been challenged theoretically by the notion of imperfect competition, monopoly and oligopoly; by the Keynesian theory of more or less chronic equilibrium (or disequilibrium, according to one's view) at levels of high unemployment and market depression on the one hand, and inflation on the other; and by variations on these themes. On the borderline of economics, social scientists have generated theories of human behaviour based on the assumptions of classical economics and classical learning theory (Homans, 1974); on exchange between actors within the context of structured roles within institutions (Blau, 1964); and on models using power and prestige as well as economic goods and services as the basis of exchange (Crozier, 1964). Parsons and Smelser (1956) identified exchange as the basis for societal process; they based their formulations, however, on exchanges between *systems* (economy, polity, integrative system, and so on), not individual actors, and perhaps that is one of the main reasons why their theory is not usually considered as being in the same family as other exchange theories.

Historically, much of the dialogue about the market has swirled around one specific kind of market — the early capitalist, or 'pure capitalist' variant — and its alternatives, most of which involve some kind of political intervention. The pure capitalist market involves exchange on prices fixed by the dynamics of supply and demand, competition for profit by sellers, the institution of private property, and a minimalist role for government captured by the slogan laissez-faire. Laissez-faire, it is now recognized, did not mean *no* government involvement in the economy; it meant government involvement in a way that would guarantee freedom of choice of economic agents and would maximize the freedom of mobility of resources, especially labour. In the late nineteenth and twentieth centuries three alternatives to the classical model emerged, all involving a different role for government, and all directed in one way or another towards ameliorating or eliminating chronic imbalances and injustices in the capitalist market.

The least radical of these three was the Keynesian, which left the main institutional structures and mechanisms of the capitalist market intact, but involved government influencing the conditions of demand and supply through monetary policy (interest rate regulation, regulation of the money supply) and fiscal policy (progressive taxation and transfer payments, public works). The second was government intervention directed at easing chronic imperfections, especially of trusts and cartels, through legislation, agency monitoring, and direct government action such as monopoly breakup; the main aim of this kind of regulation was to restore market mechanisms. The third, and most radical, was the socialist, which involved alteration of the price mechanisms (administered prices), government ownership of production (nationalization, socialization), or more or less complete government control of the economy, including distribution through bureaucratically controlled exchange associated with some phases of Soviet communism. While textbooks could describe these variants in ideal-type terms, it is now the case that the economy of almost every nation-state — in the modernized West, including Japan, in the socialist countries including the Soviet Union, Eastern Europe, and China, and in the Third World — is some mix of these principles, different and changing balances being struck in each.

The debate about markets has been enlivened in the past decade or so by developments in both West and East. Western Europe and the United States have moved towards restoration of classical market mechanisms, symbolized most dramatically in the administrations of Ronald Reagan in the United States and Margaret Thatcher in the United Kingdom but felt in other countries as well. All countries in the Eastern bloc, moreover, experienced some kind of disaffection with the role of party and state in the economy and have experimented with some reintroduction of free market (including profit) arrangements; the most dramatic move in this regard is the Mikhail Gorbachev policies of *perestroika*, or restructuring. At the time of writing (early 1990), the dramatic political collapse of many East European socialist nations has thrown the future of market structure and market policies completely open.

Two ironies strike us about the current scene. The first, a minor one, is that at the moment the 'right' is identified with the free market principle in the developed Western countries, and the 'left' is so identified in the socialist countries; this is the latest in a long line of confusing usages of 'right' and 'left' and leads us to question their usefulness as categories. The second irony is that in all the flurry of thought and debate about economic organization, almost all alternatives are envisioned in the form of time-worn dialogues. For example, almost the only vision being entertained in socialist countries is some reintroduction of well-known free-market mechanisms and the main issue in the West also has to do with the degree and kind of government involvement in markets. In the abstract, one would think that — given the great ingenuity and richness of the human capacity of institutional invention — some alternatives outside this limited scope would be on the horizon, but the 'iron cages' of capitalism vs. socialism still appear to dominate thinking of political leaders and scholars alike.

The challenge for the student of economy and society is to understand the causes, character and consequences of different types of market organization. This means, in the first instance, a search for new typologies of market organization, since the pure types, inherited from earlier thought, increasingly appear to be irrelevant. One consequence of different forms of market arrangements, of course, is their relative efficiency, but, in addition, different market systems produce different incentive systems (and here the link between the social organization of the market and the motivation of the economic actor, mentioned earlier, is clearest). They also produce different distributions of resources and rewards and, by extension, different class systems and different lines of cleavage and conflict in society.

The Structuring of Economic Activity

The foregoing discussion of market principles has led us into the idea of economic structure, but does not exhaust that topic. We continue our discussion of the problematics of economic sociology by considering the conventional economic categories of production, distribution and consumption.

Production. Under this heading we also begin with a classical model. This is the model of the individual entrepreneur who, reading and responding to actual and anticipated consumer demand, mobilizes the different factors of production to produce for a profit. In this model the main problematics about the factors are their cost, and whether, given their cost, they can be combined in such a way as to secure an edge of profit in the economy.

Within this model, the main questions that commanded the interest of scholars were the types of innovation possible, the character of the entrepreneur, and the economic dynamics generated by innovative activity (Schumpeter, 1934), as well as the motivation required for entrepreneurship (McClelland, 1961) and the social origins of entrepreneurs (Hagen, 1962). This simplified model became clouded and limited in its applicability by the rise of large corporations as economic agents and the involvement of the state in productive and planning activity; both these developments highlighted the role of the collectivity or the organization as the fount of entrepreneurship, and the eclipse of the individual heroic entrepreneur. These developments brought scholars' attention more to the entrepreneurial function rather than the entrepreneur as such, even though individual entrepreneurship (for example the 'ethnic entrepreneur': Light, 1972) is still a matter of focus. While the questions to be asked about individual entrepreneurs concerned their backgrounds, motivational characteristics and strategies, many of the questions about the 'new' entrepreneurship deal not with the individual but with a complex set of triangulated relationships among corporations (including multinational corporations), banks and states, all of whom constitute sources of and obstacles to innovation. The comparative analysis of distinctive patterns of facilitation and obstruction of entrepreneurship constitute an important item on the agenda of economic sociologists.

Much of the story of economic sociology can be told as the systematic examination of the 'black boxes' of economic theory, and changing them from repositories of simplified assumptions into research questions and empirical investigation. This statement applies clearly to the theory of the firm. In classical economic theory, the firm is an actor, and internal exigencies — such as the effectiveness of authority over workers, informal organization between workers, political conflict, compromise between managers, staff and subordinates, and adequate communication within the firm — were taken as non-problematical. Many of these items, especially the relations between managers and workers and worker morale and performance, were the main preoccupations of American 'industrial sociology', and still constitute foci of interest for industrial psychologists and economic sociologists in many countries. Recent research in the United States, influenced by neo-Marxist trends, has concentrated on conflict and consent in the work place. All these areas constitute ongoing and legitimate research questions, but in the coming years some new twists are likely to arise. Among these are the special problems of worker–management relations in multinational production, which in some cases involves management of different nationalities and cultures in labour; increasing attention to patterns of authority, influence and co-operation in the service sector, including government bureaucracies; the impact of new technologies, especially computer technologies, on the autonomy of workers; relations between supervisors and workers in the new 'cottage industries' made possible by the home use of computers; and the impact of changing patterns of gender composition among workers and managers on the functioning of firms and other economic organizations.

Another set of areas where the non-problematical has been problematical is in the generation of economic resources. In the case of labour, classical economic theory treated labour as mainly responsive to changes in the level and kind of wage offers. Economic sociology opens up a whole range of additional considerations involving the motivation of labour, its quality and its performance. One tradition of analysis, which has spun off from Max Weber's studies of religion, has to do with the cultural bases of worker commitment. The 'Protestant work ethic' has constituted a kind of starting point for analysis, but additional research has attempted to find cultural analogues elsewhere, functional equivalents to internalized cultural imperatives such as the phenomenon of group loyalty and solidarity in Japan and other Asian settings and, implicitly, the possibility of securing worker performance through authoritarian discipline where the culture of hard work among workers has not been developed historically, for example in the early phases of Western capitalism and in some contemporary socialist countries.

In contemporary times, two main institutional media through which such cultural influences are transmitted are the family and the educational system. By and large, the family is the locus for the generation of fundamental orientations of trust, co-operation, attitudes toward authority, and relevant habits of industriousness, punctuality and so on. The school setting is a supplementary institution in this regard, but in that setting skills — both generalized and work place-specific — are primary. Continuing comparative work should focus on the distinctive kinds of family structure and socialization experience appropriate or inappropriate to different kinds of labour participation, the significance of different patterns of 'sharing' of training by schooling systems and economic organizations, and the effectiveness of retraining and reallocation programmes in promoting the flexibility and mobility of labour.

With respect to the supply of capital for entrepreneurial activity and production, the contemporary economic system has become more complicated as well, and correspondingly, new lines of research are generated. The early capitalist modes of supply of capital — personal savings; reliance on kin, friends, religious brethren; loans proffered by local and national banks — have been superseded by the growth of enormous banking enterprises, an enhanced role of the state in financial affairs, and the increased salience of the international dimension in credit (including the role of the World Bank, International Monetary Fund, conglomerates of banks with international operations, and the international financial activities of national governments). A byproduct of this is the increased salience of international credit and debt in the world economy. As in so many other areas, research questions in the area of capital and credit no longer deal only with the economic orientations of economic agents (individual entrepreneurs, firms or banks), but rather with the processes of conflict, co-ordination and accommodation between a multiplicity of agencies representing massive forces. For example, development strategies for both newly industrializing countries (NICs) and less developed Third World countries involve a complex political articulation between multinational corporations, international banks, domestic banks, home governments, and governments of capital-supplying nations. The understanding of the structure and functioning of massive systems of agencies, and research activity by scholars, should reflect this change.

Finally, economic sociologists should renew their interest in questions regarding the development of science and new technologies, which have traditionally been treated as 'land' factors. Much of the relevant work in this area is being carried out by historians and sociologists of science and technology, and concerns the relative effectiveness of different structural arrangements (universities, academies, government research agencies) in the generation of economically relevant science and technology. Other relevant questions concern the processes of technology diffusion — a point of great sensitivity on the part of industrial leaders, trade unions and governments — the adaptation of the same technologies in different social and cultural settings, and the dynamics (especially obstacles) involved in the phasing out of obsolete technologies. With respect to the last of these, in capitalist societies the market has proved an only partially effective mechanism in eliminating unproductive sectors (the politics of vested interests of management and workers are also salient); and in administered economies when the effects of inefficiencies associated with obsolete technologies do not appear immediately in competitive markets, the problems involved in phasing them out are even more complex.

Distribution. Earlier a few lines of variation of exchange systems were noted, namely along the dimensions of state vs. private control and degree of regulation. In addition to these political dimensions, it is essential to note that exchange also takes place in an institutional context, which defines the property rights of use, control and disposal of goods and services, and establishes laws, rules and usages governing the contractual bases of exchange. These systems range all the way from unwritten, pre-legal customs regulating the nexus of exchange in simple tribal economies to the extremely complex and elaborated systems of contemporary developed societies.

Such property and contract systems give the general contour to exchange, and indeed they may be one of the most fruitful ways to classify different kinds of market system for purposes of comparative study. Property and contract systems are also an important part of the institutional context that shapes economic development, particularly with respect to the degree to which they permit flexibility and movement of the factors of production, the ways in which they define or restrict access to natural resources (such as minerals and oil) in laws governing appropriation and expropriation of rights, and the degree to which they permit or deny accumulation of private rewards for economic activity. In the last two instances, the laws governing taxation and eminent domain are particularly relevant. For the exchange of labour services, the laws governing rights of appropriation of labour (including slavery), legal regulation of wages and salaries, and the legal system governing state intervention and moderation of labour disputes are the critical mechanisms.

Property and contract systems have, of course, long been the subject of comparative and historical research, but their conditioning influence and impact on economic processes and economic development are not fully understood. In addition to continuing these lines of scholarship, economic sociologists and other social scientists will be called upon to turn their attention more to property and contract involving international agents and internationally integrated systems. The study of the impact of legal changes on the European common market is perhaps the most obvious example, but the development of international compacts and systems of agreement on appropriation and control of the oceans and their natural resources, control of the skyways, and even the control of outer space also demand study and explanation.

Consumption. Economists' traditional approach to consumption is to extrapolate from certain assumptions about tastes, their level of plasticity and their level of stability, to posit some type of consumption function (for example the marginal propensity to consume) on the basis of these assumptions, and then to trace their impact in combination with other economic variables — on demand and on the functioning of the economy. One task of the economic sociologist is to convert these simplified assumptions into variable factors, and thus to attempt to determine the sociological sources of various types of demand.

Four sociological factors seem important in this connection. The first is the impact of a society's dominant cultural and subcultural patterns on the overall structure of consumer demand. Societies with feudal and aristocratic heritages — even if weakened — will still be likely to place a high premium on ownership of land as a symbol of status. Some cultures may place a high premium on other types of status symbol — houses, automobiles, fine arts, gastronomy — each of which may skew consumer demand in that direction. Sometimes subcultures arise which reject the dominant cultural modes and adopt contrary or compositional modes of their own. These kinds of cultural preference are not to be regarded as immutable, by any means, and the process of modernization itself appears typically to introduce new levels of materialism into the societies that are affected. Nor are cultural tastes immune to the efforts of producers and advertisers to alter them in the direction of their own preferred lines of products. It is these dynamics of interaction between dominant culture, subculture, media and advertising that should be a main focus of the economic sociologist interested in the determinants of demand.

The second set of factors affecting consumer demand is to be found in the society's stratification system. In any society there are observable class differences in the use of language, dress, patterns of leisure, eating and drinking habits. Every society also manifests a certain class-cultural dynamic as well, exhibiting a balance between classes that attempt to guard jealously their own exclusive mode of symbolization of status, and classes that make efforts to imitate and assimilate expressive patterns of more prestigious classes. Some (Veblen, 1953; Bourdieu, 1986) have elevated class culture and its dynamic into general principles of stratification. In any event, like culture in general, class differences in expressive symbolization of their status in society have obvious and direct implications for consumer demand in any society.

The third complex is education. On the one hand, education as a consumer good becomes salient in all developed societies and has also emerged as a salient basis for training, certification, and status symbolization in newly industrializing countries and in less developed countries. In many cases the state assumes the great burden of the cost for providing education, but even in these cases education is an important component in the determination of demand, because it requires the services of teachers and ancillary personnel and an infrastructure (buildings, playgrounds, books, and so on) for the educational establishment. Even if education is entirely 'free' in the sense that it is state provided, taking advantage of it still has economic consequences, since families who send their children to school forego income-earning opportunities. In these ways education enters into consumer demand for any society. In another significance, education is important for consumption because in many ways it operates as the conduit for instilling cultural preferences and standards of class symbolization into those whom it educates. Differences in educational structure and practice, then, determine in part the pattern of consumer demand between different societies.

The fourth complex is the family. As carrier of the cultural and subcultural tastes, the educational preferences, and so on already mentioned, it is the effective vehicle for expressing the demands implied by these standards in the market. In addition, the family has its own internal dynamics that conditions demand. In particular, its own exigencies of 'communal rationality' (feeding and clothing its young, sharing in leisure) spill over into consumer demand for diverse products such as toys, sports paraphernalia, camping equipment, vehicles for transportation, and so on. Special consideration should be given to the implication of the family's life cycle for consumer demand. As the family moves through the phases of childless couple, couple with young children, couple with adolescents, couple with children in college, empty-nest couple, and grandparents, their consumption patterns alter significantly. As cohorts of different sizes move through the life cycle, societies may experience significant shifts in demand — and producers of different kinds of goods and services different fortunes.

Before leaving the topic of the structuring of economic activity, it is necessary to mention that special phenomenon referred to as the informal economy or the underground economy. The phenomenon is an important feature of both developed and less developed economies, accounting for significant percentages of the total economic activities in these societies, and has caught the attention of numbers of scholars. These kinds of economy are 'inside' the total economy in that they produce goods and services that find their way into the market structure and are sold to consumers. But they are 'outside' the main economy as well, largely because they are not chartered or registered by state agencies, operate outside the tax structure, and in some cases are semi-legitimate or even illegitimate (in the case of black markets and drug distribution). Important research topics on the informal economy are how entrepreneurs mobilize the factors of production, carry on production, and advertise and distribute their wares in the semi-shadowed existence in which they live. Another focus is on the symbiotic relationships that develop between the informal economies and the official state apparatuses of countries; in some cases these economies are tolerated, even encouraged, because of the benefits they generate for the general economy; at the same time they may become a problem (for example because they do not provide tax revenue for the government) or an embarrassment (because they become the object of criticism from tourists or from outside the country), and then become the objects of periodic regulation or crackdown.

State and Societal Modes of Regulation and Legitimation

As the discussion has proceeded, the state has appeared from time to time — the state as a source of market intervention; the state as legal and administrative environment for economic activity; the state as provider of educational goods and services. These references underscore the general point that in the recent history of the Western developed countries, in the socialist countries, and in the less developed countries, the state has become part of everything in the economy. The state emerges as a major producer of goods and services (even in the most 'free-enterprise' societies, the state is the producer of infrastructures such as the highway system, sewage system and the postal system); the state is inevitably the central actor in the economics of national defence and security; its employees are an important part of the labour force; it may be the largest consumer of goods and services in society. In all these respects the state is part of the economy.

In addition the state is manager and regulator of the economy. It influences demand and the distribution of income through taxation policies and transfer payments; as indicated, it plays a role — with varying degrees of success — in planning, stabilizing the market processes, and fostering economic competition and growth in its society; it is the guarantor of the legitimacy of the specie, and is the sometimes successful regulator of inflation and the value of money; it is both agent in and regulator of economic conflict between interest groups and social classes. Comprehending and explaining the significance and impact of all these roles of the state is high on the list of priorities for economic sociologists and other scholars.

As the state has expanded, it has taken over many of the cultural and ideological functions relating to the economy and economic life that had been the province of religion, ideological and educational leaders and intellectuals. The most evident case of this state 'takeover' is in the socialist countries, but even in these the balance between state and religion as cultural and ideological voices remains delicate and problematical. And in all societies the role of the intelligentsia (however defined) remains an open one, and stands in some degree of tension with the state ideological apparatus. These cultural-ideological roles of state and other agencies are an important component in economically relevant matters such as generating and sustaining labour motivation, defining priorities between economic and other societal goals, and securing the legitimacy of competing economic interest groups and classes.

Nowhere is the economic role of the state more critical than in the international arena. Even in the era of laissez-faire, the state was perforce involved in international affairs, minimally and necessarily because of its requirement to honour or negotiate trade deficits as guarantor of the nation's money; and the state, as legally responsible for the integrity of currency, has always maintained an interest in, if not control of, banks, including their international operations. Finally, the state has been the agent to impose and enforce tariffs and other taxes, and to enter into trade agreements with other nations.

The late twentieth century has brought new economic problems for the state, and has involved it more deeply in the international economy. In many important respects these developments have weakened the state in the late twentieth century: the increased proportion of the national income that is involved in foreign trade; the increased involvement of nations in the international financial scene, either as creditors or borrowers, accompanied by the rise of enormous banking agencies such as the International Monetary Fund and private international banks; the limited capacity of national governments and banks to control the international value of their currencies, despite periodic interventions; and the presence of multinational corporations which, despite the fact that they have a domestic base, constitute a quasi-autonomous international economic force that intervenes in the production, labour and capital sectors of those nations in which they do business. As these agencies have gained in international economic power, national states have come to have less control over the economies of those countries over which they are politically sovereign.

Almost paradoxically, this diminished level of economic control has in fact made for a larger and more active state in countries involved in the international economy. Even in the face of the increased power of non-state, international economic agencies and forces, the state remains the agency that must cope directly with trade surpluses and deficits, the execution and enforcement of trade and financial agreements, the international stability of the nation's currency, and forces generated by the presence of multinationals. It is this greater involvement and responsibility in a world increasingly uncertain and difficult to control that accounts for the paradoxical result that modern nation-states are simultaneously weakened and augmented in their role.

These remarks about the new international role of the state underscore a general message for the programme of economic sociology: it has become progressively less possible to regard economic transactions between individuals and groups within societies, and even the state regulation of economic activity, in isolation from the involvements these activities have in ever-larger systems. The international economy is the most important of those systems, and almost no aspect of economic activity can be understood or explained without ultimate reference to the conditioning or determining effects emanating from that international economy.

The Impact of Economic Processes on the Larger Society

Up to this point economic activities and the economy itself have been regarded as embedded in and influenced by a larger social, political and cultural context. To round out our account of problematics for economic sociology, we turn now to the other side of the coin, and detail the points of impact of economic processes on society.

Inequality and social classes. The Marxian and Weberian traditions have set much of the agenda for this subject; it remains for us to review those points of articulation between the economy and the systems of inequality. The first of these has to do with the fact that the production system of the economy, as a system of relations between superiors and subordinates in the factories, banks, government bureaucracies and other economic agencies, constitutes one of the central modes of organizing authority in society, and produces social classes in the sense that Dahrendorf (1959) defined them, namely those occupying differential positions in authority systems. A great deal of class conflict occurs, furthermore, concretely in the work place and office, and consists of struggle over the conditions of labour and the control of the productive process. This struggle has a formal side, situated in the relations between management and trade unions, and an informal side, embedded in the day-by-day interactions of superiors and subordinates.

Overlapping with these kinds of social classes based on authority relations are those based on inequalities in income and assets. The latter are 'economic classes' in the Weberian sense. As Weber pointed out, these classes articulate with the prestige and status hierarchy and with the system of potential authority in society. The comparative study of the dynamics of these three systems of inequality — and their changes over time — constitutes an analytic focus of the economic sociologist.

As dependency theory has instructed us, these systems of inequality have come to have an increasingly important international dimension. This dimension was self-evident in the colonial era, when foreign powers' presence established systematic political, social, economic and cultural inequalities between colonials and colonized, and affected these relations between the colonized peoples. The end of colonialism brought an end to this direct subordination, but more directly and perhaps more powerfully, the system of international production and financial systems shaped the economies of the economically powerful and economically weak alike, and thus contributed to the determination of the contours of inequality in these societies as well.

Economic interests and their mobilization. The developmental experience in all types of economy — Western, Eastern socialist, newly industrializing countries, and Third World countries — has taught us the following: economic development means above all the specialization of activities along functional economic lines (division of labour), and increasing complexity in the structure of non-economic institutions — education, medicine and, above all, the government — as well. It is mainly through this differentiation that the economic social inequality in society can be traced, because of the fact that all specialized occupational positions in society receive a certain wage or salary level, and find themselves fixed appropriately in the society's prestige hierarchy.

In addition, many interest groups and 'classes' form around these functionally differentiated positions in society. When all the incumbents of a given type of specialized position (for example nurses, engineering technicians) are aggregated, they form an economic and social category. When the members of this category develop a sense of membership of it, and some expression of their interests along with some kind of ideological elaboration of that interest, then they become an economic interest group. And finally, when these groups mobilize for action on their own or as part of a social movement, they become politically significant.

Such is the economic basis for the development of groups,

classes, social mobilization and social movements. The economy is not the only basis, however; semi-independent groups and social movements also grow up around racial, cultural and ethnic identifications; age and gender membership; regional and residential location; and around specific 'causes' such as environmentalism, life styles (for example hippies, yuppies), and moral preferences (such as anti-abortion). This mosaic of economic and non-economic interest groups and social movements constitutes a great part of the political life of any society, and dictates much of the agenda of the governing authorities in society, who are alternatively negotiating with, capitulating to, repressing, or otherwise dealing with politically significant groups, as part of their interest in maintaining political stability and order. It is the dynamics of the formation and behaviour of economic groups and classes in interaction with other groups and classes, in relation to the strategies and tactics of the state, that constitutes the main focus for economic sociologists.

Economic development and structural change. Economic development implies, above all, the efforts on the part of a nation to increase the productivity of its economy and raise its level of wealth. In the first instance this involves the application of new kinds of technology, the forging of new types of productive organization, the reallocation of resources in society, and the development of new markets and types of distribution system. The impact of development on society touches many of the same areas that have been listed in the foregoing discussion, but for the purposes of foci of research the following might be specified:

(1) Geographical redistribution of human resources, mainly through migration. Depending on the pattern of development, this migration may be from one society to another, internal to the society or, as a special case, migration to the locus of activity on the part of multinational corporations. Among the multiple consequences of this are disruption of residential patterns, culture shock and acculturation, new ethnic contacts and conflicts, different kinds of strain on infrastructure (such as transportation or education) as areas 'fill up' and 'empty out', and creation of new urban centres with their inevitable social problems.

(2) Societal struggles over how to deploy resources and wealth, as capital needs, provision of social services, and consumer demands all become more complex.

(3) Complex pressures on other institutions to change, for example the pressure on the educational system emanating from skill requirements in industry and service sectors, the pressures on family life imposed by demands for many family members to participate in the labour force, pressures on neighbourhoods and communities to modernize and accommodate to different production and transportation needs.

(4) The formation of new functional groups based on occupational and other specialization; perhaps the resurgence of racial, ethnic and regional bases of group integration; changing patterns of economic reward and the appearance of new classes and subclasses based on economic position. Of particular interest is the phenomenon of new groups (industrial proletariat, clerical and sales classes), the 'squeezing out' of other groups (artisans), and the ways in which these groups contribute to the left-wing and right-wing political tendencies of the polity.

(5) The development of new pressures on national and regional governments to co-ordinate economic development, provide social services, deal with social problems, and deal politically with the ever-changing group and political pressures in society. The latter exigency tends to set up pressures for democratization associated with development, if we consider democracy as the evolution of political mechanisms to deal with the demands from groups in the population.

International consequences. Economic activity has almost always included an international dimension (trade emporia; the search for precious metals, spices, economic domination and colonialism in the interests of securing raw materials, slave labour and so on). The rise of industrial society brought a more complex international order, involving an augmentation of foreign trade, the development of complex international finance systems, shifting patterns of stratification of nations into rich and poor, economic dependency and interdependency, shifting political alliances arising from new patterns of development and dependency, new international networks of businessmen and bankers, and the possibility of the internationalization of labour through migration and the activities of multinationals. The international economics of food, oil and illegal drugs, to name the three most obvious examples, have an evident and pervasive impact on the foreign policies and military strategies of countries in this international order.

All these consequences, both domestic and international, have forced new and far-reaching demands on scholars from all disciplines who strive to understand them. New phenomena, new relations, new forms of conflict continuously appear. Old models of economic life based on the idea of aggregated individual transactions, the nation-state as the 'natural economic' unit, may grow increasingly less relevant, and the scholarly investigation of economic activity and its social aspects may call for fundamental reorientations of theory and research, focusing most of all on the 'nations-within-systems' level of analysis.

Notes

1. In this sense it can be observed that Smith treated the problem of social integration (of the market) as non-problematical because it was solved automatically on the basis of first assumptions.

2. It can be argued plausibly that all scientific inquiry must be selective and thus simplifying in order to permit the generation of general statements; any attempt to depict all of perceived reality simultaneously must thus be regarded as at worst an impossibility and at best as indiscriminate descriptiveness.

3. To make this assertion is not to ignore other cultural influences. Many of the classical sociologists were reacting to academic developments in their own societies — for example, Weber to the German historicist tradition and Durkheim to academic psychology in France — and attempting to set scientific sociology off from them analytically.

4. For a more detailed and comprehensive analysis of the works of these and other authors, see Martinelli (1987).

Part I
Cultural and Institutional Contexts of the Economy

2

IDEOLOGY AND ECONOMIC ACTIVITY

Michio Morishima*

I

In considering ideology and economic activity, ideology is defined as a system of beliefs which binds people together into a social grouping. This is synonymous with religion as defined by Durkheim (1912) and, as a definition of religion, it may be too wide; but if this definition is adopted, both Confucianism and Marxism are 'religions'. In any case, there are two broad classes of approach to this problem, Marxian and Weberian. The former regards ideology which, together with such institutions as the state, family structure and so on, constitute the superstructure of the society, as being no more than a reflection of underlying basic material conditions. The latter, on the other hand, approaches from the superstructure to the base and establishes the reverse relationship. Obviously no comment is needed on the importance of the Marxian approach, while the following passage from Weber (1930: 68–9) serves to justify his approach:

> The question of the motive forces in the expansion of modern capitalism is not in the first instance a question of the origin of the capital sums which were available for capitalistic uses, but, above all, of the development of the spirit of capitalism. Where it appears and is able to work itself out, it produces its own capital and monetary supplies as the means to its ends, but the reverse is not true.

As will be seen later, neither of the two approaches alone can serve for the interpretation of a total historical process. To achieve this we must use both approaches and examine the interdependence and interaction of materialistic or economic factors with ideological or religious factors. In fact, as Weber himself acknowledges, the Weberian approach is compatible with the Marxian; they would and should eventually be synthesized with each other, though the task is extremely difficult and complicated.

Economic theory, Marxist or non-Marxist, assumes the rational man of the Robinson Crusoe type, hardworking, materialistic and purposefully systematic. Crusoe is an Englishman born in 1632, just before the English Revolution, his father being a native of Bremen who settled in Hull; he would probably have been a Protestant. Economists entirely ignore his religious background as well as the *Zeitgeist* of the seventeenth century. Economic laws deduced from a model consisting of Robinson Crusoe consumers and firms owned and operated by Robinson Crusoe families are applied not only to European and American economies but also often to non-occidental industrial societies, such as Japan, or even to less developed countries.

Guha (1981), for example, follows the Marxian method and compares Russia, Japan, India and China in economic development. He is seldom concerned with differences in the religious attitudes of the peoples of these countries, so that they are viewed as if they speak the same language, have the same degree of industriousness and are provided with the same kind of ethos. Guha refers to the industrial revolution which occurred in Manchuria during the 1930s (1981: 91) but makes no mention of the fact that it was mainly carried out by Japanese. Although Chinese, Manchurians, Mongolians and Koreans also lived in Manchuria, it was the Japanese who established modern industries there. Of course, these Japanese were driven along by the forces of imperialism and militarism, but it must not be forgotten that of these peoples the Japanese had the most highly developed spirit of capitalism.

Dore (1976) may also be considered as tending towards the 'Marxist' approach, although he pays some attention to the Weberian approach too. Comparing education in Britain, Japan, Sri Lanka and Kenya, Dore concludes that the later the point in world history a country starts a modernization drive, the more strongly the desire for educational qualification becomes entrenched and the more qualification-orientated schooling becomes at the expense of genuine education. In deriving this general tendency Dore bases his argument on the fact that countries in the developing world are usually constructed of dual components: a rich modern sector on the one hand, and an impoverished traditional sector on the other. The later development starts, the more the tendency to dualism is exacerbated, and those organizations belonging to the modern sector — central and local government, large multinational corporations and big private firms — usually tend to recruit by certificates. Of course, this law only operates on the assumption that other things are equal, but because the concepts Dore uses are 'basic' in the sense that they can be applied to all nations, the cultural and sociological elements specific to individual nations are considered merely as 'other things'. In Dore, therefore, the examination of the effects of superstructural elements upon the basic tendencies is minimized. Since Dore has looked at cultural differences between Japan and Britain too, it would, strictly speaking, be unfair to say that he ignores the effects of the superstructure, but it seems at least to me that he has not sufficiently emphasized the significance of these effects (Dore, 1976: 72–5).

Dore mentions that the Japan of the immediate pre-industrial period was a Confucian country where learning and scholarship carried high prestige and 'the very idea of education, therefore, was given higher value than in Britain's more philistine society' (1976: 44). Confucianism, however, is firmly rooted in Japan, and goes back far beyond the immediate pre-industrial period; it has been the moral backbone of the Japanese people since the ancient time of Shōtoku Taishi (573–621). While contemporary Japanese are perhaps more hideously and vulgarly philistine than the British, they are still Confucian in the sense that they classify people into two classes, illiterates (small men) and literati (gentlemen). The educational rat race in Japan is primarily a rat race to be classified as an educated gentleman, and not an economic race in pursuit of a higher income, although income is usually obtained in proportion to achievement in the educational race. This is evident from the case of female students, because in Japan most girls work for only a few years after college or university, yet the educational rat race among them is as severe as that among boys. It is obvious that girls take part in the entrance examination to colleges and universities, not for better jobs after graduation but to be themselves classified as a member of the upper tier of a dual-structured society; without this, it is very difficult for them to marry a man in the upper tier. Women's colleges in Japan are institutions for deciding students' social standing. Like finishing schools in Britain they are neither academic nor vocational-educational, except for a few. Likewise for boys, degrees and diplomas play a role similar to that played by genealogical charts and records in the Middle Ages. Firms recruit new members from the 'gentleman' class; in Confucian Japan candidates must be able to show diplomas in order to establish their identity as a member of that class. In fact, both boys and girls can obtain a high social standing if they receive higher education, while they can easily lose their parents' high standing if they fail to go on to a university.

On the other hand, Dore emphasizes the fact that there was no systematic general education in Britain at the time of the industrial revolution. This revolution was accomplished by craftsmen-inventors, mill-owners and so on, who had only a basic education and little specialized, scientific and technological knowledge. It seems to me, however, that what we need to explain is why general education remained so poor in Britain until the late eighteenth century that the industrial revolution had to be achieved mainly by dextrous fingers. A partial explanation may lie in the long tradition of primogeniture in England, which meant that children other than the heirs of the parents' land had to become independent at a very early stage of their life. A typical child

> is early sent to school, but at fourteen leaves home to earn his living . . . he goes to the nearest country town and stands in the market place [for a job]. . . . At sixteen or seventeen he is stalwart enough to hire as a man, and now his wages are doubled. . . . Many of the men, when about thirty years of age, are able to take small farms of their own. (Macfarlane, 1978: 77–8)

This has been a typical life style among English lads since the fourteenth or fifteenth century. In this way, 'the younger sons of the gentry, apprenticed to London masters, rose to be City managers' (Trevelyan, 1944: 100). Even the eldest son went away for several years before returning to take over a holding. 'The Statute of Artificers (1563) enacted that every craftsman in town or country had for seven years to learn his craft under a master who was responsible for him' (Trevelyan, 1944: 206). Thus, for many centuries apprenticeship was a substitute for school in England. Behind the fact that higher education has not been of particular concern in England lies the spirit of independence of English youth, of English individualism. This has been one of the most powerful driving forces in this country, and the existence of such a factor has not been emphasized by Dore. This big difference in spirit observable between Japan and England, that is, Confucian class consciousness vs. English individualism, offers a basis for developing a Weberian spiritualistic analysis, and such a consideration is necessary to complete Dore's materialistic analysis.[1]

II

Weber's studies in ideology, religion and ethics (or the national ethos nurtured by them) and their effects upon the people's secular life and economic activity, the studies which I call 'social ethology', are contained in the three volumes of his *Gesammelte Aufsätze zur Religionssoziologie* (Weber, 1920, 1921, 1922) chapter XV of his *Wirtschaft und Gesellschaft* (Weber, 1956) and part IV of his *Wirtschaftsgeschichte* (Weber, 1927). The work on the Protestant ethic (Weber, 1930) is of course the most famous and controversial. There are many critics of this long treatise, the most significant including Brentano (1923) and Tawney (1977, first published in 1922). The controversy is surveyed by Fischoff (1944).

Weber's critics are mainly concerned with the following points (Tawney, 1977: 311–13). (1) It would be untrue to say that the Protestant (or Puritan) reform was necessary for the appearance of capitalist enterprises — the woollen towns such as Ghent, Bruges and Mechelen in Flanders as well as Venetian and Florentine capitalism had already flourished in the fourteenth and fifteenth centuries (Morton, 1938: 109–10) — whereas it would be equally untrue to say that the religious reforms were produced as a result of the progress in the material lives of human beings. (2) Weber failed to appreciate intellectual movements, other than religious ones, which contributed to the promotion of individuals' rational economic behaviour. Brentano and Tawney point out that Machiavelli was at least as influential as Calvin. The studies made by St Antoninus of Florence on economic activity and processes (Schumpeter, 1954: 95–107) were a second element that Weber ignored. (3) Weber seems to have oversimplified both 'the Protestant ethic' and 'the spirit of capitalism'. Tawney says that the Calvinists of the sixteenth century were believers in a rigorous discipline and would have been horrified by the individualism ascribed to the Puritan movement in the seventeenth. Weber left unexplained what caused this change (see Robertson, 1933).

Hirschmeier and Yui (1975: 52–6) compare the spirit of the

merchant class of Tokugawa Japan with that of the city merchants in Renaissance Italy. By emphasizing the fact that capitalist activity was vigorous in Catholic Italy before the age of Luther and Calvin, these authors seem to be making a similar criticism to that of point (1) above. Schumpeter (1954) directs his attention to a different point. According to him, Weber's problem is 'a typical instance of what may be termed Spurious Problems'. In view of the fact that Weber's concepts of feudalism, capitalism, and so on are all ideal types, his problem of transforming feudalism to capitalism is a problem of replacing the 'ideal' Feudal Man by the 'ideal' Capitalist Man, neither of which have any counterpart at all in the sphere of historical fact. Thus, 'the problem of what it was that turned the one into the other vanishes completely', Schumpeter, 1954: 80–1). Similar criticisms as those made by Brentano and Tawney, Hirschmeier and Yui, and Schumpeter could all be made *mutatis mutandis* concerning Weber's other works, 'Ancient Judaism', 'Confucianism and Taoism', 'Hinduism and Buddhism' and 'Islam'.

It is true that in Weber's work both 'the Protestant ethic' and 'the spirit of capitalism' are concepts constructed on the basis of an ideal type. However, as was made clear by Ōtsuka (1955), Weber carefully distinguished between 'the spirit of capitalism' and 'the capitalist spirit', the latter being the greediness for money of, for example, merchants and usurers, military contractors and financial magnates, which is seen everywhere in the world and is as old as the history of human beings. By 'the spirit of capitalism', on the other hand, Weber meant the spirit of the modern capitalist regime (that is, 'the attitude which seeks profit rationally and systematically as the calling or job', 1930: 64) and had no intention of applying it to 'capitalism [such as] existed in China, India, Babylon, in the classical world, and in the Middle Ages' (Ōtsuka, 1955). In all these cases, Weber explicitly said, this particular ethos was lacking (1930: 52). It is evident, therefore, that criticism (1) by Brentano and Tawney as well as that made by Hirschmeier and Yui are both off the point.

Weber was concerned neither with the origination of capitalism, nor with the emergence of modern capitalism, nor with the transformation of feudalism to capitalism. His theory is not a causal analysis of history at all. We must, therefore, say that Schumpeter too has missed the point. What Weber aimed to accomplish was to reveal, by use of the ideal typical analysis, that there is a deep internal relationship between Protestantism and the ethos of modern capitalism in so far as the former is suited to the promotion and enhancement of the latter, so that it could have played the role of a driving force of capitalism (see Ōtsuka, 1955). Similarly Fischoff (1968: 77) summarizes what Weber intended to clarify to the same effect: that is, 'it was the spirit of a "methodical" *Lebensführung* which he [Max Weber] was deriving from Protestant ascetism and which is related to economic forms only through congruence [*Adäquanz*]'. Point (2) raised by Brentano and Tawney is not a criticism of Weber but merely an indication of another problem. He was perfectly entitled to neglect all the non-religious intellectual movements following the Renaissance for the simple reason that he was not interested in them, although he would have had to take them into consideration if he had been concerned with a causal investigation of the emergence of capitalism.

Despite this, we must acknowledge Brentano's and Tawney's point (3). But this does not mean that Weber's analysis was wrong; it only implies that it was imperfect. We construct various ideal types on the basis of historical, sociological or economic observations and examine the logical, phenomenological or interpretive interrelationships of these ideal types. We have to begin with a simple conceptual scheme from which only an oversimplified picture can be obtained. By using a more complicated scheme of ideal types, however, we may always arrive at a better understanding of history or the society. Thus Weber is a base for further development, i.e. a first approximation.

III

Why did 'modern capitalism' not emerge at other times and in other places than modern Western Europe? It was Weber's belief that modern capitalism was not automatically produced by the development of science and technology. Behind its emergence was also the emergence of a rational, anti-traditional way of thinking among human agents. He asked why there had been an enormous historical difference in this respect between the Orient and the Occident. For the purpose of answering this question he made a magnificent comparative study covering Europe, the Middle East, India and China and concluded that the modern Occident was provided with religious elements favourable to the rise of capitalism, while such elements were absent in other civilizations. He states, in connection with China, that 'genuine prophecy creates from within a way of life systematically oriented towards a single scale of values, and in the light of such an orientation the world is regarded as raw material to be shaped in ethical terms according to the given norm' (Weber, 1920, I: 521). Confucianism is the reverse of this. Weber considers that, like Protestantism, Confucianism is a highly rational religion, but there is an important contrast between them: 'As against the accommodation to the world found in Confucianism we find in Puritanism [or Protestantism] the task of reorganising the world in a rational manner' (1920, I: 527). Thus, whilst 'rationalism' is contained in the spirit of both ethics, the Confucian rationality is different from that of Puritanism: 'Confucian rationalism signified rational accommodation to the world: Puritan rationalism rational control of the world' (1920, I: 534). It was only the latter which fostered modern natural science and promoted the spirit of capitalism. In China not only were natural science and technology absent, but also natural law and formal logic. China, therefore, failed to achieve a shift from empirical to rational techniques: 'Everything remained at the level of sublimated empiricism' (Weber, 1920, I: 440).

Each religion has a social class which supports that religion and which therefore exerts a decisive influence on its development and propagation. In the case of Confucianism, it was the mandarins — 'earthly, rational stipend-holders of literary qualifications' — whilst in the case of Hinduism and Buddhism, it was the hereditary Brahmin caste with its knowledge of the holy books, the Vedas, and also the ascetic and meditative wandering mendicant friars. (In the case of Christianity it was itinerant craftsmen or urban citizens.) Moreover, in India the society is deeply divided into countless castes, sects, speech and blood groups. Almost without explanation, metaphysical promises given by Indian doctrines of salvation are only accessible to those of the Brahmin caste or those living monastically, though some are valid for the general populace. In India, as in China, there is a deep gulf between the educated few and the illiterate mass, and knowledge is the single absolute path to the highest holiness in this world. Indians differ from and are more faithful than Chinese in believing that this rule applies to the world beyond too.

Because of this very strong and strict dualism dividing society into two strata, the wise and educated few and the uncivilized plebeian masses,

> the factual, inner orders of the real world, that is, nature and art alike, ethics and economics alike, remained concealed from noble men, since these things were so barren as far as their particular interests were concerned. Their way of life was oriented, in striving for extraordinary things, to the example set by their prophets and wise men who were their absolute exemplars in every major respect. For the plebeian, however, there was no prophecy of ethical mission which would serve as rational formulation for their everyday life. (Weber, 1921, II: 378)

As the elite was so taken up with metaphysics and the plebeians so ignorant, one could not expect modern capitalism to emerge in India indigenously and autonomously; the natural and social sciences have been of poor quality in India throughout her history, whereas magic and metaphysics have always been rich and prosperous. The imbalance between theoretical and practical statistics in India is a mere symptom of the intellectual polarization prevailing in the society.

Weber's whole comparative study of world religions may be regarded, as he himself perceived, as a massive unified work aimed at clarifying the cultural background, spiritual backbone and the materialistic consequences of occidental civilization. From a different point of view, however, it may be seen as part of the overall task of establishing the proposition that the economic performance of various peoples or nations is unstable and influenced by the slightest change in their ethos. Weber completed only that part concerning Christianity, but he left unfinished the parts relating to other religions, for example Confucianism, Hinduism, Buddhism.

The instability (or knife-edge) thesis is based on the observation that Catholics and Protestants, who share the same Bible but interpret it differently, are significantly different in their modes of worldly behaviour. Weber sees the essential disagreement between the two as lying in the fact that Protestantism removes the barrier between layman and clergy by discarding the division of Christian ethical precepts into *praecepta* and *consilia*, while Catholicism sticks to this dualism. For all Protestant denominations 'the only way of living acceptable to God was not to outbid worldly morality by monastic ascetism, but solely through the fulfilment of the obligations imposed upon the individual by his position in the world. That was his calling' (Weber, 1920, I: 69). Thus, by interpreting the same Bible differently Protestantism produces the concept of a job as a 'calling', that is, a task set by God, by which secular life (therefore economic activity) is connected with the will of God. Then one's job becomes one's duty, and this kind of outlook on work is, at least in some stage of history necessary for the establishment of the capitalist regime and the take-off of its economic growth. The Protestant Reformation was a breakthrough by which ascetism, confined up to then within monasteries, was openly released into the outside secular world. People then began to act ascetically and rationally; rational utilization of capital was carried out and the rational capitalistic organization of labour was implemented. Protestantism thus contributed to (or is congruent with) the establishment of an efficient economic system.

As for China and India, no such instability argument is found in Weber's works. He only concludes that neither Confucianism, Hinduism nor Buddhism is suitable for promoting the spirit of capitalism; each contains some significant factors which work to prevent the emergence of capitalism. He is nearest to the knife-edge proposition when he says: 'The Chinese in all probability would be quite capable, probably as much as if not more capable than the Japanese, of assimilating capitalism which has technologically and economically been fully developed in the modern culture area' (Weber, 1920, I: 535). I have, however, found room for further investigation and developed, for the sake of comparison between China and Japan, an argument parallel to the one that Weber made with respect to Catholicism and Protestantism (see Morishima, 1982).

In my opinion, between China and Japan there is *prima facie* no significant difference in ideological layout. They are primarily Confucianist countries; Buddhism came to Japan not directly from India but always through China, and Shintoism, which is generally thought of as a religion truly indigenous to Japan, was, even in its ancient primitive form, deeply influenced by Chinese Taoism; indeed it has been suggested that it might even be nothing other than a disguised Japanese version of Taoism. In spite of this, Japan succeeded in easily assimilating modern capitalism, while China continued to be exploited by imperialists from the West and Japan. Of course, there are geographical, sociological and historical differences between these two countries which played favourable or unfavourable roles in deciding their fates in the last century. For instance, Japan is an island and did not break into fragments; China was far more vulnerable. China's big families are compared with Japan's relatively small ones. Also, throughout her history, China was almost always in the hands of civil service bureaucrats, while Japan, at the end of her feudal era, was dominated by military officers, samurai. These differences, except for those which are beyond the control of the people, such as geographical differences, can only be explained by viewing them in the light of instability theory.

It is noticeable that whereas the Chinese interpretation of Confucius' doctrines is individualistic and humanistic, the Japanese one is nationalistic and militaristic. This contrast arguably has existed ever since Confucianism first came to Japan in about the sixth century. This is not surprising, since the Japanese have suffered at all times from a sense of inferiority vis-à-vis the powerful Chinese empire, leading them to be, throughout their history, closely banded together and aggressive (Morishima, 1982: 1–19). At the end of the period of isolation which lasted for more than 200 years up to 1859, Japan was under pressure from the West. In this crisis the intelligentsia — samurai, who had been educated in the Japanese-Confucian manner — succeeded in unifying the country and finally established a new, powerful, modern government. It eventually established a nationalist capitalist economy based on a seniority system, lifetime employment and the loyalty of employees to their company, a system perfectly fitting to the ethos of Japanese Confucianism (Morishima, 1982: 52–87).

For the establishment of modern western-style capitalism, there are two preconditions: the nation state and civil society. In order for the capitalist mode of economic behaviour to prevail, an administrative organization must be established, which secures the continuance of the regime. There must be a strong government which enforces rational law in order to enable each member of society to calculate the consequences of his or her activity objectively and quantitatively. The government must have professional bureaucrats, administrative, judicial and military (Weber, 1927: 337–43). It is very much due to the nationalistic Japanese form of Confucianism that Japan, which had been split into many class and regional segments, was easily unified into a nation in a relatively short period of about twenty years, although there were obviously other favourable factors, such as Japan's being an island country and Japan's awareness that the Philippines had fallen into the hands of Spain and that China was under constant attack from western countries. In 1890 Japan already had a powerful modern government with officials recruited from among ex-samurai and new university graduates.

It was, however, very difficult for Japan to fulfil the other precondition. In contrast with Christianity, according to which everyone is equal in the sight of God, Confucianism promotes a collectivist ethic and the ethics of functional role expectation (see Hirschmeier and Yui, 1975: 44), both of which maintain and strengthen the hierarchical character of the society. Therefore, the elements of a civil society were not well developed in Meiji Japan, and it is evident that this strong nation with its weak civil society was not suited to competitive capitalism of the western type. It created a different type of production system,[2] though this can be included in the broad category of capitalism. In this economy the invisible hand is more visible, since the government always takes the initiative and plays the role of helmsman of the economy. Efficiency has been established by collaboration rather than competition, and the idea of class antagonism has not been widespread among trade unionists.

IV

We may now say that by virtue of the emergence of Japan, capitalism can no longer be monochromatic. Moreover, as the capitalism of the West, which may be called Protestant capitalism, declines as Schumpeter (1943: 61) has pointed out, because of its very achievements, its very success, so the Confucian capitalism looming in the East becomes more alarming. We will return to this later. The attainment of an economic optimum via individualistic economic competition, which is said to be the most important raison d'être of the free enterprise system, is neither the main purpose nor the prime function of the Japanese economy. Not competition among workers vis-à-vis the firm, but collaboration between workers for the benefit of the firm becomes the more important subject for analysis. In fact, in Japanese society competition prevails, not so much among adults but among children, who are selected and allocated to various firms according to the qualities of the diplomas they have received in the educational rat race; once they have been allocated to a firm, it is very difficult for them to move, especially from a small firm to a big one. In addition, Japanese society is a dual society; there is a big gulf, in wages, fringe benefits, productivity, risks and the rate of profit, between the big business sector and the small business/subcontractor sector. Compared with western firms Japanese big business operates in a very bureaucratic way, often adopting, instead of the western planning and decision making by top management, the *ringi* system (the system of 'proposal submission from below and approval by the seniors', Dore, 1973: 227–8) according to which responsibility is diffused throughout the organization and it is difficult to identify where the real responsibility lies. Moreover, the newly industrialized countries such as Korea, Taiwan, Hong Kong and Singapore are all dominated by Confucianism. For the analysis of these new capitalist societies, especially Korea, Taiwan and Japan, a new economic model emphasizing collaboration, group consciousness and nationalism should be formulated.

In order to analyse non-occidental economies Marx conceived the idea of the Asiatic mode of production (Melotti, 1977). In its typical form this mode of production develops in the vast areas of the world where the climate is intensely hot, so that such areas are likely to embrace huge tracts of desert. Land in such areas is virtually a free good, and for that reason private ownership of land does not exist. Irrigation and fertilization are the most important tasks of the state, and in these places it is the state which is the supreme landlord. In economic terms the people possess no power whatsoever vis-à-vis the ruler, and autocracy therefore prevails (Oriental Despotism). There is no question of the people in countries of this kind being civil, in the western sense of the word.

Japan and the other new industrial countries of Asia are certainly not typical of the Asiatic mode of production. In the first place they are countries whose land areas are small and where irrigation is not a matter of life and death. They are all seagoing nations with long coastlines in proportion to their total land areas; all have developed by means of foreign trade by sea. Yet the population of these countries is largely made up either of Chinese or of people who have been conspicuously influenced by the culture of China, so their manners and customs are distinctively Chinese in a broad sense. In these countries, which have developed by acquiring the greatest possible demand for their goods from abroad, home demand is not very important to their economic growth. An exception to this is Japan, which has fairly large home demand, but even in Japan domestic demand is not the main motive force behind development.

So in these countries the fact that a civil society fails to develop is not a serious matter; despite poor home demand from their poor civil societies they could still expand their economies. In this way, they embarked on a forced march of rapid growth to catch up with the West. In particular, the growth programmes of Japan and Korea were formulated in such a way that the completely modernized industrial core produced within Japan or Korea was steadily expanded at all costs. The small business/subcontractor sector was a loser at all times; it was exploited and eroded by the big business sector, which was supported by the state. For the forced march loyalty and service in the form of devotion to the state and the work place are required of the people, and throughout the period of modernization there has been little recognition that each individual has an innate right to freedom and self-enlightenment.

A strong nation-state is a precondition for both capitalism and socialism. It might be said that the nationalistic Japanese Confucianism which is not suited to the establishment of a civil society would probably accord more with socialism than capitalism.[3] At the time when the modern state was formed in Japan, however, socialism was only a theory; no country actually had a socialist economy. If the modernization of Japan had been carried out later than immediately after 1868, she might have taken a more socialistic approach, instead of taking the option of state capitalism as she actually did. The course of historical development of society is not unilinear, not only within the capitalist camp, but also over the broad spectrum of regimes from capitalism to socialism. Furthermore, the instability thesis implies that by shifting the ideological base of society a wide variety of new courses of economic development will be opened up and these may significantly differ from the course that would have been followed in the absence of such a shift.

From the point of view of instability theory it is entirely reasonable that philosophers, political leaders and revolutionaries in the Third World recognize the importance of modification or replacement of existing ideology. In the case of China Sun Yat-sen advocated the western concepts of nationalism, democracy and people's welfare. Chiang Kai-shek emphasized Confucianism and Protestantism, and Mao Tse-tung accepted Marxism. Of these three only Mao was successful in giving rise to a remarkable change in the people's attitude, which resulted, in turn, in an enormous improvement in their economic life. In India, the influence of the idea of human spiritual and social equality in missionary Christianity led Mahatma Jotirao Phule to devote himself to abolishing the Hindu caste hierarchy and forming a new religious identity (O'Hanlon, 1985), while Mahatma Gandhi, also influenced by Christian ideas, tried to improve the lot of the weak and oppressed, especially the untouchables. As a Hindu himself, Gandhi did not wish to abolish the caste system but fought its evils. He condemned modern western civilization, and wanted to preserve the Indian cultural traditions, by opposing the spirit inherent in both socialist and capitalist industrialism at the time (Buss, 1985: 17–22). He laid himself open to cross-fire from conflicting forces and was shot dead by a Hindu fanatic.

Gandhi held heredity in high regard because he believed that to disregard the law of heredity would create great confusion. This belief caused his reluctance to abolish the caste system, which is the mainstay of traditionalism in India. This attitude, despite his great desire to improve the position of the untouchables, made him very much a gradualist. He could minimize bloodshed in the Indian independence movement by his advocacy of passive resistance. In the same spirit he insisted on the importance of villages as against cities, because he believed that truth and non-violence were only possible in the context of the simplicity of the villages. He also considered that labour was more important than machines in the industrial development of India. This emphasis was shared by Mao. For Gandhi, independence by passive resistance was independence achieved through the indigenous Indian spirit; the important thing was to stand by themselves without the help of western civilization. Gandhi considered that the ancient Indian ethics, which knew nothing of rights but only duties, should be the basis of Indian development in the future. He emphasized that all rights derived from duties well performed (Buss, 1985: 17).

It is clear that this philosophy of Gandhi denounces civil society, one of the main pillars of western capitalism, and promotes nationalism. The situation is in strong contrast to that of Japan after 1868. It is true that in Japan too there were many fanatical nationalists who rejected everything western and strictly upheld Japanese traditions, but Ōkubo Toshimichi, the central figure of the Meiji Revolution, was brave enough to abolish the caste system, which had prevailed more or less rigorously throughout the Tokugawa era (1603–1867). In China Confucianism was a philosophy for feudalism and had always supported the feudal hierarchy of status, but its caste system had no metaphysical justification, unlike its Indian counterpart, which has had such a justification continuously since Aryans first came to India. So the caste system is more separable from Confucianism in China than it is from Hinduism in India. Furthermore, in Japan the system was predominant only during the Tokugawa period. By comparison with Gandhi, therefore, Ōkubo could more easily terminate a system which had been a major source of economic inefficiency. By abolishing the caste system Ōkubo could bring to an end the feudal division of society into fixed classes; this not only contributed to an upsurge of nationalism, but also released individuals from the feudalistic fetters that hindered modern individualistic competition. In this way, the Japanese gradually began to recognize the importance of civil society in modern life, though this was not openly acknowledged until the end of the Second World War.

V

From this we may conclude that the line of moderate passivity which was taken by Gandhi was not revolutionary enough to make the Indian economy move in the direction of modern capitalism or socialism. However, unlike the Chinese and the Japanese, Indians are more sincere and serious in their search for truth and salvation. In Hinduism they have developed a magnificent metaphysical theory, but unfortunately it is a religion of caste and renunciation of life. As a Hindu, Gandhi was no exception; he was possessed by the devil of caste. This is the tragedy of Gandhi, the tragedy of India. Unlike Japan but like China, the introduction of elements of western ideologies, for example Protestantism, socialism or even Marxism, into the indigenous religion is necessary, or indispensable, for India's economy to develop in a rational and secularly ascetic manner.

Myrdal (1972) is also very critical of the caste system. Given the sanction of religion (that is, of Hinduism) which is even today very powerful among Indians, the caste system is still strongly influential there, particularly in Indian villages. It divides the society and is therefore an obvious obstacle to development:

> It fortifies the contempt and disgust for manual work prevalent in all social strata. Since an orthodox Hindu regards not only those who perform this work but everyone outside his own caste as beyond the pale, it also warps and stultifies ordinary human feelings of brotherhood and compassion. (Myrdal, 1972: 147)

Naturally, this caste system creates divisions of culture and economic interests which work against national consolidation. Moreover, according to Myrdal, 'we cannot claim that this ideal of a more disciplined nation is shared by a large number of people even among the intellectual elite of South Asia' (1972: 52). Thus he concludes that under present conditions in India development cannot be achieved unless the people observe social discipline much more strictly than the prevailing interpretation of democracy in the region permits. 'Too much individual interest, too little public spirit' is the diagnosis for India; it is completely opposite to that for Japan.

In this situation, Gandhi still believed non-violent social change to be possible by persuading the privileged to abandon their privileges and enter into truly democratic co-operation with the underprivileged. Quoting from D.R. Gadgil who criticizes such optimism by Gandhi as 'little more than revivalism', Myrdal joins with him in saying that 'the failure of Gandhi's approach "lay essentially in not recognizing the need for thoroughly demolishing the older institutional and class forms before a new synthesis could be attempted"' (Myrdal, 1972: 178). On the other hand, Myrdal appreciates other aspects of Gandhism. Gandhi rejected not only European products but also the European mode of industrialization. He resembled Mao in rejecting the use of machinery in the large-scale factory mode of production in cities. As pointed out earlier, he emphasized villages and labour instead. Myrdal finds an essential element or rationality in this gospel of Gandhi: 'the programs for promoting cottage industry as they have evolved in the post-war era have come more and more to represent purposeful and realistic planning for development under the very difficult conditions that prevail' (1972: 325).

It is evident, however, that however brave, ambitious and respectable such a thing might be, it is extremely difficult and expensive to achieve such a growth programme without the help of European civilization. Gandhi's philosophy of making India Indian again by dint of the Indian spirit alone is an obvious antithesis to the Japanese slogan after the Meiji Revolution, 'Japanese spirit with Western Technology'. It is not surprising to see that the instability theory has not worked in India; for that theory to work, it requires that a new shift in ideology creates secular asceticism and rationalism among the people.

Despite the existence of many articles in search of a Protestant ethic analogy in Asia, my book (Morishima, 1982) might claim to be unique in clearly referring to the instability of secular life in response to a change in ideology or a religious reform. In the case of Japan, it has been suggested that such religious sects as Jōdo Shinshu and Zen-shu and such ethical movements as Hōtoku-kyō and Shingaku are associated with Japan's successful economic achievements (Bellah, 1957: ch. 5; McClelland, 1961: 369–70). It is true that Jōdo Shinshu can be considered Buddhism's version of Protestantism and that it has played an important role in the secularization of Buddhism in Japan. It is also true, as Bellah has pointed out, that the priests of the Jōdo Shinshu sects gave sermons emphasizing the importance of 'inner-worldly asceticism'. As a matter of fact, however, after the defeat of the Ikko uprising (1571–80) by Nobunaga, Jōdo Shinshu (sometimes called Ikko-shu) had little desire for social reform, fierce indignation against evil, nor any concept of popular salvation. Throughout the Tokugawa era, and even since then, its leaders indulged themselves in an aristocratic life style. Moreover it is certainly true that Hōtoku-kyō and Shingaku were popular among Tokugawa merchants, but Bellah's (1963) criticism of McClelland — that he is mistaken in concluding that samurai in the Meiji period were devotees of Zen Buddhism — holds just as well for his own discussion of the Hōtoku-kyō and Shingaku movements. In fact, political leaders and industrialists in the Meiji period were not much influenced by these movements. Meiji Japan was still a samurai society and it was Confucian thought which played the role of the driving force behind modernization in that period (Morishima, 1982; Golzio, 1985: 98–9).

Articles concerned with the relationship between religion and inner-worldly asceticism in the non-occidental areas seem mainly to have tried to identify those religions which have most contributed to enhancing the motivation necessary for entrepreneurial activity, but they have neglected the problem of motivation for asceticism on the workers' side (for example Eisenstadt, 1968; Buss, 1985). In Weber, as was seen in an earlier part of this chapter, both are constituent elements of the spirit of the capitalist regime. We may say, therefore, that these articles are not genuinely Weberian because they discuss only 'the capitalist spirit' but not 'the spirit of capitalism'. They are also far from realizing that Weber's Protestantism thesis is essentially an instability or knife-edge theorem. Only Bellah (1963) is near to finding the theorem (but has missed it) when he says: 'As every reader of the famous [Protestant ethic] essay knows, the material is derived from England primarily, and not from Germany, where the Reformation remained abortive in important respects and its structural consequences stunted.' Without the instability theorem it is rather difficult to understand why Japan and the two countries of Korea and Taiwan, both of which have been greatly influenced by Japan in terms of education and worldly behaviour, have been successful in breaking through the barriers to modernization, whilst China, though having once accomplished a brilliant breakthrough under the communist party since the war, was later greatly disrupted by the cultural revolution launched by the whimsies of Mao. 'The cultural revolution' and 'brainwashing' look *prima facie* like Marxist concepts, but in spite of their concern with violent activities, they are entirely in place in a Weberian glossary.

Finally I would add that the instability theorem may work not only in the Third World but also in socialist countries. Marxism might be revised in such a way as to considerably enhance their economic achievement.

VI

A dynamic congruence theory may be obtained by combining what I have called the Marxian and Weberian approaches. Let E_t and S_t represent the state of the economy in period t and the state of the superstructure in t, respectively. According to the

Marxian theory, for each E_t there is an adequate state of the superstructure S^*, while the Weberian theory says that there is also a reverse relationship of adequacy between E and S, that is, for each given S_t there is an adequate state of the Economy E^*. Let us express these two kinds of congruency as $S^* = M(E_t)$ and $E^* = W(S_t)$, respectively, and assume that there is no time lag in the realization of the Marxian congruence, so that $S^* = S_t = M(E_t)$, while there is one period of lag in the Weberian one: $E^* = E_{t+1} = W(S_t)$. (This is the assumption for the sake of simplicity. We may alternatively assume that there is some time lag in the Marxian congruence too and can *mutatis mutandis* apply the following argument to this bilaterally lagged system.) Combining these, we have $S_{t+1} = M(W(S_t))$ and find that where W is not the inverse of M, there is a dynamic movement of S and, hence, of E. With a given S_o we obtain E_1 by the Weberian theory. Then the Marxian theory tells us that S_1 is congruent to E_1. Similarly, we obtain E_2 as corresponding to S_1 and S_2 to E_2; and so forth. Thus a movement of superstructure, S_1, S_2, S_3, . . . and a movement of economy, E_1, E_2, E_3, . . . are generated from the original state S_0. In the sequence of the states of economy, E_t, $t = 1, 2, 3, \ldots$, those E_t's for all $t \leqq$ some t' would belong to the same regime, say the capitalist while E_t's for $t > t'$ might belong to another, say, the socialist. In this case we have a transformation of the economy from capitalism to socialism.

This is a scheme of historical transformation which is established by using both Marxian and Weberian components. One example of this is Schumpeter's theory of the evolution of society. Contrary to the Marxist theory of revolution which maintains that the capitalist regime will finally collapse and be replaced by socialism or communism because economic polarization becomes unacceptable and repeated crises become more and more stormy and explosive, Schumpeter develops the following argument:

> the actual and prospective performance of the capitalist system is such as to negative [*sic*] the idea of its breaking down under the weight of economic failure, but . . . its very success undermines the social institutions which protect it, and 'inevitably' creates conditions in which it will not be able to live and which strongly point to socialism as the heir apparent. (1943: 61)

In more detail,

> capitalism creates a critical frame of mind which, after having destroyed the moral authority of so many other institutions, in the end turns against its own; the bourgeois finds to his amazement that the rationalist attitude does not stop at the credentials of kings and popes but goes on to attack private property and the whole scheme of bourgeois values. (1943: 143)

In addition, there is the fact that in Europe, where nation-states competed for internationally mobile capital, they were in collusion with capital and treated the bourgeois exceedingly favourably.[4] Naturally, such a collusion could also be a target of severe criticism. Monarchs strove for the provision of infrastructural services for industry and commerce in order to gain revenue for themselves. Furthermore, 'In a purely bourgeois regime', Schumpeter says,

> troops may fire on strikers, but the police cannot round up intellectuals or must release them forthwith; otherwise . . . the freedom it [the bourgeois stratum] disapproves cannot be crushed without also crushing the freedom it approves. . . . In defending the intellectuals as a group . . . the bourgeoisie defends itself and its scheme of life. Only a government of non-bourgeois nature and non-bourgeois creed . . . is strong enough to discipline them. [1943: 150]
>
> Freedom of public discussion involving freedom to nibble at the foundations of capitalist society is inevitable in the long run. . . . The intellectual group cannot help nibbling, because it lives on criticism . . . and criticism of persons and of current events will . . . fatally issue in criticism of classes and institutions. (1943: 151)

Once the superstructure of western capitalism reaches this stage, it is obvious that the economy cannot work in the way it worked when 'the Protestant ethic' and, therefore 'the spirit of capitalism' prevailed in the society. At this stage, innovation will also have been reduced to routine. Entrepreneurship tends to be depersonalized and automated: 'Bureau and committee work tends to replace individual action' (Schumpeter, 1943: 133). As in the *ringi* system of Japanese firms, a very bureaucratic form of decision making will be adopted. Not only will the entrepreneurial function become obsolete, but other strata supporting the regime, such as aristocrats and *rentiers*, will also tend to become powerless, and will finally disappear. It will become an age of professionals and intellectuals and, as in Japan, the educational rat race will become hectic and severe.

Such a situation is very remote from that of seventeenth-century England, with which Weber is mainly concerned in his famous Protestantism essay. Let S_o be the superstructure in the seventeenth century which has the Protestant ethic as its dominant element and E_1 the modern capitalist economy which was emerging and growing at that time. Furthermore, let S_t be the superstructure with the kind of ethos which, as has just been described, Schumpeter considers to prevail in mature capitalist economy in its closing years, and E_{t+1} the new economy, which would be in accordance with the superstructure S_t. Schumpeter speculates that this new economy will be a socialist one. As has already been seen, however, the capitalist camp is no longer homogeneous now that Japan has established herself as a Confucian capitalist state. An alternative option is now available. The 'diseased' western capitalist economy in its final stage might be metamorphosed into a more socialistic variety of capitalism of the Japanese type, rather than switching immediately to socialism. Schumpeter also neglected the possibility of the appearance of someone like Mrs Thatcher, whose aim is to intervene in the process of metamorphosis in the hope of reviving the Victorian ethic and spirit in the late twentieth century. In any case, Schumpeter's scheme of transformation of a society from capitalism to socialism is too simple to be accepted without modification, because the rich menu of future economic systems now available to each modern society is likely to contain several options, from among which a society can choose without undue friction. It is not entirely inconceivable that competitive capitalism, having started with the Protestant ethic, will end in the managerial capitalism of the Confucianist or Japanese type.

Since the time t at which some kind of Schumpeterian transformation is made has not yet come and, hence, t takes on a large value belonging to the future, it is necessary for us to make an empirical analysis for the past and a deductive analysis for the future in order to fill in the intermediate stages (S_i, E_{i+1}), $i = 1, 2, \ldots, t-1$, between the Weberian age (S_o, E_1) and the Schumpeterian age (S_t, E_{t+1}). In this way we might be able to obtain a complete course of dynamic congruence of S and E from 0 to t. Moreover, in view of the fact that the superstructure S is not a single entity but a multidimensional complex consisting of religion, culture, international environment and many others, it is extremely difficult to determine the dual relationships $S_i = M(E_i)$ and $E_{i+1} = W(S_i)$ which generate sequences S_i, E_{i+1}, $i = 1, 2, \ldots, t-1$. This is a classic point raised by Brentano and

Tawney. However, despite the fact that controlled experiments are almost impossible in the social sciences, it is still possible to imagine *ceteris paribus* situations from which deductive analytical conclusions can be derived by skilfully applying the method of thought experiment based on the idea of *Verstehen*. In this way we may minimize the ambiguity and arbitrariness unavoidable in this sort of research and may at least obtain a model which is useful for interpreting (or understanding) history from the viewpoint of congruence between superstructures and infrastructures.

VII

Thus, providing we are satisfied with a rough first approximation in the form of a partial theory, the task of dynamizing the Weberian thesis may not be entirely impossible. In fact, there have been attempts to tackle this problem. For example, Wiener (1981) does deal with the cultural background of the decline of the industrial spirit in Britain in the period 1850–1980, though his work has to be carefully re-examined in conjunction with economic history analyses, such as those by Church (1980), Deane and Cole (1967) and others. Wiener develops a view which is an alternative to Schumpeter's but does not entirely contradict it. He emphasizes the ambivalent character of the English ethos and writes that this ambivalence placed lasting social and psychological limits on the industrial revolution in England and, in spite of Britain's being a pioneer of modernization, a hostility to industrialism persisted there; the prosperity of industry was shortlived and the age of post-industrialization came soon. This view is not unconnected to that of Weber, who also noticed the ambivalence of the English character: in his words,

> through the whole of English society ever since the seventeenth century we see the conflict between the squirearchy, the representatives of 'merrie' old England, and Puritan circles widely fluctuating in their social influence. Both elements, on the one hand an unspoiled naive joy of life, and on the other a strictly regulated, reserved self-control combined with conventional ethical conduct, are even to-day combined to form the English national character. (Weber, 1930: 173)

Similarly, Wiener points out that while England gave birth to the industrial revolution and exported it throughout the world, the

English themselves were not comfortable with materialistic growth. They have always had the view that England is essentially the countryside, a green and pleasant land. The English way of life stresses 'nonindustrial, noninnovative and nonmaterial qualities' (Wiener, 1981: 6). 'The English genius,' he writes, 'was (despite appearances) not economic or technical, but social and spiritual; it did not lie in inventing, producing, or selling, but in persevering, harmonizing and moralizing' (1981: 6).

As the superstructure S is multidimensional, it may contain, as it does in the case of Britain, contradictory elements, the spirit of anti-individualism as well as the spirit of capitalism, and this ambivalence creates a dynamism in the economy. Throughout the nineteenth and twentieth centuries Britain has more and more been inclined, in the choice between workshop and garden, in favour of the latter. In Wiener's words: 'the dominant collective self-image in English culture became less and less that of the world workshop. Instead, this image was challenged by the counter image of an ancient, little-disturbed "green and pleasant land".' Britain all too soon lost the position of workshop of the world in the competition for economic hegemony.

In this dynamic process, Wiener says, the 'period of recognised economic crisis in Britain was preceded by a century of psychological and intellectual de-industrialisation' (1981: 157). This view fits perfectly to our formula incorporating time lag, $E_{t+1} = W(S_t)$. Wiener resembles Schumpeter in so far as they both emphasize cultural elements as one of the major causes of the decline of industrialism in Britain: 'The politicians, civil servants, churchmen, professional men, and publicists who did so much to shape modern British political opinion and policy moved in a climate of opinion uncongenial to the world of industry' (Wiener, 1981: 159). Their images of a very attractive way of life were 'geared to maintenance of a status quo rather than innovation, comfort rather than attainment, the civilized enjoyment rather than the creation, of wealth' (1981: 159). This would obviously give rise to a decline in both Schumpeter's entrepreneurship and Weber's spirit of capitalism. By developing and improving this sort of theory we may eventually obtain a theory of history, or a dynamic theory of social economy which is better than either the Marxist doctrine of historical materialism or the Weberian social theory of the 'Protestant ethic' thesis type.

Despite its brilliance I do not entirely subscribe to Wiener's analysis; we may conceive of another plausible conjecture concerning the 'British disease'. It is true that his attempts to relate Britain's economic decline to the ambivalence which is found in the English ethos is novel and ambitious. There is no doubt about this. My own conjecture, however, is that the British two-party system is greatly responsible for the decline, though this system may of course be considered as a political reflection, or symbolization, of the ambivalence in the national ethos. Economic decay may be considered as the cost paid by the British people for keeping the two-party system for the sake of democracy, individualism and liberalism.

Finally it must be stressed that both Marxian and Weberian approaches are indispensable elements in the 'extended economics' that I propose. Where no individual is moved by the spirit of maximizing utility and no entrepreneur is strong enough to be loyal to the spirit of maximizing profits, classical or neoclassical economics is nothing more than a castle in the air. Even Marx, the most important thinker to advocate an objective theory of economic determinism, assumes that a spirit of capitalism prevails in the economy when he says: 'Accumulate, accumulate! That is Moses and the prophets' (Marx 1965: 595). Social ethology, as a comparative analysis of national ethos, though as yet very undeveloped, is an appropriate member of extended economics. In this magnificent subject, which is inevitably multidisciplinary, it is of course desirable that the component disciplines, economics proper and social ethology, should be methodologically of the same kind.

Fortunately Weber's sociology is constructed along much the same lines as Ricardo's economics, the prototype of contemporary economic theory. In regarding Ricardo as the originator of theoretical economics there is no disagreement among economists. Marxian economists and Walrasian or mathematical economists, as well as those belonging to the British classical school (including Keynes), are all Ricardian in methodology. They begin by clearly defining the concepts used in their economic analysis. These may also be called ideal types (in Weber's terminology); they are pure or abstract rather than actual or concrete. By using them an economic model is constructed. Of course the model thus constructed is an ideal type too. Such a model, though it would emphasize certain aspects of the actual economy, neglecting other aspects, could provide devices to help our understanding of the essential mechanisms of the economy. Relations between the various ideal types, or economic laws, are found by deductive logic, or often by using mathematics, without giving much consideration to historical or empirical observation. A substantial part of Weber's sociology is constructed in a more or less similar way; it would not appear to be very difficult to build a construction which incorporates deductive sociology and deductive economics.

Any theoretical description of the world based on ideal types will frequently deviate from the actual world; it is no more than a first approximation to reality. Therefore, whenever we find a serious gap between theory and reality we must be modest enough to alter the model, so as to obtain a better theory. Although economic theorists are not eager to modify their own models, the revision of a theory in the light of observation is the most essential part of scientific activity. Moreover, economists should learn how to handle historical data from Weber, who started his academic life as a historian. Then the extended economics we would establish is likely to be closer to the magnificent economics of Adam Smith and Marx than to the pure economics of Ricardo and Walras.

Notes

* I wrote this paper in December 1986. It was of course before the Ten-an Men incident and the collapse of East European countries. I wish to thank Sir John Hicks and Professor K. Minogue for valuable comments.

1. Sir John Hicks kindly commented on an earlier version of this chapter. He compared education in Europe with education in China and Japan. I found it most valuable and reproduce the relevant part of his letter to me with his permission:

> 'Concerning the division between literates and illiterates in Confucian countries. I asked myself: was there anything in Europe that corresponded? At first we would say that European scripts, going back to the Greeks and Romans, were immensely easier to read and write than the Chinese. So they should not have been responsible for a similar class-division. But of course in Europe there were language differences, which could have had the same effect. Were what corresponded to the Chinese mandarins the *clerks* in Europe who could write Latin? There could have been something of that in early Mediaeval Europe.
>
> But the rise of the nation states in the 14–15th centuries was accompanied by the displacement of Latin as ''mandarin'' language by the national languages, English and French in particular. And at much the same time came the invention of printing, which made books, now easy to read, also quite cheap. So a large part of the population, at least in towns, became in your sense literate. It is surely no accident that that was accompanied

by the Protestant Reformation. And by what Weber calls the Rise of Capitalism. For the large literate population, which could now pick up ideas from each other, and did not have to have them handed down from above, could stimulate each other, in a way that had not been possible before.

Even if one goes back to the earlier period, when I accept that in Europe there was indeed a line between literate and illiterate, there is the difference that in Europe education was not, as in China, in the hands of the State. That, from very early days had a rival, the Church. That the Christian Church, in Western Europe (not in Byzantium or in Russia) was an independent source of authority was very important. Early mediaeval Kings had to rely on churchmen as administrators — bishops and cardinals were their ministers — the educational system of the church was largely independent of the King. Then the Kings tried to develop schools which were less clerical, universities, law schools, and so on, in competition; and competition was fruitful, as it often is. Surely it is because Europe, unlike China, did not have a unified educational system, but at least two systems, that Europe in critical centuries found out so much more.'

2. See for example Hirschmeier and Yui (1975) and Morishima (1982).

3. On similarities and dissimilarities between capitalist and socialist economies, see Morishima (1976: 1–15).

4. Hall (1985: 102) and Weber (1927: 337, English edition).

3

EDUCATIONAL SYSTEMS AND THE ECONOMY

A.H. Halsey

Introduction

Whenever societies have a complex division of labour, educational systems develop, linking kinship structures to labour markets. The aim of this chapter is to review the last two decades of research on the relations of learning and work in advanced industrial societies. Perhaps the first message of the recent literature is insistence on complexity (Clark, 1987). Verbal distinctions between learning, training, education, schooling, qualification, certification, and so on refer to the many social locations of the transmission and innovation of culture in such societies. Distinctions too between work and employment, activity and occupation, jobs and careers, denote significant variations in the social locations of human labour. Even the elementary vocabulary of adult and child, family and workplace, public and private, can be a lexicon of misconception of the relations between human skills and their manifestations as goods and services. People live and learn in factories and offices and the DIY industry supports a vast amount of work in homes. There are domestic and informal as well as formal economies. Adults learn in the fastest growing of all the sectors of education and children labour competitively in school and family to acquire credentials for employment.

The Political Economy of Education

It emerges then that education is valued because it is a scarce good, so we must expect to find either or both market and political institutions for its distribution. Education can be a consumption good, as when the resident caretaker of my college goes to night school to learn modern Greek, in which case it is mainly of interest to students of culture. Second, education can

TABLE 1
UK higher education students (000s)

	1970–1	**add**	**% add**	**1983–4**
Full-time				
Total	456.8	124.8	27.3	580.6
UK origin univ.	217.2	50.8	23.4	268.0
Public sector	215.1	50.8	23.6	265.9
From abroad	24.4	23.2	95.1	47.6
Men	274.2	50.2	18.3	333.4
Women	182.6	63.6	34.8	246.2
Part-time				
Total	164.7	148.5	90.2	313.2
Univ.	23.8	12.5	52.5	36.3
Open univ.	19.6	56.6	288.8	76.2[1]
Public sector	121.3	79.4	65.5	200.7
Men	142.0	68.0	47.9	210.0
Women	22.7	80.5	354.6	103.2

FT HE home students	1970–1	1980–1	1981–2	1982–3	1983–4
New students aged 21 or under as % of 18 & 19-year-old population	13.7	12.7	13.5	13.5	13.3

[1] Includes short-course students.

be a production good, as when someone takes a degree in dentistry. It then becomes of avid interest to Chicago economists like Theodore Schultz who expounded human capital theory in his famous paper (Schultz, 1961), or to Soviet state planners like Stanislav Strumilin who in 1924 justified state investment in education by working out its rate of return (he made it eleven times its cost over a lifetime, though with diminishing returns) (Kaser, 1986). Third, education can be seen as a positional good either in the economist's sense of a screening, sieving or queuing device for selecting and allocating recruits to the labour market (Arrow, 1973; Layard and Psacharopoulos, 1974) or in the sociologist's sense of a collective negative sumgame with its associated inflationary credentialism (Berg, 1970; Dore, 1976; Collins, 1979) and intensified status competition.

The dominant empirical fact is that we have lived in a century of expansion. For example in most countries there are more than twice as many university teachers now as there were students in higher education at the beginning of the century. In terms of certification, 70 percent of British 25 to 29-year-olds now have some sort of educational qualification: among the 50 to 59-year-olds the figure is only 39 percent. Moreover even after the end of the postwar boom which ended with the oil crisis, higher education has continued to expand, as is illustrated for the United Kingdom in Table 1.

Three Political Economies

In literature on the political economy of education a spectrum is, in effect, postulated with the pure market at one extreme and the centrally planned command economy at the other. In reality there are no pure cases. Milton Friedman justifies state intervention in the name of 'neighbourhood effects' (Friedman, 1955). The USSR has had periods of fee paying for secondary and tertiary education beyond compulsory schooling. Nevertheless countries can be spread along the spectrum and fall into three discernible clusters (cf. Avakov et al., 1984):

1. At the Western extreme Group 1 is comprised by the two decentralized systems of higher education in Canada and the United States. In the United States, around 3000 degree-granting institutions and the community colleges are, as it were, small-scale capitalist entrepreneurs subject through market discipline to birth and death by contrast with their planned European counterparts — slower in gestation and even slower to die.

2. Group 2 is made up of the highly centralized higher education systems of the socialist countries of Eastern Europe where education is a creature of manpower planning (Avakov et al., 1984; Lane, 1985).

3. The third group is that of the Western European social democracies which lie in between. Higher education is mostly publicly financed but there are varying degrees of centralization and three more or less developed social markets for students, for research and for graduate labour.

Planning for these markets accordingly differs in the three groups. In the United States there is high student enrolment and much broad non-specialized education directed towards a high degree of occupational flexibility. A high adaptability and substitutability is assumed between jobs in a fuzzy occupational structure. Manpower shortages are not thought of as key problems. Manpower utilization is adjusted through large numbers of retraining programmes rather than through manpower forecasting. By contrast the USSR has an elaborate planning mechanism: long-term and short-term, macro and micro, sectoral by industry and geographical by region. As it becomes more complex the output of economists is the fastest-growing category of graduates in recent years.

Three Types of Educational Organization

Three types of educational programme correspond to the three types of political economy. At the perfect market end the rate of return approach is used; price signals are relied upon to reveal market imperfections. There is no need for macro planning. The individual university or college solves its own problems, competing with many other sellers for the favours of many student buyers. Similarly in the graduate market where the students become sellers there is competition for jobs under the sovereignty of the employers who buy their skills. Of course, in a proportion of cases, the buyers are the colleges and universities themselves. In both markets the buyers dominate the character of the product.

Second, at the other end of the spectrum to which the Soviet Union approximates, the method is manpower planning and the state determines both demand and supply. Within the elaborate planning apparatus to which I have referred, prices or rather shadow prices are used but their value as signals or economic levers is part of the planning process not a substitute for it.

Both systems, 1 and 2, can claim to work. Both the USA and the USSR, from different starting points, have traversed a long journey along the Trowian road to mass higher education (Trow, 1974, 1987), the development of high technological research and the manning of a complex division of labour. American enrolments in higher education have held up at 12.5 million despite a decline in the size of the traditionally relevant age groups. In the USSR between 1955 and 1980 the number of new admissions to higher education rose by 2.3 times to reach one million at the later date (Avakov et al., 1984).

In between are the mixed systems of Western Europe. Roughly speaking it may be said of all these countries as well as of Eastern Europe that right through the expansion of higher education in the twentieth century the supply of graduates has risen behind the demand for them until, again roughly, the end of the postwar period in the mid-1970s. There is admittedly an important exception — Germany in the 1920s. Between 1925 and 1932 the number of students in German universities rose from 90,000 to 140,000, and 60,000 graduates were out of work. The difficulty was solved in 1933 when the Nazis came to power. It was solved by a brutal act of state planning: a numerus clausus was imposed, annual entry was reduced to 15,000 with 10 percent women and no Jews. Within a few years the graduate market was, in economists' jargon, 'cleared'.

The social democracies have not found it politically possible to plan so effectively. Yet there are said to be urgent reasons for doing so which have emerged in the recession decade. Graduate unemployment is one of them and is seen as a serious problem in Germany. But there are other reasons which push and pull these countries between the two poles of market and planning strategy. The essential reason is that they are welfare states, i.e. in their varying circumstances they have sought in this century to find a compromise between the claims of equality and fairness rooted in citizenship and the claims to efficiency, freedom and property right rooted in class. As T.H. Marshall said, class and citizenship have been at war in the twentieth century (Marshall, 1950) and nowhere more so than in education. Of course neither has ever won outright victory in any field of public policy.

Higher education is an intricate example of the interplay of the forces of citizenship responding to popular political demand and accommodation to class interests through market strategies. The more obvious recent trends of the British variant of social democracy can be summarized as a westward rhetorical orientation combined with an actual net movement eastwards. The declared Robbins principle was social demand. But taking each of the three main markets in turn it appears:

First that Britain is distinctively eastern by comparison with Germany or France in controlling the demand side of the student market. The *Abitur* and the *baccalauréat* give right of entry. Britain has a political quota for home and EC undergraduates combined with an open market for overseas candidates. The supply side of the same market is as rigid as elsewhere in Western Europe, with tight overall budgetary control supplemented by the stubborn tradition of academic tenure.

Second, in research, so-called Rothschild principles are applied to construct a social market of academic clients and state customers again with severely limited government funding together with exhortation to industrial funding. On the supply side the recent novel development has been a rating of university research performance by the University Grants Committee but this is overshadowed by overall financial limitations leading to worsening staff/student ratios, registers of suspended posts, and so on — a haemorrhage inadequately stemmed by 'new-blood posts'.

Third, in the graduate market, the dominant force is laissez-faire but with increasing state intervention, for example on the supply side through extra bursaries to maths and science teacher trainees or earmarked grants for information technology courses.

Education and Stratification

On a long historical perspective economies are systems of stratification, and education prepares people for places in the stratified order of production and consumption. In Europe in the eighteenth and nineteenth centuries there were essentially two separate arrangements for the upper and lower strata. For traditional elites, educational institutions such as the German law faculties, the French *grandes écoles*, or the English 'public' schools and ancient universities were vehicles for the preservation, transmission and renewal of the styles of life rather than the occupations of the elevated strata. Primary education was for 'workmen and servants'. It eventually became free and compulsory. Education in Europe, at least up to the end of the nineteenth century, was a public stamp determined for all but a tiny minority by the circumstances of private birth. But in the twentieth century there have been fundamental changes in the formation and function of elites. They have expanded and, especially after the Second World War, have drawn in new recruits of more diverse social origin. In consequence, the traditional, but highly restricted, function of schools and universities as promoters of mobility for the gifted sons (and to an even smaller extent daughters) of the masses has been strengthened, at least temporarily. Meanwhile, elite occupational groups have become more differentiated in function, less closely knit in familial and educational origin and connections, and more specialized in their economic and social role and their basis in knowledge.

It does not follow, however, that advanced industrialism necessarily generates technocracy or a generalized meritocracy. A similar technological base can support widely different distributions of power and advantage depending on the historical, political and cultural conditions of any particular country. Elites may be more or less open. Moreover, to varying degrees, established and emergent elites accommodate one another. In the Soviet Union the accommodation seems to have taken the form of control by the political elite over bureaucratic, industrial and military organizations. In France the technocratic traditions instituted by Napoleon in the *grandes écoles* are closely assimilated to the metropolitan and governmental elite. In the United Kingdom the amateur and classical traditions of Oxford and Cambridge have hitherto largely contained the expansion of science and technology and subordinated the 'expert' to a relatively subservient role in higher officialdom and in large-scale industrial enterprise.

In the Third World, especially in the period of the widespread establishment of new states in Africa and Asia in the middle years of the twentieth century, the role of education in the formation of new elites deserves a special note. It separated them from an illiterate mass and, necessarily under the historical circumstances of empire and colonialism, the modernizing elites were heavily recruited from those with educational experience in European and North American schools and universities. On top of the characteristic fission and conflict of tribal identity new nations were plagued by wide cultural differences between the people in power and their supporters in popular political movements. Education for the masses, typically represented as investment in human capital, has been a strong motive force in modernizing movements. But there has been considerable tension between the wish on the one hand, to preserve elements of traditional cultures in educational systems and, on the other hand, to incorporate the scientific and technological culture of the richer Western countries. Thus education has been intricately involved in status struggles as educational systems have expanded all over the world (Collins, 1979).

Modernization

Independently and from the perspective of a comparative sociologist Ronald Dore has drawn on evidence from Britain, Japan, Sri Lanka, Kenya, China, Cuba and Tanzania to attack the theory of economic development current among economists and sociologists. He argues that the contribution of education to economic growth was misconceived and distorted in governmental planning so as to replace education by certification — the modern *Diploma Disease* (Dore, 1976). It was 'almost entirely in the factories and mines, the workshops and mills, not in the schools that the skills which fed Britain's industrial advance were both accumulated and transmitted' (Dore, 1976: 18). The modern trends towards raising of the pre-career qualifications of increasing numbers of trades and professions has undermined both academic education and industrial training. For advanced industrial societies the trend is a problem: for the Third World it is a disaster. Under the pressure of the late development effect, that is the later the point in world history that a country starts on a modernization drive, 'the more widely education certifications are used for occupational selection; the faster the rate of qualification inflation; and the more examination-oriented schooling becomes at the expense of genuine education' (Dore, 1976: 72).

The phenomenon of status conflict over education is not new. Durkheim (1893), for example, was able to show that the pedagogical ideals of the Renaissance in France were, at least in part, an outcome of changes in class relations which developed in late medieval society. A more recent example is Trow's (1961) demonstration of the transformation of the United States high school from a mass terminal to a mass preparatory institution reflecting changes in the occupational division of labour from one largely made up of agricultural and industrial workers to an increasingly differentiated structure in which white-collar workers were numerically preponderant. It is unclear exactly how far educational expansion since the 1930s is attributable to the effects of technology on occupational structure, or to struggles between status groups for cultural domination. But there is no doubt that both economic and cultural conflict lie behind the characteristic history of rising enrolments.

Socialization

Among Marxists, great emphasis is placed on the role of schooling in the reproduction of the social division of labour. This is the central thesis of Bowles and Gintis (1976). In their view, the essential function of schools is to prepare children for the place in the class structure which their origins have predetermined. The curriculum and ethos of a hierarchy of schools are thus fashioned in parallel to the occupational hierarchy of the wider society.

Bowles and Gintis attributed unequal education to the stratified division of labour under capitalism. These neo-Marxists were aware of the hierarchical character of schooling and the work in communist countries. But they were primarily concerned with the United States and their work was criticized for identifying hierarchy in school and work with capitalism. In fact the roots of inequality are spread far beyond private ownership of the means of production to the division of labour itself. Accordingly it was pointed out that their theory of correspondence, like Bourdieu's theory of cultural capital (Bourdieu and Passeron, 1977), might be more applicable to the Soviet Union than to the United States or France.

> Where for example is the relationship between the economy and the schools less mediated than in the USSR which has an explicit policy of manpower planning? Similarly, where is the correspondence principle more clearly exemplified than in the changes of educational policy that follow from changes in production strategies in a revolutionary socialist society such as Cuba? And where does cultural capital play a greater role in the transmission of inequality than in those societies that have abolished private ownership of the means of production? In short, whether one refers to the subordination of schools to the economy or to the cultural reproduction function of the educational system, much of the analysis of radical educational researchers is at least as applicable to socialist societies as it is to the capitalist countries upon which they focus their attention. (Karabel and Halsey, 1977)

Further work on the correspondence thesis has been published by Carnoy and Levin (1985). Its main interest is in its attempt to come to terms with these criticisms and particularly with the historical evidence that the structure of education is determined by democratic politics as well as by the imperatives of economic organization. In theoretical terms this is a large step away from orthodox Marxism. It puts in question the primacy of social relations of production in explaining 'epiphenomenal' institutions.

Nevertheless Carnoy and Levin postulate contradictory trends towards equality and democracy in education. They argue that the educational system in America has two functions: on the one hand it prepares young people for the unequal and authoritarian relations of capitalist production but on the other it socializes children for citizenship in a democratic society. Thus these authors complicate the original correspondence theory arguing 'that the relationship between education and work is dialectical — composed of a perpetual tension between two dynamics, the imperatives of capitalism and those of democracy in all its forms' (Carnoy and Levin, 1985: 4).

This modification to Marxist theory is significant but remains open to the objection which can be levelled against both the correspondence principle and liberal theories of human capital or technical functionalism that the dependence of education on economy is still assumed, even though mediated by political and cultural forces, whereas further theoretical advance invites the treatment of educational institutions as at least partially independent. Thus the mismatch between educational qualifications and labour demand in the economy — the credentialist problem analysed by Collins and by Dore — may be described in its consequences but cannot be explained in its genesis without positing independent sources of educational decision making. Paul Willis's analysis of working-class boys in a British comprehensive school (Willis, 1977) and Gambetta's study of Italian school leavers (Gambetta, 1987) are, by different methods, outstanding contributions to the understanding of such decision making.

Education and Social Selection

Public credentials or qualifications are increasingly the mark of modern societies, legitimizing inequalities of pay and controlling entry to the labour market. In broader historical perspective it should be noticed that societies may distribute their opportunities according to many different principles. Primogeniture, for example, was widespread in agrarian societies, the principle that the first-born has the right of inheritance to a defined occupational position together with the property or monopoly pertaining to it. Some form of inheritance or ascription has been the dominant traditional principle in the whole history of human society.

Education under such circumstances reproduces the stratified status quo. But modern systems of stratification might appear to permit the deliberate use of educational selection to break the traditional tie of birth to occupational destination and instead to foster meritocracy (Bell, 1973; Young, 1958).

Blau and Duncan (1967) interpret the relation between education and occupational achievement within the framework of a postulated broad movement from ascription to achievement in the allocation of jobs, and this in turn may derive from a still broader trend from particularist to universalistic definitions of social roles. The underlying theory is that the division of labour and the demands of efficiency together effectively ensure that there will be public arrangements to test competence before allocating people to positions. The role of industrialism, while generating class systems, has also been that of a catalyst, providing both encouragement towards openness and resources for political redistribution of opportunity.

Industrialism requires, or at least encourages, a more complex division of labour and a more mobile labour force: it gives opportunities to new skills, makes old ones obsolescent, releases knowledge and its acquisition from familial and quasifamilial networks, and above all generates the economic surplus which makes possible the pursuit of educational opportunities through governmental spending. At the same time, however, industrialism, especially in capitalist countries of the Western European type, generates a class system: with schools and other social organizations that are at once open in the formal and legal sense but also tending towards closure because parents seek to convert their own class advantages into enhanced opportunities for their own children. In consequence, the family and the market are pitted against the state and the bureaucracy in struggles for scarce goods and services, each acting as the agent of principles which, in the end, are contradictory. These political conflicts, set in their background of social stratification, have been much sharpened during the period of slowdown or cessation of economic growth in the Western countries in the late 1970s and 1980s.

Taking the longer view of development out of classical industrialism in the nineteenth century towards one form or another of post-industrialism in the late twentieth century, modern educational systems can be thought of as the instruments used by the state in a grand strategy of 'class abatement' by the establishment of equality of opportunity irrespective of birth. Successive education acts establishing elementary and secondary universal education as well as the expansion of higher education have all been stages in the development of that strategy. The underlying theory has been that life chances depend upon education, that education controlled by the state could overcome the inequalities of class, and that above all education could be equalized by expansion. Many modern empirical studies have been concerned with the social scientific testing of this hypothesis. Among them have been the studies of Boudon (1974) in France, Jencks et al. (1972; 1979) in the United States, and Halsey and his colleagues (1980) in the United Kingdom. At root such studies are concerned with the question of how far the state itself is an agent of the dominant class or, in different terms, how far political democracy can be successful in overcoming economic inequality.

Boudon (1974), using empirical data from a range of Western European countries, has demonstrated by a mathematical model the process through which an increase in educational equality can occur without any change or even possibly a decrease in social mobility between classes. Jencks et al. (1972) arrived at similar pessimistic conclusions from data on the experience of individuals in the United States.

People with similar family background, test scores and schooling scattered themselves subsequently over the range of occupational status and income to about three-quarters the extent of the scatter of people in general. In that sense United States society was open. By the same token the scope for social engineering on behalf of a principled allocation of life chances was woefully small. If schooling explained only 12 percent of the variance in individual incomes, then complete equalization of schooling would at the maximum reduce income inequality by only 12 percent.

The critics rightly complained that to assume it is possible to change the value of one variable without changing the totality of relations between variables in a system of plural causation is statistically convenient but sociologically invalid. If the United States gave everyone the same schooling, it would, in the process, completely change the class structure, the labour market, and indeed the general shape of society.

In the later publication *Who Gets Ahead?* (1979), Jencks et al.

reassessed the determinants of economic success in America. It turned out, in short, that family of origin, schooling, measured intelligence and personality put a heavier, and 'luck' a lighter, stamp on an individual's economic prospects than readers of *Inequality* (Jencks et al., 1972) had been invited to believe.

The old figure for the percentage of variance in occupational status explained by family background was 32; the new figure was 48. The old figure for schooling was 42 percent; the new was 55 percent. Combining the variables of family background, test scores, years of schooling and personality traits, it now appeared that the characteristics which people take into the market on first entry explain 55–60 percent of variance in adult occupational status and 33–41 percent of variance in annual earnings.

Thus the general thrust of the *Inequality* argument is not blocked by recalculation. For example, whereas in *Inequality* the expected difference between the occupational status of brothers was 82 percent of the expected difference between pairs of unrelated men, the new percentage was 72. Clearly the revised figure does not afford dramatically enlarged scope to the social engineers.

In any case the old pessimism remains. Past efforts to equalize through education have been ineffective. Moreover, as Thurow (1981) has argued, these policies were expensive and such effects as they had were to be arrested in the 1980s. In the 1970s in the United States there was an enormous difference in the educational qualifications of the cohorts entering and leaving the labour market. The leavers had experienced the relatively restricted opportunities for schooling available before the Second World War. The entrants were the beneficiaries of expanded opportunity. There was accordingly less scope for education to offset the forces of class and status which produce and maintain inequality. The problem of equality, at least in the United States, is therefore likely to turn increasingly on the distribution of market incomes. That was indeed the burden of Jencks's original arguments.

Another approach to the problem is provided by Halsey et al. in *Origins and Destinations* (1980), a study of the history of the relation between class and educational opportunity in the United Kingdom from the First World War up to 1972. A national survey of social mobility conducted from Oxford gave a sample of familial, educational and occupational biographies collected from 10,000 men in England and Wales. By arranging the records of individuals into birth cohorts, the authors were able to reconstruct the experience of successive generations passing through the educational system as it developed in the twentieth century.

The context in which this social experiment in equalization through educational expansion has taken place is roughly similar in most of the Western countries. It is a background in all of these countries of continuing economic growth and social mobility. In each succeeding decade the material circumstances of the average child has improved. The class structure itself has gradually been modified in the direction of enlarging the middle class and shrinking the working class. For example, in the United Kingdom, 10 percent of those born between 1913 and 1921 came from the middle or service class of professionals, administrators, managers, proprietors and supervisors. But for the birth cohort of 1943–52 the proportion had risen to 18 percent. In general, throughout the period, the chance of a middle-class childhood grew, and within the working class there was an increased chance that a child would grow up in a smaller family with a larger income, and with more educated parents. In the process a relatively smaller, but more hereditary and probably more culturally homogeneous, working class has evolved — what Goldthorpe calls a 'mature' working class (Goldthorpe et al., 1980). And in the same process the middle class has become more heterogeneous and diversely recruited, not so much by class heredity but more by upward mobility from other class origins.

Theoretical Challenges

So there is great existential complexity in the relations between modern economies and their educational systems. But theorists properly seek parsimony of explanation. Acknowledgement of complexity in the social scientific literature as distinct from common speech may be tacit admission of failure to invent powerful theory (Gambetta, 1987). A review of the state of the art must be in part an appraisal of attempts to bridge the gap. It was already obvious in the 1960s that the principal requirement was a bridge between the macroscopic analysis of systems and the social actions of individuals. Articulation had to be sought between on the one hand the movements of economies and their educational antechambers, and on the other, the choices of students and teachers in schools and work places. Hence the more general theoretical debate over explanations couched in terms of structure versus agency also became central to the sociology of education. The dominance of structural explanations, especially structural-functionalism, was accordingly challenged. The 'black box' of the processes of learning in classrooms and occupational choices in families and the offices of youth counsellors had to be opened.

Two new bridge-building blueprints were offered. One, announcing itself as a 'new sociology of education' was abortive. Correctly identifying the limitations of the established, mainly liberal or liberal-socialist technico-functionalist, explanations, it promised to open the black box by ethnomethodological techniques and so to transform the 'conventional' sociology of education into a sociology of knowledge (Young, 1971). But the subsequent delivery as empirical study has been meagre. The other research programme designed to link structures to individual action has been the development of rational choice theory with its roots in economic theory but with significant advances towards more sophisticated social and psychological assumptions (Boudon, 1974; Gambetta, 1987; Halsey et al., 1980; Heath, 1976). Gambetta's study of individual decision mechanisms in education, based on surveys of Italian high school pupils and unemployed youth, is a notable advance in both theory and analytical technique. Meanwhile the type of theory which seeks to derive explanations of both educational achievement and occupational placement from genetic rather than social sources remained as a continuing contributor to debate about meritocracy and the purported movement of industrial societies from ascription to achievement in the pattern of educational and occupational careers (Modgil and Modgil, 1987; Schiff and Lewontin, 1986).

However, the two main enterprises of this bridge-building industry remain the two competing giants of liberalism and Marxism with their opposed general conception of the nature and dynamics of industrial or post-industrial and capitalist or post-capitalist society. Research on the relation between education and economy over the past two decades has largely, if often tacitly, been conducted as application of these two contending traditions of social and political thought and the research outcomes have served both to expose their strengths and weaknesses and to demonstrate modifications in their essential theoretical constructs. The study of schools and labour markets and their interrelations has revealed evidence damaging to both traditional positions, forced many 'humanist' Marxists to reconsider the pre-eminence of structure as against agency, compelled many liberals to acknowledge the stubborn power of ascriptive forces in class, race and gender and challenged both in their respective versions of a 'logic of industrialism' with its underlying historicist assumptions. From recent quantitative studies of employment and mobility, John Goldthorpe has concluded that neither type of theory concerning long-term change in the class stratification of advanced Western societies stands up successfully to empirical testing and that 'the claims of both must now in fact be seen as in major respects invalid' (Goldthorpe, 1986). The theoretical error is historicism and particularly the hope of 'theorizing' the movement of history.

Out of the research evidence has come renewed justification of the liberal idea of voluntarism and renewed disconfirmation of the Marxist view that history is made 'behind men's backs'. But the same body of evidence also reaffirms the infirmity of theories of progress towards collective prosperity, social openness and individual freedom through the combination of educational expansion and technological innovation in industry so confidently proposed by the Victorian Alfred Marshall and his liberal descendants in economics and sociology (Marshall, 1872; Kerr et al., 1960, 1973; Kerr, 1983; Bell, 1973).

Liberal Utopia and Marxist Doom

The significance of education in the political economy of modern society differs sharply in liberal and Marxist theory. For liberals it is central to the determination of both production and distribution. For Marxists it is a dependent variable about which Marx himself wrote little. In more recent writing the contrast continues, mainly because of opposed interpretations of the changes in the structure of employment and the incidence of social mobility both of which entail theories of the relation between education and employment.

In liberal theory the development of industrial and post-industrial societies involves a progressive upgrading of the skills demanded in the economy (both high scientific manpower and technological culture). The structure of employment shifts with advancing technology from unskilled manual labour to diverse non-manual professional and managerial jobs, requiring ever more elaborate education and training. This upward movement accompanies the shift of modernizing economies from primary to secondary to tertiary sectors of production, that is, from agriculture to manufacture to services, reinforcing the demand for skilled labour, professionals and managers, and from private to public sector activity. The vast movement of educational expansion is partly explained in terms of burgeoning economic demand, and in the human capital theory applied to Third World planning (Schultz, 1961) the expansion of schooling came to be seen as a process whereby supply could be expected to create its own demand.

The Marxist view is completely contrary. Instead of upgrading there is degrading. In his *Labour and Monopoly Capitalism*, Braverman (1974) argued that capitalist society with its scientific management in the service of exploitation of the proletariat, systematically involves the degradation of employment. The labour process on this view must be simplified and deskilled to satisfy the employers' need for both productive efficiency and the social control of workers. The agenda for education is accordingly different. Whereas for liberals the shape, direction and pace of educational expansion is problematic, for Marxists the focus is on the internal stratification of educational systems in capitalist societies and the anticipatory socialization of workers' children for their ascribed proletarian role in the discipline of industry. Thus at the centre of the liberal literature is Martin Trow's theory of stages of expansion from elite through mass to universal higher education[1] and Dan Bell's characterization of the university as the gatekeeper to occupational placement (Bell, 1973) while at the centre of Marxist analysis is Bowles and Gintis's correspondence theory of the regime of control of schools and work places (Bowles and Gintis, 1976) and the French structuralist Bourdieu's theory of cultural capital explaining class differences in educational success and certification.

As Goldthorpe (1986) has insisted, the research evidence concerning the structure of employment effectively negates

Braverman's labour process theory and leaves the liberal problematic of expansion as a serious one. Moreover Marxist views concerning social mobility leave little room for consideration of the well-documented patterns of upward mobility through education which have been a prominent feature of the link of education to occupation and class in the twentieth century.

Nevertheless the liberal theories of meritocracy and the movement from ascription to achievement are not in themselves confirmed by the disconfirmation of Marxist belief in the degradation of labour and the unimportance of mobility. The research evidence certainly shows a great deal of movement, including intergenerational movement through education, as the structure of employment in advanced societies (and earlier in the century the differential fertility of class groupings) enlarged opportunities in the professional, managerial and technical occupations. But structural mobility has to be distinguished from exchange mobility for it is the latter, measured in relative terms, which denotes the degree of openness of a society. The evidence is disputed but certainly cannot be held to uphold the optimistic theories commonly advanced by liberals (Halsey, 1977).[2]

Liberal cheerfulness concerning upgrading towards universal, middle-class professional society cannot plausibly accommodate the re-emergence of widespread unemployment in the First World capitalist countries. Since the end of the postwar period in the mid-1970s few such countries, Sweden being a significant exception, have managed to keep their unemployment rate below 10 percent. Moreover unemployment is heavily concentrated among the young disadvantaged ethnic minorities, the educationally unsuccessful and those previously employed in manual work.

At the same time the structure of employment has become differentiated in ways which have led some analysts to characterize labour markets as dual or primary and secondary. It is not necessary to accept dual labour market theories in order to recognize the importance of the growth of insecure, part-time and temporary jobs with precarious conditions of service as a conspicuous feature of modern free-enterprise economies. But it is necessary to discard any notion of mechanical upgrading of skill, security of tenure in occupations and equalization of income and life style around middle-class norms under modern conditions of market fluctuation and the pressed strategy of employers to seek a flexible workforce. Indeed the phenomenon of labour market uncertainty in a less than full employment economy is so damaging to liberal optimism as to generate new analysis of polarization in class structures, including the identification of an emerging so-called 'underclass'. This stratum, in so far as it exists, presents urgent problems for any theory, liberal or Marxist, of the relation between education and employment. For the typical recruit to it seems to be a young person with a background of school failure who lacks the motive, the skills, the qualifications and the traits of personality to enter successfully into the formal economy. Research on the underclass to describe empirically its characteristics and prevalence is not yet adequate but began in the late 1980s.[3] It is likely, however, to undermine further the Marxist theory of an enlarging and homogenized working class as well as the liberal dream of a classless society of skilled workers.

Citizenship, Education and Employment

The phenomenon of an emergent underclass with its parallel of 'infantilism' among young people in the communist countries of Eastern Europe (Gospodinov, 1986)[4] illustrates the more general differences between liberals and Marxists in their conception of the state and the family. The liberal nostrum of advance towards affluent, free and equal society accorded a political as well as an economic role to education. In Alfred Marshall's classic formulation, the transition from an economy of low technology, long hours of work and low wages to one of high technology, short hours and high pay, would eliminate the working class by making all its members gentlemen (and presumably gentlewomen) at least by occupation. The new economy would thereby afford the conditions for extension of citizenship in the form of leisure to pursue civilized interests and energy to undertake responsible self-government in parliaments, local councils, trade unions and producer co-operatives (Marshall, 1872). Education was destined, in other words, to bring up enlightened citizens as well as efficient and skilled workers. It was precisely this utopian vision of an elevated combination of politics and economy — a prosperous democracy — that justified state 'interference' in the private lives of families to compel the freedom of school attendance and to provide educational opportunity. The subsequent official history of ministries of education in Western countries, and indeed in much of the Third World, is characteristically celebrated in these liberal terms.

But the underclass and the demonstration through social research of limits on exchange mobility, the elusiveness of meritocracy, the persistence of class difference in educability and the continuance of, albeit classless, inequality of income and status have been factors generating pessimism rather than optimism in the liberal camp. Christopher Jencks's *Inequality* called in question the whole project of social transformation through educational policy. In America and Western Europe the combined impact of liberal pessimism and aggressive Marxism resulted in the late 1970s and early 1980s in widespread retreat by governments from the previous belief in the efficacy of educational expansion either as profitable economic investment or as benign political socialization.

The reaction was, of course, exaggerated but the curve of educational expenditure as a proportion of GDP flattened in many countries, enrolments beyond school slowed their rate of growth, private education gained at the expense of state provision and resources were transferred to forms of training held to be relevant to the cure of rising youth unemployment.

There is ample research evidence from most countries that education and occupational level are strongly correlated — the thesis of a tightening bond between education and occupation is securely established. The strongest beta coefficient in path diagrams analysing the determinants of occupational position, since Blau and Duncan's analysis of American occupational structure in 1967, has been consistently drawn from respondent's education to job as distinct from father's or mother's education or job or any other background variable (Blau and Duncan, 1967; Halsey et al., 1980). More recent evidence from British studies (Payne, 1985, 1987; Raffe, 1984; Junanker, 1987; Payne and Payne, 1985) also demonstrates that school qualifications have improved the chances of avoiding unemployment in the period of economic recession from 1974 to 1981, that as youth unemployment and overall levels of certification have grown so have the differences between the job chances of the qualified and the unqualified (Payne and Payne, 1985). It does pay to stay on at school. And more generally, apropos the emerging underclass, Joan Payne has used data from the British 1980 and 1981 General

Household Surveys to show that the young unemployed are three times more likely than their employed peers to have parents or brothers or sisters who are also out of work (see also Raffe, 1984: ch. 9). The reasons are complex, including variations in local labour markets and residence in particularly deprived inner city or corporation estates (Payne, 1987) but there is also a tendency for unemployment to run in families — another facet of the survival of ascription in an achievement society.

Higher Education as a Positional Good

Finally, it is appropriate to emphasize the conception of education as a positional good (Hirsch, 1976). Expansion, as Table 1 illustrates for Britain, has been the dominant feature of the postwar period in all the three groups of countries that I identified. Absorption of the qualified has been partly through relative increase in middle-class occupations and partly through 'gradualization' of a wider range of occupations. But the correlate has been intensified class competition for access and there is evidence of a status reconstruction of higher education.

The sociological interpretation of these developments is that this positional good has been increased in supply by institutional differentiation such that the advantaged strata have secured relatively more places for their children in the more prestigious institutions of an elongating hierarchy of universities and colleges. Thus Paul Windolf, the German sociologist, has shown a trend during the expansive 1960s and 1970s towards on the one hand relatively higher rates of expansion at the lower levels, for example the *Fachhochshulen* in Germany, community colleges in the USA or the IUTs in France, and on the other hand an increase in concentration of students of advantaged class origin in the Harvards and Stanfords, the *grandes écoles*, the Japanese Imperial universities and the German faculties with a numerus clausus. In such ways is positionality transmitted to the next generation of market entrants (Windolf, 1985). If further empirical enquiry confirms this polarizing tendency the hope for increased openness by university expansion (Hout, 1987) must be disappointed.

Applying this thesis to the British case one can begin to see evidence of institutional differentiation in Table 1. The traditional male full-time undergraduate as a gentlemanly state pensioner had the smallest growth rate from 1970 to 1984. The part-time woman on short-cycle course in the Open University had the greatest rate of increase. There is a developing institutional hierarchy from the top research universities down through the lesser colleges. Social closure contends with social mobility through education. A comparison of take-up by the social classes as between 1961 and 1984 in Britain shows that the Registrar General's classes I and II have increased their share of university places from 59 percent to 67 percent. Adjusting for the changing class base, that is for the expansion of the professional and managerial classes, the familiar picture emerges of increased absolute along with stable or very slowly equalizing relative class chances of access to the highest level of education.

Educational systems stand in complex relation to modern economies. They manifest remarkable shifts of adaptation to changing circumstances. But they have yet to fulfil the social dreams of children of the enlightenment. And they still defy adequate analysis by social scientists.

Notes

1. In his most recent writing Trow disavows the impression that this thesis was advanced as an inherent law of motion in modern society. It was intended as a rough model of historical experience serving to highlight the deviation and problems of particular countries (Trow, 1987).

2. In an interesting new analysis of mobility in the United States Michael Hout (1987) puts optimistic emphasis on the random relation between social origins and occupational destinations of American graduates. But more evidence is required before the new version of social openness through educational expansion can be accepted. See my remarks on polarization (p. 97).

3. A significant funding of research on the underclass in America has recently been announced by the Russell Sage Foundation. See *Reporting* from the Russell Sage Foundation, No. 10, May 1987.

4. It is reported by Gospodinov (1986: 12), that

> 'At a seminar held in 1983 in Moscow, organized by the Institute of International Workers' Movement at the Academy of Sciences of the USSR and the European (Vienna) Coordination Centre for Research and Documentation in Social Sciences, scientists from the capitalist countries commented on a particular "cultural mutation" expressed in the fact that labour is no longer on the top rank in the value structure of contemporary youth. It would be erroneous to suppose that these problems do not concern socialist countries, whereas experts have noted, due to prolongation of the education period and isolation in the educational process from acquisition of habits of work,

tendencies of decreased interest in labour are observed among certain groups of youth. This is a complicated issue, conditioned by the forced liquidation of old motivations for work, frequently surpassing the formation of new stimuli for work based on high cultural and conscientiousness level of the working masses. As a result there was a motivational vacuum, when old stimuli were displaced and liquidated and new ones were not created. It becomes obvious nowadays in a number of vocations where high percentage of youth is employed, where the wages do not cover the existential minimum, which results in young people and young families aged up to 30 and more, living at the expense of their parents, which promotes infantilism, strengthens scepticism, lack of self-assurance, leads to a phenomenon where the wage according to labour law is transformed into a peculiar labour according to wage ''antilaw''. It is increased owing to diverse possibilities for unearned income, here we refer to the use of connections, ''protectionism'' for obtaining easy and well-paid jobs.

The processes of urbanization, ubiquitous distribution of city standards of living, higher level of comfort are intrinsically linked with scientific and technological revolution and change the role of the family in rearing the young generation. Years ago the family was the cradle of morality at work, children from an early age had to help their parents around the house, looking after animals, thus naturally gaining an idea of the necessity to work. Now, in a city apartment with all amenities, away from nature, children are redeemed of all household errands, thus deprived of these first lessons of labour education.'

Part II
Economic Co-ordination and Economic Development

4
MARKET AND STATE IN ADVANCED CAPITALIST SOCIETIES

Johannes Berger

I

The relationship between market and state is certainly one of the fundamental issues in the sociological, public finance and economic literature dealing with the central problems of present-day societies. On the one hand, the literature relates to 'demarcation problems' (cf. Lane, 1985). Up to this day, there is an on-going controversy about how active a role the government — and correspondingly the private sector — should take. To solve this question, normative criteria are required to determine the proper size of state and market activities. On the other hand unlike the normative branch of the literature, the positive one deals with the factors which determine the size and the growth of the private and the public sector. Furthermore, it is widely recognized that in the mixed economies of Western countries one major factor determining the size and the growth of the market is the state — and vice versa. State and market activities are intertwined in manifold ways. Not only does the government alter the behaviour of the private sector through a variety of laws, taxes and expenditure behaviour in general, but the private sector also exerts influence on public policy, whether passively as a 'constraint' or actively by exercising economic power.

In the course of capitalist development, the borderline between state and market has been anything but stable. During the last hundred years an essential shift took place in favour of 'big government' (cf. Rose, 1984). Not only has government grown (in terms of both state expenditure and state personnel) but it has grown faster than the economy; the classic formulation of such a tendency of the public sector to grow faster than the GNP is Wagner's 'law of an increasing state activity' (cf. Wagner, 1876).

This growth is now the reason for serious concern, not only

about the increasing problems of meeting the costs of government, but about the consequences of a growing public sector for the performance of a private market economy. Referring to the relationship between 'market' and 'state', probably the most important question is whether in a 'mixed economy welfare state' (Rose, 1984: 13) the welfare state has become a burden for the functioning of a market economy, that is, whether the interaction between market and state has possibly changed from a supportive to an antagonistic one (Offe, 1987). This change has been contended by liberals and denied by the defenders of the welfare state.

In the following I start with the assumption that the relation between 'market' and 'state' can be described — at least for the recent past — as the 'mixed economy welfare state' just mentioned or as 'welfare state capitalism'. I shall concentrate on three questions:

1. What elements of the institutional setting can be labelled as 'welfare state capitalism'?

2. Does the welfare state stabilize or destabilize a private enterprise economy?

3. If the growth potential of 'welfare state capitalism' is exhausted, what comes after it? Assuming the time of peaceful coexistence of the welfare state and a market economy is over, by what institutional setting can and will it be replaced? To discuss this question, it will be necessary to consider the arguments for and against a market economy and the state as different modes of provision of goods and services.

Let me add a brief note on terminology. In general it is advisable to draw a distinction between 'market' and 'market economy'. By 'market' is usually meant an allocative and distributive mechanism, the counterpart of which is not the state but 'hierarchy' or 'planning'. Whereas the 'unit act' of markets is voluntary exchange, the 'unit act' of hierarchies is 'command'. Markets can work only where property rights are well defined and can be enforced. By 'market economy' I mean a private enterprise economy or 'capitalism'. Here these terms (including 'private sector' and so on) are applied equivocally. Where no confusion can occur, I neglect the distinction between both 'market' and 'market economy'. 'Capitalism' is a mode of provision of goods, or a 'mode of production', but it varies its institutional structure in the course of its development. 'Welfare state capitalism' (another frequently applied term is 'Keynesian welfare state') is the institutional structure that has characterized the postwar period of capitalist development.

By 'state' I mean the public sector of the public finance literature (see for instance Stiglitz, 1986); in political sociology the language of 'government and its organizations' is preferred. These form a part of the political subsystem of the modern society. Because the term 'state' pretends a compactedness of the political realm which does not exist, in sociology this term has been replaced by 'political subsystem' (see Easton, 1953; Parsons and Smelser, 1956). The end of this conceptual dissolution of the state is to regard it only as a self-description of the 'political', a semantical artefact (Luhmann, 1984: 621). Where the boundaries of both the political subsystem and the public sector run is more or less vague. Not even the concept of the 'public sector' covers the same range as 'government'. 'Government organizations' can be defined as 'formal administrative structures established by the constitution or public laws, headed by officials elected by citizens or appointed by elected officials and/or principally financed by taxation or owned by the state' (Rose, 1984: 13). The definition of the public sector can focus more on legislation and authority or more on budget and allocation. As Lane (1985: 8) therefore summarizes, 'the public–private distinction is not one, but several'. Though disputes over the growth of the public sector or government depend to a certain degree on their measure, I do not commit myself here to a particular distinction, because I hope that the general argument is independent of terminological quarrels or of special definitions of the 'public', and so on. In order to investigate the changed relationship between market economy and state a concise description of the particular combination of both sites, which characterized the postwar period, is more relevant than a final decision on which expenditure and which organizations belong to the 'state'.

II

As a brief look at historical studies shows, the first twenty to twenty-five years of the postwar period differs essentially from former periods of economic history. During this period the advanced capitalist countries enjoyed an extended period of

TABLE 1
Phases of GDP growth, 1870–1984
(average annual compound growth rates)

	I 1870–1913	II 1913–50	III 1950–73	IV 1973–84	Acceleration from Phase II to Phase III	Slowdown from Phase III to Phase IV
France	1.7	1.1	5.1	2.2	+4.0	−2.9
Germany	2.8	1.3	5.9	1.7	+4.6	−4.2
Japan	2.5	2.2	9.4	3.8	+7.2	−5.6
Netherlands	2.1	2.4	4.7	1.6	+2.3	−3.1
UK	1.9	1.3	3.0	1.1	+1.7	−1.9
Five-country average	2.2	1.7	5.6	2.1	+4.0	−3.5
US	4.2	2.8	3.7	2.3	+0.9	−1.4

Source: Maddison (1987: 650).

prosperity for which it is impossible to find a precedent (Shonfield, 1965: 61). Taken together, at no time did the economies of the Western world grow faster and — contrary to what is regarded as a precondition of capitalist accumulation, the existence of an industrial reserve army — the period of high growth was accompanied by virtually full employment in many countries.

As Table 1 shows, in the 'post war golden age' (Maddison, 1987) growth was indeed exceptional. The growth rates of leading capitalist countries were higher than even in that twenty-year period before the First World War, which has been called *la belle époque*. Only the economy of the United States displays a different pattern. In the United States the growth rates during the long upswing, which ended with the First World War were higher than in the period of prosperity after the Second World War. This is closely connected with the fact that before the First World War the US economy was able to keep up a significantly faster rate of industrial expansion than European countries at that time.

Table 1 shows in addition that phases of acceleration are replaced by phases of slowdown. In the economic literature it has generally been agreed to call these phases 'long waves' or 'long cycles' of economic growth. Even if substantial evidence can be mobilized in favour of the existence of such 'long waves', the reasons for them are highly controversial. The only matter which seems to be clear is that it would be misleading to look for a

FIGURE 1
The social product in Western Europe 1880–1982 (1899/1901 = 100) (log. scale)

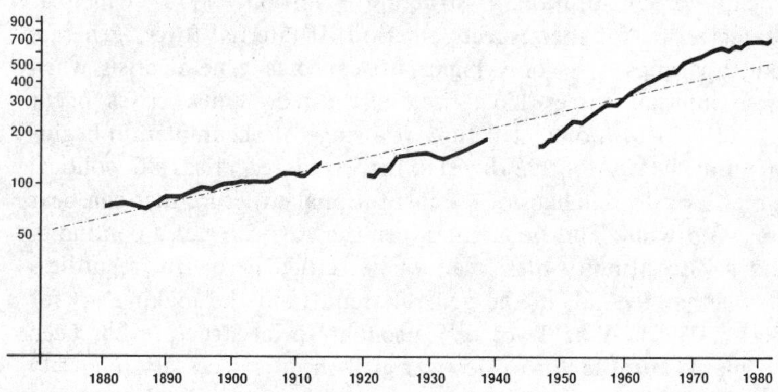

Source: Ambrosius and Hubbard (1986: 131).

common generating mechanism 'behind' the long cycles. If a particular institutional structure is responsible at all for a long period of economic growth it differs from cycle to cycle. But the main question is whether or not these cycles are based on a particular institutional setting. As far as the postwar period is concerned mainly two opposing views are held in the literature relevant to the subject. The first emphasizes the aspect of continuity, the second the aspect of a structural break. According to the first view, which can be traced back to the work of S. Kuznets, despite the rapid growth in the postwar period this phase of prosperity is not so different from former long economic upswings. The European economies could grow so fast because they were favoured by extraordinary circumstances. In this view the postwar period was a period of reconstruction, the function of which was to make good the losses caused by the Second World War. Indeed, the West European economies grew during the postwar boom faster than the trend, but when favourable circumstances ceased, the economy returned to the trend, and the acceleration phase is quite naturally followed by a phase of retarded growth which corresponds to the long-term trend (see Figure 1).

In opposition to this view the advocates of a discontinuity thesis hold that one has to refer to the peculiar institutional structure in which the economy was located. This structure has been labelled 'welfare state capitalism' or 'Keynesian welfare state'.

Deviating from Schumpeter, who regards fundamental technical innovations as decisive, accumulation is now borne by a peculiar 'social' or 'institutional' structure (Gordon, 1978) which is characteristic for the respective period. If internal forces generate long upswings, it is only logical to expect a general crisis when these internal forces have been exhausted. Thus, crises occur when the institutional structure of a stage of accumulation begins to unravel (Gordon, 1978: 31). In periods of crises all political forces look for changes of the institutional structure that can bear a new upswing. This debate between the advocates of a continuity and a discontinuity thesis cannot be settled here. But regardless of whether the fall in the general trend (and the making up for it after World War Two) or a peculiar social structure has been the main causal factor of postwar growth, it is necessary to clarify the institutional peculiarities which distinguish welfare state capitalism from earlier periods of capitalism.

If one concentrates only on domestic events,[1] then four institutional features clearly separate the postwar welfare period from preceding stages of growth. All these features imply a changed relationship between 'market and state'.

The first feature is *state management of the economy*. 'The outstanding faults of the economic society in which we live are its failure to provide for full employment and its arbitrary and unequitable distribution of wealth and income' (Keynes, 1936: 372). The interventionist welfare state can be regarded as an attempt to overcome these market failures by a commitment to full employment and growth. Even to this day there is controversy between Keynesian and neoclassical economists as to whether the state is really able to regulate the overall level of economic activity. A central difference exists with respect to the question whether there can be such a thing as 'unemployment equilibrium' at all and whether it can be removed by means of fiscal policy. In economic orthodoxy unemployment is regarded as a short-period phenomenon; correspondingly it makes no sense to use the public budget as an instrument to fight it, because sooner or later the rise and fall in wages will balance supply and demand on the labour market. The Keynesian heresy was to regard unemployment as an economic state which could occur in *equilibrium*. From this Keynes deduced the necessity of state intervention to overcome a situation which could not be changed by reliance on the working of market forces alone. Therefore the central

Keynesian message — for all practical purposes — is governmental responsibility for an acceptable level of employment. By accepting this responsibility the economic policy of social democratic governments can be called 'applied Keynesianism', taking Keynes's work as a theoretical foundation for full-employment policy (Beveridge, 1944; Crosland, 1956; Strachey, 1956). Certainly, Keynesian policies were implemented to a different degree and with timelags in the Western countries. The United States and Germany, for example, were relatively late in this respect. Nevertheless 'the social democratic consensus' (Dahrendorf, 1979), the core of which is the commitment to full employment, also dominated in countries where conservative parties were in government. This consensus distinguishes the social democratic era from former times of capitalist growth and exactly this consensus was abandoned at the end of the postwar boom.

The second institutional innovation of welfare state capitalism consists in establishing an extended system of *social security*. The main function of this system is to protect the labour force against risks in case of sickness, unemployment, old age and industrial accidents and its protective function covers virtually the whole population. The further function which is assigned to the establishment of social state principles is to correct the inequitable distribution mentioned in the Keynes quotation above. Social security embraces mainly the four social insurance schemes (occupational injuries, health, pension and unemployment insurance), but equally important is the development of public education and health systems. Along with social security these constitute the institutional core of the welfare state as a social state (Flora, 1983).

Expenditure on social security has considerably increased over time but of course the level varies from country to country (see the empirical data for Western Europe in Alber, 1982a). In the social policy literature a polar distinction is made between a 'marginal' and an 'institutional' type of social policy (Titmuss, 1985). The United States, for example, is reckoned among the former, whereas the Scandinavian countries are reckoned among the latter type. In countries with an institutionalized social policy the rate of social expenditure, defined as the relation between social expenditure in a broad sense and the GNP, has surpassed 30 percent. A fully developed welfare state belongs to the peculiarities distinguishing in particular the north-western part of Europe from other capitalist countries. So it is certainly justified to regard this region as the bastion of the welfare state (Kaelble, 1987: 73).

Thus, in welfare state capitalism the state not only takes over a role in stabilizing the economy but has a function in safeguarding certain minimum standards of living, too. In addition to the responsibility for full employment, the responsibility for social welfare also comes into effect. Marshall (1950) has summarized this development as 'growth of citizenship'. Citizenship has three components: civil, political and social; they have been institutionalized step by step in the course of history. Where social citizenship has been established, social welfare becomes a matter of rights, not of charity. Marshall clearly saw that the principle of social citizenship is in conflict with a market economy but simultaneously was convinced that a compromise between both principles can be found (Turner, 1986; Hindess, 1987). Though this compromise is not at all free of tensions, following Marshall to abolish the compromise would cause much more trouble than to stick to it.

Whether social policy is really an institutional feature peculiar to the welfare state capitalism of the postwar period without significant precursors is a question of some interest. Historians in particular have pointed to the fact that one can trace the introduction of social insurance systems back to the 1880s. But if one compares the range of coverage, amount of payment and their general efficiency, the difference between the present and the Victorian situation is more striking than the similarity (Kaelble, 1987).

A third characterizing feature of welfare state capitalism is 'mass consumption' (Rostow, 1971). By this I mean not only that in the postwar period the labour force has gained access to goods beyond the subsistence level; the term serves primarily to indicate the accumulation model which made possible increasing consumption levels. Welfare state capitalism differs from earlier modes of accumulation by the participation of the labour force in economic progress. If one wants to describe the change in terms of Marxist political economy, then the most salient feature of the relation between capital and labour is that capitalist growth is no longer based on the increase of the 'relative rate of surplus value'. This change is manifested in a wage policy which is oriented to an increase in productivity. Quite differently from Marx's assumptions, wage labour is not the source of increasing immiseration but — in comparison with other ways to participate in economic progress — a stable access to 'wealth'. This does not at all mean that poverty has been erased, but that it has turned more or less into a minority problem and a problem which typically concerns the population not belonging to the actively employed (especially the retired population).

Finally, welfare state capitalism can be defined by changed industrial relations, the core of which is *the capital labour accord* (Bowles and Gintis, 1982). This accord contains several elements of which the most important is the public recognition of trade unions and the institutionalization of class conflict (Dahrendorf, 1959), that is a system of formal regulations shaping the actions of both sides of the labour market in case of a conflict.

Again, the degree to which class conflicts have been institutionalized varies considerably, but in general, it is not an exaggeration to state that in the 'institutionalized welfare states' (Korpi, 1980) of north-western Europe during the postwar period a consensus between labour and capital predominated in which both sides of the labour market shared common aims of industrial policy. As long as an improvement of the conditions of the working class by growth was ensured, the trade unions were prepared to accept the control by private property of the economic process.

In the literature on corporatism the new type of industrial relations has been generalized to a tripartite exchange relationship of state, capital and labour in which every part can improve its situation by a *quid pro quo*. The government uses the associations as an instrument to implement its policies and the private associations are incorporated into the process of determining political goals. Indeed, the centre of politics shifts from the government to a 'system of corporatist interest intermediation' (Schmitter, 1979) but this does not necessarily mean that economic policy is now subject to the egoistic demands of private interest groups. The central effect of a corporatist interest intermediation is rather to generate a restraint on egoistic (wage) demands. Though corporatist regulations can be met in different fields of politics (for example health) the core of it is income policy. Within such a system the regulation of the conflict between capital and wage increases is subject to the general framework of macroeconomic policy. But the term corporatism is not restricted to a specification of the type of conflict regulation between capital and labour. Schmitter (1979: 64) uses the concept as a 'means of capturing fundamental changes in the nature of civil society–association–state linkages'. In the advanced industrial capitalist societies

> formally organized interest associations . . . have tended to acquire an indispensability and ubiquity in civil society, a penetration and influence within the apparatus of the state, and a presence in the formation and promotion of ideology and collective consciousness that radically alter the liberal–bourgeois–parliamentary–democratic mode of political domination.

These four features are constitutive of the social structure of accumulation in the postwar period. By these features welfare state capitalism differs fundamentally from earlier stages of growth or 'long cycles'. Against these contentions it could now be objected either that other features are more important (such as 'monopoly capitalism') or that the features mentioned already characterize the relationship between market and state in earlier periods of growth. Following this line of reasoning, the decisive historical turn in the relationship between market and state did not take place during the 'great depression', but had already taken place before the First World War. In German social history, for example (see Kocka, 1974 and as a review Puhle, 1984), there is a certain inclination to regard the shift from liberal to organized capitalism before the First World War as the decisive step in capitalist development and accordingly to furnish the concept of organized capitalism with those elements I assumed to be characteristic of the 'Keynesian welfare state'. As I see it, the quality of organization, in the sense of concentration and centralization of capital, is neither constitutive of the 'Keynesian welfare state' nor does it make sense to ascribe the commitment to full employment to the state in a period before Keynes, where this commitment — as a study of economic policy during the 'great depression' can show — did not exist. It is true that, above all, the policies intending to augment social security and the integration of the labour movement into capitalist society were tendencies effective since the end of the last century. Nevertheless, in combination with the commitment to full employment and the participation of the labour force in economic progress, these tendencies are apt to distinguish the postwar 'long cycle' from earlier capitalist cycles.

III

Surveying the economic history of the postwar period, the decade between the late 1950s and the late 1960s in particular appears to be an outstanding success. After 1950 in Western Europe real incomes increased on a scale never experienced before. The improvement in living conditions which this growth entailed is the more astonishing if one calls to mind that at the beginning of this development living conditions of the working class had been quite similar to those in 1913. From the end of the 1950s until the late 1960s unemployment in major Western European countries practically disappeared. There was no time in the history of Western countries when the level of unemployment was so low for such a long period of time (Fischer 1987: 102, Table 36).

Though it is tempting to ascribe this economic success immediately to the institutional structure of the Keynesian welfare state, the amount to which this structure contributed to it is controversial. Certainly without an entirely new wage policy, which shifted from 'exploitation' to participation in productivity increases, the rise of real wages would have been impossible. Transfer payments stabilize consumer demand during a recession while industrial peace, achieved by the integration of the labour force, certainly plays a role as a 'productive force'. Less evident is the function of economic policy in economic growth. To assess the contribution of a Keynesian full employment policy to economic performance is difficult. State commitment to full employment counts as the core of the institutional innovation and is characteristic of welfare state capitalism. Without it one could hardly speak of a paradigmatic change of direction in economic policy, that is in the relationship between 'market' and 'state'. Yet the function of economic policy in the performance of a market economy is highly controversial. First, what economic success means is not at all clear. There is a debate over whether it is measured by a high rate of active employment and growth, by low rates of unemployment and inflation, or by a combination of these goals. Judgement on whether a national economy and its economic policy is successful depends on the unit of measure of economic success. Second, one has to evaluate the contribution of accidental and external factors such as an international division of labour favourable to the old industrial nations, cheap energy prices and generally a situation of reconstruction in which the problem for the leading Western European countries consisted of returning to a long-term path of economic growth. Thus we are confronted with a peculiar and uneasy situation. On the one hand, the difference between a Keynesian welfare state and its predecessors seems to be clear; on the other hand, the function of economic policy with respect to economic growth must be regarded as unsettled.[2]

Complications increase further if one turns to the reasons for economic failure in the mid–1970s. Not even the unit of measure of economic failure is beyond doubt. To answer the question whether and to what degree welfare state regulations in the end caused economic failure, poses extremely difficult theoretical and empirical problems. There is hardly any effect for which the welfare state has not been held responsible. It has not only been accused of having weakened economic performance, but in addition was supposed to have destroyed 'life world' and 'community'. These destructive effects are linked up with an expanding welfare bureaucracy that treated its clients merely as policy takers, and with legal regulations penetrating nearly every realm of daily life. Finally the welfare state is suspect because the frequently deplored 'government overload' ultimately originates in its endeavour to intervene in different spheres of social life (for a classic statement, see Janowitz, 1976). The inbuilt inclination of the welfare state to overestimate its capacity to guide and control is finally held responsible for a situation where the government is confronted with demands it cannot fulfil.

Here I can only treat the economic aspect of the problem. In order to examine the arguments for or against the existence of an antagonistic relationship between market and state as a result of a development which predominated in the postwar period, I shall first collect some empirical evidence for tensions and contradictions of welfare state capitalism and then turn to the problem of whether and in what manner the idea of the welfare state as an obstacle to economic success can be specified.

The indicators of economic failure that usually count are rising state expenditure and a concomitant fiscal crisis of the state; productivity slowdown; declining growth rates (or even negative ones); rising unemployment, and inflation. No doubt, measured by these indicators, the efficiency of capitalist economies has abated (see Figure 2).

But as obvious as economic decline may seem to be, one should

FIGURE 2

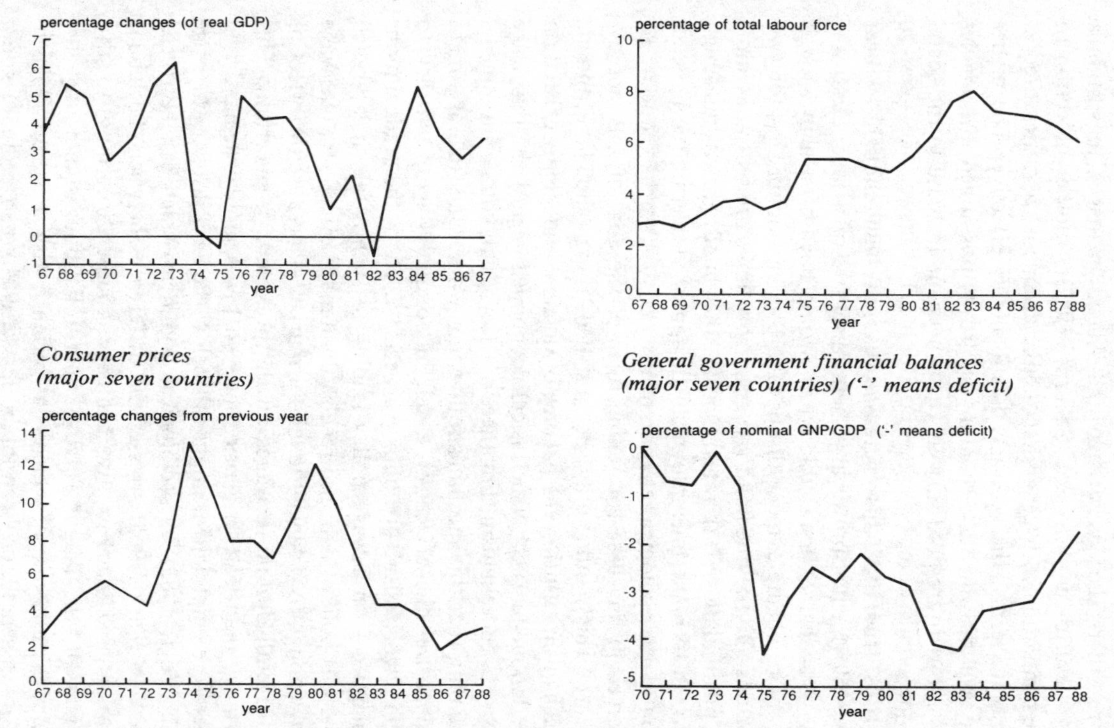

Sources: OECD *Economic Outlook* (1983–7) and OECD *Historical Statistics*

avoid jumping to conclusions. For the individual economies have nonetheless displayed different patterns since the mid-1970s. Some countries — like West Germany — managed to fight inflation; others such as Sweden and Austria managed to sustain a high level of employment (Scharpf, 1987). Another objection to the contention of a general economic decline is that, measured in absolute terms, the economy is still highly effective. The higher the level on which the economy is already positioned, the smaller the growth rate necessary to yield the same increase in the social product.

It is true that this increase was not high enough to beat unemployment. But this argument raises two questions. First, was any growth rate achievable which would have been high enough to make unemployment disappear? One can doubt this for two reasons. On the one hand rather narrow limits are set on attempts to manipulate growth rates. On the other hand, growth rates high enough to make unemployment disappear accelerate the destruction of the ecological environment. Second, can the economy be blamed in any case for failing to meet the goal of full employment? This could only be justified if an inbuilt economic mechanism ensuring the balance of demand and supply existed on the labour market. Neoclassical economists regard the real wage as such a mechanism, but there are Keynesian counter-arguments claiming that this mechanism does not work. One such argument emphasizes the effects of a fall in nominal wages, contrary to what neoclassical orthodoxy expects. Even if the trade unions complied with a wage policy leading to such a fall, it is argued that this policy might not reach the intended effect — a real wage low enough to balance the labour market — because the effect of an overall decline in wages on the price level is uncertain. This strategy may lead to a price level so low that real demand and therefore employment might fall below the level prior to the wage fall (Vogt, 1983). A sociological argument which can be traced back to Marx (1965) stresses the differences between the labour market and markets for ordinary goods. According to this argument, the labour force is only a fictitious commodity, the commercialization of which is at variance with social principles in a broad sense, so it cannot be marketed like an ordinary good.

One major line of reasoning to prove a negative impact of the welfare state on economic performance is to illustrate the consequences of rising state expenditure. Indeed, empirical data show

TABLE 2
Public expenditure in fifteen OECD countries

Year	Belgium	Denmark	W. Germany	Finland	France	UK	Ireland	Italy	Canada	Nether-lands	Norway	Austria	Sweden	Switzer-land	USA
1850						11.1									
1855		8.4													
1860		9.4				10.7									
1865		11.2									5.8				
1870		9.2	13.3[e]		11.0	8.7					5.9				
1875		8.3													
1880		8.9	9.9[c]		15.4	9.1					6.8			16.5	
1885		10.0													
1890		10.6	12.9[c]		15.0	9.2					7.4			15.0	7.1
1895		10.3				10.4									
1900		10.8	14.2[c]		15.2	14.9				8.9	9.9			11.1	7.9[e]
1905		10.0	15.1[e]		14.6[c]	12.4				8.8					
1910		12.3			14.4[b]	12.7				8.8	9.3				
1915		11.5[b]	17.0[d]			12.7[d]				9.1[b]			11.2[b]	14.0[d]	8.5[d]
1920		15.3[c]			34.2	27.4				18.5[c]	12.8		10.9		12.6[e]
1925		13.4	22.4		21.9[c]	23.6	21.5[e]			14.9			14.1[c]	17.0[b]	11.7[e]
1930		13.5	29.4		22.1[b]	24.7	20.8			15.2	17.4		14.0	17.4	21.3[e]
1935		17.5	29.8		35.4	23.7	27.8			18.0	18.1		17.1[b]	23.7[b]	
1940		19.2[b]	36.9[d]		29.2[d]	33.4[b]	26.8			18.3[b]	19.1[b]		17.7[d]	23.9[d]	22.2
1945		20.0[e]			37.2[e]	45.5[c]	22.6				29.3[c]		19.3[c]	29.3[c]	
1950	22.6	19.4	30.8		28.4	30.4	27.4			27.0	25.5	25.0	23.5	19.8	23.0[d]
1955	24.7	23.6	30.0		32.2	30.2	27.5	27.8	27.1	28.5	26.8	27.5	26.4	17.4	24.9
1960	30.3	24.8	32.0	26.7	34.6	32.6	28.0	30.1	28.9	33.7	29.9	32.1	31.1	17.2	27.8
1965	32.3	29.9	36.3	31.3	38.4	36.4	33.1	34.3	29.1	38.7	34.2	37.9	36.0	19.7	28.0
1970	36.5	40.2	37.6	31.3	38.9	39.3	39.6	34.2	35.7	45.5	41.0	39.2	43.7	21.3	32.2
1975	44.5	48.2	47.1	37.1	43.5	46.9	47.5	43.2	40.8	55.9	46.6	46.1	49.0	28.7	35.4
1980	51.7	56.0	46.9	38.2	46.2	44.6	48.9[b]	45.6	40.7	62.5	49.4	48.5	65.7	29.7	33.2

[a] in % des Bruttosozialprodukts; [b] Abweichung vom Bezugsjahr; – 1 Jahr; [c] + 1 Jahr; [d] – 2 Jahre; [e] + 2 Jahre.
Source: Kohl 1983; vor 1950 nationale finanzstatistische Quellen, ab 1950 vor allem OECD-National Accounts; Schweiz (bis 1910), Frankreich (bis 1910), Niederlande (bis 1940) mit Bezugsgröße Nettosozialprodukt.

three stable trends: (1) in the postwar period state expenditure increased rapidly; (2) state spending grew faster than the economy, and (3) the major component of state growth has been in welfare and social service expenditure (Kohl, 1985; Block, 1981; see also Table 2).

Furthermore, increasing state expenditure was accompanied by a continuously — and in some countries rapidly — increasing state debt. For example, gross federal debt in the United States rose from $544.1 billion in 1975 to $1,827.5 billion in 1985 and in 1987 had reached the fantastic figure of $2,344 billion (OECD, December 1989, pp. 49 and 109). But measured in terms relative to GDP, state debt in the United States cannot be said to be alarmingly high. For instance, it is much higher in Italy, where the general government borrowing requirement is around 12.5 percent of the GDP; the debt/GDP ratio has already risen above 100 percent.[3]

All these developments certainly exert an influence on the performance of a market economy. In principle, there are good reasons to follow Janowitz and to stress the negative impact of the trends mentioned on economic performance. Public administration and social security expenditure absorb a growing share of national income, thus leaving less for private investment. They will increase inflation if the demands on the GNP exceed the production of goods and services. Further, they force up public debt and contribute in this way to rising interest rates (see the discussion on 'crowding out', for example Placone et al., 1985). In addition, tax resistance, heightened pressure for limits on state spending as well as fiscal pressure on state and local governments are expected (Block, 1981: 5). But does all this amount to the fact that the highest explanatory power for economic decline can be attributed to rising state expenditure? In West Germany the statistical correlation of social expenditure with private investment, public debts and inflation is rather weak (Alber, 1982a). 'There is not so much evidence' — Schmidt (1983: 8ff) summarizes his own statistical analysis of OECD data — 'for the view held by the new fiscal orthodoxy according to which the economic miseries were the product of governments, particularly the rapid expansion and the excessive levels of government spending'.

Further, one has to take into account that statistical correlations conceal rather than reveal the relevant causal factors. For example, long before the economic limit of state debt is reached, psychological limits become effective. It does not matter very much if economists prove in abstract models that nothing is wrong with rising state debts, if the rise is only proportional to the increase of the GNP. Such models overlook the fact that an intermediating factor in state debt is confidence. If economic agents lose it due to a rapid increase of debt, the absolute level of which need not be at all dangerous, then this loss of confidence sets a limit more effective than so-called objective ones.

Undeniably, inflation rates grew considerably since the late 1960s and nowhere was economic policy able to reduce them before the recession of 1981–2. But behind the mere fact of rising inflation rates two theoretical problems are concealed. Does inflation have any negative impact on economic performance? And can welfare state principles be blamed for it?

As to the first problem — why care about inflation — it is argued that inflation really does matter mainly because in a money economy inflation often leads to negative reactions of property holders such as wrong allocation of resources, increased uncertainty in investment decisions and a tendency to transfer money to countries with a stable currency. On the 'system integration' level the functioning of a money economy is not endangered by unemployment, but by a continuous erosion of monetary stability. But things look different on the 'social integration' level. On this level a capitalist economy might be more endangered by unemployment than by rising inflation rates.

In textbook economics it is common to distinguish between a demand-pull and a cost-push approach to explain the causes of inflation. The conventional approach is to explain inflation by excess demand. Following this approach there is a clear causal link between demand and inflation. Wherever too much money spending bids for the limited supply of goods and labour available at full employment, prices and wages will be pulled up (Samuelson, 1973: 289). In a situation of full capacity utilization the remedy is simple: application of fiscal and monetary brakes by the government. But unfortunately, the advanced capitalist societies are involved in a much more complex situation, in which they are hit by a new dilemma distinguishable from the conventional demand-pull inflation. Where the modern type of cost-push inflation predominates, prices and wages will begin to rise before full capacity utilization is reached. Some see the causal mechanism behind cost-push inflation as exaggerated demands of the working class on the social product. Other authors prefer a more general cost-pull approach, which does not focus on wages. Be that as it may: in order to uphold a level of profitability which ensures the stability of the firm, employers are forced to raise prices. In case of a cost-push inflation the remedy effective in a demand-pull situation does not work. Samuelson has summarized the argument: 'when we apply the monetary and fiscal brakes at the same time that we limit the rate of cost-push inflation, we shall kill off the golden goose of prosperity. Many will regard the remedy as worse than the disease' (1973: 827). In addition, Samuelson has hinted at 'structural elements', which could explain that the demand-pull inflation has been superseded by the cost-push inflation. He assumes 'that the mixed economy under the prodding of populist democracy gets itself in a structural bind'. Bankers and policy makers will be thrown out of office by the electorate if they try to fight inflation with a restrictive fiscal and monetary policy. But as the recent political history of Great Britain and West Germany has shown, this did not happen. Today governments can win elections by promising balanced budgets. Therefore it remains a task for sociologists to transform the weak indicators of 'structural elements' responsible for inflation into a model with explanatory power.

A decisive step towards a sociological explanation of inflation was taken in a paper by Goldthorpe (1978). Regarding our problem — the possibility of an antagonistic relationship between market and state — a great advantage of Goldthorpe's approach is that he explicitly tries to associate inflation with a constitutive element of welfare state capitalism — citizenship. According to Goldthorpe three institutional changes must coincide to generate wage pressure. First, the market economy tends to undermine the traditional status order. To the degree that the market economy expands, it weakens the willingness of workers to accept their place in society ascribed by tradition and legitimate authority. The pursuit of interest within a market context is entirely at variance with behaviour bound by premodern norms. If these norms (including norms of fair pay) are eroded, the behavioural restrictions that a market economy relies on fades away (Hirsch, 1977). In this way the welfare state not only endangers the foundations of economic efficiency but the moral foundations of solidarity too. The weakening of traditional moral bonds is a precondition of individualization — a historical tendency first described by G. Simmel.

Second, the principle of citizenship is in conflict with the distribution of life chances in a pure labour market economy. This not only means that the more this principle is realized, the more it becomes difficult to explain social stratification by recourse to the category of classes formed exclusively on the labour market. It means furthermore that to the degree that citizenship has been implemented, the power of employees to enforce their demands has increased. This increase in power takes place in an ideological and in an objective dimension. In the ideological dimension, class inequality becomes illegitimate; in the objective dimension citizenship strengthens the ability of workers to resist, because they now dispose of — however limited — resources independent of wage payments.

The third element Goldthorpe refers to is the maturity of the working class, measured by homogeneity and organizational strength. If the actions of a mature working class find support in the breakdown of a premodern status system and the expansion of citizenship, then a situation becomes probable in which the strength of organized labour has increased sufficiently to raise wages beyond a level neutral to the value of money. The only way for capital to escape loss of income share is to take recourse to the anonymous instrument of raising prices. Then it becomes an empirical question whether the economy will accept the depreciation of the currency and whether — and for how long — the government or the central bank participates in the game. In West Germany the Central Bank refused to co-operate. Today it is — independent of the political position of the observer — broadly accepted that the recession of 1974–5 was initiated by the refusal of the Central Bank to provide the economy with a money supply big enough to finance a race between wages and prices.

Though there are some sociological arguments that a certain connection between one dimension of economic failure, namely inflation, and the Keynesian welfare state exists, these arguments cannot be generalized.[4] It is still an open question whether the impact of welfare state structures on economic performance is mainly a negative one. Still less can they serve to back the political recommendation to do without the welfare state. But before I turn to the question 'market or state' let me pursue the idea of an antagonistic economic relationship between a developed welfare state and a market economy a bit further.

To substantiate this idea it is insufficient to focus only on the link between a strong working class and inflationary tendencies. One has to focus on the valorization process of capital itself. The problem is to explain why in all major capitalist countries the long postwar upswing was replaced by a period of stagnation and crisis. For obvious reasons in a capitalist context the immediate explanation for the tendency of the economy towards stagnation is a decline in the profit rate. There can be no doubt that this is exactly what has happened since 1965 (Hill, 1979). Although there can be little controversy about the mere fact of a profit squeeze, the debate on the reasons for such a squeeze has been very intense. Similar to the dispute on the reasons for rapid postwar growth, the attempts to explain economic decline call either for external, accidental or internal structural forces. When the McCracken Report (1977) appeared, the majority of economists and politicians accepted the main finding, the explanation of economic stagnation as a result of the oil price shock. But the longer the stagnation period lasted, the greater the need for a structural explanation. Above all, Marxist economists have proposed an explanation of the fall of the profit rate which points to the workings of a mechanism central to the functioning of a capitalist economy. Following an argument which had already been elaborated by Marx and which was restated powerfully in a famous article by Kalecki (1972), cyclical growth is based on the operation of an industrial reserve army mechanism. During the upswing unemployment is reduced and wages increase to a level which finally endangers the valorization of capital. When this point is reached, the upswing ends and a phase of recession starts. The operation of the reserve army mechanism is crucial, because only increasing unemployment rates can force down wages and mitigate the profit squeeze. In this manner the reserve army mechanism creates the precondition of economic recovery. Kalecki was the first to point to the fact that in a full-employment policy environment this reserve army mechanism will be weakened. Indeed, welfare state capitalism differs crucially from a capitalist society without welfare state institutions, in that it is virtually a capitalism without a reserve army (Lutz, 1982).

This institutional change to a capitalism without a reserve army cannot be achieved without costs. 'If we are correct,' Bowles and Gintis summarize the argument, 'the ability of the reserve army to provide the conditions for restarting the engine of rapid capitalist growth has been significantly impaired in the course of the long postwar boom' (1982: 78). Welfare state institutions affect the capitalist accumulation process mainly in two different ways. First, a Keynesian demand management promising full employment obviously weakens the ability of the reserve army to discipline labour, because the goal of this policy is to avoid rising unemployment rates. Second, the power of the reserve army is weakened in addition by a process Bowles and Gintis call 'the deproletarization of labour'. This term means nothing other than Marshall's 'citizenship'. In a welfare state context 'much of the working-class standard of living is now acquired not through the sale of labour power, but through the exercise of rights of citizenship' (Bowles and Gintis, 1982: 83). The authors reject the view that the profit squeeze is caused by a wage policy of trade unions capable of enforcing wage increases above the level of productivity increase. A distributional bottleneck for capital occurs only if one takes into account wage gains and state spending together. 'The accord promoted distributional conflict as the predominant axis of class struggle, and the capitalist class lost' (Bowles and Gintis, 1982: 75). The authors maintain that the average working wage has grown relatively and absolutely. If this can be said of a marginal welfare state like the USA, one can certainly expect it to hold true in the institutionalized welfare states of Western Europe.[5]

As long as the empirical evidence of a profit squeeze being mainly caused by a rising social wage is contested and alternative explanations of economic decline are possible, this approach is also only a hypothesis. So far, this review of attempts to substantiate the idea of a destabilizing impact of welfare state institutions on a market economy has not claimed the status of an established truth, but has aimed to indicate in which way a destabilization hypothesis can be maintained and proved. Provided that this hypothesis is true and capital has really lost a distributional struggle, then a reversal of the long-term tendency of a compromise between citizenship and class presupposes a long and severe period of depression. Not surprisingly, capital will use this phase to reverse the historical tendency which resulted in its defeat. I now hold that economic and social history since the mid-1970s has to be regarded as a period of conflict centred on the articulation of state and economy, which was constitutive of welfare state capitalism. Labour's share of national income decreased and social security benefits were cut. In addition since the mid-1970s state commitment to full employment was abandoned. Indeed in mass democracies no government can afford to deny that mass unemployment is a central political problem the solution of which is on the agenda. Nevertheless, Keynesian strategies to control the overall level of economic activity are no longer regarded by the majority of politicians and economists as an appropriate tool to reach the full employment goal. Not even in Sweden is a counter-cyclical fiscal policy applied as a means to increase the employment level.[6]

Phases of downturn are not only phases of decay, but phases in which the institutional foundations of a new upswing are sought, too. With reference to this search for an institutional restructuring capable of bearing a new upswing, it is decisive, whether and to what extent the welfare state compromise can be upheld or in what direction it must be dissolved.

IV

As has been shown, there is some evidence for the contention that the welfare state has become a part of the problem whose solution it pretends to be; both theoretical arguments and empirical data — though they are not undisputed — point out that the welfare state changed from a 'solution' to a 'source' of crisis (Flora, 1981). Provided this is true, logically the follow-up questions are: what comes after the welfare state? Can its achievements simply be abandoned without any costs? Are there any reasons to believe that a market economy without a full-employment policy, guarantee of citizenship, mass consumption and capital–labour accord would work better? A complete answer to these questions would not only get us into a complex investigation of the economic and social history of the last decade, it would lead us on to the field of speculation. I therefore contain myself to dealing with remarks on three points: (1) the capacity of the state to govern the economy; (2) the pros and cons with respect to market and state (or 'hierarchy' to be more precise) as modes of integration; (3) elements of an institutional restructuring to which welfare state capitalism is subjected.

As I pointed out, in the postwar period governments accepted responsibility for full employment. Keynesian demand management was held to be the central means to reach this goal. The advocates of a Keynesian counter-cyclical policy did not waste much time on a thorough examination of the question whether the government has the competence to govern the economy. It is a precondition of the social democratic consensus to presuppose that the government is able to control the overall level of the economy. This belief is very clearly stated by Crosland. Crosland was fully convinced that there 'is now no insuperable economic difficulty about the government imposing its will, provided it has one . . .' (1956: 468). If the government does not act, this is due either to lack of information or to lack of will, but the inactivity cannot be ascribed to lack of administrative power. Crosland not only believed government could regulate the overall level of economic activity: he assumed it could 'exert any influence it likes on income distribution' (1956: 27). At the latest since the economic downturn of the mid-1970s this optimism regarding the guidance capacity of government has evaporated, to make room for a more realistic view. The research of sociologists and political scientists has contributed a good deal to this changing view. This research did not examine the relationship between economic variables (for example the relation between full employment policy and inflation) but concentrated on the political process of demand management itself, its preconditions for success and its inner organization:

(a) On a highly abstract level one can point to the problems of societal control in the context of a polycentric society (see the contributions in Glagow and Willke, 1987). Doubts of the steering capacity of the government have in particular been nourished by recent developments in sociological system theory. The idea of an *Eigengesetzlichkeit* (determination by inherent laws) to which every functional subsystem of society is subject had already been formulated by Max Weber. But in Luhmann's outline of a theory of social systems (1984) this idea had been radicalized and provided with a micro-foundation. The keywords of the new stage of system theory are autopoiesis, self-referentiality and operational closure. They circumscribe the elementary behaviour of every social system. These systems continue to exist by generating the elements they consist of (autopoiesis), through a determination of their actual state by a previous one (self-referentiality) and by the incapability of systems to transcend their own limits (closure). From all this it follows that the environment of a system can only encourage (or impair) the performance of its own operations, but can never determine these operations.

(b) In political science the preconditions of strategic choices of collective actors have attracted increasing attention. If one cannot simply impute the ability to act to a single actor (see the discussion on the 'multiple self'), this is even less feasible in the case of a collective actor. In a recent study Scharpf (1987) thoroughly investigated the preconditions and the limits of governmental capacity to formulate and implement full-employment strategy. One precondition, which is not at all self-evident but must be produced, is that all parts of the government come together in a concerted action. According to Scharpf, in Germany full-employment policy failed mainly because of the autonomy of the Central Bank and the procyclical behaviour of the regional and local governments (1987: 294). The next problem confronting a unified fiscal and monetary policy of the government is that it must not be frustrated by the wage policy of the trade unions. Specific conditions must exist in order for the trade unions to choose a co-operative strategy and check their inclination to enforce high wages in a situation where full employment is ensured by the state. Among the four countries with a social democratic government whose full employment policies Scharpf analysed, Austria came out best, because it succeeded in co-ordinating the governmental fiscal and monetary policy as well as trade union wage policy (1987: 207).

(c) Whether the state can achieve what it is aiming at depends on the means it disposes of and the special circumstances of the situation. One can leave undecided whether after the 1974–5 economic crisis the circumstances were still favourable to a full-employment policy, but since the beginning of the 1980s these favourable circumstances have vanished. Now the main obstacles to the successful application of Keynesian strategies are the internationalization of capital markets and increased inflation rates (Scharpf, 1987: 298).

(d) Finally, the capacity of governments to pursue their policy objectives will generally be restricted by the policy instruments available to them. The instruments of Keynesian demand management are fiscal (and monetary) policy; nobody can reasonably expect them to reach goals beyond the scope conditioned by the specific shape of these instruments.

Although arguments of this kind are apt to unsettle belief in the capability of the government to keep effective demand on a full-employment level, one should not exaggerate their impact. Objections to a Keynesian stabilization policy cannot be expanded without further qualification to general objections to state activities. Even though the critique of a Keynesian stabilization policy is valid, the scope of this critique is strictly limited to its subject. It is not the final proof of the 'market' being better than the 'state'.

The issue whether and in what respect 'market' or 'state' is better belongs to the 'great debate' in social sciences. This debate was opened by Mandeville's famous observation that 'private vices' can under certain conditions turn to 'public virtues'. A sufficient condition for this turn is, as Adam Smith added, the existence of a market. To describe the workings of a market, Smith used the metaphor of an 'invisible hand' leading a self-interested individual 'to promote an end which was no part of his intention'. In microeconomic theory Smith's metaphor has been elaborated to a general equilibrium model of the market. The conditions were clarified under which the price mechanism produces an efficient allocation of resources to utilizations.

But the market not only guarantees the identity of individual and collective rationality. Where markets are established, external effects are prevented from occurring. Markets are defined by the exchange of private goods, that is, goods the exchange of which does not affect 'third parties'. If such effects do occur, it need not be due to market failures, but to an incomplete realization of markets. Markets are only established if property rights can be defined and enforced.

In welfare economics the microeconomic analysis of the market as an efficient allocative mechanism has been applied to demonstrate that state intervention is superfluous. The market can do the job of regulating social pressures at least as well as any alternative mechanism. To prove this, welfare economists have established two fundamental theorems. First, in the absence of external economies or diseconomies a competitive market sustains a Pareto-efficient allocation. Second, every Pareto-efficient allocation can be sustained by a market (provided that appropriate transfers of resources are made). The thrust of these theorems is directed against planning. They serve to fight the erroneous belief that public interest necessarily requires public action and that with increasing social complexity the need for planning also increases.

Are the fundamental theorems of welfare economics a solid foundation for rejecting government actions either as superfluous or as less efficient? Even on the abstract level of a discussion of allocative or integrative mechanisms this would be conclusive only if there were no 'market failures'. The literature on this topic (for a classic treatment see Bator, 1958) deals mainly with three types of market failure: increasing returns to scale, public goods and externalities (for a longer list see Stiglitz, 1986). Increasing returns to scale exclude perfect competition as a precondition of Pareto-efficient market allocation and provide big firms with cost advantages; public goods are goods which cannot be appropriated privately. If such a good is supplied, no member of the collectivity can be excluded from its consumption.[7] Therefore public goods must be produced by institution other than a market economy and distributed by a mechanism different from markets. Externalities occur wherever private costs (benefits) and social costs (benefits) diverge. Private costs are costs imputed to a single actor, like an individual or a firm; social costs are costs imputed to the society. I cannot deal systematically with the problem of market failures here. The remark must suffice that these failures prevent us from coming to a conclusion on the 'great debate' in favour of the market. Market failures are a 'rationale for government activity' (Stiglitz, 1986: 183).

Of course, government is hit by 'failures', too. Apart from the problems I discussed with reference to government intervention in the economy, the literature stresses in particular three types of government failure: mismanagement (inefficiency), tax burden and loss of freedom. A variant of the latter is threat to the community and life world of individuals by an expanding bureaucracy (see for example Illich et al., 1977; Habermas, 1985).

This debate cannot be settled here but fortunately it need not be settled at all, if this implies the compulsion to opt for an abstract principle. This compulsion does not exist, for several reasons. First, as Hindess (1987) has pointed out, social science must avoid the failure of 'essentialism'. Indeed, both Marxism and liberalism are inclined to analyse the market 'in terms of an essence or inner principle which produces necessary effects by the mere fact of its presence' (Hindess, 1987: 149). The same could be stated for the analysis of 'hierarchy' or 'planning'. But as

March and Simon already pointed out, the question of a choice between market and state 'cannot be settled once and for all by a priori considerations, but must be decided in each case by reference to the empirical facts of the world' (1958: 204).[8]

Second, market and hierarchy (planning) are not necessarily incompatible principles. The working of the one may depend on the working of the other. Furthermore, they can be in a relation of 'reciprocal gradation'. Thus the issue is not 'market' or 'state', but where the realm of efficiency ends and the realm of equity begins (Okun, 1975), that is, what social sphere should be governed by which principle.

Third, the 'grand alternative' does not exist, because of the coexistence of two further principles or allocative mechanisms, 'community' and 'private associations' (see Streeck and Schmitter, 1985; Dahl and Lindblom, 1953 for a slightly different list). In the case of social policy this means, for example, that social welfare is produced by the interactions of markets, state, associations and private groups (Zapf, 1986: 143).

Can one already observe a shift with respect to the articulation of market and state which was constitutive for welfare state capitalism? Among the four features defining welfare state capitalism two, citizenship and mass consumption (the affluent society), have survived and seem to be able to survive (despite tendencies to dismantle the welfare state and despite the squeeze on real incomes of the dependent employed). To abolish these principles would automatically bring back the problems which were to be controlled by their implementation. The other two — state intervention and the capital–labour accord — can hardly be sustained without any substantial change. The time of a Keynesian full-employment policy seems to be gone (but the problem to which it was addressed is not). In particular the capital–labour accord is under pressure because of three important social changes.

First, the postwar growth was paid for dearly by the tremendous destruction of the natural environment. This destruction is closely linked with the fact that in the labour–capital accord no place is assigned to the interest of nature. Probably in the period after welfare state capitalism the 'quality of life' will become more important than 'mass consumption'. In the literature on the 'economics of exhaustible resources' the overconsumption of nature is attributed to the absence of markets for natural resources. In order to correct misallocation resulting from the status of natural goods as free goods, it has been proposed to charge a tax or fees on their consumption.

In addition to a policy of charging for the use of natural resources one can imagine a policy aimed at lowering the social costs of labour. In welfare state context the finance of social security is bound to wage labour. Wage labour is charged the costs for social security. If wage labour becomes cheaper, because the employment relationship is no longer burdened with the costs of social security, one can hope to reduce unemployment by decoupling social security from the employment relationship and simultaneously to stop the waste of natural resources by shifting the burden of taxation from employment to resource use. In West Germany political proposals are being discussed which amount to making social security on a basic level entirely a state function by decoupling it from the employment relationship and simultaneously introducing markets for natural resources (Biedenkopf, 1985). Such a shift certainly could be regarded as a step beyond welfare state capitalism.

Second, the labour–capital accord was an accord on the standardization and unification of work, too. One of the central topics of present discussions on the need for institutional changes is 'flexibility'. During the postwar period rigid standards with regard to work have been established in three dimensions: wages, labour legislation and working time. It is doubtful whether these standards can be sustained in all three dimensions. Trade unionists usually regard them exclusively as social achievements which have to be defended; employers stress the economic losses caused by inflexibility of working standards. If one compares tendencies to flexibilize wages, labour legislation and working time, it seems to me that there are better reasons to expect the trade unions to agree to a greater flexibility of working time rather than wage cuts and a slackening of labour legislation. The last two would definitely worsen the conditions of the labour force, whereas greater time flexibility can improve it. But of course whether more flexible working time is really able to improve work conditions is contingent on its design. Without regulations in this field of conflicting interests, the establishment of flexible working time would most probably deprive labour of the protection inherent in standardized working time without offering increased 'time sovereignty'. Be that as it may: as opinion polls show, increasing groups in the labour force are interested in a greater flexibility of working time. In Germany preferences of this kind are at variance with the strategy of trade unions to fight for a general reduction of working hours per week. However, a less rigid standardization of working time could lead to a better compatibility of different spheres of life such as work and family, provided that regulations concerning working time are established which take the time preferences of the employed into account. A greater flexibility of working time would certainly signify a considerable change in the work regulations constitutive of welfare state capitalism.

Finally, the welfare state has itself contributed to a dissolution of the unity of the working class and a corresponding individualization of life chances. Increasing incomes alienated workers from their traditional working-class background, and welfare benefits changed the pattern of social stratification. Further, the capital–labour accord destroyed proletarian consciousness, in so far as interest in socialism has to be regarded as a constitutive feature of this consciousness. As a result of the capital–labour accord, socialism as a unifying aim of the working class was abolished in return for participation in economic progress. Since the changes from free enterprise capitalism to welfare state capitalism, socialism is no longer on the agenda — but neither is a return to Manchester capitalism. The institutional changes which replace and supplement the Keynesian welfare state cannot be completely predicted yet, but I assume that ecology, flexibility and individualization will form part of them.

Notes

1. The establishment of the international economic institutions like GATT, the World Bank, IMF, the European Common Market and so on are among the major institutional innovations since the Second World War. Notwithstanding their importance I do not deal with them here nor with changes in international trade and finance in general. In the literature critical of capitalism the international economic order after the Second World War has been described as 'Pax Americana' (Amin et al., 1982); this 'Pax Americana' is assumed to have disintegrated since the termination of the Bretton Woods treaty.

2. For a critique of the view that full employment in Great Britain had anything to do with full employment policy see Matthews (1968).

3. See Saunders and Klau (1985), and for a treatment of the implications of the recent increase in the ratio of public debt to GNP, Chouraqui et al. (1986).

4. In the literature on corporatism it has been shown that 'big' and 'centralized' trade unions can be bound more to the aim of monetary stability than 'small' and 'decentralized' ones.

5. Glyn and Sutcliffe (1972) collected the data confirming the profit squeeze approach in the case of Great Britain. For similar developments in other West European countries cf. Armstrong, Glyn and Harrison (1989).

6. A full explanation of the incapacity and unwillingness of governments since the economic downturn of the mid-1970s to raise overall economic activity to the full-employment level with the help of fiscal policy certainly has to take into account not only the debate between 'Keynesians' and 'monetarists', but above all international factors like the increasing interpenetration of national economies and the rise of the level of interest rates (see for instance Scharpf, 1987).

7. See Lane (1985: 16) with reference to Pigou: 'Non-excludability implies market failure because non-excludability is only one side of the more general concept of non-appropriability . . . or externality'.

8. 'Why abolish the wage system,' Dahl and Lindblom (1953: 3), have already asked, 'if e.g. taxation will serve the purpose . . . to ameliorate income inequality'.

5
MARKET AND STATE IN CENTRALLY PLANNED ECONOMIES

Andrzej K. Koźmiński

Introduction

The very notion of a 'planned economy' may seem ambiguous and misleading to some, because of the different forms and degrees of planning practised in various economic systems at different times especially under the special conditions of war. The German economy during both world wars is undoubtedly such a confusing example. In this analysis of centrally planned economies I am referring to the Marxist economic system introduced in the countries ruled by communist parties. It is clear, however, that different types of such systems can be observed in the real world. The North Korean economic system is very different from the Yugoslav, Hungarian from East German, Polish from Romanian, and so on.

Looking for a common denominator among such differences one will quickly discover that the degree to which the economies are state controlled and market regulated best describe the differences between centrally planned economies. This statement opens enormous possibilities of comparative economic systems analysis, because these two dimensions are the most commonly addressed characteristics of all existing economic systems (Lindlum, 1977: 1).

The relative importance of the two regulation mechanisms, state and market, is different in different countries and constantly changing. The problem of the relationship between the market and the state in centrally planned economies should be formulated in process terms as a dynamic one. Driving forces and consequences of the process of change should be identified and analysed. In the present analysis I intend to deal mainly with the mechanism of change, which implies a focus on economic reforms. Such an analysis requires consideration of the sociopolitical context of the reform processes as it is known through empirical observations.

Historical Background

The history of economic reforms in centrally planned economies is already over sixty-five years old and full of dramatic changes in various directions (Nove, 1977a; Brus, 1986; *Revue*, 1975). The economic system of 'war communism' introduced in the Soviet Union in 1918, immediately after the Bolshevik revolution, can be briefly characterized as a 'proletarian state economy' without private property, without market, without money. It has to be noted, however, that even in such a system the underground economy and the black market survived and the old tsarist banknotes were widely accepted (Davies, 1958: 31; Seurot, 1983: 65). This system was dramatically changed in 1921 when Lenin introduced his New Economic Policy (NEP). Under the NEP system classical monetary reform was implemented: a strong convertible currency based on reserves of gold, was re-established. A large number of industrial enterprises became private property again; foreign capital, foreign managers and engineers were invited back to Russia. In agriculture, large farmers flourished. Market relationships dominated, while a state-sponsored system of central planning was gradually emerging (especially in the second half of the 1920s).

Around 1930 another drastic change took place in the USSR: the Stalinist system of 'forced industrialization' was firmly introduced. It took the form of an almost completely state-controlled economy totally subordinated to consecutive five-year and annual plans. The Stalinist system was based upon the early experiences of 'war communism' and was designed to enable the Soviet Union to industrialize for the anticipated war effort and to promote the new type of society of 'proletarian dictatorship'. The economy was totally subordinated to centralized planning in natural units with monetary categories (such as prices and costs) playing only a passive role and being manipulated at will by central planners. Such a system was made possible by a huge economic bureaucracy which formulated the plans, monitored and controlled their implementation and constantly interfered with the functioning of the enterprises by means of administrative measures and political pressure. The bureaucracy itself was constantly supervised by the Party apparatus and the political police. The Stalinist system was geared towards unbalanced growth: rapid extensive development of heavy industry at the expense of the consumption sector (agriculture, consumers, durable goods and services). Such a system accelerated economic growth as long as the extensive resources (natural resources and cheap, disciplined, undemanding labour) were abundant and easily accessible. The shortcomings of the system became evident with the inevitable depletion of these resources. They are more visible than in smaller countries, less privileged by nature and with a more independent and consumption-oriented population. The unsatisfactory performance of the system in such crucial areas as economic and social equilibrium, quality of life and technological progress has been generally known and widely criticized in the socialist countries themselves since the mid-1950s.

After the Second World War the Stalinist economic system was adopted in the whole socialist bloc, but not instantaneously and not without resistance. It finally prevailed at the beginning of the 1950s and its basic characteristics still remain in the USSR itself and until recently in the majority of the socialist countries.

Also in 1950, however, the first 'Yugoslav schism' came into being: the new alternative version of the socialist economy emerged, based on the principles of decentralization, workers' self-management and the growing role of the market mechanism.

The death of Stalin and the twentieth Congress of the Soviet Communist Party triggered a wave of criticism of the 'classical' Stalinist economic model as well as new attempts at economic reform. Polish discussion of the economic model of socialism (1956–8) and subsequent (only partly successful) decentralization reform pioneered this movement (Zieliński, 1973). Czechoslovakia and East Germany followed in the same direction in the mid-1960s. Around 1968, however, these two countries reversed the trend and engaged in recentralization and the re-establishment of the 'classic' model with some minor administrative and organizational improvements.

A new push was given to the reformist movement by the Hungarian reform introduced in 1969. Since that time Hungary has begun a cautious but consistent movement towards a parametric system using mainly indirect financial instruments to influence the behaviour of enterprises (which were gradually given greater autonomy and freedom of choice). In spite of some slowing down and temporary reverse trends the Hungarian reform process was accelerated in the mid-1980s and the evolution towards a market-regulated socialist economy became likely.

The Hungarian reform had a very strong impact on two Polish reforms. The first one — introduced in 1972 — was a complete failure due to cardinal mistakes in economic policy: a very strong and ill-conceived investment drive, rapid growth in the standard of living of the population combined with low economic efficiency financed through external debt (Kuczyński, 1981). The second Polish reform was introduced in the extremely difficult and tense political situation of 1982, aggravated by the accumulated results of the ill-fated economic policy of the 1970s (Koźmiński, 1986). The reform is now half completed and anti-reformist tendencies are still relatively strong (Pajestka, 1986: 385–426). But a return to the old system seems rather unlikely.

The USSR, which in the 1960s and early 1970s experienced some unsuccessful attempts to reform its economic system, seems to be entering a new period of turbulence and dramatic change called *perestroika* (reconstruction) (Manasian, 1987). Mikhail Gorbachev put it very clearly in his speech at the twenty-seventh Congress of the Communist Party of the USSR: 'The situation is such that we cannot limit ourselves to the partial improvements of the system; radical reform is needed' (*Materijaly*, 1986: 33).

Since the early 1980s the western world has become fascinated by Chinese reforms: decollectivization of agriculture, decentralization, regionalization and debureaucratization of the industrial system, new openness to the world markets, and the introduction of some elements of the capital market. The final goal of the Chinese reform once again seems to be a market-regulated, open socialist economy (Chevrier, 1986; Zafanolli, 1985).

Even such a short overview of the broad spectrum of economic reforms in centrally planned economies justifies some more general conclusions:

1. Historically socialism has developed a relative diversity in its economic mechanisms as well as corresponding organizational forms and social institutions. Such a diversity implies different and varying degrees of government control and market regulation of the economy.

2. Economic reforms were both successful and unsuccessful: some produced results completely opposite to the initial intentions. Reforms were designed in a variety of patterns: some were

based on centralization, some on decentralization, some on market or parametric regulation, some on direct economic calculation in natural units, combined with administrative management methods. All involved, however, more or less dramatic changes in the 'state–market mix of the economy'.

3. Economic reforms were implemented in varying sociopolitical conditions. Sometimes they were stable and well under control (as in Hungary in 1969), sometimes extremely tense and turbulent (Poland 1982). Economic situations varied in the same way: from relatively prosperous and stable (Hungary 1969, Poland 1972) to extremely difficult (USSR 1921, Yugoslavia 1950, Poland 1982).

4. The reforms can be attributed to various political inspirations such as Trotskyism, Stalinism, revisionism, liberalism and some other 'isms'. Political and ideological struggle was always an important part of the reform process. Sometimes it involved violence and repression (as in the introduction of the Stalinist reform in the early 1930s in the USSR). In this way such notions as the role of market and state in the functioning of the economy became ideologically based. The main purpose of this analysis is to use them as scientific categories explaining the dynamic of the socioeconomic and political systems of the socialist economies.

Such an analysis involves the following crucial issues:

— The problem of the identity of the centrally planned socialist economy.

— Identification of the main types of such economic systems and their main sociopolitical correlates.

— Identification of the main factors underlying the dynamics of the system: transition from one form to another.

The Problem of Identity

In *What is Socialism?* published as early as 1934 D. Griffith quotes 261 definitions of socialism. In most cases such definitions take the form of a list of the basic characteristic features of socialist economies. The following list, formulated by J.G. Zieliński, is a typical example of such a definition:

— satisfaction of needs of the whole society as a declared goal of the socialist economy;

— social ownership of the means of production;

— central control of economic life;
— freedom of choice of the consumer;
— freedom of employment;
— preservation of money (Zieliński, 1986: 34).

This list seems to be general enough to cover all the socialist economies existing now and in the past, both predominantly state regulated and predominantly market regulated. Some additional updating comments remain to be added to this list of characteristic features.

1. The historical experience of the socialist economy proves that private ownership of the means of production always survives to some extent within the framework of a black, grey or perfect legal economy (Aslund, 1985; Katsenliboigen, 1977). Therefore social ownership of the means of production should be considered as dominant, not necessarily exclusive. In some socialist countries (Poland, China, Hungary) the possibility of creating commercial companies issuing bonds and shares to employees and to the general public is openly discussed. Some practical experiences have already begun; the embryos of stock exchanges have already appeared in China and in Hungary (mainly in the form of bonds sold by state-owned enterprises). It means that almost certainly some new forms of ownership of the means of production will emerge in the socialist economies. These new forms of ownership could be qualified as intermediate between private and social ownership. Such a trend will inevitably lead towards the creation of a capital market in the socialist economies (Nagy, 1970). Some socialist societies can be characterized as having a relatively high level of acceptance of private ownership of the means of production. In a public opinion poll taken in Poland in December 1986, for example, 91.4 percent of workers and 95 percent of managers accepted private initiative in crafts and services. The respective figures for retailing were 78.7 percent and 84.4 percent, for small industry 60.6 percent and 66.3 percent, for medium-sized industry 36.6 percent and 29.1 percent, for banking 20.3 percent and 18.6 percent and for heavy industry 23 percent and 12.5 percent.[1]

2. Some authors strongly advocate including self-management as one of the basic characteristic features of the socialist economy (Horvath et al., 1977; Horvat, 1982). This argument cannot be defended on the grounds of the analysis of existing socialist economies: some of them were and still are organized on purely

authoritarian and totalitarian principles, with the exclusion of any kind of self-management (for example Romania and North Korea).

3. The problem of ranking the characteristic features of the socialist economies is raised by some. Such a problem can be formulated as a question: 'How far can the reforms go without losing the socialist character of the economy?' This question was seldom openly addressed, partly because of its far-reaching political implications, partly because of the fact that up to 1990 none of the existing socialist economies has ever lost its socialist character. The answer is probably most closely related to the central control of economic life and has to be formulated in terms of political science rather than economy. The Polish political scientist J.J. Wiatr (1979: 100, 115) formulates it as a 'direct link between economic and political functions of the state'. A socialist economy always remains politically centrally controlled by the state, which is in turn controlled by the Party. The preservation of this feature seems to be the limit of the reforms: beyond it the economy loses its socialist character. This means that the political authority controls the degree to which self-regulating market mechanisms, private ownership, independent initiative, self-management and so on are allowed in the economic system. Political reasons can induce dramatic changes of policy in this respect. This statement confirms once more that the spectrum of possible 'state–market mixes' is relatively broad in existing centrally planned economies.

The problem of the identity of the socialist economy is closely related to the notion of economic reform changing the system without changing its identity.

Similarly to the way the problem of identity of the socialist economy was presented we will try to establish a list of the most important features of an economic reform (Grossman, 1966; Bronstein, 1973: 3–4, 8–10; Zaleski, 1975):

1. Economic reform brings qualitative change into the philosophy, procedures and instruments of central planning. This covers the scope of planning and the type of economic calculation.

2. Economic reform changes 'the rules of the game' between the state and other economic agents: enterprises and households. It implies a change in the instruments used by the state in order to influence the behaviour of enterprises and households. The

proportion of administrative and political versus economic and monetary instruments changes, as well as the nature of both types of instrument.

3. Institutional and organizational changes should be considered an integral part of reform. Both changes in the structure of the state and its economic administration and changes in the way in which the enterprises are grouped are involved. Such a reorganization always triggers more or less drastic changes in the ruling elite, bureaucracy and managerial personnel.

4. The process of the formulation and implementation of a reform always has a very important political and ideological aspect. It assumes the form of a political campaign and very often of political struggle between the supporters of the 'old' and the 'new', and sometimes between different orientations of the 'new'. This implies a change of some ideological principles, the emergence of new forms of political and social life as well as a change in the role of the mass media and public opinion.

Such a list of the most important features of economic reform enables us to grasp the fundamental variables describing different types of socialist economy. By the same token we will be able to provide a description of three types of relationship between the state and the market in centrally planned economies.

Three Types of Centrally Planned Economy

On the grounds of the historical experience of existing socialist economies and analysis of different economic and sociopolitical theories of socialism, three main types of centrally planned economies can be indicated:

1. The centralized Stalinist system;
2. The partly decentralized parametric system;
3. The market-driven socialist economy.

The first type was introduced by Stalin and his political supporters in the late 1920s. Its theoretical foundations were laid by the Trotskyist E. Preobrazhensky who formulated the theory of 'primitive socialist accumulation' enabling rapid industrialization. According to Preobrazhensky, industrialization was made possible by an unequal income distribution between industry and agriculture in favour of industry, and the low standard of living of the working class (Preobrazhensky, 1927, 1966; Ehrlich, 1960;

Spulber, 1964). After politically eliminating Preobrazhensky, Stalin put his ideas into action (naturally without mentioning the source of his inspiration). The theory of Stalinist industrialization was further developed by such economists as S. Strumulin, G. Krzyżhanowski, L. Grinko and others (Smolar, 1974). These ideas dominated Soviet economic thought until the mid-1960s and were not completely abandoned until Gorbachev's reconstruction began in 1986. They survived until recently to some extent in the political economy of such countries as Czechoslovakia, East Germany and Romania.

The idea of a partly decentralized parametric system was developed independently in the USSR during the animated economic debates of the 1920s,[2] and in the West by O. Lange and A. Lerner (Lerner, 1936–7, 1938; Lange, 1936; Gado, 1972). The main idea behind the parametric system is the use of monetary instruments and incentives and market mechanisms in order to implement a centrally formulated economic plan. This idea was and still is widely accepted by generations of 'moderate reformers' in the USSR, Poland and especially in Hungary, where the parametric system was introduced in the 1969 economic reform (Csikos-Nagy, 1972).

The theory of a market-driven socialist economy was presented in the 1920s in the USSR by N. Bukharin and his group (Bukharin, 1928). This theory focused on the notion of economic and social equilibrium and assumed that central planners could only anticipate a structure of the economy determined by market mechanisms. The possibility of state influence on the economy was limited, then, by equilibrium requirements and the amount of resources the state could mobilize in support of its actions. Bukharin's ideas seem pretty close to the contemporary theories and practice of 'indicative planning' in the 1950s, 1960s and 1970s in some capitalist countries such as France and Holland. The theory of 'market socialism' was based on the experiences of the USSR under NEP. Introducing his system of 'forced industrialization', Stalin took a very negative attitude towards this theory and ruthlessly eliminated all its supporters. Since that time, until very recently, 'market socialism' was considered as ideological schism or 'revisionism' even in more liberal socialist countries such as Poland or Hungary. Nineteen sixty-eight and subsequent events in Czechoslovakia were classic in this respect. 'Market socialism' ideas, however, re-emerged several times in the economic thought of the socialist countries: in Poland in 1956 (Kurowski, 1956; *Ekonomiści*, 1956), in Czechoslovakia in 1966–8 (Golan, 1981), in Poland in 1981 and again in 1986–7 (*Reforma*, 1981), in the USSR under Gorbachev's reconstruction (Manasian, 1987) and in Hungary around 1985. In some countries (Hungary, Poland) it seems to have been considered a realistic alternative to the existing economic mechanism. It should be noted then that the roots of all three alternative models of the centrally planned economy lie in the Soviet economic debate and political struggle of the 1920s — a fact which was almost completely ignored in the West until the late 1950s.

Following the description just given of the fundamental features of the centrally planned economy, let us briefly describe three basic types.

In the centralized Stalinist system (Nove, 1977b; Lavigne, 1979) the philosophy and practice of central planning is based upon the theological assumption of the absolute freedom of central planners determined to achieve their political and military objectives 'at any price'.[3] This approach to planning imposes direct economic calculation, where physical quantities are directly linked and co-ordinated. The logic of such a planning methodology is most adequately represented by Leontief's input–output model, where the supply of a product represented by a physical unit is directly balanced by central planners with the demand for it by final users and other branches of the production sector (Wakar, 1965: 8–9). Monetary categories do not play any active role as criteria of choice. The whole planning process is subordinated to the political and military priorities established and followed by the state. The only limitations come from technology. Production methods are arbitrarily chosen by central planners in order to maintain the balance between input and output (Berliner, 1976; Koźmiński and Obłój, 1984). All available resources are mobilized to satisfy the needs of priority branches of production (important for political and military reasons), while the others remain deliberately undersupplied. Unbalanced growth, favouring heavy industry at the expense of agriculture and the consumption sector and compromising economic and social equilibrium, inevitably results from that kind of approach to planning. It is based on the absolute domination of political priorities represented by the state.

The rules of the game between the state and other economic

agents can be briefly described as state domination achieved through coercion and administrative means. The centralized Stalinist system implies rationing of all important production factors and centralized distribution of scarce consumer goods. Some consumer items are rationed or allocated through administrative procedures and the bureaucratic apparatus. Wages are centrally controlled, plan targets are formulated as military orders expressed in natural units. The performance of enterprises is evaluated by supervising administrative authorities as a percentage of plan fulfilment.

The administrative and political authorities constantly interfere with the functioning of the enterprise. That kind of system leads managers on the enterprise level to adopt purely defensive strategies in order to obtain easier plan targets and generous allocation of resources (Koźmiński, 1976; Berliner, 1957). This can be obtained through a 'quasi-political game'.[4] In the centralized system the share of market relations is limited to the 'shadow economy' which grows rapidly along with the degeneration of the system (Cassel and Cichy, 1987). The role of the monetary and banking system is purely passive, limited to accounting and financial control (Wakar, 1969; Seurot, 1983).

The classical Stalinist system developed its own specific institutional structure well fitted to the logic of its functioning. This type of structure can be described as follows:

1. The Central Planning Office linked with rationing agencies administratively allocating resources (such as GOSSNAB in the USSR) plays a key role in formulating plans, changing and adjusting them, co-ordinating and evaluating plan proposals submitted by various sectors and branches of the national economy and local governments.

2. Sectors of the national economy are supervised by corresponding ministries. The number of such ministries grows with the increase in the scope and complexity of the system. Ministries have a double and basically contradictory function. On the one hand they belong to the state apparatus and represent the general interest of society embodied in a central plan. On the other hand they represent the particular interests and development needs of a given sector of the economy (in other words a particular group of enterprises). Needless to say, these particular interests tend to be contradictory: ministries compete among themselves for scarce resources and the most powerful lobbies,

representing 'priority' sectors, successfully promote their own extensive growth at the expense of the others. In that way they contribute to the 'arhythmia' of economic development.[5]

3. The whole system is highly centralized: all resource allocation decisions and all adjustments are made or at least approved at the top level. A high degree of formalization follows, promoting 'trained incapacity' and bureaucratic games within the system.

4. Enterprises are grouped in 'unions', producing homogeneous groups of products, or sometimes established on a territorial basis. They can be considered as 'administrative monopolies'. Every such union of enterprises is supervised by one ministry protecting its monopolistic position, as its own 'turf'.

The hierarchical character of the institutional structure of the economy is correlated with the social stratification and unequal distribution of income, housing, medical care, education and prestige.[6]

The political and social climate of the centralized Stalinist system is characterized by the ideological domination of 'Stalinist Marxism' adjusted to the needs of 'forced industrialization', and by the police state. The whole of cultural and social life is subordinated to one goal: mobilization of the masses around the plan targets (Roberts, 1971). A new style in art: 'socialist realism', is created and forcefully imposed on cultural life. Such a sociopolitical system is called by some authors 'monocentric' (Koźmiński, 1982: 32–48).

A partly decentralized parametric system introduces some changes into the planning philosophy and practice without changing its fundamental logic. Planning remains highly centralized and direct economic calculation in natural units prevails. The scope of central planning is, however, gradually reduced: the number of plan indicators and centrally allocated resources decreases.[7] In the new parametric system introduced in Poland in 1987, for example, only basic raw materials, energy, centrally financed imports and important investment projects were centrally planned in natural units. The plan loses its total character but remains the principal regulator of the macrostructure of the economy. As B. Csikos-Nagy puts it: 'The market has an active role in the formation of the micro-structure but is not a principal regulator of the macro-structure' (Csikos-Nagy, 1972). Plan priorities change under the parametric system: the standard of living of the population is given much more attention by central planners in order to avoid a political and social crisis gradually intensifying with the decline of the centralized Stalinist system (Berlin 1954, Poland 1956, Hungary 1956). The Hungarian economist J. Kornai explains this change of priorities in the following way:

> Hungarian economic policy was more oriented toward the consumer and the standard of living than the economic policy of the other East European countries. This decision was taken under the influence of the events of 1956. The historical lesson drawn from 1956 was that a socialist government has to satisfy the material needs of the people and to avoid periods of intense dissatisfaction. (Kornai, 1984)

In such a way 'goulash socialism' was born.

Partial abandonment of central allocation of resources and partial reorientation of the economy toward consumption considerably increase the importance of economic equilibrium (inflation) and price formation. Central financial planning covers such areas as prices (centrally established or at least centrally controlled), the level and structure of incomes and expenditure of the economic agents: state, enterprises and households (Gado, 1976; Górski and Jedrzejczak, 1987: 204–86). Financial planning existed under the Stalinist system but it was perceived as a simple, formal consequence of direct economic calculation in natural units. A parametric system makes it much more important and much more sophisticated. Monetary equilibrium is often achieved by administrative means, and this is why a monopolistic and bureaucratic structure of banking is maintained: banks play an important role as a part of the state economic bureaucracy (Zwass, 1978–9).

A parametric system changes the relationship and rules of the game between the state and other economic agents. It is based on the principle of decentralization. Managers are free to choose between various courses of action in order to maximize performance indicators imposed by the system. The complexity and scope of the performance indicators set has an inherent tendency to grow. In order to induce the enterprises to behave according to the expectations of the state organs and the plan targets natural indicators (such as production volume and structure, volume of exports, norms of raw materials and energy use) have to be combined with financial ones (such as profit, profitability before and after taxes). Such complex systems enable enterprises to 'cheat' and to 'play' some performance indicators against the others.[8] More advanced parametric systems reduce and simplify the sets of performance evaluation criteria, focusing mainly on profitability and self-financing. This does not completely exclude, however, bargaining and 'games with the indicators' (Antal, in Kornai and Richet, 1986: ch. 3; Lipiński and Wojciechowska, 1987).

A parametric system increases the freedom of choice of the consumer because it provides for a wider selection of consumer items. At the same time it can create social tensions because of cyclical shortages (Wiles, 1982).

A parametric system introduces changes into the institutional structure of the economy:

1. The number of ministries supervising sectors of the national economy is consistently reduced in order to achieve a more unified economic policy and to avoid conflict of interests and too much lobbying. In both Hungary and Poland, for example, since 1988 there have been only two such ministries: Industry and Agriculture.

2. The importance of the Central Planning Office diminishes and functional ministries (such as ministries of Finance or Foreign Trade) become more important.

3. Ministries lose some of their authority over enterprises, and the organizational form of branch unions of enterprises ('administrative monopolies') is replaced by looser structures such as voluntary associations or joint ventures.

4. Ministries lose some of their authority over the enterprises they supervise, since the parametric system requires that considerable freedom of choice be given to managers. The behaviour of the enterprises is influenced by centrally determined parameters such as prices, interest rates, currency exchange rates and taxation rates. This means (at least in theory and by law) that a ministry can interfere with the functioning of an enterprise or a group of enterprises only in clearly defined situations. The funds accorded to them to reallocate resources and to 'assist' financially unstable enterprises are also gradually reduced.[9]

Answering the question about the state–market relationship in parametric systems, one comes to the conclusion that they are somewhat relaxed and liberalized forms of the classic Stalinist system. Among the reasons justifying that statement let us mention the most important.

— The basic philosophy of planning based on direct economic calculation in natural units remains unchanged.

— Vertical hierarchical relationships between the organs of the state and the other economic agents (enterprises and households) still predominate over horizontal, market-regulated relationships between enterprises and households.

The rules of the game between the state and other economic agents are unstable and often subjected to sudden changes, due to the fact that the state cannot meet its plan targets formulated in natural units. Such arbitrarily formulated plan targets still represent political preferences on the part of the state.

The political and ideological aspects of the system also clearly demonstrate its relaxed and liberalized but still authoritarian character. The political climate accompanying the implementation of the parametric system can be characterized as follows:

— Political liberalization, enabling the emergence of different orientations within the party. Some of them represent strong pro-reform tendencies and can be characterized as 'quasi political opposition' (Tomas, 1970; Korbonski, 1975).

— More technocratic and less ideological orientation of political leadership (Farrell, 1970: 88–107, 157–94).

— National differences play an increasingly important role as one of the factors shaping different types of socialist economic mechanisms.

— Socialist societies become less and less egalitarian. Individual success and even entrepreneurship gradually gain official recognition as factors differentiating the standard of living (Connor, 1975; Lauter, 1972; Kende and Strmiska, 1984).

— Market socialism and political pluralism are still ideologically condemned as 'anti socialist'. The repression which follows such condemnation becomes, however, less and less rigid and brutal (at least in the countries implementing a parametric system, such as Hungary and Poland).

The description of a market-driven socialist economy is more difficult than an analysis of the Stalinist or parametric model. Since NEP such an economic system has not existed in reality, if we do not take into consideration the specific case of the self-managed Yugoslav economy. Hungary only recently (in 1985) took the first step towards a market-regulated economy when it abandoned central planning in natural units. We can only outline, then, the most important features of such a system of socialist economy:

— A market driven system in a way reverses the planning-plan implementation relationship existing in both centralized and parametric systems. The market mechanism determines the plan: planning decisions have to be accepted and verified by the market. A market driven system cannot coexist with direct economic calculation in natural units. The bureaucratic procedure of formulating five-year and annual plans will have to be replaced by industrial policy in its contemporary western version (Koźmiński, 1986: 113–17; Magaziner and Reich, 1982; Bienayme, 1982).

— New rules of the game between economic agents will have to be established, based on the principle of the equality of the participating parties. Such relationships are regulated by civil commercial law, while administrative law dominates in both centralized and parametric systems.

— The Central Planning Office and the sectoral ministries have to disappear. The role of money, banking and credit institutions must be radically changed:

— an at least partly convertible currency is considered a necessary condition of an open market economy;

— a network of profit-driven, competitive commercial banks has to be developed;

— the Central Bank has to gain independence from the state budget; maintaining the value of money is to become its only responsibility (which means inevitably hard budget constraints imposed on state-owned enterprises);

— capital market institutions have to be developed (Backai and Varhegyi, 1983).

— A pluralist model of socialist society and socialist politics will probably emerge. It will be based on the official recognition of different interest groups and different political orientations. New political platforms will have to be created in order to facilitate negotiations and compromises. Workers' and territorial (local) self-management organs will probably play an important role in this process. A monopoly of information and interpretation could no longer be granted to the official fully state-controlled media promoting official ideology. An increasing degree of pluralism in the area of information seems inevitable (Morawski, 1983: Part I).

System Dynamics

Economic reforms changing the state–market relationship in centrally planned economies are introduced for political reasons. A need to reform the economy arises when at least one of the three following reasons becomes evident to the political elite:

— Lack of an economic foundation for the implementation of the political programme of 'socialist reconstruction of society' and for the corresponding military strategy (this was the reason behind 'Stalinist reform' of the late 1920s);

— Dissatisfaction and unrest causing political instability in the system (Hungarian reform and Polish reform);

— Sudden changes in the political situation, both internal and international (Yugoslavia 1950).

The political origin of the reforms is reflected in the process of their implementation. Reforms are always directly or indirectly linked to some kind of political crisis. Public debate on the deficiencies of the 'old system' brings out possible remedies and solutions. The impact of such a debate is not limited to the closed circles of professional politicians, experts and managers; the general political climate and the opinions and attitudes of the general public are also strongly affected (Adamski et al., 1986). The case of Poland after 1980 is classic in this respect. Preparation of the project of the new reformed system always involves political struggle between promoters of the reform and its enemies. The implementation of the project triggers even more visible antagonistic games and political manoeuvring. In Poland after 1982, for example, strong pressures promoting a more egalitarian income policy and government price controls are considered to be one of the main factors inhibiting the process of reforming the economy (Lipiński and Wojciechowska, 1987: 271–80). Similar processes were observed in Hungary in the 1970s (Koltay, 1986; Soos, 1985). In the USSR at the end of the 1920s the NEP was abolished with the help of spontaneous political pressures from an impoverished working class shocked by the luxurious life of the new breed of capitalists the NEP had created. The bureaucracy often uses quite sophisticated strategies to protect its own interests and to stop the reform. Monopolistic groups within the system (such as industrial lobbies representing heavy industry or mining, or bureaucratic lobbies grouped in such organs as the Central Planning Office, protecting its monopoly of economic initiative) try to control the reform implementation process and to use it to their own advantage. They often appeal to the political elite's fear of losing control over the economy (Rychard, 1980a, 1980b; Iwanowska, 1982).

The political crisis accompanying the reform process has an economic origin, which might be called the 'vicious circle of socialist industrialization'. In general terms it can be described as follows:

A centralized Stalinist system is introduced to facilitate industrialization and to liquidate the industrial gap between advanced capitalist countries and socialist countries. As a consequence of industrialization plans are developed.

The number and total value of investment projects rapidly grows as a result of intensive lobbying by powerful industrial pressure groups. Heavy industry is a winner in this game.

Principles of liberal financing by the state budget and easy credit are applied to these projects. As a result, demand grows rapidly in such areas as:

— consumer goods and housing (new industrial workers and new bureaucrats are employed and relatively highly paid);

— construction services and materials, transportation and energy;

— imported capital goods and technology;

— imported components.

Such an excessive demand cannot be met within reasonable time limits. Shortages accumulate in all the areas listed here and completion of investment projects is increasingly delayed.

Shortages create strong pressure to increase the output of operating industrial enterprises and to intensify exports. Such a pressure takes a 'natural' administrative form. Since operating enterprises are also subjected to soft budget constraints, this pressure results in an increasingly wasteful use of resources and unexpected wage increases. Both contribute to increased shortages.

As a result, the centrally planned economy becomes nearly uncontrollable. Plan targets are not met, up to 60 percent of GNP is frozen in uncompleted investment projects; production costs and material input run out of control. Popular unrest, dissatisfaction and lack of motivation follows, triggering the political crisis mentioned earlier. The political elite is divided over the issue of responsibility for ill-conceived projects, the growing technological gap, low performance in exports, low quality of products, underdeveloped agriculture, devastation of natural resources, and so on.

There are two possible system answers to that situation:

— extensive use of easily available natural resources, manpower and foreign credit;

— rigorous administrative control and arbitrary cuts imposed on investment, wages and production costs;

Both answers appear simultaneously in different proportions and in consequence create new shortages and add new factors to unbalanced growth. A new investment programme then has to be undertaken, to eliminate some of the shortages and all previously described consequences inevitably follow (Kornai, 1980).

Such a mechanism is typical of the centralized Stalinist model. An immensely rich country like the USSR could bear for a long time its astronomic costs and still achieve some economic and social progress. In other countries, especially those with more demanding and less disciplined populations (like Poland and Hungary), a parametric system is introduced to improve the economic and sociopolitical efficiency of the centrally planned economy. Let us discuss to what extent this is possible.

All the observers of economic reforms in socialist countries confirm that in reality parametric systems are never pure. They always have to be assisted by such administrative measures as direct orders, rationing and different forms of subsidies. This can be explained by the following reasons:

Parameters determined at the central level cannot be adjusted to all possible plan targets (still formulated in natural units) and all possible local conditions of plan fulfilment.

Lack of coherence in the sets of artificially established performance evaluation indicators induces the enterprises to 'play games' and to vary their output considerably from the central planners' expectations.

The bureaucracy has an inherent tendency to use and abuse administrative measures.

Parameters influence enterprise behaviour with time lags. Unexpected shortages and changes of political priorities often require quick adjustments and resource reallocations, which can only be achieved by administrative measures.

Such administrative adjustments contradict the basic principles of the parametric systems:

— stable limits on the autonomy of the enterprises respected by administration;

— promotion of self-financing by enterprises;

— commercialization of bank credit.

These principles are only partly respected (budget constraints become somewhat harder but not really hard) and the system is not stable: the degrees of autonomy and self-financing constantly change following the needs of short-term adjustments of economic policy (Koźmiński et al., 1982). This happens especially in times of economic difficulties and sociopolitical tensions (for example in Poland between 1976 and 1980 and in Hungary between 1980 and 1985).

All the above observations lead to the conclusion that a parametric system is not a realistic alternative to the centralized Stalinist system. It can only be perceived as a temporary, transitional solution leading backwards to an administrative system, or forward to a market-driven one. Its relatively low economic efficiency, combined with the lack of coherence and instability built into the system, provide arguments for a political rhetoric of 'good old days'. Such rhetoric often seems appealing to a public opinion afraid of losing such achievements of the socialist system as job security, subsidized prices for foodstuffs and housing, free education and medical care, and egalitarian principles of income distribution.

These advantages, however, tend to vanish with the increasing inefficiency caused by accumulated shortages. The ruling elite, or at least a part of it, realizes, then, that more radical reforms have to be undertaken in order to change the uncontrollable and nearly anarchic character of the economic system. Additional pressure is put on socialist governments by the international financial community because of the socialist countries' constantly growing foreign debt. It is well known that the International Monetary Fund played an important role in promoting more radical reforms in Poland in 1987 and in Hungary in 1985.

Such a pressure from a part of the political elite, and from outside, activates two additional possible reinforcements of pro-reform tendencies.

The first is the mobilization of self-management and expert public opinion against the return of 'good old days' of bureaucratic rule, and the corresponding development and reinforcement of the new institutions of 'socialist democracy', as for example in Poland after 1982: a new, enlarged and much more active role of the parliament, the creation of new consultative bodies grouping people of different opinions and political orientations, and considerably increased freedom of expression, especially in economic matters.

Second is more freedom for private entrepreneurship, small and medium-sized firms, joint ventures with foreign capital, commercial law companies and so on. Such, for socialist economies, unconventional forms of economic initiative can serve the purpose of training people in effective market-driven economic behaviour, getting them accustomed to competition and market constraints, promoting technological progress and new management methods and techniques. In Poland, for example, the microcomputer market is dominated by such firms. Concrete results and rewards for entrepreneurship can also help to remove some of the prejudices against a market-driven socialist economy.

Both types of reinforcement of pro-reform tendencies are at present used to different degrees in the USSR, Hungary and Poland. Up to the end of 1987, however, only Hungary had made a decisive move towards a market-driven socialist economy. This is based on two fundamental principles introduced in 1985 in the form of new legislation concerning planning, finance and local governments.

— The principle of 'decentralized planning' openly declares the complete independence and autonomy of enterprises and local governments as planning subjects. The state budget is no longer required to finance automatically all the plan targets. Planners are expected to show flexibility and to adjust to the changing economic situation. The concept of decentralized planning implies the use of flexible time horizons in various areas and stages of the plan, which differs from the rigid one- and five-year planning periods still used in all other socialist countries. The most important difference is that in the new Hungarian system no plan targets are formulated in physical units. The new Hungarian concept of planning should be perceived as an attempt to reconcile the market mechanism with the incentive and dynamizing role of the plan. The plan represents the macroeconomic intervention (industrial policy) of the state and the market mechanism is meant to shape the final decisions of the economic agents.

— The principle of the monetarization of the economy implies commercialized financing and hard budget constraints imposed on all economic agents. The bankruptcy of inefficient enterprises is openly admitted and even welcomed under the new system. The capital market is intended to regulate all non-budget-financed capital flows within the system. The role of the state budget in redistribution of income is considerably reduced. A network of competitive commercial banks is created. The opening of the economy should push Hungarian enterprises towards competition on world markets (Csaba, 1986b).

The Hungarian and Polish experiences show clearly that, in spite of all the weaknesses of the parametric system and its vulnerability to anti-reform attack, it should be considered a necessary and practically unavoidable transitional stage on the path from the centralized Stalinist system towards a market-driven socialist economy. Instantaneous change would jeopardize the sociopolitical stability of the system and dramatically alter its identity. It should also be remembered that long years of a centralized and bureaucratized natural (non-monetary) economy eradicated cultural patterns of market-driven behaviour and discontinued its social and moral legitimation. A business and banking community is practically non-existent in centrally planned economies and there are no skills easily available in such areas as business strategy, finance or marketing. Gradual decentralization of the system over a long period of time seems the only way to develop new attitudes, motivations and skills enabling an economically efficient but also politically and sociologically feasible state–market mix. Events of 1989 and 1990 showed that such a long period of grace was not given to centrally planned economies.

Notes

1. Quoted by *Miesiecznik Literacki*, August 1987, relating figures of the Polish Government Centre of Public Opinion Surveys.
2. By such economists as A. Ajchenwald, I. Smilga, J. Repsze and L. Jurkowski. See for example Smilga (1926), Repsze (1926), Wakar (1969: 269–74).
3. As S. Strumilin, one of the early representatives of the centralized system, put it: 'we don't have to study economy but to change it' (Smolar, 1974: 110).
4. Empirical results presented in Koźmiński and Obłój (1983).
5. The Polish economic, sociological and management literature of the 1980s is full of empirical descriptions of this kind of structure and its functioning in practice. See for example, Karpiński (1986), Gliński (1985, ch. 2: 54–86), Morawski (1983, chs 1–2: 23–116).

6. Comparative analysis of concepts and empirical data related to the issue of equality and inequality in Eastern Europe is presented in Kende and Strmiska (1984).

7. For example in Poland in 1982–5, 30 percent of resources were centrally allocated. See Pajestka (1986: 149). Similar trends were observed in Hungary in the late 1960s and early 1970s. See Gado (1972).

8. For an empirical analysis of such 'early decentralized systems' see Fick (1965).

9. Empirical research shows that ministries often act against the new parametric system. See Dulski (1984) and Malinowski (1986: 48–70).

6
THE INFORMAL ECONOMY

Arnaldo Bagnasco

A Problem of Calculation?

The question we are going to deal with would, at first sight, appear to be simple. It is easily noticeable how, even in our societies of organized capitalism, certain transactions involving goods and services evade national accounting and remain hidden. This applies especially to illegal activities such as contraband, drug smuggling, tax frauds and infringement of labour laws. In attempting to study this invisible economy, the biggest problem seems to be of a technical nature: what means can we adopt to uncover transactions that are hidden from view? It is by no means easy to solve this problem and yet it is not impossible to attempt reasonable approximations on the basis of indirect methods. Things get more complicated when we observe the existence of perfectly legal exchanges of goods and services that are not accounted for in money terms — an exchange of labour regulated by custom, an interest-free loan between relatives, voluntary services and so on. Even in cases such as these we might seek to give a value to the transactions and relate them to national accounting. We realize, however, that the more we venture into intimate social or culturally complex relations, the less prepared we are to consider the exchange a transaction or to highlight and isolate its specifically economic content. When a friend comes to our aid economically we tend to make a rough mental calculation as to when we will be able to pay him or her back. This is much less likely, however, between fathers and sons. And what view are we then to take of a woman's housework? Today many would still readily object that, in such cases, it is wrong to speak of labour. It would be preferable to refer to relations based on affection, relations which, by their very nature, cannot be imagined or construed in monetary terms. After all, love for money has always gone under a different name! The conclusion might be that the woman can still continue to play her role as a sort of angel of hearth and home: or, on the other hand, that it is necessary, from a moral standpoint, to review the domestic responsibilities of man and woman alike, albeit avoiding any calculation of 'assets and liabilities', something which intimate relations exclude by definition.

Thus, the more we stray from the market, the more this apparently simple issue is subject to conceptual complications. As long as money and free bargaining are involved, we can attempt to use appropriate techniques to count something that is not immediately apparent. Beyond this level, however, we are unable to relate the economic content of the more complex social relations to money as such, nor do we have an exact idea of what is economic and what is not.

And the picture does not change if we move on to the borderline between economy and political system. In contemporary societies, the state provides a whole range of services that are neither bought nor sold on the market, some of them seen as constituting citizens' rights. Political decisions — which may vary with time — must establish whether certain services are to be bought on the market or provided by the administration or whether parallel administrative and market circuits are to be set up. It thus becomes evident — as in the previous case of exchanges in the context of complex cultural relations — that the hidden economy stands head-on to a *normal* economy which is defined as such on the basis of accepted rules and the borderlines of which are variable.

Having set out to quantify part of the hidden economy, we are now confronted by serious theoretical problems. The non-recorded, or hidden, economy becomes an indefinite object. We realize that to be concerned with the hidden economy is to be concerned with a whole range of different things: illegal markets and moonlighting, the public economy and the domestic economy, the off-market in the public sector and 'do it yourself' and so on. These phenomena are so vastly different one from the other that all we can do to hold them together conceptually is to label them with a negative term, not because of what they are but of what they are not. In view of what has already been said, we may consider them to be types or aspects which fail to correspond to a certain form of economy perceived by us to be normal. This form will, in turn, identify itself in real processes or the way in which we define such processes.

Throughout the long historical cycle which has seen the development of large-scale industrial systems, the economy has always tended to assume the specific form we attribute to it. This is due to three main factors:

(a) its differentiation from the rest of society — a specialized, essentially market-regulated system of action has been formed whereby production and consumer decisions are made in accordance with the prices fixed by formally free bargaining:

(b) the development of specific organizations geared towards profit and based on a rational division of labour-enterprises:

(c) the way in which complex sets of laws create links between the economy and the rest of the system. The term 'formal economy' may be used to define the production processes and exchanges of goods and services regulated by the market and typically performed by profit-oriented commercial enterprises acting in compliance with trading, tax and labour laws. 'Informal economy' may thus refer to all those production and exchange processes which, in some way, fail to comply with the distinctive features described above.

Although we have now made some headway, we will soon find ourselves confronted once more by the very obstacles we have been trying to get round. Our calculation problems began just as we were starting to realize that actually the economy is not completely differentiated from other systems of action. More precisely, the market is a mechanism which regulates production and exchange but is less exclusive than may be imagined. Hence, for example, the domestic production of goods and services for self-consumption — which varies from state to state, from country to town — has always been high. This also means that the regulating mechanism of *reciprocity* has been at work. The economic content of the rules of exchange, in this case, is not made explicit and classified as such but is part of more complex cultural contexts. On the other hand, state intervention in the economy has not, as already observed, been confined merely to a handful of basic laws nor to the simple bolstering up of the free market: it has instead explicitly modified the constitution and working of the market itself. In the final analysis, it has also highlighted the regulating mechanism of *political exchange* based on agreements designed to give advantages to certain categories and create political loyalties.

A Field of Highly Diversified Phenomena

Let us now take stock of the situation. First of all, it seems clear that we must leave aside calculation problems for the moment. Although it is already possible to make the calculations that are conceptually the simplest (on tax evasion, for instance), others which presuppose conceptual definition of the relevant fields will have to be put off until later: they are bound to entail more indeterminate conceptual options which, in some cases, will rule them out altogether. In the meantime, our discussion of the informal economy has shifted attention from problems of calculation to interesting theoretical problems, the overall significance of which, however, we are still unable to grasp. Indeed we still have not answered the question: what sense is there in attempting to discuss such a diverse phenomenon in a unitary fashion? And how can we frame the conclusion we have just reached; namely, that the kernel of the question is the relationship between formal and informal?

Let us try to ask another question. Why is discussion arising at the present moment? This is a way of finding the theoretical significance of our research work, starting from its historical significance. Let us then return to the historical process of formalization. Can we be more specific about it?

If we leave aside national differences for the moment and consider only the main trend, we can say that, on the whole, mass production organized into big enterprises has been a typical feature of the economy over the last century. The combination of mechanized production processes and a generally unskilled labour force have meant increased productivity and larger overall production volumes. In order to achieve this, not only rigid, concentrated investments in plant but also consistent expanding market demand were required. Thus, while the organizational regulation of production processes tended to increase on a microeconomic level, political intervention created the development of stabilizing procedures on a macroeconomic level. A system such as this may count full employment and social equity among its aims: indeed it is completed by policies designed to control the economy through public expenditure which, in turn, aims to develop the welfare state. This arrangement allows the market to gain new ground with the increased supply of standardized goods, traditional forms of labour tend to be replaced by formal production activities, urbanization breaks down the fabric of community and family relations and so on. Most of the goods and services consumed are produced by enterprises buying and selling on goods and labour markets in compliance with formal legal regulations.

Nonetheless, while this arrangement imposes a strong differentiation between the economy and family and community structures and relations, at the same time, it deeply involves the economy itself in political and organizational relations. So, when speaking of this arrangement, we might once more bring up the question of the borderlines of the economy and the interplay of formal and informal. The problem we are dealing with, however, arose in the 1970s, at a time when large-scale economies were experiencing a critical situation: that is, after thirty years of development they were tending to show signs of stagnation, inflation and unemployment. This is when questions were asked about the invisible economy and its growth was charted. Studies showed how it was often linked to aspects of, or reactions to, the crises undergone by previous systems based on mass production and Keynesian regulation. Due to the indeterminateness of the concepts involved, it is impossible to say whether informal processes increased during this phase. One thing may be inferred from the data available, however: during this period of deadlock, and in the course of attempts to emerge from it, the borderlines of the formal economy were altered and the interplay of formal and informal changed to a large extent. This conspicuous process had an undoubted influence on the development of research in this area we are concerned with, tending to unify a very broad set of phenomena (probably excessively judging by the misunderstandings that have arisen). It should not be taken for granted that all types of informal economy stem from the same ultimate cause nor that they are all new to us. The conclusion we arrive at, therefore, is that, often for diverse reasons, the current economic situation has, in many cases, created the conditions for non-normal economic behaviour — that is, the informal economy we have been speaking about.

In some cases, the difficulties enterprises have had to deal with when confronted by greater constraints on the use of resources and labour and by more diversified, unstable markets, have given rise to types of behaviour which, in turn, have developed the informal economy directly. An example might be the decentralization of production, an issue we shall return to later. But in general the development of small enterprises (which initially, in particular, bears with it whole chunks of the informal economy) is not generated directly by the crisis in big industry. The state, in turn, finding it harder and harder to control and hierarchize expenditure and to make the latter compatible with the process of accumulation, has often resorted to deregulation. It cannot necessarily be said that this has caused the informal economy to increase but it has changed the interplay of formal and informal. In many cases, the informal economic strategies adopted by individuals and families are clearly a means of adapting to worsening conditions: a second job to make ends meet, for example. In others, however, modifications of the general situation have brought about the emergence and growth of patterns of production and consumption based on criteria other than mere market purchase: nor can we consider this an *effect* of the general condition. The growth of voluntary work in certain services, such as the health service, is not simply a consequence of the fiscal crisis in the welfare state: it also reflects cultural changes that are part of a more general trend involving transformations in the way in which interpersonal relations, life styles, consumption, work, and so on are seen. If a technician refuses standardized factory labour and opens a small business of his own, perhaps evading taxes and irregularly employing workers who also refuse work in the factory, are we to consider this an effect of the crisis in big industry? If so, it is in a more complicated sense than we have encountered up to now.

Although the picture is clearly muddled, we can see, in conclusion, why research into the informal economy, albeit problematic, has had such a great power of aggregation. It has provided us with crucial insights into the development of ideas about adaptation and social change over the last few years. It is also an overcharged, unstable area of research. Its interest is also its weakness. The best results concern precise aspects of the interplay of formal and informal. A general theory based on a residual category would, however, appear to be unthinkable: in this way we would run the risk of confining to a unified pattern of interpretation phenomena that are probably symptoms of large-scale diversification of the principles of social structure. We shall be returning to this point at the end of the chapter.

Different Lines of Research: Some Examples

As national economies differ in structure and performance, so different types of informal economy emerge in varying proportions. The differences increase if, besides large-scale economies, we also consider underdeveloped economies, and they increase just the same in both capitalist and socialist industrial countries. Different nations face problems in different ways and the problems themselves tend to depend upon the economic phenomena emerging. In wealthy nations such as Germany, Canada and France researchers are frequently faced with the attempts of individuals or groups to reclaim their participation and personal autonomy from the intrusiveness of the state and the market. In countries most affected by the economic crisis — Britain, for instance — the adaptive strategies adopted by families come into view. In countries in which there are many small enterprises, such as Spain and Italy, priority is given to the relationship between informal and formal production. Of course these differences are relative and, indeed, research carried out in the United States, for example, deals with phenomena that are familiar in Europe too. Nonetheless, national differences do help to increase the dispersion of interest and angle in research work. Studies conducted in underdeveloped countries may indeed resemble those made in developed countries in issues and methods. They often differ, however: often it is necessary to consider the aspects of the interplay of formal and informal peculiar to backward or dependent economies.

Here we receive substantial confirmation of the difficulty that exists in imagining a theory of the informal economy. It is certainly preferable to study the informal aspects of specific processes and economic structures. In these circumstances it would be useless to present a long — and not necessarily organic — catalogue of research work. Instead, I shall first present patterns in which the informal economy is defined and typologies constructed: the two presented here are among the most useful currently available. While failing to constitute the basis for a theory of informal economy (as we have seen, this would be impossible) they are, nonetheless, useful devices for the orderly construction of those problem areas of economic research that contemplate significant informal aspects. A concrete example of this type of problem area will then be given.

FIGURE 1
Typology of formal and informal economic activities

	labour	goods and services
off-market	1, 6, 3, 7	
market	2, 5, 4	

The first pattern is the brainchild of I. Sachs (Sachs, 1981). Its aim is to establish 'a sort of typology of situations that go together to create the field of investigation of the hidden economy and which should facilitate comparative study'. The term 'hidden economy' refers to everything the national accounting system fails to register either for conceptual reasons or because the relevant data are concealed. It covers, on the one hand, phenomena of *off-market* production (the *domestic economy*, for example) and, on the other, *parallel markets* (legal and illegal alike). The cross-tabulation pattern shown in Figure 1 illustrates the extent of relationships between market/off-market and labour-goods/services.

Line 1 refers to the domestic economy: here labour is not registered and the goods and services produced are consumed within the family environment.

Line 2 is the private and public market economy. It may include the co-operative sector, although the latter also contains components of 4 and 6.

Line 3 is the sector of direct state intervention, including both its traditional functions and modern forms of welfare. It may generally be regarded as 'off-market' in the public sector.

Line 4 refers to small autonomous producers and the economy of farming families, including elements of 7.

Line 5 refers to parallel markets and most moonlighting as such. Type of parallel market and the boundary between official and parallel markets may entail wide empirical variability according to their institutional and legal context.

Line 6 represents the communal economy: charity work, exchanges at a grassroots level, and so on.

Line 7 defines the domestic economy 'colonized' by market economy supply (do-it-yourself) and its simple appendix. If domestic consumer goods are taken into account — electrical appliances, cars and so on — the economy shown by line 1 would today tend to include elements of line 7.

In practice, the pattern displays traces of all the main components of the informal economy question. Since it is essentially descriptive, it gives no idea of the links between the various types. The second pattern I shall present is less analytic but does cover the relationships existing between different types. It has been designed and revised on various occasions by J.I. Gershuny and R.E. Pahl (Gershuny and Pahl, 1980). The term 'informal economy' is used to include three areas of phenomena:

(1) *household economy*: production, not for sales purposes, by members of a family largely for the family itself;

(2) *underground, hidden or black economy*: production — wholly or partly for sale or barter — liable to declaration for tax or control purposes which is, instead, wholly or partly hidden;

(3) *communal economy*: production by an individual or group — not for sale or barter — of a product which might be procured in a different manner and of which the producers are not the main consumers.

Although economies such as these have always existed, the relationship between them varies: formal and informal economies develop at different speeds and 'there are grounds for believing that the informal economy will grow at the expense of the formal' (Gershuny and Pahl, 1980: 7). The argument goes as follows: over the last 150 to 200 years increase in production has been associated with technological development and large-scale organization. Today this trend is coming to an end. New technology makes production cheaper, more efficient, and even more profitable when organized on a small scale: legal-institutional changes (such as social insurance, labour laws and taxation) encourage the trend which the production of services, in turn, appears to follow. Other conditions (for example labour costs) being equal, the cost of services is rising faster than the cost of industry thanks to the low growth of productivity: consequently, informal production procedures are once more likely to intervene.

As a result, transfer processes are created between the formal and informal economies. They may be shown in a three-dimensional pattern in which hidden economy, on the one hand,

FIGURE 2
Transfer processes between the formal and informal economies

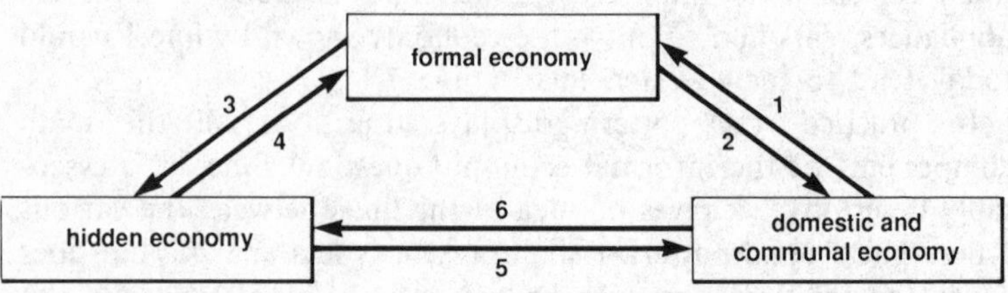

and domestic and communal economy, on the other, are separated under 'informal economy' (see Figure 2). Six directions of flow are possible between the three sectors, each being determined by the technical and social conditions behind the production of particular goods and services at any given moment. A few examples: washing is first taken to laundries (line 1), but later the diffusion of electric washing machines restores the production of this service back to the family (line 2). The availability of sophisticated devices for the production of goods and services on a small scale means it is possible to restore a whole series of activities to the context of the domestic economy or else perform them as communal economy, either to save or to earn money (the passage is from formal economy to hidden economy here) or to achieve the job satisfaction that formalized activities no longer provide. The increased cost of labour and the legal protection of labour itself (line 3) shift from the formal to the hidden economy. If unemployment increases, however, the cost of labour in the hidden economy may decrease and part of domestic and communal production might shift to the hidden economy too (line 6). The central thesis claims that, whereas, over the last two centuries, the trend shown by lines 1 and 4 has prevailed, the most significant transformations in the future may be in the direction of lines 2 and 3.

The pattern described is useful mainly because it raises a series of questions about why transfers take place between one activity and another. The main issue at stake, however, is the relationship between certain types and processes of formal economy and certain types and processes of informal economy in that *they are interlinked in a particular, stable relationship structure*. In other words, it is not only a question of seeing whether an activity is transferred from the formal to the informal. We must also establish how certain formal and informal activities are interlinked and interwoven.

It is impossible to study these problems in terms of a general theory of informal economy. They must be interpreted through the study of particular problem areas of specific aspects of the economy. Let us look at a typical case in this perspective, an example of how informal factors may be an organic part of analysis of economic structures: namely, small industry-based regional development in Italy (for a relevant bibliography, see Bagnasco, 1986). In terms of Sachs's pattern, the structure of the relations that will be created will have an essential effect on the processes described by lines 2 and 5 (market economy and parallel markets), although practically all the other processes will be specifically related to these too. In terms of Gershuny and Pahl's pattern, all three terms (formal, hidden and domestic economies) will be considered. But rather than perceiving passages from one type to the next, it will be important to pinpoint the stable relations between types or the tendency to change of these relationship patterns.

The research into the small enterprise we are concerned with here started as an analysis of the decentralization of production, from the big factory to small units. The problem tended to be defined, at the start of the 1970s, in terms of the following pattern: the cost of labour and its rigid use grew as a result of the new relationships arising between capital and labour. The reactive strategy of big industry did not at first envisage great changes in products or technologies. The aim was to get round the new constraints and to recover low labour costs and elasticity in the use of labour by exploiting the lack of trade union representation in small production units. The interpretation was simple but, at that time, extremely effective. The informal economy was closely linked to a certain interpretation of the structure of the formal economy in that it was the fruit of infringement of labour laws. On a conceptual plane, however, there was a clear paradox: that is, the economy regained its typical regulating mechanism — the market — by hiding itself and by evading legal connecting links. What does this mean? Simply that the social process had enervated the economy within organizational and political relationships involved to such a degree that the latter's tendency to be structurally differentiated from the rest of society — a central trend in the old normal economy — was the fruit of illegality. And this was a symptom of the tensions and instability of the system, one of the first traces of the general changes that currently challenge any well-defined idea of formal economy. It is thus possible to have an initial concrete perception of the crisis which Fordism and Keynesianism have suffered in Italy.

Increased sensitivity to the problems of the small enterprise shifts our attention to a different phenomenon, but one that is often confused at first with the previous one: that is, the wide-ranging economic development of Italy's north-east and central regions based on sectors normally regarded as traditional. The most interesting aspect of this new form of development (something which was totally unexpected and perceived only when it was too evident to be ignored any longer) was its continuity with old economies: and, more generally, localized social and cultural formations which became resources for a special type of development. The growth in demand for non-standardized consumer goods caused a reappraisal of the advantages of the small enterprise's elasticity, an advantage which was exploited by breaking through the boundaries of the formal all across the board. Tax evasion and infringement of labour laws ensued: most of all, the free products and labour markets were combined with production and consumer processes that were deeply rooted in family and community relations and based on flexible forms of organization.

As research shows, market mobilization gave rise to an economy regulated by the market itself and by a combination between market and mechanisms of reciprocity. In the background were the farming families that were already a market-oriented production unit and the old local communities that had become areas of skilled industrial production. And, in the mean time, the commercial and craft centres of the old Italian cities activated the process. It is important here to emphasize how this economy not only had the capacity to grow quantitatively: it was also able to modernize its own structure at a moment when the relationship between informal and formal was undergoing important transformations. The unexpected consequences of new technologies played a leading part in all this. It soon became clear that they could be applied in small plants too and that the old equation between technological modernization and big plant was erased. Technological innovation, higher wages, the increased complexity of local systems, bigger capital investment, changes in the cultural fabric, class differentiation and other factors have created a situation in which the market is related less to reciprocity and more to organization and political exchange. Family structures still counterbalance wages and community codes still facilitate relations between entrepreneurs. But, on the other hand, trade union organization has increased in importance with its demands for political mediation, and forms of 'appropriate organization' (long-term contracts, consortia and so on) now stabilize the systems of small enterprises which had become too complicated to be regulated by an unstable market alone. These are but two of the examples that might be chosen to show the important changes that the diffuse economy system has undergone. We have followed this evolution for long enough to be able to affirm that it is now directed towards normalization and modernization without taking in the big organization. As was already the case for the development of the big Ford-style enterprise, diffuse economic development sets organizational regulation and political exchange side by side with the market, but the types and combinations of these mechanisms are new and unusual. Here it is likely that the hidden part has progressively diminished in relation to the visible.

The model of the institutional structure of the economy summarily presented here is the synthesis of a number of pieces of research on the informal aspects of economic institutions. It is one example among many of work in which a research interest in the informal aspects of the economy stands out and is hence maintained, albeit without a general theory of informal economy. An important conclusion emerges from all this research and offers food for thought on the meaning of the informal in society today. Observation of the development of the small enterprise shows that important de-differentiation and deregulation processes are currently on course. Whereas a small entrepreneur performs a wide range of activities, managers in big companies have more specialized roles: or, in the case of families, individual roles are less differentiated from the nuclear family model where the man procures the means of subsistence and the woman takes care of house and children. We have also seen the trend to deregulate economic activities and the move towards different regulation based on economic context: for example, special regulation of the part-time work of women.

In view of all this, it would appear that the formal economy is being challenged across the board: the very principles used earlier to define normalization are the ones that are most affected. There are, therefore, a whole series of reasons why we should seriously begin to reflect on the meaning of all this in relation to our way of understanding economic and social development. What are the consequences we can draw on a theoretical plane?

From Calculation Problems to Development Theory Problems

I shall now discuss development in a very general sense with regard to the continuing transformation that characterizes contemporary societies. Economic development, social modernization and political modernization are all the same process but seen from different angles. Yet these are the terms in question: in other words, our theories of development. The processes of de-differentiation and deregulation mentioned earlier seem to indicate a decisive change of direction. From a sociological point of view, they are indeed a change of direction in the process of modernization. Or is it just that our concepts make us see things in this way? Is society, so to speak, actually going backwards, or do our concepts, and the way we use them, just give this impression? And if society is not 'going backwards', what concepts and theories do we need to understand the new directions of development? The aim here will be to show that a by no means secondary effect of research on the informal economy has been the trend towards a critical reframing of these theoretical problems. If the dichotomy between traditional and modern has any use at all it is simply as a conceptual aid in understanding concrete variability.

The essential nucleus of the concept of modernization includes three types of change: the passage from the predominance of prescriptive action to the diffusion of elective action, the institutionalization of change, and the process of institutional differentiation and specialization. This conceptual nucleus is used to identify the features peculiar to the society in which we live in comparison with the societies that have preceded it, although, of course, these characteristics may also have been partly present in the past too. The polar concept suggests that evolution in this direction has been intense and rapid in our era. Elective action is, for example, the occupying of a professional position by choice, or enjoying one kind of life style rather than another, or freely choosing a husband or wife. Of course this does not mean that such action is not influenced, above all, by structures of social control and inequality. Indeed, we may observe that prescriptive values persist on a normative plane but, in elective action, prescription is the very fact of having to make a choice since individual freedom is a socially sanctioned value. In the same way, change is also accepted as a social phenomenon in that it is envisaged and legitimate. New patterns of behaviour or preference can never be excluded as a matter of principle but only for the sake of argument: is it also possible, in principle, to question the forms of control that block change and take the measures that are consequently necessary. A decisive expression of the institutionalization of change is the very process of differentiation and specialization we have seen at work in the economy.

If we reduce the question to these essential terms, we may ask whether, in the economy, the development of the informal challenges this nucleus of the concept of modernization. Does it have a heuristic role in society today? Let us try to answer analytically, point by point. First of all, informal behaviour, in all its various forms, does not generally seem to affect the principle of elective action. Hidden markets may be entered out of necessity, but in any case strategically. Even more evident still is the case in which the supply of one's skills on the market depends on the need for self-realization which is denied in the formal economy. Informal, non-market activities, such as voluntary social work, are also the fruit of individual choices of commitment geared towards normative models which the formal economy is unable to achieve. When people, especially young people, do work in a religious context, this is the result of free personal choice rather than of rigid normative prescription. In many cases at least, even the tendency towards deregulation may be seen as the individual's regaining of room for choice that had been reduced excessively in relation to changing economic and cultural conditions.[1]

As to the institutionalization of change, the informal economy does not seem merely to reintroduce previous forms even when it relates to traditional structures and relations. Combinations of formal and informal — or the parallel trends of formal and informal — may only be justified on markets if they can fight off competition in changing situations. In practice, thanks to the forms they assume and the resources they exploit, these combinations are, nonetheless, innovations in traditional economic structures. The move away from standardized normative patterns, or even from positive law, does not generally prejudice cultural acceptance of such forms of behaviour in relatively large communities of individuals who are perceived as normal. In this sense, the structures of the informal economy often appear to constitute a *transition* towards non-hidden and fully institutionalized forms: the case of part-time work, for example, is paradigmatic here. And of course, even in informal market behaviour many perceive signs of the affirmation of the self-determination of labour, something surrounded by ambiguity but which seems to be a part of profound processes of cultural change. The informal economy is probably a field in which different normative principles conflict but which does not seem to involve the blocking of social change. If anything, the opposite would appear to be true.

The question of differentiation and specialization is more difficult. Processes of de-differentiation and despecialization are evident in the informal economy, as we have already seen. But these trends should be assessed together with other factors. The first is the fact there here once more we might imagine that the informal, in many cases, represents a transitional phase towards more formalized systems. For example, research into diffuse industrialization shows that the worker-peasant or the working-class family with members in farming has become the exception, whereas ten years ago, at the start of this type of industrialization, such families were probably more common. The fact remains that small enterprise production generally entails more unspecific functions and is more linked to traditional relations. We may also observe that non-standardized economic activities had the same characteristics in the past too, and that the development of production with the aid of the informal economy has been more a process of differentiation-specialization than of de-differentiation of the previous situation. The pullovers we wear today are mostly manufactured in small enterprises — the latter sometimes resorting to work at home — but our parents used to wear pullovers made at home by our grandmothers: this does not mean, however, that in the informal economy we are not generally confronted by rather unspecific structures.

And so we come to the most important factor: that different degrees of informal are to be found in different types of production of goods and services. For example, the chemical and nuclear industries currently maintain highly specialized and specific structures. Fashion, leather goods, quality furnishings, certain foodstuffs and so on are, on the other hand, more tied to traditional procedures and have structures that are much less specific. This means that different types of production are organized and institutionalized in different manners. In other words, faced with changing conditions — the state of technology, demand, the evolution of life styles and so on — it is the production system itself which becomes more differentiated and specialized. At a certain point it may no longer be related to a single organizational and institutional model and this sometimes means that it maintains a certain degree of non-differentiation *within* single sectors.

The following conclusions may be drawn. On a very abstract level, the informal economy in itself would not seem to threaten the process of modernization as it is defined by the relevant concept. But it does cast doubts on the idea of a continuous, unlimited process of, so to speak, progressive 'purification' of the social structure to achieve a perfect, ideal-typical, and hence unique, modernity. The concept of modernization clearly appears useful as a grand historical dividing line beyond which society may continue to achieve changes which are, however, difficult to organize in terms of the simple concept of modernization precisely because the concept itself is not specific enough. Concepts should be made more positive: they must be able to embrace the complex combinations of old and new (it must also be remembered that today's new is tomorrow's old), between specific and diffuse, and between differentiated and non-differentiated. The existence of the informal economy is awkward for theory but it is a strong reminder of how the economy is rooted in society and in politics. Looking back, it makes us realize that there has never been complete differentiation, and, looking forward, that we must not expect any.

It is perhaps a paradox that studies of the informal economy are never a self-sufficient theoretical field even though they are highly capable of revealing trends of social change. Indeed research into the informal economy shows that discussion of the theory of development has actually been resumed.

Note

1. Illegal activities, such as drug-pushing and drug consumption, also entail pressure for deregulation (i.e. the legalization of the use of drugs). Cases such as these, however, involve a largely unproblematic cultural definition of the issue in the extreme terms of the non-availability of life.

7
INTERNATIONAL LABOUR MIGRATION AND CLASS RELATIONS

Ayşe Öncü

Nearly all reviews of the international labour migration field share one point in common. They begin by underlining the phenomenal growth of a voluminous literature, highly uneven in theoretical and methodological sophistication, fragmented along disciplinary lines, patchy in results, diverse in topical concerns and often contradictory in political premisses and interpretations. Indeed, the field has emerged as a veritable growth industry in social science research, its broader contours shaped by the changing political itineraries and policy priorities of national governments and international agencies.

One advantage of attempting yet another review in such a far-flung field is that it relieves the author of the obligation to provide exhaustive coverage. The present review is thus a highly selective one, aiming to identify some of the salient theoretical issues that have become crystallized in the 1980s and empirical research relevant to them. Or perhaps more accurately, salient issues as seen through the filtering lens of a social scientist located in a major labour-exporting country, Turkey. For while references to the Turkish migration research figure only tangentially in the following pages, the case informs much of what are selected as important and challenging new developments in the field. The present chapter thus represents a search for new conceptual openings in the international comparative literature, by an author well familiar with the existing bottlenecks of a country-specific body of research and writing.

To provide an outline of what follows, I will first briefly touch upon the two major contending conceptual frameworks in contemporary international labour migration research: the behaviourist (equilibrium) tradition and the historical-structural (conflict) school. To the extent that these alternative perspectives represent broader currents of dominant social and economic thought, the issue is an old one and to my mind a moot controversy. The lines of dispute are well marked, differences solidified into adherents of alternative camps. Thus beyond outlining the contrasting paradigms of global inequality these schools are embedded in, I will make no attempt to review the variants of the classical tradition. Instead, I will address myself to a series of theoretical issues which have moved to the foreground within the structuralist paradigm.

The intellectual frontiers of the international labour migration field over the past two decades have been the attempts to link labour flows to the historical-structural processes of the world economy. What began in the early 1970s as a critical reaction to classical, behaviourist models progressively gave way to analyses based on the premisses of an international political economy and a global system of inequalities. Thus throughout the 1970s, questions of labour migration across national boundaries were framed within the context of structurally uneven patterns of accumulation on a world scale. The emphasis was on the development of a macroanalytical framework within which interlinkages between labour migration and reproduction of asymmetrical growth patterns between the core and periphery of a global system could be interpreted.

The challenge of the 1980s has been to step beyond such elegant and sometimes formalistic global analyses, toward formulations which take into account and try to explain variations between advanced industrial economies of the core in their recourse to foreign labour as well as alternative patterns of accommodation of immigrants. Hence the salient trend of the 1980s has been away from a blanket approach to labour importing (core) and labour exporting (peripheral) societies, to more delimited attempts to try to account for systematic variations. On the forefront of the research agenda have been issues related to the heterogeneity of labour-importing economies, differences in the social, economic and political contours of their labour markets. In the second section, I will focus on a series of concepts — such as labour market segmentation, immigrant enclaves, modes of incorporation of foreign labour — which have gained increasing currency in the 1980s and represent attempts to come to grips with changes in the internal structure of labour markets in advanced industrial economies and the role of immigrant labour within them.

The *variable* impact and implications of labour exports on peripheral societies has remained a largely unexplored topic, despite an abundance of empirical material on individual countries. Very broad formulations which emphasize the asymmetrical gains to the core and periphery in the international migration process, while useful, lose sight of the enormous variation between the so-called peripheral societies. In the absence of conceptual handles which serve to disaggregate the 'periphery', enabling us to delineate major theoretical axes of comparison between labour-exporting societies, the available empirical material goes begging for interpretation. This issue will be taken up towards the end of the present chapter, with a view to charting impending avenues of future exploration.

The Two Contending Traditions in Migration Theory

Many of the current theoretical and methodological issues in the field of international labour migration can be traced back to the perennial debate between two contending currents of social and economic thought: equilibrium (behaviourist) and historical-structural (conflict) schools (Wood, 1982; Bach and Schraml, 1982; Papademetriou, 1983b).

Variants of equilibrium models include the cost-benefit analyses and human capital models in neoclassical economics as well as 'push-pull' analyses in sociology. In both, migration is treated as a voluntary and rational calculus by individuals seeking to enhance their economic position. Migration flows are the cumulative result of such individual decisions based on the evaluation of the benefits to be gained and the costs entailed in moving. The direction and magnitude of the aggregate process of labour mobility is determined by the imbalances in the spatial distribution of land, labour, capital and natural resources. By redistributing human capital, labour migration restores the balance (equilibrium) between unequally distributed resources across space and hence serves development by correcting rural–urban, interregional and by extension, international differences in the geographic location of factors of production (Lewis, 1959; Sjaastad, 1962; Spengler and Myers, 1977). Since workers seek out those employment opportunities which give them the greatest return, their prospects for long-term economic and occupational advancement are also enhanced. In sum, sending regions and countries, receiving regions and countries, as well as the migrants themselves, benefit in the long term.

This putative harmony of interests implicit in variants of human capital models in neoclassical economics finds its counterpart in the push-pull analysis of sociologists (Lee, 1966; Jackson, 1969; Jansen, 1970; Mangalam and Schwartzweller, 1970). Given the presupposition that societies are fundamentally self-equilibrating and that migration is instrumental in achieving an optimal distribution of population and other resources, the key issues centre on the questions of selectivity (differences in the social and psychological attributes of migrants and non-migrants) at the sending end and adaptation and/or assimilation at the point of destination.

Global patterns of labour movements are viewed, from within this perspective, in terms of the balance sheet of advantages and disadvantages for individual countries. In the case of labour exporting, less developed countries, such advantages and disadvantages are formulated with reference to basic conditions and strategic factors for economic development. Benefits or gains include the hard currency remitted by migrant workers, which relieves balance of payments difficulties and enables imports of raw materials, capital goods and technology needed for development. On their return, migrants serve as agents of change by applying their newly developed skills and ideas acquired abroad to establish enterprises conducive to growth. These advantages offset possible losses in skilled and educated manpower, hence the balance sheet appears, on the whole, positive (Paine, 1974; Todaro, 1976). In stimulating savings and investments in the country of origin, labour emigration enhances the potential for self-generating growth. What is required is the will and the ability to utilize this potential, i.e. the right, governmental policies.

This essentially optimistic vision, reminiscent of the modernization theories of the 1960s with their promise of self-sustained growth, remained virtually unchallenged during the period of active labour recruitment in Western Europe. It is only in the latter half of the 1970s that more sober assessments, emphasizing unintended and unanticipated consequences for labour-importing and exporting countries begin to appear in the literature. And the overall tenor of the 1980s in the aftermath of economic crisis and closing doors is definitely gloomy (Miller Mark, 1981; Rogers,

1985; Miller Mark, 1986). But the potential contribution of labour emigration for exporting countries is rarely questioned in this context; the emphasis is on lost opportunities, analysed and interpreted in terms of misguided government policy and paucity of planning (e.g. Adler, 1981). Even in its most perceptive and sophisticated versions, various strands of the equilibrium tradition are concerned with the question of what went wrong, without probing the central premisses of the model itself. The methodological orthodoxy and empirical emphasis of the approach also contribute, since operational definitions and proxy indicators of conceptual variables at various levels of analysis can be associated with one another through statistical techniques, without contradicting the underlying assumptions of the model itself.

Clearly, equilibrium models of labour migration are rooted in a set of theoretical and methodological premisses that define a broader tradition in social science research. It is important to recognize the appeal of this tradition with its voluntaristic, ameliorative assumptions and sophisticated methodological tools, since it continues to define the current profile of international labour migration literature. But the intellectual frontiers of the field in the past decade reside elsewhere, in the attempts to link migration flows to the historical-structural processes of the world economy.

The historical-structural approach shifts the focus of analysis in migration from the individual to the level of regional, national and international politico-economic forces. At issue is not the assumption that individuals behave rationally, seeking to maximize their economic advantages through migration. Nor is the problem one of constraints on individual rationality such as social information networks, family bonds, attitudinal propensities and so on, all of which are extensively elaborated and often quantified in the behaviourist tradition (see review by Kubat and Hoffman-Nowotny, 1982). Rather, the point is that analysis of migratory movements cannot be reduced to the sum total of such individual decisions and constraints thereupon. Hence the emphasis is upon the broader historical-structural forces which define the preconditions and directionality of labour flows, rather than the micro-context of individual decision making. Labour migration is treated, not as a discrete phenomenon to be subjected to separate analysis, but as an integral component of the evolution of disparities between sectors, regions and national units at the global level.

Within the structuralist paradigm, both the causes and effects of labour movements are sought in the deepening process of combined and uneven development of regions and nations (Castells, 1975; Portes, 1978a; Petras, 1980a, 1981; Zolberg, 1981; Sassen-Koob, 1980, 1981; Portes and Walton, 1981; Walton, 1985). The concept of uneven development implies that inequalities or gaps between sectors, regions or countries derives *not* from disparities in the distribution of resources or factor endowments, but from 'the logic of capitalist accumulation and the division of labour it commands according to the imperatives of the rate of profit' (Castells, 1975: 35). The implications of viewing labour migration as integral to uneven development are thus twofold. First, it means that the differences in levels of development which produce labour flows are continuously recreated by the same process. To put it differently, labour flows do not lead to equilibrium, but reinforce existing sectoral imbalances and regional inequalities, widening the gap between sending and receiving areas. Viewed from this perspective, labour migration is not simply a product, a result of differences in levels of development, but an indispensable component of the capital accumulation process and hence one of the motors of uneven growth. It leads to the progressive subordination of the weaker regions to the stronger ones (Damette, 1980; Lapple and Hoogstraten, 1980; Lapple, 1985; Slater, 1985); it results in the weakening of less developed countries vis-à-vis more economically developed ones (Chaney, 1979; Ward, 1975; Arrighi, 1985; Sassen-Koob, 1987; Boyd et al., 1987; Cohen, 1987a).

Viewing labour migration as integral to uneven development has a very important secondary implication as well. It means that labour flows represent more than a dictate of economic logic, a function of supply and demand in a laissez-faire market. To the extent that the territorial and social effects of accumulation are interrelated (Henderson and Castells, 1987), movements of labour and capital are inextricably bound to class struggles, and hence subject to 'political logic'. And the role of the state as a political actor in shaping the economic and spatial arrangements of production, circulation and consumption comes to the foreground (Peek and Standing, 1982; Aymard, 1985; Slater, 1985). Not only do state policies of trade, protection and profit define the broad outlines of capital investment and production, but the state also regulates the conditions of labour and organizational strength of labour organizations (Evans et al., 1985; Bergquist, 1984). Needless to point out, the nature, role and autonomy of the state vis-à-vis class struggles is a sharply contested issue among proponents of the historical-structural perspective. But such differences in the conceptualization of the state notwithstanding, the historical-structuralist perspective frames the analysis of labour migration in the context of state and class conflicts on the one hand, and processes of territorial and social accumulation on the other. The regional and spatial facets of uneven development become the key referent in the study of labour flows; its origins (state–class struggles) and effects (socio-spatial distribution of inequality) embrace multiple levels of causation, ranging from the global to the local.

Within this macroanalytical framework, labour migration across national boundaries is viewed as a process generated by structurally uneven patterns of accumulation on a *world scale*. The point of departure is a global system of vertically integrated control and accumulation, of production and distribution, that is, a world division of labour. A complexity of cross-national movements of capital, labour and commodities become interlinked processes in the reproduction of asymmetrical growth patterns between the core and periphery of this global system; integral to the evolution of worldwide inequalities. The emphasis is thus upon the dynamics of change on a world scale. Analysis is couched at the level of global transformations, historical and contemporary, generated by the cyclical rhythms, trends and crises of accumulation on a world scale. Historically specific, locally particular movements of labour are situated and interpreted in terms of their linkages to major shifts in the direction of capital and labour flows at the global level. Thus a wide range of concrete labour flows across particular national boundaries become the microcosm of changes and crises on a world scale, ranging from Caribbean or Mexican migration to the USA (Bonilla and Campos, 1982; Cockcroft, 1982) or immigration to Switzerland from southern Europe (Casparis, 1985) to labour immigration to OPEC countries (Sassen-Koob, 1981, 1982).

The somewhat synthetic tone of the paragraphs above arises in part from an effort to encompass the multiple strands of the historical-structural school. Within its rubric one finds not only studies grounded squarely on the basic tenets of Marxism-Leninism but also adherents of the world system perspective or more broadly neo-Marxist, political economy approaches as well as many structural sociologists. Thus many of the studies already cited one after another in the time-honoured review article tradition, often represent different conceptual and theoretical starting points. Any attempt to suggest certain broad generalizations which cover these important differences is bound to sound synthetic. But the diversity and complexity of various strands within the historical-structural paradigm is only one aspect of the problem. Part of the difficulty arises from the global reach of the approach itself. For while its macroanalytical framework has been and continues to be a potent point of departure in critical assessments of the equilibrium perspective, its totalizing language generates its own burden. The emphasis on the general, the whole, the universal means that analysis takes the form of a logical discourse based on a series of abstract concepts often embedded in ideological controversies (for example internationalization of the labour struggle; transnational circulation of capital; inter-state system; global restructuring; recomposition of capital and reindustrialization in the core; world market production in the periphery, to cite a few). Concrete labour movements across specific boundaries are then used to illustrate deductive arguments. As expressed by one of the leading proponents of the paradigm itself, 'Facts and figures are cited more as an illustration of an argument than as a way to understand what is happening. . . . We do not have to choose between surrendering to irrelevant empiricism or dealing with social analysis in careless terms' (Castells, 1982: 117). Furthermore, the emphasis on neat generalizations in terms of global mechanisms means that there emerges a large category, 'local variations', which do not merit explanatory attention on their own. While it is important to understand different forms of labour migration at various stages of capitalist development, every occurrence of labour migration has its own history and its own outcomes as well as being part of the more general process of uneven capitalist development. The danger of relying on universal generalizations alone is that such concepts as incorporation into the world economy, underdevelopment of the periphery etc., can become substitutes for explanation, avoiding the need to account for what is actually happening. And within the historical-structural paradigm, the search for a global logic tends to become more prestigious than explanations of the particular. As Walton, another leading proponent of the perspective puts it, 'In the early enthusiasm for critical views of the development process, theoretical fashion shifted, perhaps, too far in the direction of neat mechanisms of metropolitan-satellite extractions or the totalizing language of a world system' (1985: 5).

Obviously, to account for the whole as well as the particular is no mean task. It should be clear by now that the two broad paradigms outlined all too briefly earlier, representing different streams or currents in international migration research, err in opposite directions. While in the macroanalytical framework of the historical-structural perspective the complexity and diversity of reality is often glossed over, the equilibrium perspective's sophisticated methodology and empirical emphasis lends itself to the multiplication of often disparate research findings which simply do not add up to a vision of the whole. But to suggest some sort of a modified position wherein the two perspectives could converge; to search for a realm wherein they could meet, so to speak, is not meaningful. To the extent that these perspectives are embedded in different currents of dominant social and economic thought, and represent contending traditions, there is, in effect, no golden mean. Not only because differences are solidified into adherents of alternative camps with their embedded ideologies such that to seek a meeting ground is not practical; but also because it is not necessarily desirable. In the vast and diverse literature on international migration, where the implicit and explicit assumptions of the equilibrium perspective continue to prevail, the conflict school, with its critical stance, has proved fertile ground for germination of new concepts. And its shortcomings, subject to debate within the paradigm itself, have brought into the foreground a number of issues which continue to define the intellectual frontiers of international migration research. One such issue concerns the role of immigrant labour in the labour markets of advanced industrial societies, that is, attempts to come to grips with the empirically frustrating, heuristically appealing concept of the 'core' and to concentrate on the economic and political processes which define the contours of labour markets of different labour-importing core countries, attempting to account for variability as well as uniformity.

Immigrants in the Labour Markets of Core Economies

Why do advanced industrial economies of the core exhibit differences in their recourse to foreign labour? How can the differential demand for foreign labour in various sectors or industries *within* core economies be explained? Why do immigrants of the same nationality encounter different experiences in various countries of the core? Or alternatively, how can we account for the different patterns of incorporation of various nationalities in the same labour-importing country?

Variants of the classical reserve army of labour thesis in the international labour migration literature are of limited analytical utility in providing answers to such questions. The principal function of the reserve army, as it is usually described, is to keep down labour costs by confronting employed workers with the threat of easy replacement (Baran and Sweezy, 1966: ch. 6; Amin, 1976: 351–64). Hence the notion that the unemployed masses of dependent capitalist countries act as a veritable world reserve army on the working class of the advanced capitalist countries, to be recruited or sent away as the needs of core states dictate, has occupied a solid place in Marxist and neo-Marxist theories of imperialism, dependency and global inequality. The specificity of *foreign* labour in the context of advanced capitalism, according to such formulations, derives from the politico-legal status of immigrants. Extensive legislation on selective criteria for immigrant status means that foreign workers are recruited from among the young, healthy and most reproductive age groups; and their costs of reproduction, as well as their families who succeed in accompanying them, are below the average standards of indigenous workers (Castles and Kosack, 1973; Ward, 1975; Buraway, 1976). They are willing to work in the worst safety and health conditions for lower wages, with little immediate potential for political organization because of their ideological isolation. Most importantly, given their legal status as temporary aliens, they are particularly easy to lay off when industry faces recession. Hence in addition to suffering excessive exploitation, foreign migrant labour functions as a regulator of capitalist crises, cushioning the impact of the expansion and contraction of capital. To quote from Petras (1980b: 176), 'the advantage is that (foreign) labor can be recruited, restrained or expelled from entry according to sectoral, cyclical and secular demands of capital'.

Moral stance and political merits aside, such global formulations based on the reserve army thesis do not provide *conceptual* handles in approaching the sorts of questions posed above. The unquenchable thirst of capital for a steady and docile yet expendable and infinitely flexible labour supply, assumed to be a 'natural' tendency, explains everything and hence very little. Indeed, in its cruder versions, it lends itself to vacuous functionalist arguments of the sort discredited by an enormous amount of critical writing in the last two decades.

The emerging trend of the 1980s within the historical-structural paradigm has been away from very broad, facile generalizations to more delimited attempts to develop concepts which deal with the diversity of labour markets in industrial economies and the role of immigrant labour within them. Rethinking along these lines has generated a stream of writing and research on the relationship between large flows of foreign labour and the nature, sources and consequences of labour market segmentation in core economies.

Secondary Labour Markets and the Demand for Foreign Labour

The current debate on labour market segmentation in industrial market societies dates back to the 1970s when a number of studies in the United States proposed a dual structure of primary and secondary labour markets; a dichotomization based on technology, skill and worker characteristics (for example Edwards et al., 1975; Doeringer and Piore, 1971). Such studies challenged the premiss that dualism is exclusively associated with underdevelopment; and that market rationality tends to integrate all economic activities into a homogeneous whole in the advanced industrial society, allocating persons and resources in a continuous array. They suggested instead that contemporary Western market societies tend to be divided segmentally, i.e. are characterized by radical discontinuities. The ensuing debate on the general applicability of models based exclusively on the United States experience brought into the foreground questions about variability between industrial societies and has since then generated a series of studies concentrating on sectoral variations, inter-industry differences and more broadly on the dynamics of labour market segmentation in European countries as well (for example Berger and Piore, 1980; Wilkinson, 1981; Solinas, 1982; Grant and Streeck, 1985; Morokvasic et al., 1986; Goldthorpe, 1984).

The relationship between large flows of foreign labour and market segmentation in Western capitalist economies came on to the agenda in international labour migration research through the initial formulations of Piore (1979) and Portes (1978a) whose original conceptualizations and later refinements (Berger and Piore, 1980; Piore and Sabel, 1984; Piore, 1986; Portes, 1981; Portes and Bach, 1984; Portes and Sassen-Koob, 1987) constitute landmarks in the ongoing debate.

The conceptual framework originally proposed by Piore in his seminal work *Birds of Passage* (1979) was based on a dual-labour-market formulation. The upper tier of this dual market (primary market) is made up principally of monopoly or oligopoly firms, while the lower (secondary market) is composed of competitive firms. The former exercise significant control over their markets; they utilize high capital intensity to enhance productivity and are able to pass wage increases to consumers through control of markets. Accordingly, jobs in the monopoly/oligopoly sector are characterized by stability, tenure and high wages. The secondary, competitive sector is by contrast faced with economic uncertainty, demand unpredictability and offers low wages, substandard working conditions and irregular tenure.

Given two distinct types of job associated with dual labour markets, Piore proceeded to argue that national workers, because they are interested in long-term career prospects, shun the secondary labour market where instability of employment is coupled with menial status and lower wages. Such work is accepted only by native marginal workers — such as students, housewives, retired workers — whose labour force commitment is temporary and who tend to view their income as supplementary. When such marginal native workers are limited in number or tied down geographically, filling secondary jobs with foreign labour is one solution to the problem. Immigrant labourers tend to view their stay as temporary and hence are undeterred by lack of long-term career prospects or job instability; they are also untouched by menial, demeaning work since they derive social status from their roles in their country of origin; they frequently come from areas where wages are so low relative to those of the immigrant-receiving industrial country that the work seems much better paid than it does to national workers. Thus the demand for low-cost labour in the secondary sector and the attractiveness of such jobs to immigrants is viewed as the engine of the migration process.

The key line of reasoning followed by Portes (1978b) in his original analysis of illegal (undocumented) migration in the United States, was again based on a two-sector model, but his emphasis was on the informal hiring practices among small and very small enterprises, notably in agriculture and a variety of urban consumer services which, by their very nature, cannot be relocated to areas of abundant, inexpensive labour. The survival of such small enterprises depends on employment practices which take place at the margins of the law because they entail savings on tax and social security obligations; since they can easily escape government regulation, they provide a congenial setting for casual hiring, non-reporting of income etc. The notion of a thriving informal urban economy in the midst of industrial societies has since then been followed up by studies exploring what may be termed an underground labour market (see Portes and Sassen-Koob, 1987 for a recent review). Also, research on clustering of illegal immigrants in such sectors as garment, footwear, construction, etc., characterized by the prevalence of very small enterprises where informal hiring practices tend to be widespread, has brought to the fore questions of immigrant enterprise and ethnic enclaves.

The term enclave economy was coined by Portes (1981) to refer to immigrant groups that have managed to gain control over a significant segment of a local industry such that the immigrant labour force works in enterprises owned by other immigrants. The proliferation of immigrant business and upward mobility opportunities within such enclave economies suggests a pattern distinct from secondary sector employment, commonly associated with bottom-rung, dead-end jobs. Following the line of reasoning offered by Portes, it thus seems meaningful to talk about three analytically distinct patterns of immigrant incorporation. The first pattern, associated with primary sector employment is characterized by job security, wage levels defined by collective bargaining, and working conditions comparable to native workers. Skilled immigrants arriving with secure legal status, subject to official recruitment policies, thus constitute one distinct mode of insertion of foreign labour into the industrial economy. The second pattern, associated with secondary labour markets as originally outlined by Piore, stems from inelasticities in the domestic supply of labour, i.e. consists of unskilled immigrants hired for transient, short-term jobs of menial status, detached from the main lines of structured mobility within the primary sector of the labour market. The third — the enclave pattern suggested by Portes — brings to the fore economic niches captured by immigrant groups based on ethnic communal ties.

Once these distinct patterns or modes of incorporating foreign labour are identified, there arises a series of analytical questions about when or where one or the other might prevail. Recent research suggests several observations. First, the pattern of incorporation into the secondary labour market, which appears to be the significant pattern in the United States, does not seem on balance to have been the prevailing trend in continental Europe. Böhning's (1983) cross-national comparisons for instance, based on the relationship between firm size and proportion of foreign labour employed in different industries in France and Germany, point towards the importance of primary sector employment in manufacturing. Böhning underlines the importance of institutional factors, such as industry-wide rather than craftsman-type unions in continental Europe, as well as the political screening of economic demand in more general terms. His point is that economic demand for foreign labour (in the primary or secondary sector) is a necessary but not sufficient cause of large-scale immigration; whether and how much borders will be opened to which type of foreign labour depends on domestic political configurations. The possibility of different political and institutional responses to similar economic constraints is a point reiterated in much current labour migration literature. Morokvasic et al. (1986) for instance, in their comparative analysis of the clothing industry in Germany, France and Britain, point out the significance of state policies in defining the contours of the secondary labour market. All three countries experienced similar problems of declining profitability and massive job losses in their clothing industry in the face of diminishing international markets since the 1960s. But while protectionist state policies in France and Britain enabled the maintenance of a large secondary sector of production based on immigrant labour and entrepreneurship, in

Germany by contrast immigration policy and a strategy of relocating production left little room for the growth of a secondary sector. The legal/institutional barriers to small business and terms of entry for migrant workers which restrict self-employment in many parts of continental Europe appear to have held back the growth of a secondary labour market associated with immigrant labour in the United States, Britain or, to some extent, France.

That there exist important differences in the size and significance of secondary sector employment and its role in incorporating immigrant labour between advanced capitalist societies seems clear. Whether, these current differences notwithstanding, there is a common, long-term trend toward more flexible (i.e. casual or informal) employment practices as the labour force composition shifts from smokestack industries and manufacturing as a whole towards services, is much more controversial. Available evidence points towards a renewed viability for small business coupled with casualization of employment, not only in the United States (Fain, 1980; Granovetter, 1984; Portes and Sassen-Koob, 1987) but also in Britain and other continental European countries (Gerry, 1984; Boissevain, 1984; Scase and Goffee, 1982). Whether this is a temporary phenomenon corresponding to the mid-1970s recession, or the harbinger of a fundamental restructuring in the labour markets of advanced capitalist societies, historically shaped by the technical imperatives of mass production (Piore and Sabel, 1984; Piore, 1986) continues to be debatable. If indeed, decentralization of production, flexible labour arrangements and subcontracting down to low-cost small enterprises are rooted in global processes of restructuration as technological dynamism shifts from mass production to information technologies, then current differences in the structure of labour markets in advanced industrial societies can be interpreted as conjunctural variations of timing and strategy. A wider discussion of different lines of thinking on this issue is beyond the scope of this review. Of more immediate relevance is that changing economics of small business in Western societies in an era of slow growth and massive technological change, coupled with the transformation of Europe's temporary workers into permanent ethnic communities, has brought the question of ethnic enterprises on to the research agenda. Thus paradoxically perhaps, a current keyword in recent research in the historical-structural tradition is 'ethnicity' rather than class. Before moving on to discuss the growing body of research on determinants and implications of immigrant enclaves in advanced economies however, a note must be added on 'project-tied labour' or 'contract labour' as a distinctive pattern within the Middle Eastern context.

Literature and research on the flow of immigrant labour from South-East and East Asia to oil-producing Arab states in the 1980s emphasizes imports of labour as part of a complete package supplied by foreign contractors in the region's construction market. The development, administration and characteristics of such collective contract or project-tied labour have been examined in detail in studies on South Korea (Kim, 1982, 1983; Chough, 1983) as well as the Philippines (Lazo et al., 1982; Tomas, 1983). For instance, Kim (1982) reports that 98 percent of South Korean workers employed in the Middle East in 1980 were engaged by South Korean companies. Similarly, Huan-Ming Ling (1984) notes that Chinese labour is employed by other East Asian, notably Japanese, firms working in the Middle East. Again, the competitive edge of Turkish contractors in Middle East markets was based on project-tied Turkish labour until the inflow of cheaper Pakistani and Bangladesh workers began to erode it in the 1980s. (See Keyder and Aksu, 1986, for a review of literature on Turkish workers in Middle Eastern labour markets.) In the 1980s, continuing labour shortages in oil-exporting countries, alongside declines in oil revenues, appear to have increased the attractiveness of contract labour from South and South-East Asia, both because these workers accept lower wage rates and poorer conditions of employment (Nagi, 1983) and also because repatriation of contract workers is easier, a factor of importance as concern over the long-term implications of immigrant ethnic communities in the Gulf states mounts. Project-tied labourers live in camps provided by the companies which employ them on the basis of two- to three-year contracts, with no dependants and no life outside the camp and hence with little possibility of willingness to stay on.

While project-tied import and export of labour appears to be confined to intra-periphery migration flows, it seems worth taking into account as an analytically distinct mode of insertion of foreign labour in comparative perspective. It has been suggested for instance (Keyder and Aksu, 1986), that Turkish labourers employed on a contract basis in Libya have become radicalized politically, their anger directed towards the government and employing firms alike, in contrast to the European experience which has led many Turkish workers to xenophobic reactions and to taking refuge in either religious tradition or reactive nationalism. Such suggestions, however tentative they may be in the absence of rigorous research, point towards fruitful possibilities of comparative analysis on the variable experiences of immigrants from a single nationality under different conditions of labour market incorporation.

Immigrant Enclaves and Ethnic Business

Students of migration have long been interested in the emergence of ethnic communities in the context of large-scale immigration. But the emphasis has traditionally been on factors which facilitate or hinder assimilation, the assumption being that ethnic communities are temporary — albeit important — way stations to eventual integration. Hence questions of ethnicity have been formulated in terms of social and cultural barriers to adaptation on the part of migrants themselves (such as inadequate job or language skills, low levels of education, differences in cultural values) as well as ethnic discrimination on the part of the native born (based on negative stereotypes of race, colour, religion, national origin, and so on), which hinder assimilation. 'Assimilation', 'adaptation' and 'integration' have thus been key concepts (see review by Morokvasic, 1984b, on the continuing salience of the assimilation framework in European migration research).

Current interest and growing research on immigrant enclaves and ethnic business in advanced capitalist societies within the historical-structural paradigm proceeds from a different set of issues in approaching questions of ethnicity. The central problematic is framed in terms of how and why some immigrant groups are able to capture a niche and exploit business opportunities in economies that are dominated by large-scale, technologically advanced concerns. The key issue is when, where and which immigrant groups are able to utilize communal resources such that ethnic business proliferates to gain control of a significant portion of the market. The emphasis is on the resilience of ethnicity; on the reproduction of communal distinctiveness and identity of national origin within enclave economies.

Since the formation of immigrant enclaves is contingent on immigrant entrepreneurship, the question of the conditions under which immigrant enterprise grows and prospers is of crucial interest. But available research indicates that immigrant business does not automatically lead to an enclave. First, almost every immigrant community provides minimal business opportunities for its own members, stores for special ethnic products, travel and moving agencies involved in the immigration process itself, legal and medical services — but none of these are potentially large employers and furthermore the limits of such a protected market tend to be reached very quickly. Similarly, the residential concentration of immigrant populations tends to generate opportunities for immigrant small business. When an immigrant population gradually begins to take over a residential area, native small businesses seek opportunities outside the neighbourhood, creating vacancies for immigrant businesspeople. Thus for instance, Aldrich and his associates (1985) in their extensive research on Asians in British cities, have found a strong association between Asian small business and the proportion of Asians in various neighbourhoods. Their explanation emphasizes the high rates of failure among such small businesses in general, and in the absence of white proprietors willing to open up new firms in 'changed' neighbourhoods. Some of the shops are bought by immigrants, others are simply left empty or converted to non-business uses. It is difficult to speak of a competitive edge to immigrant small business in such a context, although the phenomenon has been observed in other European cities, for example among Turks in Berlin (Hoffmeyer-Zlotnik, 1982). It is only when immigrant entrepreneurs, by mobilizing the informal resources of the ethnic community, gain a favourable position in competition with native proprietors and hence manage to control a significant portion of a local or regional industry, that we can speak of an immigrant enclave as originally proposed by Portes (1981).

Lines of activity in which immigrant enterprise thrives to grow and prosper appear to be those in which small-scale enterprise is viable to begin with, that is, situations where heterogeneity of markets is coupled with flux and instability of demand. The garment industry is a prime example where much of the research on immigrant enterprise has been focused (Hoel, 1982; Anthias, 1983; Werbner, 1984; Waldinger, 1984: 85; Morokvasic et al.,

1986). Fragmentation of markets, seasonality of demand and rapid fashion changes in many sectors of the garment industry make short runs imperative and the production process has to remain flexible. Large wholesalers, retailers and manufacturers faced with unpredictable demand and erratic work flow tend to shift their risks to small inner-city firms through various subcontracting arrangements, resulting in a proliferation of small-scale enterprises. Thus for instance, close to 80 percent of London's clothing industry is accounted for by firms employing fewer than fifty people, according to Morokvasic et al. (1986: 411). Portes and Sassen-Koob (1987: 47) underline the prevalence of very small firms employing fewer than ten people among apparel and clothing firms in central New York and Miami.

The prevalence of small-scale enterprise lowers capital barriers, enabling immigrants with limited resources to draw upon ethnic bonds of solidarity based on loyalty, obligation and honour, in both capitalizing and organizing neophyte concerns. Bonnett (1981) and Laguerre (1984) have shown how rotating credit associations continue to funnel capital to West Indian and Haitian businesses in New York City. 'Business on trust', appears to be the keyword in all cases where immigrant entrepreneurs have made substantial inroads into local business, ranging from Pakistanis in the Manchester garment trade (Werbner, 1984) to Cuban-owned businesses in Miami (Wilson and Portes, 1980) or Korean grocery stores in New York (Kim, 1981). Once in business, immigrant entrepreneurs recruit labour through immigrant networks. And it is in the ready access to a cheap and stable supply of immigrant labour that the competitive edge to immigrant enterprise resides. Hiring through informal networks not only provides a privileged conduit to a cheaper source of labour — a crucial advantage in competition with non-immigrant firms — but also enables owners to define employment in terms of ethnic loyalties and paternalistic relationships, thus strengthening attachment to the firm. Native-owned firms which rely on market mechanisms for recruitment are plagued by low levels of labour commitment and by absenteeism, ethnic differences between management and labour exacerbating conflicts over production quotas and further contributing to labour turnover (Waldinger, 1985). Immigrant enterprise thus has a distinctive advantage in industries traditionally associated with small-scale enterprise, low pay and high failure rates. Use of labour from within the ethnic community enables immigrant owners to surmount the organizational problems traditionally associated with small firms in such industries, leading to the development of an enclave wherein possibilities of accumulation are contingent on continued isolation of the immigrant community from mainstream society. Hence in industries where the labour force is *immigrant* and *female*, that is, doubly vulnerable, as documented in studies of contemporary sweatshops in the garment industry (Hoel, 1982; Anthias, 1983), immigrant entrepreneurship appears to find the most fertile ground.

Interpreting the broader significance of available case studies on immigrant enclaves and the opportunity structures they provide for immigrant entrepreneurship is much more difficult. Most existing research is focused on successive waves of immigrants to North America, where Asians are the most recent group to establish a foothold in small-scale industry, replicating a pattern followed by earlier groups such as Jewish, Italian and Irish immigrants (Light, 1984). Whether the increasing permanence of settlement of initially temporary migrant streams to continental Europe is the harbinger of a similar pattern of incorporation is open to some question. Heisler (1986) for instance, offers a strong argument against the generalizability of the enclave phenomenon by underlining political and legal arrangements which set the European context apart. She points out that a host of official or quasi-official service agencies, some initiated by European welfare states, others subsidized by governments of sending countries, have from the very beginning provided a wide range of social and political benefits to European immigrant groups. Coupled with the fact that very few immigrants are self-employed, the majority working in medium and large firms and increasingly unionized, Europe's immigrants have failed to develop their own autonomous institutions. Such independent communal organizations as mutual aid societies or revolving credit funds which have been identified as the hub of immigrant communities elsewhere have simply not emerged. While there do exist differences in the communal organization of various immigrant groups in continental Europe, these differences appear to stem from the variety of organizational arrangements directly instituted and subsidized by sending governments, rather than support systems and/or intermediary networks developed by the immigrants themselves. Even the social, cultural and recreational clubs which have increased in recent years are often initiated and indirectly maintained by governments. The contrast between Great Britain, with its strong ethnic communal organizations, and continental Europe where informal immigrant networks have been very slow to develop is striking (Rex et al., 1987). Immigrants in continental Europe continue to channel their savings into investment at home and do not appear to be interested in obtaining citizenship, despite the fact that many — perhaps most — do not plan to return in the foreseeable future. Governments at both ends remain committed to an official policy of promoting return. Sending countries generally oppose large-scale settlement of their citizens since it would entail a loss of remittances. European governments are in the process of implementing a variety of return-incentive schemes, albeit with limited success so far.

These differences in the formation and structure of immigrant communities which set the continental European context apart from other advanced industrial countries are obviously not immutable. But any conjecture as to future developments would take us once again far afield into broader questions of global economic restructuration, industrial relocation, technological changes and so on, which have a bearing on the future contours of labour markets in Europe and hence on the fate of immigrants in them. It therefore seems best to conclude this section on immigrants in the labour markets of core economies by re-emphasizing the current *diversity* of industrial economies and the role of immigrant labour within them.

Concepts such as labour market segmentation, dualism, informal economy and ethnic enclaves are certainly not new to those familiar with development literature. Indeed, these concepts appear to have acquired a second lease of life in the literature on international labour migration, at a time when their usefulness in development studies is being seriously challenged (see Peattie, 1987). Their increasing currency in the analysis of immigrant labour in core societies reflects a search for analytical tools for grasping and explaining the historical and contextual variations in the insertion of foreign labour into advanced industrial economies. And their merit rests in developing hypotheses for comparative analysis. They suggest fruitful lines of exploration such as comparison of immigrants from the same nationality in different labour market segments of the same industrial society (for example Turkish workers in the French garment and automotive industries) or the same industry in different countries (Turkish workers in the French and Dutch garment industry) or comparisons between different nationalities in the same industry (Turkish and Yugoslav workers in the German steel industry). In sum, they enable us to ask new questions at a time when the theoretical sterility and repetitiveness of mainstream literature on the plight of immigrants would have us believe there is little more to be studied.

Labour Exports and Peripheral Societies

On the variable impact of labour exports on peripheral societies, there is an abundance of empirical material on individual countries which remains largely unexplored from a comparative perspective. Thus we have, on the one hand, broad formulations that focus on labour export as a process which reinforces global inequalities and emphasize the asymmetrical gains of the periphery and the core, already reviewed above. We also have case studies which delve into and document how labour exports serve to further distort the internal parameters of economic growth in various national contexts by reinforcing the unequal growth of sectors, regions and classes within them, to be reviewed below. What we are lacking is a range of concepts capable of specifying major axes of comparison between labour-exporting peripheral societies. That there are wide differences in the socioeconomic and political trajectories of countries which have been major labour exporters in the postwar decades is self-evident. On the differential impact of labour exports on societies with different patterns of capital accumulation, state and class structures, and external constraints (such as Egypt, Turkey or Mexico) we know next to nothing. The lacuna is theoretical rather than empirical and is not confined to the international labour migration literature. For we have not yet moved beyond a blanket approach to the periphery, to develop analytical tools which will enable us to account for *divergence* between societies essentially similar in their location in the world system, that is, peripheral. In sum, we do not have a theory of 'paths of peripheralization'. In the absence of an analytical framework within which meaningful questions on the variable impact of labour exports can be posed and hypotheses formulated, what we are left with is a series of empirically informed observations which emerge as common themes in the available country-specific literature.

At the most general and broadest level, the common theme to emerge from attempts to assess the impact of labour exports and return is that the process tends to accelerate mechanisms of change already in motion, without altering the dynamics of change itself. Ranging from studies of the impact of capital flow from remittances and returns from abroad on the macroeconomy, to studies of regions and local communities where migration abroad and return have been concentrated, to surveys of individual households whose members work abroad, the general conclusion appears to be that the migration process tends to reinforce existing trends without making a strategic difference in patterns of change, or altering the social system significantly. I will elaborate this briefly.

With regard to the large inflow of remitted and transferred savings of emigrants, there appears to be little question that it has served to provide much-needed foreign currency to alleviate balance of payments problems in the macroeconomy of most labour-exporting countries. In the case of southern Europe for instance, Hudson and Lewis (1985) emphasize the structural dependence of the Greek, Portuguese and Turkish economies on migrant remittances, and hence upon changes in the labour markets of northern Europe. The figures they cite for 1979, based on World Bank estimates, indicate that remittances in Turkey were equivalent to almost 60 percent of the value of exports, those in Portugal to over 53 percent and those in Greece to almost 23 percent; in contrast, in Spain and Italy the comparable figures were a little more than 8 percent and less than 4 percent respectively (Hudson and Lewis, 1985: 8–9). Tsakok reports that in the case of Pakistan, remittances of Pakistani workers in the Middle East amounted to almost 80 percent of total merchandise export earnings in 1980–1 (Tsakok, 1982). Such figures reveal the short-term significance of remittances in terms of the hard currency they represent. But they also pinpoint sharp contrasts in the extent to which governments of various labour-exporting countries have become dependent on the inflow of migrant remittances for alleviating immediate social, economic and perhaps political pressures. Indeed, the contrasts appear to be much more significant than the similarities, cautioning against blanket interpretations.

A second broad generalization which is reiterated in much research on the impact of the large inflow of remittances, is that figures which appear to be vast sums of capital at the aggregate level are actually composed of relatively small budgets of individual households. And to the extent that attempts to pool and channel the savings of individual migrants through schemes intended to foster foreign worker-led industrial ventures or agro-industrial enterprises have in general either failed, or have been of marginal importance, the significance of remittances has not extended beyond the hard currency they represent. (See Papademetriou, 1984 and Van Amersfoort et al., 1984 for review and assessment of such government-sponsored schemes in labour-exporting southern European countries.) Once again, there are important differences in the extent to which governments have actively pursued policies aimed at channelling workers' remittances into priority investments. But even in the case of Yugoslavia, noteworthy for programmes which assign high priority to remitted emigrant funds and channel them in employment-generating directions, governmental schemes appear to have remained limited in scope and effectiveness (Morokvasic, 1984a). Hence accumulated savings of returnees, spent in small change in the hands of many, has in most countries become absorbed into the existing system, thereby losing its strategic importance. In other words, highly rational investment behaviour on the part of individual migrant households appears to have added up to a picture of wasted resources in the aggregate.

Studies on saving and investment patterns of migrant households in a variety of national contexts emphasize two salient trends: increasing consumerism on the one hand, and growing tertiarization through self-employment in petty commodity production and services on the other. Thus for instance, in southern European societies, the purchase or construction of a new house, together with expenditure on consumer durables ranging from cars to video recorders, appears to be the first common choice of investment for migrant households. Then depending on such factors as length of stay abroad, age of return, level of accumulated savings, investments in small trade or service establishments ranging from taxis and bars to haberdashery shops or the establishment of small manufacturing establishments of the craft type, primarily in construction-related sectors such as making doors, furniture and so on, appear to be the typical pattern (for reviews of country-based research see for instance, King, 1979; Reyneri and Mughini, 1984; King et al., 1985, on Italy; Papademetriou, 1983a, and Unger, 1984, on Greece; Morokvasic, 1984a, on Yugoslavia or Öncü, 1987, on Turkey). Remarkably similar findings emerge from research on investment patterns of migrant households in Jordan, Egypt and Syria, countries of the Middle East which have become heavily dependent upon outside employment. In the case of Jordan for instance, where Birks and Sinclair (1980) estimate that as much as half of the labour force may be working abroad, surveys (Keely and Saket, 1984; Findlay, 1984) underline substantial increase in the consumption expenditure of migrant households as well as proliferation of small-business ventures or self-employment, feeding into the ongoing building boom and population concentration in Amman. The prevalence of this pattern in a variety of national contexts suggests that regardless of whether emigrants gain industrial experience abroad, or attain new skills and formal qualifications, their future aspirations are shaped by the petty-bourgeois dream of self-employment. Industrial skills go to waste, not necessarily because of lack of will on the part of emigrants but because, given the very few areas of coincidence between the two economies, they cannot be put to use upon return. So long as the very conditions of stagnation and unemployment that led emigrants to search for work abroad in the first place continue to prevail, accumulated savings continue to be channelled towards houses, shops and services — the most 'rational' choice from the point of view of improving family welfare and security.

The aggregate result is that villages and towns where emigration and/or return is concentrated undergo commercial expansion; creating what Abu-Lughod (1985: 133) characterizes as 'an illusion of economic prosperity within unviable economies', or 'cosmetic development in the countryside' as described by Hudson and Lewis (1985: 25). The considerable social reordering in such communities, with some families moving into social prominence and others experiencing status reduction related to the 'luck' of going abroad, is very rarely accompanied by changes in productive structure, except in areas which already have the most dynamic economic environments.

The preceding paragraphs, intended to briefly suggest some of the common themes which run across the country-based literature on the impact of labour exports, hardly do justice to the richness of available research. Yet delving further into the voluminous literature on individual countries, while it would provide an opportunity for citing some of the best scholarly work in the field, would not necessarily add up to a new vision. So long as we lack concepts which will allow meaningful comparisons, much of the richly textured information provided by such studies would remain relegated to an uncomfortably large category of 'local' variations. The chasm between very broad generalizations on the one hand, and finely textured case studies on the other poses a theoretical impasse that has yet to be transcended on the question of labour exports from the so-called periphery.

Concluding Remarks

Over the past decade there has been a major shift in the salience of analytical issues in international migration research. What began in the 1970s as a critical reaction to classical models of migration in sociology or economics has progressively given way to analyses and research based on the premisses of an international political economy and a global system of inequalities. The challenge of the 1980s has been to step beyond elegant — and sometimes formalistic — models emphasizing the asymmetrical gains of the core and periphery in the international labour migration process, towards formulations which take into account variations in the incorporation and role of migrant labour among core economies, as well as the differential consequences of labour exports for countries of the periphery.

What the present review reveals is that only half of this challenge has been met. On questions such as alternative responses of the advanced industrial societies of the core to global crisis; differences in their recourse to foreign labour; as well as the variable experiences of immigrant labour within and among them, the conceptual groundwork has already been laid. The available literature provides fertile ground for developing hypotheses for comparative analysis, much of which is already on the research agenda.

By contrast, the dearth of analytical formulations on the variable consequences and impact of labour exports upon the so-called peripheral societies is striking. To lament the spurious character of research that does not take into account 'global structural determinations' has become almost platitudinous in international labour migration research. What has been ignored is that there is also *analytical* scope for different outcomes in societies under similar structural constraints and location in the global system, i.e. peripheral. In so far as we have not as yet stepped beyond a blanket approach to peripheral societies, the voluminous country-specific research findings which have accumulated over the past twenty years remain a veritable pool of factual information in search of a comparative framework.

8

TRANSNATIONAL CORPORATIONS*

Volker Bornschier and Hanspeter Stamm

Introduction

What is specific about transnational corporations (TNCs), what is their 'distinctive nature' (Dunning, 1981)? Aren't they simply firms like the many others that flourish in the capitalist world? Maybe TNCs are simply bigger and command more economic resources than the others, but do not represent a species of their own. Obviously, the business of TNCs is highly concentrated, but so is business in many economic fields that are organized only nationally. For example, the eight leading world manufacturers of passenger cars — all TNCs according to the standard specification (see below) — accounted for 75 percent of the world output of passenger cars in 1980. But it is not difficult to find higher concentration ratios of supply in more local or regional markets. Thus, neither size nor concentration, nor the command over technology *as such* represents any specificity on its own. What seems to make TNCs worth a chapter of their own in this volume is the fact that they represent organizations designed for capital accumulation on a world scale. This fact is also reflected in the most simple definition of TNCs: decision-making centres owning income-generating assets in at least two countries. Many researchers in the field suggest the more stringent criterion of owning income generating assets in six or more countries.[1]

Accumulation on a world scale implies that there exists a system and social processes beyond individual societies organized as (nation) states in the modern world. Joseph A. Schumpeter was an early proponent of such a conceptualization, arguing that 'capitalism itself is, both in the economic and sociological sense, essentially one process, with the whole earth as its stage' (1939, II: 666). Hence the link with the overall theme of the volume 'Economy and Society' appears. The modern world system does not simply consist of a great number of societies. Beyond these coexisting societies there are economic processes at the level of the world economy that affect all these societies and their states. At the same time, the rather decentralized social and political structure of the world system shapes the very logic of the overarching world economy, too.[2]

Transnational capital accumulation as the *differentia specifica*, however, is by no means a modern phenomenon. Various types of transnational business have existed throughout the course of history. First, the trade diasporas of ethnic groups must be mentioned as early organizers of exchange in world economies which seem to be traceable back to the Mesopotamian systems and were still of importance in recent times (Curtin, 1984). Second, the big chartered companies of the early centuries of the modern world system should be noted. These companies produced their own protection (Lane, 1979), built their own colonies and were active throughout all three main economic sectors: primary, secondary and distribution. They were especially important outside the domain of the emerging national states in Europe. Third, the transnational corporations of the nineteenth and twentieth centuries, with which we will deal here, came to the fore.

Thus, the specific feature about TNCs is their double nature: the combination of transnational business — which itself is nothing new — with a certain organizational form. The scholar who elaborated this organizational feature of the phenomenon and directed the research community to it was the late Stephen Hymer, to whom contemporary theory of TNCs owes a lot.

Theoretical Views on Transnational Corporations

Theoretical investigations of TNCs can be seen as closely related to the perception of their phenomenal growth and the problems arising from their activities. While up to the 1950s the (neo)classical theories of trade and direct investment[3] (Ricardo, Ohlin and others) seemed to be adequate for the treatment of the phenomenon of TNCs, the situation changed radically in the early 1960s. In 1960 a new era in the discussion of TNCs was triggered by Stephen Hymer's seminal dissertation thesis 'The International Operations of National Firms'[4]. Hymer, inspired by the work of Bain (1956) and Dunning (1958), pointed, for the first time, to the specific features of TNCs. Among these he identified monopolistic advantages, which allow TNCs to survive in foreign markets where domestic firms have — other things being equal — advantages. The advantages of TNCs — stemming, for example, from economies of scale in production or the control over resources and patents — help them to overcome barriers to entry in foreign markets as well as to protect their market position vis-à-vis local or TNC competitors once they have got hold in a foreign market. So monopolistic advantages allow TNCs to create and exploit imperfect markets.

Especially in economic theory, Hymer's ideas have been widely acknowledged, improved and refined, which has led to the emergence of a variety of more or less original and autonomous theories of TNCs, generally stressing the economically positive side of their activities. At the same time, researchers outside the classical economic sciences became aware of the growing weight of TNCs in the world economy and consequently included this phenomenon in the broader framework of theories of development and underdevelopment. Therefore, the present body of theory can quite simply be classified according to two main orientations, 'neoconventional' and 'critical' (Biersteker, 1978). Although the critical perspective does not represent a homogeneous theoretical body, it still owes much to the Latin American *dependencia* approach, which itself cannot be described as one uniform theory. The *dependencia* approach suggests an answer to explanatory shortcomings of older theories of modernization in Latin America. It offers a 'broad set of contemporary discussions about imperialism, global inequality and underdevelopment, that focus on the economic, social and political distortions of peripheral societies' (Duvall et al., 1981), which have their roots in the writings of such authors as Marx, Baran and Prebisch. It must be stressed that critical approaches in general are not theories of TNCs; rather, they represent more encompassing historical-structurally oriented approaches, aimed at explaining the 'development of underdevelopment' (Amin, 1974). Development thereby is not understood simply in terms of economic growth but also as social and political progress.

One of the common features of the critical perspective is its division of the world into a (developed) core and an underdeveloped periphery, which are entangled in a network of unequal, capitalist exchange relations.[5] This interdependence, however, leads to a permanent reproduction of dependence, which in turn hinders or even blocks development in the periphery. A great deal of the differences between various critical theories arise from their perception of the degree of possible development in this situation. While some authors believe 'associated-dependent development' to be possible (Cardoso, 1973), the stagnationists see the only solution for the periphery as revolutionary change (see for example Dos Santos, 1970 or Frank, 1969) and/or radical withdrawal from the capitalist world economy and 'autocentric development' (see for example, Amin, 1974; Senghaas and Menzel, 1976).[6] Within those theoretical perspectives TNCs become important as mediators of capitalist dependency relations. It is difficult to derive explicit hypotheses about their activities and effects from those general frameworks. Nevertheless, with reference to the conceptualization of Theodore Moran (1978), three broad hypotheses can be set out.

1. The advantages of transnational direct investments are unequally distributed between TNCs and host countries, because TNCs have the ability to absorb gains that could otherwise be reinvested.[7]

2. TNCs create distortions in the economy by displacing domestic production, utilizing inappropriate technology and distorting consumer tastes. In addition their behaviour leads to a worsening of income distribution.

3. TNCs may pervert or undermine the political system of host countries.

While in the *dependencia* approach the nation-state stood at the centre of analysis — external dependence was therefore taken more or less as given — in some new theoretical perspectives more weight is attached to the unity of the world system. In this perspective there is no distinction between processes internal and external to the system as they are all internal to the overarching world system.[8] So this approach allows a more general interpretation of the processes and the dynamics of the capitalist world system than the geographically limited framework of other approaches. Within such a framework TNCs, too, have been studied in more detail (see for example Bornschier and Chase-Dunn, 1985).

Some other approaches have further stimulated discussion in recent years, as for example the concept of the 'new international division of labour', which regards differential labour costs between centre and periphery as the most important determinant of dependence (Froebel et al., 1980). At this point one should also mention the more recent contributions of Stephen Hymer (1979), who at the beginning of the 1970s turned to a Marxist view of the problems attached to TNCs and addressed his theory of monopolistic advantages more and more to questions of underdevelopment. Those contributions, however, were quite sparsely noticed by other authors.

The line of argument against the critical perspective was often directed towards the conceptual shortcomings of the various approaches, which have prevented their systematic empirical testing. But in current research there have been some attempts at conceptualizing and testing critical perspectives as a whole (Moran, 1978; Duvall et al., 1981) and with special regard to TNCs (see Biersteker 1978; Bornschier and Chase-Dunn, 1985; Gereffi, 1983; Newfarmer and Topik, 1982; Newfarmer, 1985).

One of the more important disadvantages of critical research lies in its absolute orientation to development problems at the periphery. Implicitly assuming a balancing of effects in the core, critical writers seem to forget that the overwhelming part of foreign direct investment takes place in the core zone.[9] Even where research is concerned with less developed countries (LDCs), the simple zero-sum contention that if TNCs are to win, other actors — for example the host country — have to lose may not hold true (Biersteker, 1978).

The extensive criticism of TNCs arising in the 1960s and early 1970s brought many replies, mainly from business schools and the TNCs themselves. As stated earlier, economic theorizing on TNCs had begun in the early 1960s. As opposed to critical theories, 'neoconventional' writings offer a large variety of directly testable hypotheses on various issues. Their disadvantage lies in the preoccupation with purely economic questions such as growth, efficiency or organization of activities, and their confinement to the micro-level.

Since it is impossible to describe the development of neoconventional theories in detail, the following paragraphs name only the most influential contributions to the stream of theorizing. One is Raymond Vernon's seminal product cycle model which links the internationalization of firms to the developmental sequence of their products. New products (innovations) emerge in highly developed countries and spread from there all over the world through exports. This development is accompanied by a process of diffusion of the know-how of production: similar products are developed and sold by other firms, in turn lowering the profitability of investments. However, as production becomes standardized, its shift to more peripheral areas allows the maintenance of profits (Vernon, 1971, 1973).

For some time this theory was one of the most important instruments for explaining foreign direct investment by US firms. But as German and Japanese TNCs became able to reduce the technological gap between themselves and US TNCs in the late 1970s, Vernon's model showed some explanatory shortcomings, which at last led Vernon himself to doubt the viability of his product cycle model for the 1980s (Vernon, 1979, 1985).

During the 1970s, an influential group of economists around John H. Dunning refined and extended Hymer's concepts. Their effort resulted in a number of theories, which for Charles P. Kindleberger (1984b) are all more or less unoriginal replicas of Hymer's ideas — a fact that makes it rather difficult to distinguish between them.

Various approaches in industrial organization theory emerged in direct succession to Hymer's ideas. They treat questions of imperfect markets, oligopolistic competition and reaction (Caves, 1971, 1974; Knickerbocker, 1973). Theories which emphasize internalization of market functions as the central feature of TNCs (Buckley and Casson, 1976) aim in a similar direction. Such theories argue that internalization — that is, the vertical and horizontal integration of operations — and markets represent alternative ways of organizing economic activities (Hennart, 1982). It is argued that internalization of activities lowers transaction costs in imperfect markets.[10] Yet internalization may in turn lead to even more imperfect markets, for example where it is put into effect by mergers or unfriendly takeovers. In this context, location theory also received some consideration. Unlike other approaches, it is closely related to the classical theory of trade and explains foreign investment by pointing to features of host countries.[11]

For the present, the discussion seems to end with Dunning's (1981; Black and Dunning, 1982) integration of those different approaches into his 'eclectic theory', which combines owner-specific advantages, location theory and internalization-specific advantages[12] in an impressive mix, which now apparently belongs to the standard research equipment of economists interested in the study of TNCs.

Reviewing the theoretical discussion reveals the interesting fact that the vehement exchange of arguments between critical and neoconventional researchers of the late 1960s and the early 1970s has significantly calmed down. There may be different reasons for this. To begin with, public interest in TNCs seems to have declined[13] and it is not difficult to conclude that academic interest correlates considerably with this. Furthermore, some resignation among scholars in the critical camp may be observed. This is paralleled by the recent development towards theoretical perfectionism that has occurred in the neoconventional camp. Although the neoconventionalists have turned away from discussions with theorists of other schools of thought, even among the neoconventionals there have recently been signs of theoretical stagnation (Schlupp, 1985).

Stagnation, however, does not mean that the theories offered are already perfect. And in fact there are some avenues for possible further development and improvement. Apart from the long overdue integration of critical and neoconventional knowledge, as has for example been suggested by Biersteker (1978) or Newfarmer (1985), there are some other interesting ideas which surely deserve more attention. For example, Robert Gilpin, a political scientist, points to one fundamental problem in theorizing: 'the fact that economists don't believe in power; political scientists, for their part, do not really believe in markets' (Gilpin, 1976: 5). As a consequence he offers a politico-economic model postulating interdependent relationships of political and economic (TNCs) actors. Within this model, Gilpin is able to explain the growth of US TNCs as a result of favourable factors, both in the US and abroad, that is, the establishing of the Bretton Woods system and the rise of the United States to hegemony. The work of Stephen Krasner and others on international regimes also draws attention to global political conditions that favour or hinder world economic processes (Krasner, 1983). In addition, the contributions of economic historians, such as Mira Wilkins, Alfred D. Chandler Jr, Stephen J. Nicholas or Oliver E. Williamson, should be mentioned. Some of those approaches allow a possible reconciliation of the different theories. Economic historians generally point to the institutional and organizational roots of the foreign expansion of industrial firms, and in doing so they sometimes draw heavily on the writings of already mentioned neoconventional authors. The concepts of Williamson (1981) and Nicholas (1982, 1983), for example, are inspired by Caves's (1982) transaction-cost approach. The work of Alfred D. Chandler Jr points in somewhat the same direction (1969, 1977, 1980). In his approach, national growth of firms is a consequence of vertical integration and the formation of a multidivisional structure among the leading business firms. In this process, administrative activities are centralized and production is rationalized, which leads to the emergence of managerial hierarchies that are able to replace the classical family entrepreneur. This transition from family to managerial capitalism is also stressed in the later writings of Hymer (1979: 58ff.) and Bornschier (1976). The concept of managerial capitalism, however, has been challenged on theoretical and empirical grounds lately (Nyman and Silberston, 1978, see also Mizruchi, 1982), which in some instances has led to an integration of managerial capitalism in the framework of corporate elite approaches (Useem, 1980; Fennema, 1982).

Closely related to Chandler's theory is Mira Wilkins's (1974) interpretation of the expansion of US TNCs as a three-step process. The first step is characterized by foreign investments with little complexity. With the growing number of affiliates the establishment of an administrative supervising organization becomes necessary. In the second phase, the original monocentric approach is replaced by a polycentric system in whose setting the affiliates get (back) a certain autonomy which allows them to begin expansion on their own.[14] The growth of the affiliates and their own partial internationalization generate an even more complicated structure in the third phase: the conglomerate entangled structure. According to Wilkins, the model holds for TNCs in different sectors and times.

Findings

Transnational Business over Time

Although the extraordinary growth of the modern TNC represents a relatively new phenomenon, the historical roots of direct control over the production of goods and services in foreign countries can be traced back several hundred years. In historical perspective, TNCs are merely a new organizational form of the capitalist world economy, the origin of which has been dated to the long sixteenth century (1450–1640) by several authors (see, for example, Wallerstein, 1974, and other scholars in the world system perspective). Initially, exchange in this system of worldwide division of labour was confined to trade relations in the first place. Historical analyses, however, show that even under merchant capitalism big chartered companies, for example the British East India Company in the seventeenth century, already exercised some direct control of production processes (Choudhuri, 1978). In the eighteenth century big trading companies began founding foreign agencies, but most of the responsibility was in the hands of family members or independent agents (Wilkins, 1970). With the growth of world trade and industrial production — and the simultaneously growing importance of technological know-how — in the nineteenth century, the pressure to found affiliates increased, due to the need to open up new attractive markets and to secure access to raw materials. Independent agents played a major role in such activities, too, but as they were often unreliable they were replaced more and more by directly controlled affiliates (Nicholas, 1983; Williamson, 1981; Wilkins, 1970: 207).

British capital exports in connection with the construction of railways in Britain's colonies and in Latin America boomed in the second half of the last century. Yet these capital exports consisted in large part of portfolio investment which does not involve direct control (Edelstein, 1982). Direct investment by industrial enterprises in the US and Europe dates back in some cases to the early nineteenth century, but it was, with some exceptions,[15] restricted to small family entrepreneurs or licence arrangements with independent firms (Wilkins, 1970: 15ff).

The emergence of TNCs in the modern sense can only be traced back to the late nineteenth century. The lead was taken by big industrial enterprises in the US and Germany and in some smaller continental European countries, like The Netherlands, Belgium and Switzerland (Wilkins, 1970, 1974; Chandler, 1977, 1980; Franko, 1976). Transnationalization in Great Britain and several other European countries began somewhat more slowly, a fact that Chandler (1980) explains as the hesitating transformation of family to managerial enterprises. Apart from internalization of national operations and the emergence of the multidivisional structure as a result of the growth of the domestic market (Wilkins, 1974: 436; Chandler, 1977, 1980),[16] external factors have also been important. Export opportunities as well as the threat of loss of established export outlets, the desire to secure access to raw materials and the growth prospect of foreign markets have been fundamental preconditions for transnationalization; in addition, improved international transport and communication facilities have been favourable to the decision to go abroad (Wilkins, 1974; Nicholas, 1982, 1983; Chandler, 1977, 1980). All in all, 'aggressive and innovative enterprises' (Wilkins, 1974) and firms from highly concentrated sectors (Nicholas, 1982; Chandler, 1980; Bornschier, 1976) generally took a marked lead in going transnational.

While the already mentioned model of Mira Wilkins (1974) seems to have some validity in explaining the growth of American TNCs, the development of continental European TNCs shows, according to Franko (1976: 187ff.) a somewhat different pattern. Here, the monocentric structure — Franko calls it the 'mother-daughter structure' — was maintained longer because of personal or familial relationships between presidents of parent companies and affiliates, and the more personally structured pattern was only slowly given up in favour of impersonal managerial hierarchies because of the success of the US corporate structure.

The importance of transnationalization at the turn of the century can be illustrated with figures for the stock of US foreign direct investment in 1914. Although total stock was only about $2.65 billion, this figure equals about 7 percent of the US GNP at that time — a share that was only slightly higher in 1966 (Wilkins, 1970: 201–7).[17] While the foreign activities of mining, agriculture and petroleum corporations were concentrated in underdeveloped areas, manufacturing industry had its operations in Europe and Canada. Nevertheless, it seems necessary to point out that — at the turn of the century — a large number of foreign affiliates were still merely sales companies.

Contrary to the widespread opinion, US TNCs by no means had a monopoly of transnationalization in this early phase. Of the estimated total stock of direct investments of $14.3 billion in 1914 about $11 billion were held by firms in European countries, with Britain in a dominant position in terms of stocks (Dunning, 1983).[18] A look at the number of European TNCs in manufacturing shows that in 1914 a total of 37 mostly chemical or electrical enterprises had affiliates in at least one foreign country.[19] Contrary to US TNCs, European firms were almost exclusively confined to the European market and only hesitatingly ventured into other areas, especially into the USA (Franko, 1976). Nevertheless, for that early time Franko (1976: 8) concludes that German TNCs in manufacturing had a competitive edge over US TNCs.[20]

As noted earlier, transnationalization was not always successful. Examples like that of Dunlop, whose American affiliate operated only one year without loss between 1923 and 1936 (Jones, 1984), also reveal aspects neglected by the 'success story' (Nicholas, 1982: 630). In addition, the expansion of transnational business did not take a continuous course. There is a close relationship between waves of transnationalization, merger waves and economic stagnation (Bornschier, 1976: 482–91), and Franko (1976: 10) has pointed to the cyclical pattern in the founding of foreign affiliates by European TNCs. The generally more continuous evolution of US TNCs — favoured by European self-destruction in two wars and the shift of hegemony in the world system over the Atlantic — has made them the leaders in international direct investments over time: their share in the total stock of direct investments increased from 19.5 percent in 1914 and 30.4 percent in 1938 to 56 percent in 1960. At the same time the share of Western European TNCs dropped from 76.9 percent in 1914 to 39.8 percent in 1960 (Dunning, 1983). Since the early 1970s, however, this trend has been reversed again. The share of the US in the total stock of $386.2 billion in 1978 not only decreased to 47 percent (with the European share recovering somewhat to 41 percent), but also their share in the 50 largest industrial corporations went down drastically from 43 in the late 1950s to 21 in the late 1970s (Bergesen and Sahoo, 1985). During the 1980s the 50 largest industrials of the world distribute among headquarter regions as follows: 21 are US, 20 European, 5 Japanese and about 4 from semiperipheral countries.[21] This indicates a marked loss of the former US position. Furthermore, during the world recession the US turned from the leading capital exporter to an important importer of foreign capital. While only 2.6 percent of world capital flows between 1961 and 1967 went to the US, this share rose to about one-third in the period 1978–80 (OECD, 1981: 13; UN, 1983: 18ff.). With regard to capital exports, West Germany and Japan have markedly increased their shares[22] and other European countries have either increased (France) or at least stabilized (United Kingdom) their shares. In addition, TNCs from developing countries are now appearing on stage (see Lall, 1983; Wells, 1983). Yet, the operations of those (mainly Indian, South-East Asian and South American) firms are still of modest size and almost exclusively limited to investments in other LDCs.[23] The data on the changing relative shares of headquarter countries in total TNC business, should not obscure, however, the general growth of TNC activities in the post-Second World War period. The quite modest initial growth rates virtually 'exploded' in the 1960s, but declined again from the mid-1970s on. The sharp increase in foreign direct investment around the 1960s can largely be explained by an interaction of push, pull and rivalry factors, and this constellation was bolstered by the generally favourable economic and political environment as established for example by the Bretton Woods system, the functioning of which also reached its peak in the 1960s. While push forces arise from the concern of TNCs for new market outlets, which cannot be serviced easily by exports, pull forces stem from host countries' policies of industrialization. The last factor — rivalry — is a consequence of oligopolistic reaction among TNCs, that is, a follow-the-leader effect, as analysed by Knickerbocker (1973, see also p. 208).

The annual growth rate of total foreign direct investment from 13 OECD countries amounted to an average of 12 percent between 1960 and 1973 (OECD, 1981: 6). That figure approximately equals the growth of world trade and is about one and a half times larger than the GNP growth rate of the capital-exporting countries. Although the growth rates remained of this order up to the mid-1970s, real growth has slowed down due to increasing inflation (OECD, 1981: 12; UN, 1983: 18).

Capital flows to LDCs stand out against this world pattern. Between 1960 and 1968 flows from Development Assistance Committee (DAC) countries to LDCs grew at an average annual rate of only about 7 percent. This figure increased sharply to 19.4 percent p.a. in the period 1973–8 (OECD, 1981: 43). This increase of foreign direct investment in LDCs did not, however, affect the share of the LDCs in the total stock of foreign direct investment. At the end of the 1970s, this share amounted to about 30 percent, a figure similar to that at the beginning of the 1960s (Dunning,

1983). Although the LDCs do not play an overwhelming role in the transnational network, one still has to stress the comparatively more important role of TNCs in LDCs. This is manifested by the fact that in 1966–7 LDCs produced only 15 percent of world GNP, but hosted 30 percent of the total stock of foreign direct investment (Bornschier, 1976: 349).[24] Even more important is the LDC share in world payments for foreign direct investment (dividends, royalties and fees and related categories). The annual figure for such payments from LDCs was about $12.8 billion, which was about half of the world total of such payments, and these annual outflows were larger than the annual figures for fresh capital inflows, which amounted to about $8 billion per year (see UN, 1983: 19ff.).

In talking about capital flows, one should also mention the growing importance of reinvested earnings — which provide about 50 percent of the increase in the stock of foreign investment — and the financing of TNC activities with loans in host countries (about a quarter of the total increase in capital: see Vernon, 1973: 69; Niedermayer, 1979: 51ff.; UN, 1983: 19ff.). In addition, one has to mention a tendency, which has recently been observed, away from wholly owned affiliates to majority or minority participations, joint ventures and licence agreements. The kind of engagement, however, seems to differ according to technology (UN, 1978: 229; UN, 1983: 40–6; OECD, 1981: 31–5). Such observations reveal that a mere examination of international capital flows and stock measures underestimates the real impact of TNCs in the world as well as in the host country economy.

The sectoral distribution of TNC operations has also been subject to some changes. At the beginning of the 1970s, raw materials and services each held about a quarter of all foreign direct investment, with the rest being made up by manufacturing. Since then, the trend to investments in the services sector has continued while in manufacturing there is a tendency to divide production into separate production steps which may even be located in different geographical regions (Helleiner, 1973, 1975). Assembly production has become important in some low-wage countries of South-East Asia and Central America and leads — according to some authors — to a new form of dependence (Grunwald and Flamm, 1985: Froebel et al., 1980).

In global figures, the importance of transnational business is documented by a growing share of foreign affiliates in the overall sales of TNCs. By 1980 this figure had amounted to 40 percent of total sales (UN, 1983). In general, the foreign activities of TNCs have grown much faster than their activities in their country of origin.

The importance of TNCs as organizers of world trade has also increased. Trade between affiliates and the parent firm (intra-firm trade) has become more important, but estimates of its share in total world trade differ between various sources. Yet, one may at least impute about one-quarter to one-third of total world trade to intra-firm transactions (Berthold, 1980; Lall and Streeten, 1977).

There has been a growing number of small and medium-sized firms taking part in the process of transnationalization lately, yet the largest TNCs have a high and increasing share in total transnational business. The overall concentration is shown by the fact that the largest 350 TNCs of the world owned about a quarter of the total of about 100,000 foreign affiliates. These largest 350 had approximately 25 million employees worldwide. Their world sales were about $2635 billion, according to the UN (1983: 46ff.), a figure that equals 28 percent of the GDP of developed and less developed countries together. Furthermore, the largest hundred TNCs are growing even faster — at about 17 percent a year 1971–80 — than the rest of the TNCs (UN, 1983: 47; Dunning and Pearce, 1981). Finally, there is a growing number of public enterprises which have also started to go transnational.

This short overview of the development and size of TNCs shows only part of the their economic significance and their considerable power in the modern world. In order to obtain a more complete picture we must now turn to some particular questions.

Analytical Questions and Empirical Studies

Over the past twenty years a vast number of empirical studies addressing various subjects has been published. It is thus almost impossible to present an overview in a short chapter. Credit is due here to Peter B. Evans (1981), who did an excellent job in reviewing the vast literature that had appeared up to the late 1970s. As it is not possible to plunge as deep into the material as he did, it seems adequate to divide the empirical material into four, partly overlapping subject areas: 'TNCs and development', 'TNCs and labour', 'TNCs and the nation-state' and 'TNCs as organizations and control within TNCs'.

As already mentioned, research has been especially preoccupied with LDCs, a fact that limits the possibilities of generalizing several of the following findings. Whenever possible and of interest, however, we try to mention empirical material pertinent to core countries, too.

TNCs and development. Questions concerning the developmental impact of TNCs have received special interest from researchers in the past. Regardless of the underlying concept of development, studies addressing the growth effects of TNCs seem to be an adequate starting point in the discussion of development problems in general.

A large body of studies address the impact of TNCs on overall economic growth. An overview of these studies seems to suggest, however, contradictory results.[25] Yet many of these differences can be reconciled since they are in part due to insufficient design, lack of adequate control variables and differences in indicators and samples used in the various analyses.[26] The lack of distinction between short-term and long-term effects on growth is of particular importance for reconciling discrepant findings. A detailed look at all available studies and a reanalysis by Bornschier and Chase-Dunn (1985)[27] with an improved design and using large country samples (101 countries) confirm the evidence and conclusion of several earlier studies — that penetration by TNCs adds to overall economic growth in the short run while it reduces growth performance in the long run. This holds for world samples and for LDCs, while the effect for core countries is small or absent. In more technical terms, this finding is established as follows: if growth rates of GNP per capita over 6 to 20 years are regressed together with several control variables on weighted stocks of TNC capital at the beginning of the growth period and on TNC investment during the growth period, one observes a significant negative effect of stocks on subsequent growth and a significant positive one for investment on growth. The design to disentangle short-term from long-term TNC effects on growth was suggested independently by researchers in Great Britain, the United States and Switzerland, in 1975. Meanwhile these different effects on overall growth belong to what may be called a fairly consolidated finding for growth periods from 1950 to the mid-1970s. During the world recession starting in 1975 almost all previous predictors of growth in cross-national studies lost their predictive power, and so did TNC variables (Bornschier, 1985).

Negative effects of TNCs on growth in industrialized countries have been found by Hammer and Gartrell (1986) in their time series analysis of Canada. They suggest that Canada is a special case of 'mature dependency', since it is characterized by a long-lasting penetration, mainly by US firms. More research, however, is necessary in order to clarify the issue of whether and why effects of TNCs differ in core countries.

The impact of TNCs on changes in the industrial structure which may have effects on the performance of the economy as a whole has been repeatedly studied. The issue under debate is whether or not TNCs increase market concentration and/or competition. From the observation that TNCs prevail in highly concentrated sectors in their home markets (Buckley and Dunning, 1980; Bornschier, 1976; Caves, 1974) it has been concluded that they will also be active in highly concentrated industries of host countries. This contention seems to hold true for both industrial (Fishwick, 1982) and less developed countries (Newfarmer and Marsh, 1981; Lall, 1978, see also Newfarmer, 1985). Yet it remains unclear whether TNCs are only attracted by oligopolistic markets, which does not preclude that they may enhance competition once they have penetrated these industries or if they themselves increase concentration leading to negative effects as, for example, by means of oligopolistic pricing (Biersteker, 1978; Dunning, 1981; Caves, 1982). Empirically it seems difficult to establish a causal relationship which could allow one to evaluate the balance of negative and positive effects (Fishwick, 1982). Yet, on the whole, TNC activities seem to lead to higher industrial concentration. This is illustrated for example by Blomström's (1986) analysis of the manufacturing sector in Mexico or the various sector studies in Newfarmer's 1985 volume on South America, which, in addition, points out important differences between sectors. Data on the market entry behaviour of TNCs fits into this picture. Often entry takes place by the acquisition of existing domestic firms, and later acquisition of domestic firms is also quite common (Evans, 1977; Lall, 1978; Newfarmer, 1985). Nevertheless, for the method of entry the literature also reports differences according to industrial sector.

The question of displacement of domestic production and employment enters here. But still we have little conclusive evidence. Biersteker (1978: 103–18) finds only weak displacement effects in his case study of Nigeria, but points to an important relationship between displacement of domestic production and imported consumption patterns.[28] Closely related to these problems are questions of whether and to what extent local backward linkages are created by TNC investment, and of the influence of TNCs on entrepreneurial capabilities in the population of the host country. One may argue that growth-stimulating effects of TNCs in segments of the host economy do not add to balanced overall growth as long as backward linkages in the economy are lacking. Under such conditions, growth spurred by TNC investment may even lead to greater dependence and distortions in the structure of society (Biersteker, 1978). Again there are sectoral differences. Assembly production is a special case in so far as linkage and displacement effects are rarely associated with it (Helleiner, 1973, 1975), while in certain other branches of manufacturing industry linkage effects rarely seem to occur (Lim and Fong, 1982).

Related problems are technological dependence (Meyer-Fehr, 1980) and inappropriate technologies that may be introduced by TNCs in LDCs. The lack of systematic evidence seems to preclude any generalization (Lall, 1978). Effects of TNCs on trade and on trade dependence, and the question of decapitalization of host countries due to TNC activities have also received some attention. One of the main arguments in favour of TNCs is their alleged positive contribution to the trade and capital accounts of LDCs. Yet various studies (Reuber, 1973: 162; Lall and Streeten, 1977: 134ff., 142ff.; Bornschier, 1976: 384) have reported a negative overall effect on the balance of trade and the balance of payments of host countries, even if one restricts the analysis to export-oriented TNCs (Reuber, 1973). This unfavourable effect may be largely due to two syndromes: (a) the affiliates' high propensity to import factor inputs, and (b) the possibilities of using transfer pricing mechanisms within TNCs across countries. Conclusive findings on the extent of transfer pricing devices are still lacking. While Müller and Morgenstern (1974) and Niedermayer (1979) find significant transfer pricing effects, Biersteker (1978: 87ff.) and Lall and Streeten (1977: 153ff.) are not able to establish the systematic use of this mechanism to shift income across countries, except in the pharmaceutical industry.[29]

The previously mentioned observations combined with findings for effects of TNCs on capital imports and exports strengthen the point of the decapitalization hypothesis (Ochel, 1982; Bornschier, 1976, 1980; Committee on Finance, 1973; Biersteker, 1978; Lall and Streeten, 1977). The relationship between foreign direct investment and foreign borrowing has been analysed, too (Rothgeb, 1984; Pfister and Suter, 1986; Bornschier, 1982a). These studies suggest that capital penetration by TNCs adds to the increase in foreign debt of host countries (which may differ according to regions, as Rothgeb suggests). Such a relationship is indirectly supported by findings in an analysis by Schneider and Frey (1985), who identify the extent of bilateral and multilateral aid as important determinants of TNC investment.

The catalogue of questions relating to the influence of TNCs on growth could easily be extended, but we prefer to turn attention to some of the 'social effects' which are, however, related to growth problems, and, at the same time establish a link to the next section (TNCs and labour). Income inequality and development have received considerable attention (see Gagliani, 1987, for a recent review). Numerous studies have analysed the effect of TNCs on income distribution.

A review of fifteen studies on the question of the effect of TNCs on income inequality reveals that all except one report a positive relationship between TNC penetration and income inequality (see Bornschier and Chase-Dunn, 1985). A reanalysis by Bornschier and Chase-Dunn (1985) confirms these earlier findings in a sample of seventy-two countries. But while TNCs are associated with higher income inequality in LDCs, the opposite holds for core countries. Moreover, sectoral differences again seem to be important to the relationship in LDCs. TNC penetration of the manufacturing sector is significantly related to higher overall income inequality in LDCs, while no such relationship exist for the penetration of agriculture (see also Sullivan, 1983). The findings for TNCs and income distribution do not permit causal conclusions since sufficient cases for cross-national time series analyses on distribution data are lacking. One has to note also that in some theoretical approaches income inequality may be both a consequence and a precondition for TNC investment in LDCs. Other aspects of social structure have also been studied. TNCs were found to have an influence on overurbanization (Timberlake and Kentor, 1983). This may be related to the fact that TNCs operate in core areas of host countries (Blackburn, 1982). The unbalanced growth this implies is connected with a growing marginalization of broad segments of the population (Evans and Timberlake, 1980; Michel, 1983). Effects on gender inequality have been found in empirical studies, too (Michel, 1983; Froebel et al., 1980).

In theoretical contributions, distorting effects of TNCs on traditional culture are often mentioned. The problems extend from imported, inappropriate consumption patterns — often mediated by the international advertising industry — to influence by the international media business (Mattelart, 1983; Reiffers et al., 1982). Systematic empirical studies that address such problems are still lacking.

TNCs and labour. It is often argued that one of the most important incentives to invest abroad is labour cost differences between countries. This may hold true in the case of assembly production and related labour-intensive manufacturing activities, but not necessarily in more capital-intensive sectors. The observation that TNCs on average seem to pay somewhat higher wages than domestic firms applies for LDCs as well as for industrialized countries (Dunning, 1981: 272–303). This finding can largely be attributed to the fact that TNCs generally operate in modern industrial sectors. Yet high wages in the leading sector do not imply more social equality in the society as a whole. Higher wages paid by TNCs may strengthen the segmentation of the labour market, and a mere comparison of wages neglects the question of total employment. Actually, the already mentioned figure of 25 million people employed by the largest 350 TNCs worldwide seems quite modest when compared to their contribution to world production. According to estimates of the ILO (1981a, 1981b) about 45 million people work for TNCs, of whom only about 10 percent are employed in LDCs,[30] mainly in the semi-periphery. Although employment by TNCs has increased two and a half times between 1960 and 1977 (ILO, 1981a), a complete evaluation of their labour market effects must also take into account indirect effects which can arise from linkage and displacement processes (see p. 219). In an overview of existing studies the ILO (1976) is unable to suggest a conclusive answer to the employment effects, although positive effects may exist in some sectors (for example in the food industry). Similar conclusions are drawn by Meller and Mizala (1982) for South America and by Enderwick (1985), who reviews different studies. Positive employment effects, however, may be outweighed by distortions of the traditional labour market structure. Evans and Timberlake (1980), for example, suggest that according to their findings the negative effect of TNCs on equality is mediated by a disproportionate growth of the tertiary sector. Sullivan (1983) points to the negative consequences of sectoral income differences and Bornschier and Ballmer-Cao (1979) mention structural unemployment.

While these questions address LDCs, some research has been inspired by the so-called job export debate in core countries. The central issue here is whether the shift of production to other countries lowers domestic employment or, indeed, increases it by indirect feedback effects. Such studies are necessarily tied to various (sometimes rather problematic) assumptions. It is thus not astonishing that the evidence is mixed. In his sophisticated analysis of West Germany covering the period 1975–80, Olle (1983) estimates a net loss of 300,000–400,000 jobs caused by TNCs investing abroad, while estimates for the US reach from a gain of 279,000 to a loss of 660,000 jobs (ILO, 1976).

In connection with problems of the labour market, the bargaining position of labour unions deserves attention. Unions normally take a rather critical stance towards TNCs because they have no adequate organizational structure to cope with transnational business. Lately, however, one has observed a certain internationalization of the labour movement (Baumer and von Gleich, 1982) together with an intensification of the dialogue between unions and TNCs in industrialized countries (De Vos, 1981). But in some instances TNCs are still able to pursue explicit policies against labour unions (Hood and Young, 1983).[31]

TNCs and the nation-state. Researchers usually assume a conflictual relationship between TNCs and the nation-state which arises from the contradictions of national (development) policies and global profit-maximizing strategies pursued by TNCs (see for example Vernon, 1973; Barnet and Müller, 1974). A more thorough analysis of power structures, however, reveals possible alliances between TNCs, official and local elites (Evans, 1979). Thus a state's actions may be limited by the selfish interests of its own elites. Yet, this perspective does not contradict the observation that conflicts and hard bargaining between TNCs and state officials are relatively frequent because alliances of actors and the distribution of the gains between them are different things. Furthermore, alliances of the state and local capital against TNCs may also be possible (Evans, 1986).[32] Alliances between TNCs and local elites tend to favour the political exclusion of the masses. In cross-national studies there seems to be a positive empirical relationship between the dependence on TNCs and political exclusion (Timberlake and Williams, 1984), and social conflicts and political instability are higher when TNCs have a stronghold in a society (Ballmer-Cao, 1979).[33] Although political instability may be the consequence of a social setting to which TNCs contributed, it represents at the same time an important factor in the relocation decision of TNCs. In cross-national research one has observed that fresh foreign direct investment is negatively affected by political instability (Schneider and Frey, 1985), while contrary to common expectations the ideology of governments does not play an important role in the worldwide process of allocating TNC investment (Schneider and Frey, 1985).

The last few years have witnessed an improvement in the bargaining position of states vis-à-vis TNCs, which is reflected in more stringent codes of conduct regulations and tougher contractual terms as well as in the numerous nationalizations that have occurred (UN, 1978, 1983). Nevertheless, we have concluded from cross-national research over the 1960–76 time span that restrictive government policies against TNCs have often been contradictory (stop-and-go interventionism) and thus government measures in LDCs in general have not been very successful; indeed, the immediate impact of restrictive policies has been disadvantageous to overall growth (Bornschier and Hoby, 1981; Berweger and Hoby, 1980; Bornschier, 1982b). Although 'sovereignty at bay' (Vernon, 1971) has not become a reality, the ability of TNCs to shift their activities from one country to another still imposes severe restrictions on the policy alternatives of LDCs. The actual policy mix in LDCs may thus be contradictory.

TNCs as organizations and the control within TNCs. We have already mentioned important organizational changes that are suggested as necessary preconditions for the growth and the internationalization of firms. The literature has pointed to the emerging separation of ownership and control in large corporations since the 1920s (Berle and Means, 1967; Useem, 1980). Hence the problem of control in TNCs has at least two dimensions: first, one must ask who owns the shares of TNCs, and second, who actually decides on their business activities. Research in this field rarely considers TNCs explicitly; rather, it is concerned with large business firms. But, as we have seen, the correlation between size and transnationalization is very strong (Bornschier, 1976; Dunning and Pearce, 1981).

It has often been argued that, with the increasing dispersion of the ownership of corporate shares, top management has gained control over large firms at the expense of the classical family entrepreneur. In this line of reasoning, the separation of ownership and control has been accompanied by a transition from short-run profit maximization goals to long-run growth strategies. Recently the hypothesis of managerial control has been subject to criticism on various grounds. First, the question has been raised whether managers really act differently from family entrepreneurs who have certainly no less interest in securing the long-run existence of the firm. Furthermore, it has been possible to show that managers themselves obtain a growing proportion of their income in the form of company shares and dividends. Thus, they also earn elements of classical entrepreneurial income (Useem, 1980; Allen, 1981).[34]

Other challenges to the separation thesis (family versus managerial capitalism) stress the concept of financial capitalism.[35] Financial control exercised through the shareholdings of financial institutions (mainly large banks) is likely to limit the sovereign decision-making capability of managers similarly to the way in which big private shareholders are supposed to. In their analysis of the 224 largest British firms, Nyman and Silberston (1978) found only a very small proportion of firms that could not be labelled as owner controlled, that is, controlled by families, by other firms or by financial institutions. The importance of financial capitalism has also been stressed by other authors. In his research Mizruchi (1982) furthermore found a cyclical pattern of shifts between managerial and financial control in the United States since the turn of the century that was influenced by political conditions.[36] With regard to control patterns, the work of Grou (1983) points to national differences. While American, British and, to a smaller extent, German firms are able to finance themselves on their own, Japanese firms are directly linked to big financial conglomerates. Contrary to this, many large Swiss firms are still under direct family control.

Apart from formal capital participation which is obvious in interlocking directorates (Fennema, 1982; Ornstein, 1984; Stokman et al., 1985) informal and personally based networks have also been identified in the research. This has been termed a 'corporate elite'. It is constituted by family ties, and by membership of business associations and exclusive social clubs, and it exhibits features of a new capitalist class (Useem, 1980). Recently research has gone a step further, also studying articulations between this corporate and the political elite (Useem, 1984). This brings research back to the already mentioned question of the relationship of state, local and transnational capital.

Concluding Remarks

Having reviewed the research on TNCs over the last decades we would like to add some general observations which may also point to future areas of research not satisfactorily dealt with in the past.

The perspective opened by Stephen Hymer left unanswered an important question in his research as well as in that of his colleagues and followers. Some corporations command monopolistic advantages, but why should they not exploit them simply by exporting from one country to another? One conventional answer is to stress labour cost differentials. Yet this is limited, at least in general. Low labour costs do not necessarily imply low costs of labour per unit of production. John H. Dunning goes further in his integration of location theory into the eclectic approach, although not far enough. What we suggest as a future area of research is to look at the spread of TNCs as a joint result of two sets of monopolistic strategies: one pursued by corporations and the other by states. The interface of these two strategies seems to be the most fertile ground for the spread of TNCs.

Unfortunately there are several arguments against monopolistic practices, even among liberal economists. Thus the interaction of *two* monopolistic practices may be particularly unfavourable since they involve the risk of accumulating the disadvantages of both types of monopoly. Thus the claim of TNCs to bring progress to the world and the claim of the nation-state to be the natural and legitimate organizer of society — although they may have some truth — are frustrated by the very existence of this modern marriage.

Yet the problems involved may be especially pertinent to LDCs, where the rent-seeking character of the state seems to have produced problems of development that interact with the TNC as organizer of world production.

Obviously TNCs did not prevent economic development at the periphery. Having extended the layer of the semiperiphery, they may be considered to have introduced a more continuous ladder of levels of development. But, overall, development gaps in the post-Second World War world system have remained relatively stable.

For world development as a whole, however, and especially for Western core societies, TNCs may be looked at as a progressive force in the emergence and evolution of the capitalist state, a complementary institution to accumulation on a world scale. Thus, Raymond Vernon's vision of 'Sovereignty at Bay' may appear to be mistaken. In a sense, TNCs have made states stronger as supporters of capital accumulation. Whether TNCs have made states stronger at the periphery remains unclear, but there the subordination of states to the capitalist logic of accumulation remains more problematic.

If one looks at the world system in terms of a conflictual merger of two logics — the states' and corporations' — the role of TNCs in the rise and decline of countries as well as industries needs further study. Thus more studies over longer periods of time seem necessary, also in order to put current big business into perspective. TNCs after all are mortal, even if John K. Galbraith argued the contrary. In the long run, the once prospering steel giants, for example, have become weak and almost dying bodies that yearn for public subsidies.

While problems of overcoming underdevelopment have received much attention in the literature on TNCs, looking at world development and at core countries remains a vast field for future research.

Notes

* This chapter was prepared in the spring of 1987.

1. There are other, more specific definitions of TNCs as well, which will not be discussed here. For an overview see for example Dunning (1981) or Lall and Streeten (1977).

2. One of the most widely known writers who stress this structure of the 'world system' is Immanuel Wallerstein (1984 and various of his other writings).

3. The term *direct* investment refers to the direct control associated with the ownership of income-generating assets, i.e. it involves direct control of the entrepreneurial decision-making process. Foreign direct investment is then the term to characterize cross-national acquisition of income-generating assets by TNCs.

4. The doctoral thesis (on microfilm) was, despite its theoretical impact, not published until 1976. Charles Kindleberger, who supervised the thesis, was the popularizer of Hymer's ideas.

5. The concept of 'unequal exchange' has been elaborated in depth by A. Emmanuel (1972).

6. For this classification see Evans (1981) and Bornschier and Chase-Dunn (1985: 4).

7. This leads to the creation of a redistributive economy on a world scale.

8. The most prominent author in the world systems approach is certainly Immanuel Wallerstein (1974, 1979, 1980), but others such as Charles-Albert Michalet (1976) or Samir Amin et al. (1982) have also made important contributions to this kind of analysis.

9. One exception is the world system perspective, which suggests a further structural differentiation, the stratification inside the core which, however, fluctuates between periods of hegemony and periods of a more equal distribution of power among core states. Yet a lot of work in this theoretical tradition is still concerned with the periphery or with core–periphery relations.

10. See for example Rugman (1981), who especially stresses the financial diversification of firms and Caves (1982) who offers a good overview of the transaction-cost approach, which states that market functions are increasingly internalized as the new organizations turn out to be more efficient and less costly in transactions.

11. For a more detailed overview of economic theories see for example Buckley and Casson (1985), Dunning (1974) and Black and Dunning (1982).

12. The combination of the first letters of those three concepts leads to another term for the eclectic theory: OLI paradigm.

13. In addition, Cotteret et al. (1984), for example, show a significant improvement in public opinion towards TNCs between 1976 and 1982 in France.

14. This process can be described as the implementation of the multidivisional firm structure at the international level.

15. The earliest 'real affiliate' in manufacturing seems to be the Prussian daughter of the Belgian firm Cockerill, which was established in 1815 (Franko, 1976: 3). The first affiliate of an American firm was the — unsuccessful — London affiliate (1882) of Colt (Wilkins, 1970: 30). It must be pointed out that — following the information on France given by Kindleberger (1984a: 118–45) — enterprises engaged in the services sector originally took a certain lead in transnationalization, which later turned into a lag. Only recently has the service sector again become very prominent in TNC business.

16. See also Fligstein (1985) for recent findings on the reasons for implementation of the multidivisional structure.

17. The geographical distribution of this amount was concentrated in the closely neighbouring countries of Canada, Mexico and the Caribbean and the Central

American area (in total about $1.6 billion), but also Latin America ($323 million), Europe ($573 million) and Asia ($120 million) had substantial shares. Looked at by industrial sectors, raw materials (mining, agriculture and oil) were by far most important ($1.5 billion). The rising oil industry was especially important, with a stock of $343 million.

18. For Great Britain Svedberg (1978) estimates the share of direct investments in the stock of total foreign investments before the First World War at 53 percent.

19. The importance of European TNCs is illustrated furthermore by a comparison of the number of affiliates in manufacturing: up to the First World War American TNCs had founded 122 affiliates, continental European TNCs 167 and British TNCs 60 (Franko, 1976: 10).

20. See also the contributions in Chandler and Daems (1980), in which the common organizational features of American and German firms are stressed.

21. *Informationen über Multinationale Konzerne* (periodical appearing in Austria), various issues.

22. The share of West Germany in the flows of direct investments has increased from 7.2 percent (1961–7) to 17 percent (1974–9). The figures for Japan look quite similar: they increased from 2.4 percent to 13 percent during the same period (OECD, 1981: 11ff.).

23. UN data (1983: 19, 31) estimate the share of TNCs from LDCs as about 2 percent of total direct investment flows. Dunning (1983) calculates their share in the stock of direct investments in 1978 as 3.8 percent.

24. If one takes the stock of investment of TNCs in their home countries into account — a figure normally not included in TNC-statistics — the share of LDCs in total TNC-controlled capital is reduced and corresponds to the LDC share in world production.

25. Bornschier and Chase-Dunn (1985) review and reanalyse 28 studies that appeared between 1972 and 1983.

26. Especially important seems to be the distinction between stock and flow measures as well as regional differences. The latter, however, turn out to be affected by different weights of very poor countries in regional samples.

27. This reanalysis includes, apart from an indicator for TNC-penetration, measures of the per capita income, the domestic investment rate, exports and internal market size.

28. Biersteker (1978) distinguishes four possible ways of displacement: (1) displacement of small, artisan firms; (2) displacement of manufacturing firms by TNCs which produce similar goods; (3) change (shrinking) of market shares by indigenous firms; and (4) anticipated displacement in the sense that barriers to entry are raised by TNCs.

29. On the special role of the pharmaceutical industry see Helleiner (1981), Gereffi (1978, 1983) and Kirim (1986).

30. Again there are important differences between industrial sectors: the employment effects of TNCs in the mining sector are generally very limited, but in manufacturing they can be significant, depending on the technology applied.

31. In their analysis of the United Kingdom, Hood and Young (1983) find this behaviour especially relevant for American TNCs.

32. See also the vast literature on the protection of indigenous industries against foreign competitors (Krueger and Tuncer, 1982; Lall, 1978).

33. In addition Bollen (1983) demonstrates a negative relationship between

economic dependence and political democracy.

34. The article by Useem (1980) represents one of the best overviews of the state of the art in this field of research.

35. This concept dates back to Marxist theorists (like Hilferding) and has recently experienced a renaissance.

36. He demonstrates a drastic increase in managerial control at the beginning of the century, following the implementation of very stringent antitrust laws. The share of managerial control, however, has dropped since.

9

INTERNATIONAL ECONOMICS AND DOMESTIC POLICIES

Gary Gereffi

Industrialization has been the hallmark of national development in the twentieth century. The timing, geographical spread and consequences of this industrial growth have been uneven, however. The United States rose to a position of unparalleled economic and political dominance in the two decades after the Second World War, but by the 1970s the hegemonic role of the United States in the capitalist world economy was being challenged by Japan and the Federal Republic of Germany, which surpassed the United States in economic competitiveness. In addition, a number of newly industrializing countries (NICs) in Asia, Latin America and elsewhere have succeeded in significantly expanding their world share in the production and export of manufactured goods, which has allowed them to penetrate key markets in the advanced industrial countries and rival the global dominance of producers from the core nations (see OECD, 1979). This dispersion of manufacturing activities throughout the Third World, based initially on low-cost, labour-intensive processes, has also weakened the bargaining power of the shrinking numbers of industrial workers in the advanced economies, who face increasing pressure on their jobs, wages and working conditions.

These changes in the global economy have interacted in complex ways with domestic policies, especially in the developing world. The emergence of a global manufacturing system followed a period of world economic slump (the Great Depression of the 1930s, when most countries turned inward) and the severe disruption of the Second World War. Many Third World nations responded to the plummeting commodity export prices of the late 1920s and early 1930s by moving quickly towards systematic policies of import-substituting industrialization (ISI).[1] While the manufacturing output of advanced countries declined precipitously during the 1930s, the Second World War production demands actually had an expansive impact on the Third World countries who helped supply the belligerent powers (Gordon, 1988: 34–5).

The postwar economic expansion of the United States as the hegemonic leader of the capitalist world economy was fuelled by a decade of reconstruction in Europe and Asia. The revitalization of direct foreign investment (DFI) and international trade laid the groundwork for a new international division of labour, based on increasingly complex networks of industrial production and sourcing and new forms of geographical specialization (Froebel et al., 1981). The leading economies in Latin America (Argentina, Brazil and Mexico) sought to deepen their industrialization in the mid-1950s by opening their doors to new waves of DFI from the United States, Western Europe and eventually Japan. Whereas foreign investors in Latin America had traditionally concentrated on export-oriented projects in mining, oil and agriculture, postwar DFI emphasized import-substituting investments in advanced manufacturing industries like automobiles, chemicals, machinery and pharmaceuticals, whose output was destined primarily for the relatively large domestic markets in Latin America.

A set of East Asian NICs (Hong Kong, Singapore, South Korea and Taiwan) took advantage of the extraordinary dynamism in the world economy in a different way in the 1960s, and began to pursue policies of export-oriented industrialization (EOI) in order to generate foreign exchange via manufactured exports. During this initial phase of export expansion, the high growth of the East Asian NICs was founded on light, labour-intensive industries like textiles, garments and electronic equipment. In subsequent phases, however, South Korea, Taiwan and Singapore achieved success in much heavier industries less well suited to their natural factor endowments (limited raw materials, unskilled labour, and small markets), such as steel, petrochemicals, shipbuilding, vehicle manufacture and computers.

The development experiences of the Latin American and East Asian NICs raise a number of important issues about the relationship between economy and society. They show, first of all, that economic and political development cannot be examined in isolation from each other. International economic factors have shaped in significant ways the paths of national development in the NICs, but at the same time one needs to look closely at the role played by domestic policies, institutions and social coalitions in order to understand how individual countries responded to the opportunities and constraints presented by the global economy.

An interventionist, developmentally oriented state is common to all of the NICs, with the exception of Hong Kong (for the East Asian cases, see Johnson, 1987; Cheng, 1990; and Wade, 1990). Initially, strong state action was required to implement the economic policies associated with the early stages of ISI and EOI development strategies. In the recessionary environment of the 1970s and early 1980s, however, it soon became clear that ISI and EOI were complementary rather than mutually exclusive approaches, and a more flexible set of state policies was needed. Import-substituting governments were forced to promote exports, and export-promoting governments generally controlled imports, in order to earn or conserve scarce foreign exchange. State intervention thus was a means by which individual countries could transform their ties to the international economy, presumably to their benefit. A comparative historical analysis of the NICs allows us to examine, therefore, the possibilities and limits for restructuring domestic policies and institutions in order to create new bases of comparative advantage in the world system.[2]

This chapter will focus on the four most prominent NICs in Latin America and East Asia: Brazil, Mexico, South Korea and Taiwan. These countries have been selected for several reasons. First, they have achieved the levels of economic growth, industrial diversification, and export potential that define relatively successful industrialization in the Third World (see Gereffi and Wyman, 1990). Secondly, as regional pairs these countries are usually taken to represent two distinct development orientations: Mexico and Brazil have given primacy to an inward-oriented (import-substituting) model of development, while South Korea and Taiwan are associated with an outward-oriented (export-promoting) model (Balassa, 1981: 1–26).

These countries vary not only in their broad development strategies, but also in the ways they are linked to the world system. Foreign aid, DFI, international debt, foreign trade, and geopolitical factors have all played distinctive roles in shaping each nation's development trajectory. We can thus examine the degree to which these external linkages are opportunities for or constraints on national development.

This chapter is organized in three parts. First, the phases of industrial development in the Latin American and the East Asian NICs are compared, with an emphasis on their periods of commonality, divergence and convergence. This overview identifies several critical turning points in each country's industrialization experience, which are related both to the international context and to the domestic underpinnings of their national development strategies.

In order to help account for the similarities and differences in the development trajectories of the Latin American and East Asian NICs, the second section outlines a crisis-induced model of policy change that focuses on the international and domestic constraints associated with inward-oriented and outward-oriented industrialization. Standard economic explanations emphasize market size, natural resource endowments and human capital as the main determinants of the ISI and EOI development paths of the Latin American and East Asian NICs, respectively. An emphasis on these factors alone, however, is inadequate as a characterization of policy shifts in these countries. I propose, in contrast, a more political and institutionally based explanation of the development trajectories of the NICs. Economic policy changes and industrial shifts, in this view, are seen as a response to recurrent and often predictable crises in ISI and EOI development strategies.

The third and final section of this chapter uses this crisis model of policy change as a basis for providing a systematic explanation of both the divergence and convergence in Latin American and East Asian development patterns. In particular, I argue that the foreign exchange bind associated with the early phases of ISI was handled in quite different ways in each region. A key factor was the ability of the Latin American NICs to finance ISI from land-based rents (natural resource export revenues and tax proceeds), as opposed to the reliance of Taiwan and South Korea on massive infusions of foreign aid from the United States in the 1950s and 1960s to cover their sizeable trade deficits and fixed investments in import-substituting industries. This contrast had profound implications for the subsequent divergence of development strategies in the two regions (ISI deepening in Latin America and the growth of manufactured exports in East Asia). Similarly, the convergence of the Latin American and East Asian NICs toward 'mixed' strategies of import-substituting and export-oriented industrialization in the 1970s and 1980s is also attributable to inherent limitations within each strategy that make an exclusive reliance on either unsustainable in the long run.

Development Patterns in Latin America and East Asia: Commonalities, Divergence and Convergence

The NICs in Latin America and East Asia vary in both the timing and sequences of their industrialization efforts. A useful way to conceptualize their trajectories is in terms of historical-structural *development patterns*. These have three dimensions: (1) the leading industries that structurally define the development process; (2) the transnational economic linkages that are used to finance it; and (3) the major economic agents relied on to implement and sustain development.

Based on a broad historical view of industrialization in Mexico, Brazil, South Korea and Taiwan, one can identify five main phases of industrial development. Two of these are inward-looking: primary ISI and secondary ISI. The other three are outward-looking: a commodity export phase, and primary and secondary EOI. The subtypes within the outward and inward approaches are distinguished by the kinds of product involved. In the *commodity export phase*, the output typically is unrefined or semiprocessed raw materials (agricultural goods, minerals, oil and so on). *Primary ISI* entails a shift from imports to the local manufacture of basic consumer goods, and in almost all countries the key industries during this phase are textiles, clothing, footwear and food processing. *Secondary ISI* involves using domestic production to substitute for imports of a variety of capital- and technology-intensive manufactures: consumer durables (e.g. automobiles), intermediate goods (e.g. petrochemicals and steel), and capital goods (e.g. heavy machinery). Both phases of EOI involve manufactured exports. In *primary EOI* these tend to be labour-intensive products, while *secondary EOI* includes higher value-added items that are skill intensive and require a more extensively developed local industrial base. The principal phases of industrial development for the Latin American and East Asian NICs are outlined in Tables 1 and 2.

Each regional pair of NICs has followed a sequence of development phases that closely approximate the import-substituting and export-oriented ideal types outlined here, plus a 'mixed' strategy

TABLE 1
Development strategies in Latin America and East Asia: commonalities, divergence and convergence

Mexico and Brazil: 1880–1930	Mexico and Brazil: 1930–55	Mexico and Brazil: 1955–73	Mexico and Brazil: 1974–82	Mexico and Brazil: 1983 to present
		Secondary ISI	Debt-led secondary ISI	
				Diversified export promotion and continued secondary ISI
Commodity exports	Primary ISI			
		Primary EOI	Secondary ISI	Secondary EOI
Taiwan: 1895–1945 Korea: 1910–45	Taiwan: 1950–9 S. Korea: 1953–60	Taiwan: 1960–72 S. Korea: 1961–72	Taiwan and S. Korea: 1973–9	Taiwan and S. Korea: 1980 to present

ISI = Import-Substituting Industrialization
EOI = Export-Oriented Industrialization

in the most recent period. An analysis of these sequences, as shown in Table 1, suggests the following conclusions.[3] First, the contrast often made between Latin America and East Asia as representing inward- and outward-oriented development models, respectively, is oversimplified. While this distinction is appropriate for some periods, an historical perspective shows that each of these regional pairs of NICs has pursued *both* inward- and outward-oriented approaches. Rather than being mutually exclusive alternatives, the ISI and EOI development paths in fact are complementary and interactive.

Second, the initial phases of industrialization — commodity exports and primary ISI — were common to all four of the Latin American and East Asian NICs. The subsequent divergence in the regional sequences stems from the way in which each country responded to the basic problems associated with the continuation of primary ISI. These problems included balance of payments pressures, rapidly rising inflation, high levels of dependence on intermediate and capital goods imports, and low levels of manufactured exports.[4]

Third, the duration and timing of these development patterns vary by region. Primary ISI began earlier, lasted longer, and was more populist in Latin America than in East Asia. Timing helps explain these sequences because the opportunities and constraints that shape development choices are constantly shifting. The East Asian NICs began to emphasize the export of manufactured products during a period of extraordinary dynamism in the world economy. The two decades that preceded the global economic crisis of the 1970s saw unprecedented annual growth rates of world industrial production (approximately 5.6 percent) and world trade (around 7.3 percent), relatively low inflation and high employment rates in the industrialized countries, and stable international monetary arrangements. The expansion of world trade was fastest between 1960 and 1973, when the average growth rate of exports reached almost 9 percent. Starting in 1973, however, the international economy began to enter a troublesome phase. From 1973 to the end of the decade, the annual growth in world trade fell to 4.5 percent as manufactured exports from the developing countries began to encounter stiffer protectionist measures in the industrialized markets. These new trends were among the factors that led the East Asian NICs to begin to modify their EOI approach in the 1970s.

TABLE 2
Patterns of development in Latin America and East Asia

Mexico and Brazil

Development strategies	**Commodity exports**	**Primary ISI**	**Secondary ISI**	**Diversified exports (1983 to present)**
Main industries	*Mexico*: Precious metals (silver, gold), minerals (copper, lead, zinc), oil *Brazil*: Coffee, rubber, cocoa, cotton	*Mexico and Brazil*: Textiles, food, cement, iron and steel, paper, chemicals, machinery (Brazil)	*Mexico and Brazil*: Automobiles, electrical & non-electrical machinery, petrochemicals, pharmaceuticals	*Mexico*: Oil, silver, apparel, transport equipment, non-electrical machinery *Brazil*: Iron ore and steel, soybeans, apparel, footwear, transport equipment, non-electrical machinery, petrochemicals, plastic materials
Major economic agents	*Mexico*: Foreign investors *Brazil*: National private firms	*Mexico and Brazil*: National private firms	*Mexico and Brazil*: State-owned enterprises, transnational corporations, transnational banks (after 1973), and national private firms	*Mexico and Brazil*: State-owned enterprises, transnational corporations, national private firms
Orientation of economy	External markets	Internal market	Internal market and external market (Mexico's oil exports since 1975)	Internal and external markets

Taiwan and South Korea

Development strategies	Commodity exports	Primary ISI	Primary EOI	Secondary ISI & EOI (1973 to present)
Main industries	*Taiwan*: Sugar, rice *Korea*: Rice, beans	*Taiwan and S. Korea*: Food, beverages, tobacco, textiles, clothing, footwear, cement, light manufactures (wood, leather, rubber, and paper products)	*Taiwan and S. Korea*: Textiles and apparel, electronics, plywood, plastics (Taiwan), wigs (S. Korea), intermediate goods (chemicals, petroleum, paper, and steel products)	*Taiwan*: Steel, petrochemicals, computers, telecommunications, textiles & apparel *S. Korea*: Automobiles, shipbuilding, steel and metal products, petrochemicals, textiles and apparel, electronics, video-cassette recorders, machinery
Major economic agents	*Taiwan and Korea*: Local producers (colonial rule by Japan)	*Taiwan and S. Korea*: National private firms	*Taiwan and S. Korea*: National private firms, transnational corporations	*Taiwan and S. Korea*: National private firms, transnational corporations, state-owned enterprises (Taiwan), transnational banks (S. Korea)
Orientation of economy	External markets	Internal market	External markets	External and internal markets

ISI = Import-Substituting Industrialization
EOI = Export-Oriented Industrialization

Fourth, the development strategies of the Latin American and East Asian NICs show some signs of convergence in the 1970s and 1980s. To support this convergence thesis, it is necessary to distinguish two sub-phases during the most recent period. In the 1970s Mexico and Brazil began to expand both their commodity exports (oil, soybeans, minerals, and so on) and manufactured exports, as well as to accelerate their foreign borrowing, in order to acquire enough foreign exchange to finance the imports necessary for furthering secondary ISI. South Korea and Taiwan, on the other hand, emphasized heavy and chemical industrialization from 1973 to 1979, with a focus on steel, automobiles, shipbuilding and petrochemicals. The objective of heavy and chemical industrialization in East Asia was twofold: to develop national production capability in these sectors, justified by national security as well as import-substitution considerations; and to lay the groundwork for more diversified exports in the future. Thus the Latin American and East Asian NICs felt the need to couple their previous strategies from the 1960s (secondary ISI and primary EOI, respectively) with elements of the other strategy in order to derive the complementary benefits from simultaneously pursuing inward- and outward-oriented approaches.

There were further pressures in the 1980s towards convergence. The oil price shock of 1979–80, rising international interest rates, and growing protectionism in the advanced industrial countries combined to push all four of the Latin American and East Asian NICs to adopt similar adjustments in their development strategies (see Cheng and Haggard, 1987; Kaufman, 1990). These domestic policy shifts may be described as efforts to promote stabilization, privatization and internationalization. *Stabilization* measures sought to reduce inflation in the NICs by using the conventional policy tools of fiscal restraint and monetary control, together with restrictions on wage increases. *Privatization* meant a turn in all four countries to a more market-oriented style of economic management. This involved a move away from discretionary, sector-specific interventions and toward indirect, non-discretionary supports (such as incentives for research and development, and manpower training), deregulating foreign exchange controls, liberalizing imports, limiting the role of state-owned enterprises, and lessening government influence over banks and credit. *Internationalization* refers to measures taken in all four NICs to open up their domestic markets by removing restrictions on direct foreign investment, especially in the service sector (including banking, insurance, hotels and retail stores).

Notwithstanding these notable forms of convergence, there were also significant national variations among the NICs during this period. Heavy and chemical industrialization in the East Asian nations had similar goals, but in Taiwan the principal domestic agents were state enterprises, while in South Korea this phase of development was primarily carried out by large private industrial conglomerates (*chaebols*). This also had implications for the kind of industrial restructuring that was emphasized in each country in the 1980s. There were common export promotion efforts focusing on a new range of 'strategic' high-technology industries, such as semiconductors, computers, telecommunications and computerized numerical-control machine tools. In this phase of secondary EOI, there was less of a concern with export volume from labour-intensive industries, and much more emphasis on increasing the value-added in capital- and technology-intensive industries. In Taiwan, however, industrial restructuring also implied a rationalization in which mergers and joint ventures were encouraged in sectors like automobiles, advanced electronics and heavy machinery in order to overcome the limitations of the predominantly small-scale manufacturing firms on the island. In South Korea, industrial restructuring had an opposite meaning: namely, reducing the level of concentration among the *chaebols* by giving greater attention to small and medium-sized firms which are central to the diversified export of light manufactures.

Whereas exchange rate liberalization in East Asia led to the appreciation of local currencies in Japan, Taiwan and South Korea, in the Latin American NICs there was a sharp devaluation of their currencies. In Mexico, this led to a spectacular increase of labour-intensive manufactured exports from the *maquiladora* (bonded-processing) industries located along the US border, and also a renewed inflow of direct foreign investment in the mid-1980s. Brazil has had a more diversified profile in terms of manufactured exports, especially in consumer durables (like automobiles and auto parts), steel, capital goods and armaments. This reflects Brazil's more successful and sustained secondary ISI investments in the late 1970s. Thus the East Asian and Latin American NICs still show some differences in emphasis with regard to production structures, but all four NICs have moved to a more advanced stage of industrialization in which secondary ISI and secondary EOI are combined.

A Crisis Model of Policy Change in the NICs: The Limits of ISI and EOI

This overview of the development sequences of the Latin American and East Asian NICs has brought to light several critical turning points in each country's industrialization experience. This raises a number of key questions. What causes the broad cross-regional development patterns — commonalities, divergence and convergence — that have been noted? When a particular development approach is no longer viable, what factors influence a country's choice of subsequent strategy? In particular, why did Latin American NICs respond to a crisis in primary ISI by a continued emphasis on supplying the domestic market through secondary ISI, while the East Asian NICs responded to a similar crisis by adopting an export-oriented approach? Why did the NICs in both regions appear to be converging toward a 'mixed' model in the 1980s which is simultaneously inward- and outward-oriented?

To answer these questions one needs a comparative perspective on policy change that is both historical and structural. As a starting point, it is important to distinguish between development 'patterns', which are clusters of interrelated economic outcomes (see Table 2), and development 'strategies' (Table 1), which can be defined as 'sets of policies that shape a country's relationship to the global economy and that affect the domestic allocation of resources among industries and distinct social groups' (Gereffi and Wyman, 1987: 11). Development strategies thus define and mediate a country's relationship to the international environment, as well as embodying domestic priorities regarding economic growth and equity.

Government decision making in capitalist societies is often pragmatic and incremental rather than strategic, responding to immediate crises and short-term dilemmas rather than to long-range plans and comprehensive schemes for change (see Kaufman, 1990; Cheng, 1990). With regard to the NICs, the discussion of 'import substitution' and 'export promotion' is frequently misleading because this distinction is ignored: the domestic policies associated with ISI and EOI can refer to short-term defensive tactics as well as long-term development strategies. The fact that many economic policies are motivated by crisis situations does not invalidate the notion of development strategies, though, since they still retain much of their capacity to influence subsequent decisions even if they emerge as post hoc constructs.

The main crisis situations that generate defensive reactions or strategic shifts are of two sorts. There are *external crises*, such as wars, world economic depressions, or severe raw material shortages (for example the oil crisis of the 1970s). These crises test a country's capacity to adjust to a radically changed external environment, but they are not usually predicted or planned for in advance. In addition to these catastrophic external events, there are also *developmental crises* inherent in particular development strategies, such as ISI or EOI. These developmental crises are the result of systematic constraints that lead countries periodically to modify or adapt a given economic orientation.

To better understand this process of crisis-induced policy change, one must examine both the motives and the limits associated with ISI and EOI. The original justification given for ISI in Latin America was not that it was an economic panacea, but rather that it allowed nations in the region to take advantage of particular opportunities presented by their abundant natural resource base and relatively large domestic markets. Thus it presented greater possibilities for industrial diversification and increases in GDP per capita than the commodity export model did.

Similarly, the East Asian nations had varied motives for undertaking EOI. For Taiwan and South Korea, it was primarily a means of acquiring needed foreign exchange when the US government announced in the late 1950s that it planned to reduce official aid disbursements to these countries; Hong Kong, as a commercial entrepôt, had no industrial alternative to EOI because it had a small domestic market and no agricultural hinterland; Singapore turned to EOI for reasons similar to Hong Kong's when it was dissociated from Malaysia; one of Malaysia's primary goals in adopting EOI was employment creation; and Indonesia was strongly inclined to move toward EOI when its oil revenues began to fall. The fact that countries adopted EOI for different reasons is important in order to know the conditions under which this strategy is viewed as successful by the countries pursuing it. The choice of EOI or ISI for whatever purpose, however, implies potential constraints.

As a development strategy, ISI confronts four main limitations. The first is that, paradoxically, given its advocacy on the grounds of enabling countries to escape from the foreign exchange bind associated with late industrialization, it tends to cause even greater foreign exchange vulnerability. This is because ISI is import intensive, and gives rise to the need for more intermediate and capital goods imports to the extent that consumer goods production advances. Indeed, secondary ISI was relatively successful in Latin America because it was implemented during a period of unusually favourable commodity prices induced by the Korean War (Fishlow, 1985: 128). A related problem is that standard ISI policies like overvalued exchange rates tend to discourage exports.

Second, import substitution also gives rise to sectoral imbalances. Industrial production tends to be emphasized at the expense of agricultural output. Food production in Latin America has not been able to keep pace with urban demand, and industry has been unable to generate enough jobs to absorb the effects of rapid population growth and migration to the cities. In addition, agricultural exports have a tendency to fall, thus further reducing the availability of foreign exchange.

Third, ISI tends to generate fiscal disequilibria as the state has increasingly been called upon to subsidize the continuing investments in industry from its own revenue. This leads to a vicious circle: increased government expenditure fuels accelerating inflation, which aggravates the balance of payments problem by further overvaluing the exchange rate, thus curbing the appetite of private sector entrepreneurs for productive investment in export industries.

Finally, there were real limits to ISI's potential as a source of continuous economic growth, given the severe income inequalities that characterized Mexico, Brazil, and most of the other Latin American nations. In addition, the capital-intensive technology used in advanced ISI industries diminished its job creation impact (Sunkel and Paz, 1970: 361–3). Paradoxically, the export sector not only induced the ISI process, but also constituted a real limit on it. The success of ISI in the finished consumer goods sector did not truly *substitute* for imports in an absolute sense, but rather *displaced* imports toward the intermediate and capital goods industries that would become the ultimate target of ISI efforts.

Although EOI has been viewed by some as the new 'development orthodoxy' for Third World nations based on the extraordinary dynamism achieved by the so-called 'Gang of Four' (Hong Kong, Singapore, South Korea and Taiwan) in East Asia, it should be emphasized that EOI is not a universal route to success either. Three conditions must be present for EOI to produce good results: (a) the maintenance of favourable prices for exports and stability in the prices of imports; (b) continued economic growth in key overseas markets, typically the United States, Western Europe and Japan; and (c) a non-protectionist world trading atmosphere. By the late 1970s, the existence of each of these conditions was being called into question.

There are also other vulnerabilities inherent in EOI. The first is what can be called a 'fallacy of composition' — if all developing countries tried to pursue export-led growth at the same time, the ensuing competition would drive down the gain for all (Fishlow, 1985: 138). A high degree of openness has two related disadvantages: it makes an economy more susceptible to external shocks, and the marginal gains from trade tend to diminish as economies become progressively more open. It is also important to note that EOI, like ISI, is import intensive. It requires a high volume and diverse range of imports to satisfy the input needs of a rapidly expanding export economy, especially one that is small or lacking in natural resources. Finally, EOI employment is often more unstable than traditional manufacturing employment, particularly if foreign-dominated export-processing zones are a main component of a country's export structure.

An analysis of the constraints inherent in ISI and EOI is crucial in order to clarify the nature of the development choices facing the NICs. Both ISI and EOI are susceptible to recurring balance of payments problems, rooted in a negative trade balance, heavy foreign indebtedness, the flight of substantial amounts of private capital, and so on. When confronting a balance of payments problem, a nation has a variety of possible options. The most obvious are: (a) *increase exports* via primary commodities or manufactured items; (b) *decrease imports*, which could involve import-substituting local production (by foreign or local companies), the restriction of imports (for example to essential items), or simply doing without most imported goods which runs the risk of a severe recession; and (c) *finance imports* through economic aid, borrowing from abroad, or domestic savings. These options will be examined below in terms of the different industrial paths the Latin American and East Asian NICs took after primary ISI.

Explaining Divergence and Convergence in Latin American and East Asian Development

Thus far I have identified key turning points or periods of transition in the development patterns of the Latin American and East Asian NICs (Table 1), with the preceding section indicating that these structural choice points are in part the product of systematic constraints or vulnerabilities inherent in the particular development strategies pursued by each country. Attention will now be focused on two major transitions highlighted by this cross-regional comparison: the *divergence* of the secondary ISI and the primary EOI approaches favoured by the Latin American and East Asian NICs respectively, following their common experience with primary ISI; and the *convergence* of the Latin American and East Asian NICs around 'mixed' ISI and EOI strategies in the 1970s and 1980s which nonetheless retain strong elements of national diversity.

An analysis of these turning points is important because it sheds light on the elements of domestic policy choice that shaped the decisions that pushed the development process in one of several possible directions. Whether these decisions are strategic or incremental, they reflect the kinds of internal and external pressure that lead nations along different industrial paths.

Cross-Regional Divergence: Secondary ISI in Latin America vs. Primary EOI in East Asia

The fact that the Latin American and East Asian NICs went through a similar phase of primary import substitution is not unusual, since every country except Great Britain began its industrialization efforts this way. What differentiates countries is how and when they first experienced ISI, and what ISI led to. My central argument is that we cannot understand the cross-regional divergence in development strategies in the Latin American and East Asian NICs without first examining how primary ISI was carried out in these countries. More specifically, given that one of the distinguishing (and limiting) features of ISI is its import-intensive nature, the subsequent evolution of a nation's industrial development will be strongly influenced by how 'early ISI' was financed.

A standard explanation of why the Latin American and East Asian NICs diverged after primary ISI would focus on certain country-specific characteristics, especially natural resource endowments and internal market size. Economists have long argued that foreign trade is much more important to small economies than to large ones. With few natural resources and relatively small markets, this argument goes, the East Asian countries had no choice but to pursue primary EOI. The Latin American countries, in contrast, were thought to have had large enough potential markets, coupled with their diverse array of export commodities (for example minerals, petroleum, agricultural goods), to make secondary ISI feasible.

It would be foolish to argue that factors such as natural resource endowments or size of the internal market do not play a major role in the determination of national development trajectories. Confining oneself to these factors alone, however, asserts too narrow an explanation for the outcomes of policy deliberations. The correlation between a country's size and its economic policies, for example, is far from perfect. Furthermore, the East Asian NICs are not really small in market terms, relative to many other developing countries. A comparative analysis of the causes and consequences of development strategies must consider choice as a real phenomenon to be explained.

The persistence of ISI in Latin America and the turn to EOI in East Asia are both related to how primary ISI was paid for in the two regions. The existence of plentiful natural resources in Mexico and Brazil provided the wherewithal for deepening ISI (that is, carrying it into its consumer durable, intermediate and capital goods phases) in the late 1950s and 1960s, as export revenues and tax proceeds helped maintain very respectable growth rates. Financing ISI from land-based rents, however, shaped the style of industrialization in these countries in several major ways (Keesing, 1981; Ranis, 1981).

First, abundant natural resources allow a country to postpone or avoid making its industries competitive at a world level, since resource-rich economies are often characterized by overvalued exchange rates, protected domestic markets, relatively high wages in the non-agricultural sector, low real interest rates, and inflationary pressures generated by monetary expansion. Hence it has proven difficult for the Latin American nations to expand their manufactured exports amidst booming commodity exports.

Second, even when episodes of policy liberalization are recorded in an effort to improve competitiveness, the system is much more vulnerable to backsliding in response to inevitable oscillations in the terms of trade. This produces the familiar liberalization/interventionist cycles in Latin America as external shocks are felt and then recede.[5]

Third, when the state decides to use a country's resource wealth to subsidize ISI, a particularly durable supporting social coalition tends to be formed, including not only the raw material exporters themselves but also urban industrialists, organized labour, and the civil servants who parcel out the specific benefits of ISI. This reduces the willingness or capacity of the state to withdraw the 'goodies' from the major vested interest groups when a change is deemed necessary.

Finally, ISI in the Latin American NICs has tended to exacerbate rather than ameliorate their dismal income distribution situation. It did nothing to improve the sectoral articulation within these economies, it was insufficiently labour intensive and decentralized to have much of a job creation impact (especially secondary ISI), and ultimately it led to the deterioration of the agro-extractive export sectors that were its main domestic source of economic backing.

The financing of primary ISI in the East Asian NICs was radically different. Taiwan and South Korea, lacking an abundance of traditional natural resources, paid for ISI in the 1950s and early 1960s with massive inflows of foreign aid from the United States. It is widely acknowledged that the Korean and Taiwanese economies could not have survived in the 1950s without American assistance. Between 1951 and 1965, $1.5 billion in economic aid and $2.5 billion in military aid was sent to Taiwan by the United States; South Korea received a similar amount of American aid in the 1953–61 period, with $2.6 billion earmarked for economic assistance and $1.6 billion for military assistance. Aid financed 40 percent of fixed investment in Taiwan and 80 percent in South Korea. Concessional capital flows were used to purchase 70 percent of the imports coming into South Korea, as well as to pay 90 percent of the balance of trade deficit in Taiwan (Jacoby, 1966; Cole, 1980).

Despite the geopolitical importance of these two nations to the United States as bulwarks against Asian communism, as articulated by George Kennan's famous 'containment doctrine', American aid of this magnitude could not continue indefinitely. When US aid officials announced in the late 1950s that this foreign assistance was going to be curtailed, it forced Taiwan and South Korea to address the question of where they would obtain needed foreign exchange once the aid flows ceased. The US government took advantage of the vulnerability of these two countries and lobbied hard to make continued aid conditional on a two-pronged shift in strategy in Taiwan and South Korea: a greater role for exports, thus replacing the ISI approach, followed in the 1950s; and more openness to private capital, especially direct foreign investment.[6]

The differences in how the Latin American and East Asian NICs financed primary ISI had profound implications for their subsequent development strategies. Mexico and Brazil could continue to rely on natural resource exports to help pay for ISI after 1955, although an important new actor joined the coalition that supported ISI 'deepening' — transnational corporations (TNCs). These large foreign manufacturers were prominent in the industries that were to be the new sources of dynamism in the Latin American NICs: automobiles, electrical appliances, chemicals, pharmaceuticals, heavy machinery and so on (see Table 2). The hope was that by broadening the range of local production to include the consumer durable, intermediate and capital goods that were causing a big drain on these countries' balance of payments, continued economic growth would be assured (Gereffi and Evans, 1981). While these expectations were overly optimistic, since the balance of payments deficits endemic to ISI have continued to plague Mexico and Brazil, the key point is that none of the main economic actors in these countries had a strong interest in changing the logic of ISI in order to promote competitive manufactured exports.

Foreign capital, private and public, thus played very different roles in the Latin American and East Asian NICs during and after primary ISI. The TNCs that came into Mexico and Brazil to help implement secondary ISI were initially content to supply protected domestic markets, while some of these same firms entered the newly established export-processing zones in Taiwan and South Korea in the late 1960s and early 1970s to produce manufactured items for export. The lesson here seems to be that economically powerful TNCs, under the right conditions, are susceptible to political pressures to contribute to either ISI or EOI development objectives. Thus Brazil and Mexico had some success in the 1970s, requiring foreign automobile manufacturers to generate increasing export revenues as a condition for continuing to supply their domestic markets (Gereffi and Evans, 1981; Bennett and Sharpe, 1985).

In Taiwan and South Korea, the foreign capital that financed primary ISI was public (government-to-government aid) rather than private (see Haggard and Cheng, 1987). This meant that the US government had considerable leverage over economic policymaking in these countries. It was, therefore, much more difficult for the East Asian NICs to politically justify or 'afford' the continued protectionism implied by ISI because it contravened the interests of their principal financier (the United States government).

Despite the influence of the United States, Taiwan and South Korea did not simply succumb to US pressures. Vulnerability does not assure compliance, and there were several indications that both East Asian nations worked hard to expand their room for manoeuvre and choice. Contrary to the prevailing impression that Taiwan and South Korea moved inevitably and directly from primary ISI to primary EOI in the early to mid-1960s, in fact both countries, motivated by defence considerations, flirted with the idea of secondary ISI before making the transition to primary EOI. Korea's first Five-Year Plan (1962–6) was adapted from an earlier plan that stressed ISI deepening as the best means to achieve an integrated industrial structure, and between 1961 and 1963 the military regime considered the option of self-sufficiency. In Taiwan, as well, state technocrats tried secondary ISI: automobile assembly plants were built and a large steel mill conceived, both justified on national security grounds. However, the cost inefficiency of advanced ISI, an unfavourable balance of payments situation, and an increasingly acute problem of surplus labour militated against this choice (Cheng, 1990).

The decision to adopt EOI in Taiwan and South Korea was neither inevitable nor easy. But it did have a number of positive consequences for these countries. The economic gains in industrial competitiveness, full employment and steady growth in manufactured exports[7] are among the most obvious, but equally important perhaps is the fact that EOI liberated the East Asian NICs from their sense of acute vulnerability vis-à-vis US aid officials. By the end of 1965 South Korea had already reached a settlement with Japan that called for sizeable financial flows from Japan over the next decade,[8] thus beginning the process of reducing its dependency on the United States.

The Convergence of ISI and EOI in the 1970s and 1980s: Recapturing National Diversity

By the early 1970s the Latin American and East Asian NICs were confronted by a series of difficulties generated by the inherent constraints of secondary ISI and primary EOI respectively, and were thus forced to consider modifications of these approaches. Mexico and Brazil found their chronic balance of payments deficits growing larger in the late 1960s and inflation was getting worse in both countries. At the start of the 1970s Taiwan and South Korea were facing a three-dimensional challenge: from *below*, by emerging NICs like the Philippines, Indonesia, Malaysia and Thailand who were competing in many of the same low-wage manufacturing export industries that East Asia's 'Gang of Four' so successfully exploited during the previous decade; from *above*, creeping protectionism in the major markets for their industrial exports (the United States and the nations of Western Europe); and from *within*, the shrinking labour pool, and hence rising wage levels, especially in Taiwan, coupled with growing political unrest in South Korea.

Each country, as it turns out, tried to resolve the problems of secondary ISI and primary EOI by incorporating elements of the other approach. The Latin American NICs adopted the strategy of diversified export promotion, but with continued ISI deepening. In contrast to the commodity export model, the key feature of this approach was its emphasis on a diversification of exports, especially manufactures, rather than the quantitative expansion of a single commodity or a small number of commodities. In

Mexico, this meant maintaining and even extending its extraordinary export variety (prior to the oil boom of the 1970s no single product, with the exception of cotton for a few years, had accounted for more than 10 percent of Mexico's postwar exports); for Brazil this meant a decline in the share of coffee from 42 percent of exports in the mid-1960s to 13 percent in 1974 (Gereffi and Evans, 1981: 42). Secondary ISI efforts continued in this phase, especially in the intermediate and capital goods sectors.

The East Asian NICs were motivated to go into heavy industries, especially steel and heavy machinery, in part by defence considerations. In 1973–4 both South Korea and Taiwan launched heavy and chemical industrialization (HCI) programmes to upgrade their industrial structures. In both countries secondary ISI was selective rather than systematic, and it was designed to sustain rather than supplant national exports as the basis for growth. The East Asian NICs used secondary ISI to deepen EOI in different ways, however. South Korea followed a 'big push' approach, in which HCI was turned into the new centrepiece of the country's export structure, while Taiwan pursued a 'gradualist' approach, based primarily on the strengthening of existing industries with the state becoming the principal producer in HCI (Cheng, 1990).

As in the preceding section, our understanding of the dynamics of these new development phases requires us first to return to the prior phase in order to highlight shifts in the key economic actors who were responsible for carrying these strategies out. Secondary ISI in the Latin American NICs tended to rely on TNCs as a primary agent of change because they possessed the requisite technology, capital and managerial and marketing expertise for establishing the consumer durable, intermediate input and capital goods industries implied by this approach. Nonetheless, the attempt at deepening was initiated without necessarily halting the expansion of primary ISI in response to growing consumer demand.

Secondary ISI in Mexico did not advance as far as it did in Brazil, partly for geographical and historical reasons. Both its stable currency and its geographical proximity to the United States permitted Mexico to rely far more during the late 1950s and 1960s on imports of intermediate and especially capital goods in order to maintain high rates of growth, whereas Brazil had greater incentives to push for domestic production of machinery and assorted intermediate items. Mexico also had less room to manoeuvre because its economic ties with the United States were much closer.[9] In Brazil as well as Mexico, ISI industries had similar patterns of ownership: local private companies were prominent in the consumer non-durable goods sector, state-owned firms tended to produce intermediate products such as steel, fertilizers and basic chemicals, while the TNCs were concentrated in the consumer durable and capital goods sectors (Evans and Gereffi, 1982).

The export diversification/ISI-deepening strategy adopted by Mexico and Brazil in the 1970s is one obvious response to the balance of payments deficits created by secondary ISI, since it aimed to increase export revenues from two already established sources: the traditional natural resource industries, and the industrial TNCs who were being encouraged to add manufactured exports to an expanding list of national 'performance requirements' upon which access to the domestic market and local incentives was conditioned. But a tremendous new opportunity presented itself in the 1970s. The main actor in this case was not TNCs, but rather large international commercial banks (see Table 2) which had access to a seemingly inexhaustible supply of loan capital in the form of petrodollars following the 1973–4 oil price increases by the Organization of Petroleum Exporting Countries. The Mexican and Brazilian governments increasingly turned to loans to finance the investments required by their two-pronged strategy — i.e. a further deepening of their industrial sectors and an increase in exports.

The new opportunity soon turned sour, however, as soaring interest rates led many borrowers into an escalating debt crisis, with Brazil and Mexico leading the pack as the Third World's largest debtor nations. The International Monetary Fund (IMF) became the key actor in managing the international debt crisis, and it made access to its structural adjustment loans contingent on sweeping policy reforms in the debtor countries. Ironically, the IMF, with its stabilization programme requiring economic liberalization and government austerity as a precondition for renegotiating a country's debt, has come to play a policing function in the current Latin American policy-making arena analogous to that asserted by US aid officials in Taiwan and South Korea in the 1950s and 1960s.

Although they are facing a similar constraint with their massive debt burdens, Mexico and Brazil have responded to the situation very differently. In the late 1970s Mexico opted to turn to an oil-led development strategy, with a curious twist. Petroleum became the country's dominant export item, accounting for two-thirds of total exports by 1980, with taxes paid by PEMEX, the state oil monopoly, accounting for one-quarter of total government revenue. Although a sudden export boom of this sort usually leads to the accumulation of considerable foreign exchange by the resource-rich country, Mexico by contrast never permitted its imports to fall behind the rapidly growing oil exports. The result was a process of 'import *de*substitution', with imports accounting for an increasingly important portion of total domestic supply for consumer, capital and intermediate goods alike (Hirschman, 1987; Villarreal, 1983). Mexico's trade balance was consistently negative throughout the 1970s, with imports occupying an ever larger share of GDP from 1976 until 1981, when drastic import cuts were imposed.

Unlike Mexico, which utilized foreign loans to purchase imports, Brazil used its debt primarily to finance ISI deepening in large-scale industrial and infrastructural projects in the 1970s. This process of 'forced-march industrialization' (Hirschman, 1987: 19–22) has resulted in a very large export surplus since 1983, attributable both to a vigorous expansion in exports (mostly of manufactures) and to a deep cut in imports. The paradox is that, in a period of high petroleum prices (1973–85), oil-rich Mexico has suffered serious economic setbacks, while oil-poor and oil-hungry Brazil has made notable industrial advances.

The attempt of the East Asian NICs to combine EOI with ISI has run into problems of its own. For example, the export superiority of the East Asian NICs does not necessarily translate into a positive trade balance. South Korea's trade balance was negative *every year from 1957 until 1984*. Taiwan performed much better than its East Asian neighbour in this regard, with positive trade balances in all but two of the years from 1970 to 1984.[10] Thus while EOI has succeeded in generating substantial exports for the East Asian NICs, this has often been counterbalanced by an even greater need for imports, confirming the assertion that EOI, like ISI, is import intensive.

In the mid-1980s there were signs that the export strategy of the East Asian NICs might be facing serious difficulties on the horizon. The possible EOI demise was based on several short- and medium-term tendencies: a recession in the United States, a longer-term slowdown in the computer and electronics industries (which are leading components of East Asia's global export performance), and the perception of rising protectionist sentiments in the US Congress. By September 1985, 300 pieces of trade legislation were coming up for congressional debate; retaliatory sights were focused not only on Japan (with whom the US ran a $50 billion deficit), but also Taiwan (a $13.6 billion deficit), Hong Kong ($5.8 billion), and South Korea ($4 billion). There were strong protectionist pressures for heavy restrictions on imports of textiles and footwear (*Far Eastern Economic Review*, 1985a).

The United States is the region's largest trading partner, taking half of Taiwan's exports, 44 percent of Hong Kong's, 40 percent of South Korea's and 20 percent of Singapore's. As a result of this trade dependence, slow growth in the US economy has made deep cuts into the imports of many Asian-made goods. Singapore was perhaps the hardest hit country, registering a 2 percent growth rate during 1985, with an 18 percent drop in exports. South Korea registered a 26.6 percent fall in exports of colour television sets to the United States, and a 47 percent drop in orders to its shipbuilding industry (*US News and World Report*, 1985).

The problem is one of increasing competition, involving not only other NICs but also developed countries. Lack of adequate financing from foreign sources could undermine the East Asian NICs' ability to make the transition to automation of manufacturing plants that would allow these nations, which have undergone consistent increases in their labour costs, to face competition from the United States and Western Europe. Recent efforts by South Korea to expand finished exports into Japan were countered by US intentions to enter the Japanese market as one of the results of their bargaining over protectionist measures (*Far Eastern Economic Review*, 1985b). The tide may turn yet again, however, as the dramatic strengthening of the Japanese yen is shifting the price advantage in export markets to the East Asian NICs. South Korea shapes up as the biggest winner because it competes most directly against Japan in autos, steel, and videocassette recorders (*Business Week*, 1986). Korea's Samsung and Goldstar built 3.5 million VCRs in 1986, instead of the projected

2.2 million. Perhaps the key to South Korea's bid for increased sales in the United States is the huge export drive surrounding the introduction of the Hyundai car on to the American market (*Business Week*, 1985). If successful, this would further South Korea's reputation as one of the world's premier export economies.

Conclusions

This review of current development strategies of the Latin American and East Asian NICs shows these strategies to be in flux and subject to a considerable amount of tension and potential conflict. The NICs continue to confront a variety of challenges, and how they respond to these will shape their development paths in the future. One of Mexico's biggest long-term economic challenges, beyond its current debt bind, is industrial competitiveness. Although Mexico is located next to the world's biggest economy and it has a long standing border industrialization programme to provide easy access for manufactured exports to the US market, the inefficiency of Mexican industry has traditionally hindered it from being a major producer of industrial exports. But recently Mexico's performance in this area has improved dramatically, with manufactured exports growing by 45 percent between April 1986 and April 1987 (de María y Campos, 1987: 94). For Brazil, massive income inequality continues to be a brake on its efforts to become a fully integrated industrial nation, since the effective internal demand for middle- and high-income products is severely restricted. In addition, there are the social and political tensions that this crippling poverty generates, especially in a society undergoing the pressures associated with redemocratization (O'Donnell et al., 1986).

South Korea and Taiwan both face serious political challenges, but of different sorts. South Korea's problems are largely internal, given the rapidly escalating pressures to open the society politically. The recent wave of redemocratization experiences in Latin America almost surely has a profound demonstration effect elsewhere in the world, and nowhere is this of greater interest to the local population than in South Korea, where increasing economic prosperity has whetted people's appetite for greater political participation. Taiwan's primary problem, by contrast, is one of international legitimacy. It withdrew from the United Nations in the early 1970s over the issue of its relationship to mainland China, and while its economic successes can function temporarily as a surrogate for fully recognized political sovereignty, Taiwan's future will be clouded until some form of mutually acceptable accommodation is reached with the People's Republic of China.

What can ultimately be learned from a cross-regional comparison of development patterns in Latin America and East Asia? This analysis, at the very least, should lead us to reject the false dilemmas that are commonplace in discussions of the development experience of these countries. Growth vs. equity, ISI vs. EOI, agriculture vs. industry, market vs. the state — all are sterile distinctions that greatly oversimplify the process of rapid economic transformation that has characterized the NICs.

The dichotomy between market forces and government intervention misconceives the fundamental motivating principle at work in both regions, which revolves around their ability to forge flexible and beneficial linkages with the world economy. What seems to distinguish the East Asian development experience is the effective and highly dynamic relationships that have been established between the state and the private sector (see Johnson, 1987), *not* the dominance of market forces, free enterprise and internal liberalization. The contrast between the Latin American and East Asian NICs highlights the fact that domestic policies, local institutions and social coalitions play a major role in determining whether external linkages become opportunities and not just constraints on developing countries.

This chapter has not sought to extol the virtues of either the Latin American or the East Asian paths of development, nor does it advocate the adoption of 'correct' economic policies or institutional arrangements. Historically conditioned patterns cannot be repeated, and policies or institutions that work well in one national setting may have quite different consequences elsewhere. Countries are capable of learning from each other, and highly selective adaptation or emulation may prove successful. Whatever is 'learned', however, must be adapted to particular historical, cultural and political circumstances. The goals, needs and resources of the Latin American NICs are quite different from those of the East Asian NICs. The value of comparative and historical research is to show how the experiences of the past in these nations can lead to a better appreciation of the possibilities in the present.

Notes

An earlier version of this chapter was presented at the American Sociological Association annual meeting in Atlanta, Georgia 24–8 August 1988. I would like to thank Christopher Ellison, Stephan Haggard, Miguel Korzeniewicz, Stephen Krasner, Ellis Krauss, Paul Lubeck and Mitchell Seligson for their helpful comments.

1. In Latin America, 'the world slump of 1929–33 cut the purchasing power of the continent's exports by 60 percent, and ended the possibility of much borrowing abroad. Most countries were obliged to suspend the convertibility of their currencies, cut imports radically and take measures to stimulate the production of domestic substitutes' (Harris, 1987: 17; also 74).

2. The approach adopted in this chapter is compatible with 'the new comparative political economy' perspective discussed in Evans and Stephens (1988).

3. This section draws on Gereffi and Wyman (1987).

4. The problems associated with ISI in Latin America are discussed in Baer (1972) and Hirschman (1968). For an account of similar problems in the East Asian countries, see Lin (1973: 68–74) and Deyo (1987).

5. Mexico's inability to maintain a consistent set of policies to promote manufactured exports since 1970 is a classic case of backsliding (see Villarreal, 1983; Mares, 1985).

6. Beginning in 1957, for example, the US government was able to force South Korea to agree to a series of annual stabilization programmes as a prerequisite for continued aid. And when Korea was faced with a food shortage and rapidly declining foreign exchange reserves in 1962–3, the United States conditioned its grain supply for the coming months on a 50 percent devaluation, a balanced budget and severe limitations on credit expansion (Cole, 1980: 22–3; also see Stallings, 1990).

7. Actual exports during the 1960s far outstripped the expectations of Korean planners. Moreover, the most productive sectors did not involve primary goods (such as fish, tungsten, raw silk, and swine), as the planners had predicted. Instead, roughly two-thirds of the total exports were manufactured goods, including a number of 'unexpected' items such as textiles, clothing, plywood and steel (Hong, 1979: 61–72). Thus the results of primary EOI were impressive, but largely unanticipated.

8. The Japanese agreement with South Korea called for $300 million in grants, $200 million in 'soft' loans, and $300 million in commercial credits (Cole, 1980: 23n).

9. The US market has consistently accounted for between two-thirds and three-quarters of Mexico's import and export trade. Transnational corporations from the United States represent about 75 percent of total direct foreign investment in Mexico.

10. For South Korea, see IMF (1987: 494–5). The data for Taiwan comes from the *Taiwan Statistical Data Book* (1987: 208).

10
INTERNATIONAL FINANCIAL NETWORKS AND INSTITUTIONS

Richard Swedberg

In a chapter of this kind, it might be good to start with some definitions. By 'international financial institution' (also known as IFIs in the literature) is basically meant official international financial organizations like the International Monetary Fund, the World Bank and the Bank for International Settlements. 'International financial networks' can be defined as those webs of interaction that develop between international financial intermediaries (mainly banks) and their customers. From these definitions, it is clear that the international financial networks constitute a much larger topic than the IFIs. The latter basically consist of a handful of organizations, most of which came into being after the Second World War. International financial networks, on the other hand, can be found very far back in history, from at least the Middle Ages onwards.

When one goes through the classics in economic sociology — Marx, Weber, Simmel and Sombart — one finds little on international banking, and the concept of international financial network is basically missing (for example Swedberg, 1987). The contemporary sociological literature is unfortunately not much richer. A search in *Sociological Abstracts* for 1953–86 turns up a few scattered references to international banking but not much more.[1] Articles and books which deal directly with international financial networks are missing. The literature on IFIs, on the other hand, is more satisfying.[2] Here, as will be shown, there are some well-made studies, and sociologists can be said to have made an interesting contribution to the debate.

Given this state of affairs, this chapter then sets itself the two following tasks: (1) to review the existing literature on the IFIs and — to the extent that it exists — on international financial networks; and (2) to outline how sociologists can go about studying international financial networks. The latter task has been judged especially important since international financial networks constitute a much broader and fundamental area of study in economic sociology than the IFIs.

On a general level, it should be added, this chapter is also intended as a polemic against the current use of the notion of 'network' in economic sociology. This concept has mainly been used by today's economic sociologists to denote the kind of structure that emerges when a number of interlocking directorates is traced. The task of the sociologist interested in economic networks, then, essentially boils down to analysing interlocks with the help of increasingly sophisticated quantitative measures, which have been developed for this explicit purpose (see, for example, the literature cited in Mintz and Schwartz, 1985). In my opinion, however, the current analyses of interlocks present a very impoverished version of what economic networks actually look like (see also Granovetter, 1985). What is needed — in the analysis of international financial networks as well as in economic sociology in general — is a much broader and richer notion of networks in the economy.

In order to show what such a notion of economic network can be like, I have chosen to present here a couple of concrete examples of international financial networks. This way I hope that the reader will gain more of an idea of the problems that face economic sociologists than if I had centred the discussion exclusively on the few sociological analyses that exist on the topic. The examples chosen are from three different periods: the fifteenth century, the nineteenth century and the period after the Second World War. It should be mentioned that these three networks are generally considered the most important from a historical viewpoint. By choosing the postwar period as one example we shall also, it can be added, get an opportunity to touch on the relationship between the IFIs and the current international financial networks.

In discussing each of the three examples, I shall try to use the existing sociological literature as much as possible. I shall, however, also look at a variety of factors which are important to any network and which tend to be ignored in the current literature on interlocks. These include, among other things, the spatial location of the networks, the means of communication and the content of communication. For information on these aspects of the international financial networks, I have drawn mainly on historical works on international banking, such as those by David S. Landes (1958, 1969), Raymond De Roover (1963b) and S.D. Chapman (1984). Much of the information on the current network comes from financial journalists, such as M.S. Mendelsohn (1980).

The International Financial Network in the Middle Ages

Our first example of what an IFN can look like is from the Middle Ages. The specific example we shall use is the international banking network that existed in fifteenth-century Europe. During this time the leading international banking house was that of the Medici family, and I shall take the opportunity to present the general organization of the Medici bank inside as well as outside Florence. Had I instead chosen to focus on some other of the legendary banking houses during the Middle Ages, such as the Fuggers or one of the more outstanding Genoese families from the sixteenth century, it is clear that the details would have been different. The general picture, however, would have remained more or less the same: in the sixteenth as well as the fifteenth century, banking was closely connected to international trade; the main financial instrument was the bill of exchange; and the major customers of the international bankers consisted of a small circle of wealthy merchants, aristocrats and representatives of the Church. In choosing fifteenth-century international banking one also has the advantage of being able to draw on Raymond De Roover's superb scholarship. The following discussion, unless otherwise indicated, is based on his works (De Roover 1948, 1955, 1963a, 1963b, 1974).

In the fifteenth century international banking was totally dominated by the Italians or, more precisely, by around 200 merchant bankers from cities like Venice, Florence, Pisa, Siena and Genoa. In comparison to other merchants of the time, such as the Hanseatic merchants who controlled the Baltic trade, the Italians were very sophisticated in their business methods. They made use of double-entry book-keeping and the bill of exchange, and they developed the rudiments of commercial law. Their activities consisted of a mixture of trade and banking (hence the term 'merchant banker') and reflected that great change in medieval trade, which N.S.B. Gras (1939: 33–81) has called the transition from 'the traveling merchant' to 'the sedentary merchant'. In the fifteenth century the merchants had thus stopped travelling themselves with their merchandise; they could now simply send it somewhere abroad, where a buyer was located with the help of an agent. Banking changed in a similar way; there was now a main office at home and special branches or correspondents abroad. Fairs, at which the travelling bankers and the merchants could meet and which had been so popular earlier in the Middle Ages, were on the decline in the fifteenth century.

International banking was carried out in a small number of European cities. Which these were is clear from the commercial manuals of the time. In Italy the merchant bankers could mainly be found in Bologna, Florence, Genoa, Milan, Naples, Palermo, Pisa, Venice and the Court of Rome (or wherever the Pope was in residence). Spain, France, England, Savoy and Flanders had a similar number of banking centres. There were Barcelona, Palma de Majorca, and Valencia in Spain; Avignon and Montpellier in France; Geneva in Savoy; Bruges in Flanders; and London in England. Paris was a major banking place for some years at the beginning of the fifteenth century; and Lyons after 1465. Constantinople disappeared from the international network in 1453, when it was conquered by the Turks. There was no international banking facility east of the Rhine; the Italians had tried to make Lübeck into a banking town but failed because of opposition from the Hanseatic league.

In each of the foreign banking cities there were groups of Italians organized into special 'nations' according to their city of origin. These organizations usually demanded official recognition of their incorporation as well as certain commercial privileges, such as protection against arbitrary arrest, seizure of property and the like. Each 'nation' had from 12 to one or two hundred members. In general, all bank employees abroad were also Italians, and on principle foreigners were not employed. As a rule, the members of the 'nations' tended to keep clear of the local population.

What characterized a major banking place in the Middle Ages was first and foremost that it had an organized money market. This basically meant that it was easy to change foreign currencies and to buy and sell bills of exchange. Usually these activities took place in a public square, where daily meetings between bill-brokers and merchant bankers were held. In Bruges one met at Place de la Bourse; in London at Lombard Street; and in Venice on the Piazza del Rialto.

Between the various banking places there seems to have existed a regular service of couriers (the so-called *scarcella*), while special couriers were very rarely used. All the banking centres were, however, not connected to each other. London, for example, was in direct contact only with Bruges, Florence, Genoa and Venice. Florence, on the other hand, was directly connected to many more cities, since it was the major banking centre in Western Europe during the fifteenth century. In general, the mail was very slow in the fifteenth century. The customary usance on the bills of exchange (which was mainly decided by distance) was a couple of days for other Italian cities; thirty days for Avignon; and ninety days for London. Research on the elasticity of news in the fifteenth and sixteenth century has also shown that there was great variation in the time it took for a letter to reach its destination (Braudel 1975: 361–3). Between Florence and Venice, for example, the average time for a letter was four days; the minimum was one day, and the maximum thirteen.

Outside the international financial network the traffic in money was considerably slower. This was something that the Pope often experienced since he had funds coming in from all over Europe. When money was transferred from Cracow in Poland to his court in Avignon, it took eleven months just to get the money to Bruges. First it had to be transported to Bruges in the form of merchandise, which then had to be sold. From Bruges to Avignon — a distance not much further than that between Cracow and Bruges — it took only a month. All that was needed to execute the operation at this point was a letter of advice and two book-keeping entries.

During the fifteenth century Geneva also played a special role in the international financial network as a clearing centre for international settlements. Bankers wanted to avoid shipping specie as much as possible, since it was expensive, risky and bulky. Instead they tried to settle international balances through bills of exchange at a special fair held in Geneva throughout most of the fifteenth century. A specific measure — the goldmark — was also devised to facilitate these operations.

A few of the basic aspects of the international financial network in the fifteenth century have now been touched on: its geographical location; communication between its parts; and the organization of banking communities in the various cities of the network. We shall now look at two more important aspects of the medieval network: the way the international banking houses were structured, and the role that specific financial instruments played in structuring these networks.

The so-called bill of exchange was the most important financial instrument in fifteenth-century international banking. The *lettera di cambio* had emerged in the fourteenth century as a way of circumventing the prohibition on usury (see Nelson, 1949). The way a medieval bill of exchange was constructed may at first seem complicated but was in reality quite simple. Instead of just giving the borrower an ordinary loan with a certain rate of interest attached to it, the medieval merchant banker carried out an exchange of currency for the customer. He gave the borrower a specific sum in one currency and this had to be repaid in a different place and in another currency. The lender got his rate of interest in the form of a higher amount in the foreign currency which, however, first had to be transported back to the original lender and changed back into the original currency. The medieval bill of exchange was, in other words, literally a 'bill of exchange'; and the way it operated was consequently very different from an 'ordinary' bill of exchange today.

What is of special interest about the medieval bill of exchange, from the viewpoint of international financial networks, is of course that a simple transaction such as a loan, which today usually takes place in one place in one currency, in those days took the form of a transaction in *two* currencies between *two* places. It is indeed true that the merchant bankers of the fifteenth century occasionally did away with the trouble of sending the money abroad and then taking it back just to earn some interest (so-called 'dry exchange' and 'fictional exchange'). This, however, was fairly rare according to De Roover (1963b: 14), since the banks wanted to be on good terms with the Church and therefore respected the prohibition on usury. In general the medieval bill of exchange thus 'require(d) the banker to operate with a network of correspondents in other places' (De Roover, 1963b: 13).

Having correspondents abroad caused many difficulties for the individual banking firms. If we take the Medici bank (1397–1494) as an example, it can first be noted that it was represented in most of the leading banking centres of the day. In 1455, at the

TABLE 1
Size of three major international banking houses of Florence in the fourteenth and fifteenth centuries

Office or branch	Peruzzi 1336 No. of staff	Acciaiuoli 1341 No. of staff	Medici 1469 No. of staff
Florence	11	11	12
Avignon	5	3	5
Barletta	5	4	No branch
Bologna	No record	1	No branch
Bruges	4	2	8
Castello di Castro (Sardinia)	1	No record	No branch
Chiarenza (Greece)	No record	2	No branch
Cyprus	4	3	No branch
Genoa	1	6	No branch
London	7	2	4
Lyons	No branch	No branch	8
Majorca	2	No record	No branch
Milan	1	No branch	8
Naples	8	5	No record
Paris	3	1	No branch
Pisa	7	2	No record
Ravenna	No branch	1	No branch
Rhodos	3	3	No branch
Rome	No record	2	8
Sicily	7	3	No branch
Tunis	3	2	No branch
Venice	3	No branch	7
Unidentified	13	0	0
Total	88	53	60

Source: De Roover (1963a).

height of its power, the bank had branches in eight places and correspondents in eleven more. In each branch the Medicis kept an office, which was run by a manager and a few clerks. The whole office did not exceed ten people, except in Florence where twelve people were employed in 1469. That international banks were not huge operations in the Middle Ages is clear from the fact that the Medici bank did not employ more than about sixty people at its height. The giants of international banking in the fourteenth century were also fairly small operations in terms of size (see Table 1).

The main problem with having branches abroad in the Middle Ages was in controlling them. The branches could not be visited very often since it took far too long to travel back and forth. The mail was also so slow that a local manager could hardly be expected to wait to hear from headquarters whenever an important decision had to be made. But ways had to be found to avoid local managers mismanaging the funds. Special 'partnership agreements' were thus drawn up in the Medici bank. These contained a variety of rules to ensure prudent decisions by the branch manager. He was, for example, forbidden (at the price of a severe fine) to make loans to royalty on his own initiative. Neither was he allowed to do business for himself, stand surety for his friends or engage in gambling. The people who worked at a Medici branch abroad were always hand-picked by the headquarters in Florence in order to minimize any bonds of loyalty between the staff and the branch manager. The fact, finally, that the Medici bank was legally constructed as a kind of holding company made it possible for one branch to disavow the debts of another branch. At least on one occasion, the Bruges branch refused to honour debts that had been incurred by the London branch.

The International Financial Network in the Nineteenth Century

It is clear that there are certain similarities between the international financial networks in the fifteenth and nineteenth centuries. The core of each, for example, consisted of a handful of places with small communities of international bankers. The differences, however, are enormous. In the Middle Ages the nation-states had just been formed; the economy was undeveloped; and international trade was fairly insignificant. As a result, the network was small and its influence inside the individual countries was limited. In the nineteenth century, on the other hand, the process of industrialization had started with all that this entailed in terms of economic undertakings (Gerschenkron, 1962; Landes, 1969). Foreign trade had nearly exploded; in 1880 it was more than twenty times as great as in 1780 (Kuznets, 1966: 306–7). Capital had also started to move across the borders in larger quantities than ever before. The three leading exporters of capital — Great Britain, France and Germany — trebled their investments abroad between 1880 and 1914. When the First World War started, their claims amounted to more than 34 billion dollars (Kuznets, 1966: 322–5).

The international banks naturally played an important role in all of these foreign affairs. The discussion of the international financial network in the nineteenth century will therefore be centred on the question of how it was influenced by foreign trade, by investments abroad, and by loans to foreign governments. First, however, a few words need to be said about the geographical location of the network; the kinds of communication that existed within it; and the role played by certain ethnic groups, especially among the merchant bankers.

In comparison to the network of the fifteenth century, it is clear that the Italian bankers had played out their role by the nineteenth century. When David S. Landes (1979: 16), in *Bankers and Pashas*, enumerates the leading banking cities of the nineteenth century he includes only Amsterdam, Boston, Frankfurt, Paris, Liverpool, London and New York. To these should perhaps be added a few more, such as Vienna, Frankfurt, Geneva, Berne and (after 1870) Hamburg. The undisputed financial centre in the nineteenth century was London, which had taken over this position from Amsterdam during the Napoleonic wars (see McMichael, 1985: 134–6).

The leading international banking city in a country was also usually the centre for local banking. Germany, however, was an exception to this rule; after the unification in 1870 Berlin became the local centre and Hamburg the international one (Kindleberger, 1978: 71). The way the international network branched out into the individual countries in the nineteenth century was also influenced by the way in which the national banking systems were structured. In the US, for example, legislation prevented the formation of branches abroad. And while the British banks in the early 1800s were scattered all over the country, in France they were concentrated in Paris. During the nineteenth century the international financial network also reached practically all countries in the world (see Table 2). British banks, for example, had branches in such distant countries as China, India, Brazil and Uruguay.

Individual banking firms sometimes conducted business in a multitude of countries but usually concentrated on one or two.

TABLE 2
Origin and sphere of interest of key merchant bankers in London, 1914

	Origin	Sphere of interest
Arbuthnot, Latham & Co.	Agency house	India, South America
Baring Bros & Co. Ltd	German (via Exeter)	Latin America, Far East, France, Russia
Arthur H. Brandt & Co.	German	Russia
Wm Brandt, Sons & Co.	German	India, Russia
Brown Shipley & Co.	US	USA, Mexico
Cunliffe Bros	English	India, Natal
Frühling & Goschen	German	West Indies, Egypt
Anthony Gibbs & Sons	South American	Chile, Australia
C.J. Hambro & Son	German (via Copenhagen)	Scandinavia, USA
Horstman & Co.	German	Germany
F. Huth & Co.	German (via Spain)	South America, USA
Kleinwort, Sons & Co.	German (via Cuba)	Cuba
König Bros	German	Germany
Lazard Bros & Co.	French–Jewish	Paris, New York, Far East
Morgan, Grenfell & Co.	US	USA
Neumann, Luebeck & Co.	South African	South Africa, Rhodesia
N.M. Rothschild & Sons	German–Jewish (via Manchester)	USA, continental Europe
A. Rüffer & Sons	German (via Lyons)	France, Spain
J. Henry Schröder & Co.	German	South America, Chile, Cuba, Russia
Seligman Bros	US–Jewish	USA, Germany
Wallace Bros & Co. Ltd	Agency house (Scots)	India, Far East

Note: The twenty-one merchant bankers in this table formed the first Accepting Houses' Committee on 5 August 1914.
Source: Chapman (1984: 55, 201–4).

This was especially true for the British merchant banks. The leading banking house of the time — the Rothschilds — was strong enough to build up a very wide geographical network (Born, 1983: 54–6). By 1820 the Rothschild firm was represented by the five sons of Meyer Amschel in five different countries: Nathan Rothschild in London (1803); James Rothschild in Paris (1812); Salomon Rothschild in Vienna (1816); and Carl Rothschild in Naples (1812). Amschel Rothschild had remained in Frankfurt, where the parent firm was located. In 1830 the Paris branch of the Rothschild firm opened an office in Brussels, and the London and Paris branches later established agencies in

Madrid (1833–4), New York (1835–6), New Orleans (1843), Havana (1843) and Mexico (1843). To get a full picture of the geographical network of the Rothschilds one also has to include their many correspondents all over the world. The most famous of these was undoubtedly Gerson Bleichröder, who was Bismarck's private banker (Landes, 1960).

Within the network communication was usually fast and efficient. The impetus behind this was, of course, that whoever is first in the know has an advantage in the market. The Rothschilds especially were famous for their well-functioning intelligence network and the wide variety of means they used: diplomatic pouches, balloons, pigeons, special couriers, and the like. In *Gold and Iron*, Fritz Stern's well-known biography of Gerson Bleichröder, Bismarck is quoted as saying, 'Through Bleichröder (my private banker) I am accustomed to receive important political news from Paris and St. Petersburg, usually eight days earlier than through my ambassadors' (Stern, 1979: 311).

The great event in the nineteenth century, as far as financial communications were concerned, was the invention of the telegraph. The telegraph was first used — by the Rothschilds and the Behrens — in the early 1840s but did not come into regular use until a couple of decades later (Chapman, 1984: 108). The Atlantic cable was successfully completed in 1866, and by the early 1880s London was in direct contact with all the major continents. The effect of this development on the structure of the international financial network is not clear. It has been suggested that the telegraph helped to displace the family as a working unit in international banking (Chapman, 1984: 67). With instant communication between various places the family suddenly seemed to become a relatively inflexible unit, especially in comparison to fast-moving 'loners' like Sir Ernest Cassel and Jacob Schiff. Whether this is indeed the case is hard to say. It is, however, clear that foreign branches could be controlled much more easily now that headquarters could be instantly consulted on all important questions.

The great role that ethnic bonds played in nineteenth-century banking, especially in merchant banking, has often been commented upon. David Landes (1979: 19), in *Bankers and Pashas*, says that, 'in a profession that was of its nature international and depended on the closest mutual confidence, the dispersion of certain persecuted or disfavoured groups with common values and ways of life to cement them from within, and common pressures and prejudices imposing unity from without, was a positive advantage'. The examples Landes gives are the Huguenots, the Jews and the Greeks from the Ottoman Empire. These groups had typically been expelled and persecuted a number of times and as a result were scattered throughout Europe. But Landes (1979: 28) also warns that one should not overestimate the importance of ethnicity. While ethnic bonds might help a banking firm to establish itself, in the long run it was usually profit and pragmatism that counted.

Little of novelty since Landes's work had been said about the role of ethnicity in nineteenth-century banking till the early 1980s. At that time S.D. Chapman, a business historian, and Michael Lisle-Williams, a sociologist, got involved in a debate in *The British Journal of Sociology* about the merchant bankers in England. Lisle-Williams (1984a, 1984b, 1984c) argued that since the nineteenth century the British merchant bankers had come to constitute a very cohesive and aristocratized group, which eventually melted into the English upper class. To S.D. Chapman, author of *The Rise of Merchant Banking* (1984) and the foremost authority on British nineteenth-century banking, this theory of an aristocratized banking elite smacked of cheap Marxism. He (1986) first of all reaffirmed Landes's opinion that ethnicity played a key role in merchant banking (see Table 2). He also pointed out that only a small number of the merchant banks, such as the Rothschilds and the Barings, actually fitted Lisle-Williams's description of an aristocratized elite. This, however, did *not* apply to the Anglo-German and the Greek houses, which were very careful to retain their ethnic identity well into the twentieth century. Figures showing that the acceptances of the Anglo-German group clearly surpassed those of the 'aristocratic' banks from 1900 onwards sealed Chapman's case.

The three major activities of the international banks in the nineteenth century were to help finance foreign trade, to arrange for the export of capital to private investors abroad and to put together loans for individual states. As far as foreign trade is concerned, the international bankers had developed a number of sophisticated financial instruments, which simplified trade between two distinct places and thus made possible a very extended international network (Landes, 1979: 14–15; 1969: 115–16). The basic problem with foreign trade, then as now, was that the exporter cannot afford to produce the merchandise without first getting paid; and that the importer cannot afford to import the merchandise before it has been sold. The merchant banker of the nineteenth century consequently directed his energy to finding a solution to this problem and to making money from the solution. This was done in a variety of complicated ways. The basic idea was to arrange for an advance to the exporter and to supply the importer with ready funds via a bill of exchange (for technical details, see especially Hidy, 1949: 124–63). The nineteenth-century bill of exchange, it should be noted, was very different from the medieval bill of exchange. It was typically drawn on sixty days on sight but could be discounted immediately, especially if it had been vouched for ('accepted') by a well-known banking firm; it was constructed as a short-term advance, not an exchange of currencies.

The basic kind of network needed to conduct foreign trade in the nineteenth century was a familiar one: a banking firm in a financial centre linked to trustworthy partners or correspondents abroad, who were familiar with the foreign market. To export capital for private investments, however, demanded a quite different network structure (Landes, 1969: 118). Here the nineteenth-century banker essentially operated as an intermediary between the investing public at home and a corporation abroad. The investment banker had to understand the workings of the stock market as well as the psychology of the investing public. The latter of these two tasks, especially, constituted a change for the private banker, who was used to dealing with a small circle of wealthy clients rather than a large number of small investors. The fact that the money was going to be used for an investment in some kind of industry also meant that the banker had to be in contact with some technical experts. When banks started to have technical departments is not known (Gille, 1973: 289–90). It should also be noted that the relationship between banks and industrialists at this time was filled with mutual suspicion.

From a network perspective, it is of special interest that investment banking often entailed syndication. Banks were thus forced to co-operate with other banks. David Landes (1979: 30) explains the rationale for this:

> the very nature of investment banking necessitated the formation of syndicates that were wider and more heterogeneous than the nuclear commercial team.

> There was the scope of the ventures: the risk had to be divided. There was the need for access to several markets to insure a good sale. There was the problem of competition for contracts and concessions; it was easier to absorb rivals than to fight them.

The third major activity of the international bankers consisted in arranging loans to foreign governments. This activity, it should be noted, had little in common with the personal loans that the medieval bankers arranged for princes in the Middle Ages. Loans in the nineteenth century were actually more similar to private investment banking in that the funds were usually supplied by a large number of small investors through the Stock Exchange. Loans to governments also often implied syndication.

Especially through the loans to various governments (as well as through loans for private investments abroad) private bankers came in contact with the political authorities. What effect this had has been much discussed, though not very much researched (Chapman, 1984: x). Briefly, there exist three positions on the political impact of the international banks in the nineteenth century: (1) they helped to cause the First World War (Lenin, 1985); (2) they did *not* cause the First World War (Staley, 1935; Kindleberger, 1984b: 255–6); and (3) they helped to maintain peace in the nineteenth century (Polanyi, /1944/ 1957: 3–19). To arbitrate between these three positions exceeds my present task and will therefore not be attempted. It should, however, be noted that Lenin's theory is much too simple: the available facts point to the need for a far more complex theory. For example, it is clear that the French tried to use foreign credit as a direct instrument of foreign policy during the nineteenth century, while the Foreign Office in England often felt that it was not their task to protect the loans of the City bankers (Chapman, 1984: 161).

The International Financial Institutions and the Current International Financial Network (1945–)

The international financial institutions (IFIs) were essentially created in the period after the Second World War. Since the 1960s a new international financial network has also emerged. If we start with the IFIs, it can be noted that these have attracted some attention from sociologists, especially since the 1970s. This is especially true for the International Monetary Fund (IMF) and the World Bank (International Bank for Reconstruction and Development: IBRD), while the Bank for International Settlements (BIS) and the less well known IFIs like the Paris Club have not been looked into at all. The most important contribution by sociologists to the understanding of the IFIs has clearly been to explore the history surrounding their creation. The more recent activities of the IMF and the IBRD — and by this I essentially mean their loans since the 1960s to Third World countries — have not really been researched even though they occasionally have been touched upon.

In *The Origins of International Economic Disorder* (1977) the sociologist Fred Block discusses the birth of the IMF and the World Bank as part of his general analysis of US international monetary policy between the Second World War and the 1970s. During the 1940s the US government spent a lot of energy in creating an international economic order with a high degree of 'openness' in order to ensure that there would be foreign markets for US products once the war was over. In Block's version, the US strategy was basically to eliminate the desire by European countries to introduce some form of 'national capitalism'. The idea that a nation could be 'closed' was quite popular in countries like Britain before as well as after the Second World War, since this meant that they would be less exposed to international economic forces. The IMF and the World Bank, in Block's account, were thus created as part of the US effort to institutionalize an 'open' world economy. The task of the IMF was to prevent individual countries from having managed currency rates, exchange controls, and the like; while the task of the World Bank was to finance and shape the reconstruction of Europe's industry in such a way that 'national capitalism' would not appear an attractive option.

A somewhat different version of how the IMF and the World Bank came into being can be found in an important article by Laurence H. Shoup in *Insurgent Sociologist* (1975; see also Shoup and Minter, 1977). Shoup's major finding is that planning in the US during the 1940s for a new world order was decisively influenced by the ideas of a small lobbying group, the Council on Foreign Relations. The reasoning of its members, which was essentially accepted by the Roosevelt administration, was that the

US must create a worldwide empire of free trade. This 'grand area', as it was called, included Western Europe, the European colonies, China and South-East Asia. Again the reason was to ensure the existence of foreign markets for US products after the Second World War. To help integrate this 'grand area', it was realized as early as 1942, specific international financial institutions had to be created. In Shoup's version, the IMF and the World Bank were consequently the brainchild of the Council of Foreign Relations rather than of Harry Dexter White and John Maynard Keynes, as is commonly assumed.

It is clear from Block and Shoup's accounts that the IFIs were the result of conscious actions by political institutions. In this sense they can be said to constitute 'enacted' rather than 'crescive' institutions as international financial networks. This should however not be interpreted as meaning that the IMF and the World Bank actually came to play the key roles in constructing the American empire, as the US planners had originally envisioned. The economic reconstruction of Western Europe, as it turned out, was not handled by the World Bank but through the Marshall Plan. And the IMF did not become *the* decisive institution in international financial affairs. It was quickly relegated to the background, and the important decisions in international financial affairs were instead made by the US government itself.

What eventually happened was that both the IMF and the World Bank (including its two sister organizations, the International Finance Corporation and the International Development Authority) were assigned new roles in the world economy. In the 1960s the World Bank essentially became a supplier of long-term capital to Third World countries and the IMF a supplier of balance of payments loans to approximately the same group of countries. In the early 1970s social scientists of a radical persuasion started to criticize the IMF and the World Bank for the way they carried out these activities (Hayter, 1971; Payer, 1974; cf. Payer, 1982). Their argument was basically that the IMF and the IBRD used their loans to strong-arm Third World countries into accepting the kind of free trade capitalism that the US had promoted since the Second World War and that only favoured the powerful Western nations. To show this, it was pointed out that the World Bank was not allowed to give loans to countries which reneged on their international debts, which expropriated foreign property without 'adequate' compensation or which failed to honour their agreements with foreign corporations. To get a loan from the IMF, it was argued, a country typically had to cut back on its public sector, show greater hospitality to foreign investors and abolish subsidies for food and housing. To challenge the World Bank and the IMF was a sure way for a country to be cut off from the international capital market.

Soon this type of criticism also became popular in sociology, and when the IFIs are discussed among sociologists, it is usually in a critical manner. This is as true when post-Second World War capitalism in general is discussed (for example Makler et al., 1982: 13–23) as when some particular aspect of IMF-IBRD's policies is under scrutiny (Wood, 1985; Swedberg, 1986). What is perhaps lacking in these analyses is more of an orientation to research on the actual social mechanisms that are at work in particular, concrete examples. For an example of how this type of research can be done, the reader is particularly referred to Albert Hirschman's excellent analysis of World Bank projects in *Development Projects Observed* (1967). Hirschman shows that one has to look at the interaction of a specific project with its social and geographical milieu — and not only at the policies of the Bank — in order to understand what actually happens.

While sociologists have made a contribution to the understanding of the IFIs, they have paid little attention to the new international financial network that has come into being since the early 1960s. It is true that a few analyses touch upon the contemporary network in one aspect or another (see Wachtel, 1980; Stallings, 1982; Hawley, 1984; Meyer, 1986; Wood, 1985). None, however, directly address the key questions of how the new network has developed and what its general structure is like. In this, it should be added, sociologists are not alone. When, for example, economists have discussed the growth in international banking since the 1960s they have avoided analysing the social structure of the international network and have stuck to more conventional economic perspectives.[3] A special mention should finally be made of the work by the Dutch political scientist Meindert Fennema and his study *International Networks of Banks and Industry* (1982; see also Fennema and Schijf, 1985). Fennema (1982) analyses the interlocking directorates of about 200 of the world's largest corporations (including banks) in a variety of countries. His general conclusion is that there is a loose international network between banks and industries, and that this has grown denser between 1970 and 1976. The key roles in this network, he shows, are played by a few New York banks and some Dutch multinationals.

To get a full picture of the international financial network which has developed after the Second World War one has to go beyond the restrictions imposed by conventional analyses of interlocking directorates. One must look at the specific history of the network, its geographical location, its structure of communication, and so on. When this is done, as I shall show, it will be clear that the international financial network looks very different to the one that can be reconstructed on the basis of an analysis of interlocks.

The general framework for the international financial market, which grew up in the 1960s, is in broad lines the following (see Mendelsohn, 1980). Most of the international capital movements between 1945 and 1965 were made directly through governments and the IFIs. A true international capital market with private actors consequently did not exist. Such a market, however, came into being in the mid-1960s with the birth of the so-called Euromarkets in which currencies were borrowed and lent ('the Eurocurrencies market'), loans put together ('the Eurocredit market') and bonds issued ('the Eurobond market'). These markets grew explosively during the 1970s as did the foreign bond market and the trade in foreign exchange. There were many reasons for this: the need to recycle the giant OPEC funds; the growth in international trade; the introduction in 1971–3 of floating exchange rates; and the general need in the postwar period for world reserves. Hundreds of banks now hurried to open branches abroad. The sums involved were soon truly astronomical. Foreign trade was estimated in 1977 at a value of around $2 trillion and foreign exchange transactions as $50 trillion (Moffit, 1983: 136). The international financial market was estimated to be worth around $500 billion in the same year (Mendelsohn, 1980: 37). Development since 1977 has continued to be equally dynamic (*The Economist*, 1987a: 3–7).

In the international network of interactions that was soon to be the result of all these developments there were several different types of actor. The international banks were obviously key players. In 1977 it was estimated that somewhere between 500 and 1000 banks were active in the Eurobond and Eurocredit markets. Of these, around 50 did most of the business (Mendelsohn, 1980:

67, 148). If one also adds minor banks, the number probably increases to a couple of thousand. By 1977 most central banks and governments were also part of the international scene, as well as a number of institutional investors. To this should be added the IFIs and, since the early 1980s, a number of giant corporations, which have started to sell securities directly on the international market rather than take loans from the banks ('securitization').

From a geographical viewpoint, the new international financial network is extremely complex and wide-ranging. A bank like Barclays has today more than 5000 branches worldwide, and it is not uncommon for an international bank to have a couple of thousand correspondent banks. The international financial network today reaches most corners of the world, including some of the socialist states. A novelty in the post-Second World War network is the emergence of certain offshore centres, where banking regulation is particularly lax or non-existent. Among the more famous of these are Bahrain, the Cayman Islands and Panama. The centre of the whole system is generally considered to be London, closely followed by New York. Exactly which cities constitute the core of the new network is debated and depends on whether one uses external assets or number of foreign banks as a criterion (see Davis, 1976: 28; Mendelsohn, 1980: 259). External assets is more frequently used, sometimes in combination with the number of foreign banks (see Table 3).

An important policy problem connected with the geographical distribution of the new international financial network is the question of which country is responsible for which banks. In 1975, one year after the collapse of Bankhaus Herstatt, it was decided by BIS that the host country was responsible for foreign subsidiaries; foreign branches remained the responsibility of the home country ('the Basle Concordat'). But in 1982, when Banco Ambrosiano failed, the Bank of Italy refused to honour the debts of its Luxemburg subsidiary, and this has thrown doubt on the efficiency of the Basle rules. The question of 'lender of last resort' is therefore still something of a problem in today's international network.

Communication between the various parts of today's international financial network is extremely fast. Depending on the market, different means of communication are used: telephones, telexes, faxes or various computerized systems. Eurobonds and

TABLE 3
World financial centres in 1978

	External assets* ($ billion)	Number of foreign banks**
London	173	308
New York	78	274
Bahamas**	83	285
	161	559
Frankfurt	61	172
Luxemburg***	53	67
	114	239
Zurich	73	111
Paris	58	194
Amsterdam	35	73
Brussels	31	68
Toronto**	20	90
Milan	18	40
Tokyo	17	137
Panama	10	111

*The information on external assets comes from IMF's *International Financial Statistics*, March 1979, where they are given per country. To equate the assets for a country with a specific city, as has been done in this table, presents problems in the cases of the US, West Germany and Canada, each of which has several financial centres.
**This information, from *The Banker*, April 1979, includes branches, subsidiaries, other offices and shareholdings in consortium and domestic banks.
***The information on the Bahamas is here lumped together with that of New York, since most of the business in Bahamas is done by US banks. The same reasoning is behind lumping together Frankfurt and Luxemburg.
Source: Mendelsohn (1980: 259)

TABLE 4
Members in the Society for Worldwide Interbank Financial Telecommunication (SWIFT)

Year	Member banks	Member countries	Directly connected bank locations
1977	519	21	505
1978	586	24	619
1979	683	29	659
1980	768	35	748
1981	900	39	917
1982	1017	44	1239
1983	1063	53	1699
1984	1084	54	1853

Euroequities are, for example, a telephone market (*The Economist*, 1987b: 13). In 1973 a worldwide electronic system for interbank communication called SWIFT was introduced, and today it connects some 2000 banks in more than 50 countries (see Table 4). This system is mainly used for various forms of specialised international financial transaction, such as customer transfers, bank transfers and foreign exchange deals (*The Banker*, 1984). Agencies like Reuters also supply the international banking community with instant news on foreign exchange rates, stocks on foreign exchanges and the like. The social consequences of these new means of communication are several. One that is fairly obvious is that they have enabled a much more complex and far-reaching international network to come into being. Another is that it has become increasingly difficult for nation-states to control the activities of the international banks within their borders.

The new ways of doing business since the 1960s have also had a direct impact on the network structure. In particular there is the fact that international banks for various reasons borrow from each other and keep short-term deposit funds with each other. The market for so-called international interbank lending amounted to around $2.5 trillion in 1986 (*The Economist*, 1987a: 28). A danger here is that when one bank gets into trouble, a chain reaction is set off and the whole system of international banking is endangered. Eurobonds and Eurocredits, it can also be noted, are primarily group activities. They are typically arranged by one or several big banks ('the managing bank(s)') and then parcelled out to a number of smaller banks ('the participating banks'). New groupings are formed for each new loan, and no bank is responsible for the commitments of the others. Often only the big banks make a profit from these activities; the smaller banks mainly participate to get into the market and to improve their relationship with the bigger banks (Mendelsohn, 1980: 71–91, 183–97).

On the future development of the current international financial network, there is much to say. Here it must suffice to note that new financial innovations are constantly occurring, something which gives both a dynamic quality and a certain instability to the international financial market. To the economic sociologist this, among other things, raises the question of *social control*. Which institutions, for example, are needed to ensure a minimum level of stability? And how is the correct balance between national and international supervision to be struck?

Concluding Remarks

My general conclusion, as far as economic sociology is concerned, is that while the study of IFIs can be said to be basically well under way, research on the international financial networks constitutes more or less virgin territory. Much of this chapter has consequently been devoted to an attempt to outline how this research can be done. For reasons of space it has not been possible to scrutinize any one network in great detail. The three examples which have been discussed, however, indicate some of the elements that are important to the way an international financial network is structured. When studying an international financial network, one thus has to look at:

its geographical location;
its means of communication;
the financial instruments used;
the content of the financial transactions;
the organizational structure of the banking firms;
the relationship of the network to the political system.

In certain cases one should also pay attention to the ethnicity of the people involved and the interlocks in the network.

Each of these factors, in my opinion, needs to be much further researched. Some good starting points for this can no doubt be found in the existing sociological literature. If we take ethnicity as an example, it is clear that Edna Bonacich's (1973) essay on 'middlemen minorities' or ethnic trading peoples is relevant here. In this context one can also mention Lewis Coser's (1974) analysis of the relationship between German rulers and their 'court Jew' bankers in the seventeenth and eighteenth centuries. The social mechanism that Coser lays bare is that of a ruler who exploits the isolation and financial resources of a group of outsiders in order to get an ally in the fight against vested interest groups in his country.

In other areas, however, there is little useful literature, and the researcher will mainly have to rely on his or her sociological imagination in combination with historical data. This is true of such topics as the organizational structure of international banking firms and the kinds of financial instrument used in international economic transactions. But given the present level of creativity in economic sociology, this should not present insurmountable difficulties. The important thing, when it comes to international financial networks (as well as any other area of the economy which has not yet been analysed by economic sociologists), is simply to put the topic on the agenda for research that needs to be done. The way for today's economic sociology to advance and to prove that it has an important contribution to make is constantly to confront new and challenging topics.

Notes

I thankfully acknowledge the support for this research by Humanistiskt Samhällsvetenskapliga Forskningsrådet in Stockholm, Sweden (Project F 50/86).

1. A computerized search was made in *Sociological Abstracts* on 30 January 1987 on BANK? as a title, descriptor and identifier. A manual search was made for the years 1953–62. The result was that between 1953 and 1986 only six articles on international banking had been published in professional sociological magazines: Schmidt (1969); Michalet and Cohen (1978), Michalet (1979), Lisle-Williams (1984a, 1984b, 1984c). Some information on international banking can also be found in works which do not appear in *Sociological Abstracts*, for example Wallerstein's (1974, 1980) volumes on 'the modern world system'.

2. The search in *Sociological Abstracts* described in note 1 turned up only two references in professional sociological journals to the IFIs: Yudelman (1976) and Holman (1984). But on this topic, as I shall show later, there exist a few additional, important studies by sociologists.

3. According to Robert Z. Aliber's (1984) survey of international banking — which is considered to be the first of its kind — economists have advanced several different theories to explain the growth in international banking after the Second World War. One can quickly gain an idea of their general content through their names: the follow-the-leader theory, the theory of direct investment, the cost of capital theory ('Q theory'), and the theory of superior technology.

Bibliography

ABU-LUGHOD, J. (1985) 'Urbanization and social change in the Arab world', in J. WALTON (ed.) *Capital and Labor in the Urbanized World*. Newbury Park, CA: SAGE Publications.

ADAIR, P. (1985) *L'économie informelle. Figures et discours*. Paris: Anthropos.

ADAMSKI, W., K. JASIEWICZ and A. RYCHARD (eds) (1986) *Polacy 84 — Dynamika Konfliktu i Konsensusu* (Poles 84 — Dynamics of Conflict and Consensus). Warsaw: Institute of Philosophy and Sociology, Polish Academy of Sciences.

ADLER, S. (1981) *A Turkish Conundrum: Emigration, Politics and Development, 1961–80*. World Employment Programme Research Working Paper 52. Geneva: ILO

ALBER, J. (1982a) *Vom Armenhaus zum Wohlfahrtsstaat. Analysen zur Entwicklung der Sozialversicherung in Westeuropa*. Frankfurt: Campus.

ALBER, J. (1982b) 'Der Wohlfahrtsstaat in der Krise? Eine Bilanz nach drei Jahrzehnten Sozialpolitik in der Bundesrepublik', *Zeitschrift für Soziologie* 9: 313–42.

ALDRICH, H., J. CATER, T. JONES, D. McEVOY and P. VELLEMAN (1985) 'Ethnic residential concentration and the protected market hypotheses', *Social Forces* 63(4): 996–1009.

ALIBER, R.Z. (1984) 'International banking: a survey', *Journal of Money, Credit and Banking* 16(4): 661–78. (See also 'Literature cited' and comments on Aliber's article by L.S. GOODMAN, H.S. HOUTHAKKER and J.D. MURRAY in the same journal.)

ALLEN, M.P. (1981) 'Power and privilege in the large corporation: corporate control and managerial compensation', *American Journal of Sociology* 86: 1112–23.

AMBROSIUS, G., W.H. HUBBARD (1986) *Sozial- und Wirtschaftsgeschichte Europas im 20 Jahrhundert*. Munich: Beck.

AMIN, S. (1974) *Accumulation on a World Scale: a Critique of the Theory of Underdevelopment*. New York: Monthly Review Press.

AMIN, S. (1976) *Unequal Development: an Essay on the Social Formations of Peripheral Capitalism*. New York: Monthly Review Press.

AMIN, S., G. ARRIGHI, A. GUNDER FRANK and I. WALLERSTEIN (1982) *Dynamics of Global Crisis*. New York: Monthly Review Press.

ANTHIAS, F. (1983) 'Sexual divisions and ethnic adaptation', in A. PHIZACKLEA (ed.) *One Way Ticket*. London: Routledge and Kegan Paul.

ARCHAMBAULT, E. and X. GREFFE (1984) *Les économies non officielles*. Paris: La Découverte.

ARIZPE, L. (1983) 'The rural exodus in Mexico and Mexican migration to the United States', in P.G. BROWN and H. SHUE (eds) *The*

Border that Joins: Mexican Migrants and US Responsibility. New Jersey: Rowman and Littlefield.

ARMSTRONG, P., A GLYNN and J. HARRISON (1984) *Capitalism since World War II*. London: Fontana.

ARRIGHI, G. (ed.) (1985) *Semiperipheral Development: the Politics of Southern Europe in the Twentieth Century*. London: SAGE Publications.

ARROW, K. (1973) 'Higher education as a filter', *Journal of Public Economics* 2(3): 193–216.

ASLUND, A. (1985) *Private Enterprises in Eastern Europe*. London: Macmillan.

AVAKOV, R., M. BUTTGEREIT and U. TEICHLER (1984) *Higher Education and Employment in the USSR and in the Federal Republic of Germany*. Paris: Unesco, International Institute for Educational Planning.

AYMARD, M. (1985) 'Nation states and interregional disparities in development', in G. ARRIGHI (ed.) *Semiperipheral Development: the Politics of Southern Europe in the Twentieth Century*. London: SAGE Publications.

BACH, R.L. and L.A. SCHRAML (1982) 'Migration, crisis and theoretical conflict', *International Migration Review* 16(2): 321–41.

BACKAI, T. and E. VARHEGYI (1983) 'Monetization of the Hungarian economy', *Acta Oeconomica* 1/2.

BAER, W. (1972) 'Import substitution and industrialization in Latin America: experiences and interpretations', *Latin American Research Review* 7(1): 95–122.

BAGNASCO, A. (ed.) (1986) *L'altra metà dell'economia. La ricerca internazionale sull'economia informale*. Naples: Liguori.

BAIN, J.S. (1956) *Barriers to New Competition*. Cambridge, MA: Harvard University Press.

BALASSA, B. (1981) *The Newly Industrializing Countries in the World Economy*. New York: Pergamon Press.

BALLMER-CAO, T.-H. (1979) 'Système politique, repartition des revenues et pénétration des enterprises multinationales', pp. 153–79 in *Annuaire suisse de science politique*.

BARAN, P. and P. SWEEZY (1966) *Monopoly Capital*. New York: Monthly Review Press.

BARNET, R. and R. MÜLLER (1974) *Global Reach: the Power of Multinational Corporations*. New York: Simon and Schuster.

BATOR, F.M. (1958) 'The Anatomy of Market Failure', *Quarterly Journal of Economics* 72: 351–79.

BAUMER, J.-M and A. VON GLEICH (1982) *Transnational Corporations in Latin America*. Diessenhofen: Ruegger.

BECKER, G.S. (1976) *The Economic Approach to Human Behavior*. Chicago: University of Chicago Press.

BECKER, G.S. (1981) *A Treatise on the Family*. Cambridge, MA: Harvard University Press.

BELL, D. (1973) *The Coming of Post-Industrial Society*. New York: Basic Books.

BELLAH, R.N. (1957) *Tokugawa Religion*. New York: The Free Press.

BELLAH, R.N. (1963) 'Reflection on the Protestant ethic analogy in Asia', *Journal of Social Issues* 19(1): 52–60. (Also included in EISENSTADT [1968].)

BENNETT, D.C. and K.E. SHARPE (1985) *Transnational Corporations versus the State: the Political Economy of the Mexican Auto Industry*. Princeton, NJ: Princeton University Press.

BERG, I. (1970) *Education and Jobs: The Great Training Robbery*. Boston: Beacon Press.

BERGER, S. and M.J. PIORE (1980) *Dualism and Discontinuity in Industrial Societies*. Cambridge: Cambridge University Press.

BERGESEN, A. and C. SAHOO (1985) 'Evidence of the decline of American hegemony in world production', *Review* 8(spring): 595–611.

BERGQUIST, C. (ed.) (1984) *Labor in the Capitalist World-Economy*. London: SAGE Publications.

BERLE, A.A. and G.C. MEANS (1967) *The Modern Corporation and Private Property* revised edition. New York: Macmillan.

BERLINER, J.S. (1957) *Factory and Manager in the USSR*. Cambridge, MA: Harvard University Press.

BERLINER, J.S. (1976) *The Innovation Decision in Soviet Industry*. Cambridge, MA: MIT Press.

BERROCAL, L. (1984) 'The Spanish Euromigration: returnees and the domestic labor market', in D. KUBAT (ed.) *The Politics of Return: International Return Migration in Europe*. Rome: Centro Studi-Emigrazione.

BERTHOLD, N. (1980) *Multinationale Unternehmen und nationale Währungspolitik*. Freiburg im Breisgau: Haufe.

BERWEGER, G. and J.-P. HOBY (1980) 'Nationale Wirtschaftspolitik und multinationale Konzerne', pp. 263–302 in V. BORNSCHIER (ed.) *Multinationale Konzerne, Wirtschaftspolitik und nationale Entwicklung*. Frankfurt: Campus.

BEVERIDGE, W. (1944) *Full Employment in a Free Society*. London: Allen and Unwin.

BIEDENKOPF, K. (1985) *Die neue Sicht der Dinge. Plädoyer fur eine freiheitliche Wirtschafts- und Sozialordung*. Munich.

BIENAYME, A. (1982) *Entreprise, Marché, Etat*. Paris: Presses Universitaires de France.

BIERSTEKER, T.J. (1978) *Distortion or Development?* Cambridge, MA: MIT Press.

BIRKS, J.S. and C.A. SINCLAIR (1980) *International Migration in the Arab Region*. Geneva: ILO.

BLACK, J. and J.H. DUNNING (eds) (1982) *International Capital Movements*. London: Macmillan.

BLACKBURN (1982) 'The impact of multinational corporations on the spacial organization of developed nations: a review', pp. 147–57 in M. TAYLOR and N. THRIFT (eds) *The Geography of Multinationals*. London: Croom Helm.

BLAU, P. (1964) *Exchange and Power in Social Life*. New York: Wiley.

BLAU, P.M. and O.D. DUNCAN (1967) *The American Occupational Structure*. New York: Basic Books.

BLOCK, F. (1977) *The Origins of International Economic Disorder: a Study of United States International Monetary Policy from World War II to the Present*. Berkeley, CA: University of California Press.

BLOCK, F. (1981) 'The fiscal crisis of the capitalist state', *Annual Review of Sociology* 7: 1–27.

BLOMSTRÖM, M. (1986) 'Multinationals and market structure in Mexico', *World Development* 14(4): 523–30.

BÖHNING, W.R. (1981) 'Elements of a theory of international migration to industrial nation states', in M.M. KRITZ, C.B. KREELY and S.M. TOMASINI (eds) *Global Trends in Migration: Theory and Research in International Population Movements*. New York: Center for Migration Studies.

BÖHNING, W.R. (1983) 'Guestworker employment in selected European countries — lessons for the United States?', in P.G. BROWN and H. SHUE (eds) *The Border that Joins: Mexican Migrants and US Responsibility*. New Jersey: Rowman and Littlefield.

BOISSEVAIN, J. (1984) 'Small entrepreneurs in contemporary Europe', in R. WARD and R. JENKINS (eds) *Ethnic Communities in Business: Strategies for Economic Survival*. Cambridge: Cambridge University Press.

BOLLEN, K. (1983) 'World system position, dependency and democracy: the cross-national evidence', *American Sociological Review* 48(4): 468–79.

BONACICH, E. (1973) 'A theory of middleman minorities', *American Sociological Review* 38: 583–94.

BONILLA, F. and R. CAMPOS (1982) 'Imperialist initiatives and the Puerto Rican worker: from Foraker to Reagan', *Contemporary Marxism* 5: 1–18. (Special issue on 'The new nomads: immigration and changes in the international division of labor'.)

BONNETT, A. (1981) *Institutional Adaptations of West Indian Immigrants to America*. Washington DC: University Press of America.

BORN, K.E. (1983) *International Banking in the 19th and 20th Centuries*. Leamington Spa, Warwickshire: Berg Publishers. First published 1977.

BORNSCHIER, V. (1976) *Wachstum, Konzentration und Multinationalisierung von Industrieunternehmen*. Frauenfeld/Stuttgart: Huber.

BORNSCHIER, V. (1980) 'Multinational corporations and economic growth: a test of the decapitalization hypothesis', *Journal of Development Economics* 7(June): 191–210.

BORNSCHIER, V. (1982a) 'The world economy in the world-system: structure, dependence and change', *International Social Science Journal* 34(1): 38–59.

BORNSCHIER, V. (1982b) 'World economic integration and policy responses: some developmental impacts', in H. MAKLER, A. MARTINELLI and N. SMELSER (eds) *The New International Economy*. Newbury Park, CA: SAGE Publications.

BORNSCHIER, V. (1985) 'World social structure in the long economic wave'. Paper presented at the Annual International Studies Association meeting, 5–9 March, Washington DC.

BORNSCHIER, V. and T.-H. BALLMER-CAO (1979) 'Income inequality: a cross-national study of the relationships between MNC penetration, dimensions of power structure and income distribution', *American Sociological Review* 44(3): 487–506.

BORNSCHIER, V. and C. CHASE-DUNN (1985) *Transnational Corporations and Underdevelopment*. New York: Praeger.

BORNSCHIER, V. and J.-P. HOBY (1981) 'Economic policy and multinational corporations in development: the measurable impacts in cross-national perspective', *Social Problems* 28(4): 363–77.

BOTTOMORE, T. and R. BRYM (eds) (1989) *The Capitalist Class: An International Study*. New York: Harvester Wheatsheaf.

BOUDON, R. (1974) *Education, Opportunity, and Social Inequality: Changing Prospects in Western Society*. London: Wiley.

BOULDING, K. (1973) *The Economy of Love and Fear: a Preface to Grants Economy*. Belmont, CA: Wadsworth.

BOURDIEU, P. (1986) *Distinction*. Cambridge, MA: Harvard University Press.

BOURDIEU, P. and J.-C. PASSERON (1977) *Reproduction in Education, Society and Culture*. London: SAGE Publications.

BOWLES, S. and H. GINTIS (1976) *Schooling in Capitalist America: Educational Reform and the Contradictions of Economic Life*. New York: Basic Books.

BOWLES, S. and H. GINTIS (1982) 'The crisis of liberal democratic capitalism: the case of the United States', *Politics and Society* 11: 51–93.

BOYD, R., R. COHEN and P. GUTKIND (1987) *International Labour and the Third World: the Making of a New Working Class*. Aldershot: Gower.

BRAUDEL, F. (1975) *The Mediterranean and the Mediterranean World in the Age of Philip II* 2 volumes. London: Fontana. First published 1966.

BRAVERMAN, H. (1974) *Labor and Monopoly Capitalism*. New York: Monthly Review Press.

BRENTANO, L. (1923) *Der wirtschaftende Mensch in der Geschichte, Gesammelte Reden und Aufsätze*. Leiden: E.J. Brill.

BROMLEY, R. and C. GERRY (eds) (1979) *Casual Work and Poverty in Third World Cities*. New York: John Wiley and Sons.

BRONSTEIN, M. (1973) 'Introduction', in M. BRONSTEIN (ed.) *Plan and Market: Economic Reform in Eastern Europe*. New Haven, CT: Yale University Press.

BRUS, W. (1986) *Histoire économique de l'Europe de l'Est*. Paris: Editions la Découverte.

BUCKLEY, P.J. and M. CASSON (1976) *The Future of Multinational Enterprise*. London: Macmillan.

BUCKLEY, P.J. and M. CASSON (1985) *The Economic Theory of Multinational Enterprise*. New York: St Martin's Press.

BUCKLEY, P.J. and J.H. DUNNING (1980) 'The industrial structure of US direct investment in the United Kingdom', *Journal of International Business Studies*, 5–13.

BUKHARIN, N. (1928) 'Zamietki Ekonomista' (Economist's remarks), *Pravda* 228, 30 September.

BURAWAY, M. (1976) 'The functions and reproduction of migrant labor: comparative material from Southern Africa and the United States', *American Journal of Sociology* 81(5): 1050–87.

BURNS, S. (1977) *The Household Economy*. Boston, MA: Beacon Press.

Business Week (1985) 'The Koreans are coming', 23 December.

Business Week (1986) 'The "four tigers" are pouncing on Japan's markets', 24 March: 48–9.

BUSS, A.E. (ed.) (1985) *Max Weber in Asian Studies*. Leiden: E.J. Brill.

CAMERON, D. (1984) 'Social democracy, corporatism, labour quiescence and the representation of economic interest in advanced capitalist society', pp. 143–78 in J.H. GOLDTHORPE *Conflict and Order in Contemporary Capitalism*. Oxford: Oxford University Press.

CARDOSO, F.H. (1973) 'Associated dependent development: theoretical and practical implications', in S. ALFRED (ed.) *Authoritarian Brazil: Origins, Policies and Future*. New Haven, CN: Yale University Press.

CARNOY, C. and H. LEVIN (1985) *Schooling and Work in the Democratic State*. Stamford, CA: Stamford University Press.

CASPARIS, J. (1985) 'The core demand from Southern Europe: the case of Switzerland', in G. ARRIGHI (ed.) *Semiperipheral Development: The Politics of Southern Europe in the Twentieth Century*. London: SAGE Publications.

CASSEL, D. and E.U. CICHY (1987) 'The growing shadow economy in socialist planning systems: causes and consequences', *Nauki o Zarzadzaniu* 1: 49–63.

CASTELLS, M. (1975) 'Immigrant workers and class struggles in advanced capitalism: the Western European experience', *Politics and Society* 5(1): 33–66.

CASTELLS, M. (1982) 'Commentary' in *Contemporary Marxism*, No. 5. (Special Issue on *The New Nomads: Immigration and Changes in the International Division of Labor.*)

CASTLES, F.G. (ed.) (1982) *The Impact of Political Parties*. Newbury Park, CA and London: SAGE Publications.

CASTLES, S. and G. KOSACK (1973) *Immigrant Workers and Class Structure in Western Europe*. Oxford: Oxford University Press.

CAVES, R.E. (1971) 'International corporations: the industrial economics of foreign investment', *Economica* 38: 1–2.

CAVES, R.E. (1974) 'Multinational firms, competition and productivity in host-country markets', *Economica* 41: 176–93.

CAVES, R.E. (1982) *Multinational Enterprise and Economic Analysis*. Cambridge: Cambridge University Press.

CHAMBERLAIN, E.N. (1948) *The Theory of Monopolistic Competition* sixth edition. Cambridge: Cambridge University Press.

CHANDLER Jr, A.D. (1969) *Strategy and Structure: Chapters in the History of the American Enterprise*. Cambridge, MA: MIT Press.

CHANDLER Jr, A.D. (1977) *The Visible Hand: the Managerial Revolution in American Business*. Cambridge/London: The Belknap Press of Harvard University Press.

CHANDLER Jr, A.D. (1980) 'The growth of the transnational industrial firm in the United States and the United Kingdom: a comparative analysis', *The Economic History Review* 33: 396–410.

CHANDLER Jr, A.D. and H. DAEMS (eds) (1980) *Managerial Hierarchies: Comparative Perspectives on the Rise of the Modern Industrial Enterprise*. Cambridge/London: Harvard University Press.

CHANEY, E. (1979) 'The world economy and contemporary migration', *International Migration Review* 13(summer): 204–12.

CHAPMAN, S. (1984) *The Rise of Merchant Banking*. London: George Allen and Unwin.

CHAPMAN, S. (1986) 'Aristocracy and meritocracy in merchant banking', *British Journal of Sociology* 37: 180–93.

CHENG, TUN-JEN (1990) 'Political regimes and development strategies: South Korea and Taiwan', in G. GEREFFI and D. WYMAN (eds) *Manufacturing Miracles: Paths of Industrialization in Latin America and East Asia*. Princeton, NJ: Princeton University Press.

CHENG, TUN-JEN and S. HAGGARD (1987) *Newly Industrializing Asia in Transition: Policy Reform and American Response*. Berkeley, CA: University of California at Berkeley, Institute of International Studies.

CHEVRIER, Y. (1986) 'Réformes économiques en Chine: crise de croissance ou blocage de la modernisation', *Revue d'études comparatives Est–Ouest* 2: 89–105.

CHOUDHURI, K.N. (1978) *The Trading World of Asia and the English East India Company 1660–1760*. Cambridge: Cambridge University Press.

CHOUGH, IL-LAE (1983) 'The overseas employment policy of Korea', *Conference on Asian Labor Migration to the Middle East*. Honolulu: East–West Population Center.

CHOURAQUI, J.C., B. JONES and R.B. MONTADOR (1986) 'Public debt in a medium-term perspective', *Economic Studies* 7: 103–53.

CHURCH, R. (1980) *The Dynamics of Victorian England*. London: George Allen and Unwin.

CLARK, B.R. (1987) *The Problem of Complexity in Modern Higher Education* Working Paper 9. Los Angeles, CA: Comparative Higher Education Research Group.

COCKCROFT, J.D. (1982) 'Mexican migration, crisis and the internationalization of labor struggle', *Contemporary Marxism* 5: 48–61. (Special issue on 'The new nomads: immigration and changes in the international division of labor'.)

COHEN, R. (1987a) *The New Helots: Migrants in the International Division of Labor*. Aldershot: Gower.

COHEN, R. (1987b) 'Policing the frontiers: the state and the migrant in the international division of labor', in J. HENDERSON and M. CASTELLS (eds) *Global Restructuring and Territorial Development*. London: SAGE Publications.

COLE, D.C. (1980) 'Foreign assistance and Korean development', pp. 1–29 in D.C. COLE, YOUNGIL LIM and P. KUZNETS (eds) *The Korean Economy — Issues of Development*. Berkeley, CA: Institute of East Asian Studies.

COLEMAN, J.S. (1990) *Foundations of Social Theory*. Cambridge: Belknap Press.

COLLINS, R. (1979) *The Credential Society: An Historical Sociology of Education and Stratification*. New York: Academic Press.

COMMITTEE ON FINANCE (1973) *US Senate: Implications of Multinational Firms for World Trade and Investment and for US Trade and Labor*. Washington DC: US Government Printing Office.

CONNOR, W.D. (1975) 'De l'utopie à la société pragmatique: les conséquences sociales des réformes économiques en Europe de l'est', *Revue d'études comparatives Est–Ouest* 1.

COSER, L.A. (1974) 'The alien as a servant of power: court Jews and Christian renegades', in *Greedy Institutions: Patterns of Undivided Commitment*. New York: The Free Press.

COTTERET, J.-M., G. AYACHE and J. DUX (1984) *L'image des multinationales en France dans la presse et l'opinion publique*. Geneva/Paris: Institut de recherche et d'information sur les multinationales.

CROSLAND, C.A.R. (1956) *The Future of Socialism*. London: Cape.

CROZIER, Michel (1964) *The Bureaucratic Phenomenon*. Chicago, IL: University of Chicago Press.

CSABA, L. (1986a) 'La réforme hongroise et son évolution possible en 1985–1987', *Revue d'études comparatives Est–Ouest* 2: 7–12, and pp. 23–5 commentary by X. RICHET.

CSABA, L. (1986b) 'New features in Hungarian economic mechanism in the mid-eighties', *The New Hungarian Quarterly* 90(summer).

CSIKOS-NAGY, B. (1972) 'La politique économique de la Hongrie: ses objectifs et ses moyens', *Revue l'Est* 1.

CURTIN, P.D. (1984) *Cross-cultural Trade in World History*. Cambridge: Cambridge University Press.

DAHL, R.A. and C.E. LINDBLOM (1953) *Politics, Economics and Welfare. Planning and Politico-Economic Systems Resolved into Basic Social Processes*. New York: Harper Torchbooks.

DAHRENDORF, R. (1959) *Class and Class Conflict in Industrial Society*. Stanford, CA: Stanford University Press.

DAHRENDORF, R. (1979) 'Am Ende des sozialdemokratischen Konsensus? Zur Frage der Legitimität der politischen Macht in der Gegenwart', in R. DAHRENDORF (ed.) *Lebenschancen. Aufsätze zur sozialen und politischen Theorie*. Frankfurt: Suhrkamp.

DAMETTE, F. (1980) 'The regional framework for monopoly exploitation: new problems and trends', in J. CARNEY et al. (eds) *Regions in Crisis: New Perspectives in European Regional Theory*. London: Croom Helm.

DAVIES, R.W. (1958) *The Development of the Soviet Budgetary System*. Cambridge: Cambridge University Press.

DAVIS, S.I. (1976) *The Euro-bank: Its Origins, Management and Outlook*. London: Macmillan.

DEANE, P. and W.A. COLE (1967) *British Economic Growth, 1688–1959* second edition. Cambridge: Cambridge University Press.

DE MARÍA Y CAMPOS, M. (1987) 'El cambio estructural en la evolución reciente de la economía mexicana', in M. DE LA MADRID et al. *Cambio estructural en México y en el mundo*. Mexico, D.F.: Fondo de Cultura Económica.

DE ROOVER, R. (1948) *Money, Banking and Credit in Medieval Bruges — Italian Merchant Bankers, Lombards and Money-changers: a study in the Origins of Banking*. Cambridge, MA: The Mediaeval Academy of America.

DE ROOVER, R. (1955) 'New interpretations of the history of banking', *Cahiers d'histoire mondiale* 2(1): 38–76.

DE ROOVER, R. (1963a) 'The organization of trade', pp. 42–118 in M.M. POSTAN, E.E. RICH and E. MILLER (eds) *The Cambridge Economic History of Europe III. Economic Organization and Policies in the Middle Ages*. Cambridge: Cambridge University Press.

DE ROOVER, R. (1963b) *The Rise and Decline of the Medici Bank*. Cambridge, MA: Harvard University Press.

DE ROOVER, R. (1974) *Business, Banking and Economic Thought in Late Medieval and Early Modern Europe: Selected Studies of Raymond de Roover*. Chicago, IL: University of Chicago Press.

DE VOS, T. (1981) *U.S. Multinationals and Worker Participation in Management: the American experience in the European community*. London: Aldwych Press.

DEYO, F.C. (ed.) (1987) *The Political Economy of the New Asian Industrialism*. Ithaca, NY: Cornell University Press.

DOERINGER, P.B. and M.J. PIORE (1971) *Internal Labor Markets and Manpower Analysis*. Lexington, MA: D.C. Heath.

DORE, R. (1973) *British Factory, Japanese Factory*. London: George Allen and Unwin.

DORE, R. (1976) *The Diploma Disease: Education, Qualification and Development*. London: George Allen and Unwin.

DOS SANTOS, T. (1970) 'The structure of dependence', *American Economic Review* (Papers and Proceedings) 60: 231–6.

DOWNS, A. (1957) *An Economic Theory of Democracy*. New York: Harper.

DULSKI, S. (ed.) (1984) *Reforma Gospodarcza. Zmiany w Strukturze Podmiotowej Gospodarki Narodowej* (Economic Reform. Changes in the Industrial Structure of the National Economy.) Warsaw: SGPiS.

DUMONT, L. (1977) *From Mandeville to Marx: The Genesis and Triumph of Economic Sociology*. Chicago, IL: University of Chicago Press.

DUNNING, J.H. (1958) *American Investment in British Manufacturing Industry*. London: George Allen and Unwin.

DUNNING, J.H. (ed.) (1974) *Economic Analysis and the Multinational Enterprise*. London: George Allen and Unwin.

DUNNING, J.H. (1981) *International Production and the Multinational Enterprise*. London: George Allen and Unwin.

DUNNING, J.H. (1983) 'Changes in the level and structure of international production: the last one hundred years', pp. 84–139 in M. CASSON (ed.) *The Growth of International Business*. London: Allen and Unwin.

DUNNING, J.H. and PEARCE, R.D. (1981) *The World's Largest Industrial Enterprises*. New York: St Martin's Press.

DURKHEIM, E. (1912) *The Elementary Forms of the Religious Life*. London: George Allen and Unwin.

DURKHEIM, E. (1893) *De la division de travail social. Etude sur l'organisation des sociétés supérieures*. Paris: Presses Universitaires de France (1960) *The Division of Labor in Society* second edition. Glencoe, IL: The Free Press.

DURKHEIM, E. (1948) *The Division of Labor in Society*. Translated by George Simpson. Glencoe, IL: The Free Press.

DURKHEIM, E. (1969) *L'évolution pédagogique en France*. Paris: Presses Universitaires de France.

DURKHEIM, E. (1976) *The Elementary Forms of the Religious Life* second edition. London: George Allen and Unwin.

DUVALL, R., S. JACKSON, B.M. RUSSETT, D. SNIDAL and D. SYLVAN (1981) 'A formal model of "dependencia theory": structure and measurement', pp. 312–50 in R.L. MERRITT and B. RUSSETT (eds) *From National Development to Global Community*. London: George Allen and Unwin.

EASTON, D. (1953) *The Political System*. New York: Knopf.

EDELSTEIN, M. (1982) *Overseas Investment in the Age of High Imperialism*. London: Methuen.

EDWARDS, R., M. REICH and D.M. GORDON (eds) (1975) *Labor Market Segmentation*. Lexington, MA: D.C. Heath.

EHRLICH, A. (1960) *The Soviet Industrialization Debate 1924–1928*. Cambridge, MA: Harvard University Press.

EISENSTADT, S.N. (1968) *The Protestant Ethic and Modernization*. New York: Basic Books.

Ekonomiści Dyskutuja o Prawie Wartości (Economists Discuss Value Law) (1956). Warsaw: Ksiażka i Wiedza.

EMMANUEL, A. (1972) *Unequal Exchange: a Study of the Imperialism of Trade*. New York: Monthly Review Press.

ENDERWICK, P. (1985) *Multinational Business and Labor*. New York: St Martin's Press.

ETZIONI, A. (1988) *The Moral Dimension*. New York: Basic Books.

EVANS, P.B. (1977) 'Direct investment and industrial concentration', *Journal of Development Studies* 13: 373–86.

EVANS, P.B. (1979) *Dependent Development. The Alliance of Multinational, State and Local Capital in Brazil*. Princeton, NJ: Princeton University Press.

EVANS, P.B. (1981) 'Recent research on multinational corporations', *Annual Review of Sociology* 7: 199–223.

EVANS, P.B. (1986) 'State, capital and the transformation of dependence: the Brazilian computer case', *World Development* 14(7): 791–808.

EVANS, P.B. and G. GEREFFI (1982) 'Foreign investment and dependent development: comparing Brazil and Mexico', pp. 111–68 in S.A. HEWLETT and R.S. WEINERT (eds) *Brazil and Mexico: Patterns in Late Development*. Philadelphia, PA: Institute for the Study of Human Issues.

EVANS, P.B., D. RUESCHMEYER and E.H. STEPHANS (1985) *States versus Markets in the World System*. London: SAGE Publications.

EVANS, P.B. and J.D. STEPHENS (1988) 'Development and the world economy', pp. 739–73 in N.J. SMELSER (ed.) *Handbook of Sociology*. Newbury Park, CA: SAGE Publications.

EVANS, P.B. and M. TIMBERLAKE (1980) 'Dependence, inequality and the growth of the tertiary: a comparative analysis of less developed countries', *American Sociological Review* 45: 531–52.

FAIN, T.S. (1980) 'Self-employed Americans: their number has increased', *Monthly Labor Review* 103(12): 3–8.

Far Eastern Economic Review (1985a) 'Retreat from reason: protectionism now a political rallying point in the U.S.', 5 September: 520.

Far Eastern Economic Review (1985b) 'NICs in a twist', 26 September: 99–100.

FARRELL, R.B. (ed.) (1970) *Political Leadership in Eastern Europe and the Soviet Union*. Chicago, IL: Aldine Publishing Co.

FEIGE, L. (1981) *The Theory and Measurement of the Unobserved Sector of the US Economy*. Leiden.

FENNEMA, M. (1982) *International Networks of Banks and Industry*. The Hague: Martinus Nijhoff.

FENNEMA, M. and H. SCHIJF (1985) 'The transnational network', pp. 250–66 in F.N. STOKMAN, R. ZIEGLER and J. SCOTT (eds) *Networks of Corporate Power: an Analysis of Ten Countries*. Cambridge: Polity Press.

FICK, B. (1965) *Bodżce Ekonomiczne w Przemyśle* (Economic Incentives in Industry). Warsaw: Państwowe Wydawnictwo Ekonomiczne.

FINDLAY, A.M. (1984) 'Migrations de travail dans le golfe et croissance des quartiers périphériques d'Amman', *Etudes Méditerranéennes* 6: 205–24.

FIRTH, Raymond (1971) *Elements of Social Organization* third edition. London: Tavistock Publications.

FISCHER, W. (ed.) (1987) *Handbuch der Europaischen Wirtschafts- und Sozialgeschichte* volume 6. Stuttgart: Klett-Cotta.

FISCHOFF, E. (1944) 'The Protestent ethic and the spirit of capitalism: the history of a controversy', *Social Research* 11: 54–77. (Also included in EISENSTADT [1968].)

FISHLOW, A. (1985) 'The state of Latin American economics', pp. 123–48 in INTER-AMERICAN DEVELOPMENT BANK *Economic and Social Progress in Latin America — External Debt: Crisis and Adjustment*. Washington DC: IADB.

FISHWICK, F. (1982) *Multinational Companies and Economic Concentration in Europe*. Aldershot: Gower

FLIGSTEIN, N. (1985) 'The spread of the multidivisional form among large firms 1919–1979', *American Sociological Review* 50(3): 377–91.

FLORA, P. (1981) 'Solution or source of crisis? The welfare state in historical perspective', in J.W. MOMMSEN (ed.) *The Emergence of the Welfare State in Britain and Germany*. London: Croom Helm.

FLORA, P. (1983) *State, Economy and Society in Western Europe 1815–1975* volumes 1 and 2. Frankfurt: Campus.

FRANK, A.G. (1969) *Latin America: Underdevelopment or Revolution?* New York: Monthly Review Press.

FRANKO, L.G. (1976) *The European Multinationals: a Renewed Challenge to American and British Big Business*. London: Harper and Row.

FRIEDMAN, M. (1955) 'The role of government in education', in R.A. SOLS (ed.) *Economics and the Public Interest*. New Brunswick, NJ: Rutgers University Press.

FROEBEL, F., J. HEINRICHS and O. KREYE (1981) *The New International Division of Labour: Structural Unemployment in Industrialized Countries and Industrialization in Developing Countries*. Cambridge: Cambridge University Press.

FULTON, O. (ed.) (1981) *Access to Higher Education*. Research into Higher Education Monographs series. Guildford, Surrey: SRHE.

FURTADO, C. (1983) *Accumulation and Development: the Logic of Industrial Civilization*. Oxford: Martin Robertson.

GADO, O. (1972) *Reform of Economic Mechanism in Hungary: Development 1968–1971*. Budapest: Akademiai Kaido.

GADO, O. (1976) *The Economic Mechanism in Hungary: How It Works in 1976*. Budapest: Akademiai Kaido.

GAGLIANI, G. (1987) 'Income distribution and economic development', *Annual Review of Sociology* 13:313–34.

GALASI, P. and E. SIK (1982) 'Allocation de travail et économie socialiste: le cas de la Hongrie', *Economies et Sociétiés* 10.

GAMBETTA, D. (1987) *Were They Pushed or Did they Jump?* Cambridge: Cambridge University Press.

GEREFFI, G. (1978) 'Drug firms and dependency in Mexico: the case of the steroid hormone industry', *International Organization* 32: 237–86.

GEREFFI, G. (1983) *The Pharmaceutical Industry and Dependency in the Third World*. Princeton, NJ: Princeton University Press.

GEREFFI, G. and P. EVANS (1981) 'Transnational corporations, dependent development and state policy in the semiperiphery: a comparison of Brazil and Mexico', *Latin American Research Review* 16(3): 31–654.

GEREFFI, G. and D. WYMAN (1987) 'Determinants of development strategies in Latin America and East Asia', *Pacific Focus* 2(1): 5–33.

GEREFFI, G. and D. WYMAN (eds) (1990) *Manufacturing Miracles: Paths of Industrialization in Latin America and East Asia*. Princeton, NJ: Princeton University Press.

GERRY, C. (1984) 'How important a factor will the urban informal sector be in the UK crisis management strategy?', *The Urban Informal Sector: Recent Trends in Research and Theory*. Conference Proceedings, Baltimore, Sociology Department, Johns Hopkins University.

GERSCHENKRON, A. (1962) 'Economic backwardness in historical perspective', pp. 5–30 in his *Economic Backwardness in Historical Perspective: a Book of Essays*. Cambridge, MA: Harvard University Press. First published 1952.

GERSHUNY, J. (1978) *After Industrial Society? The Emerging Self-service Economy*. London: Macmillan.

GERSHUNY, J. and R. PAHL (1980) 'Britain in the decade of the three economies', *New Society*, January.

GILLE, B. (1973) 'Banking and industrialization in Europe, 1730–1940', pp. 301–57 in C.M. CIPOLLA (ed.) *The Fontana Economic History of Europe* third volume. London: Fontana/Collins.

GILPIN, R. (1976) *US Power and the Multinational Corporation — the Political Economy of Foreign Direct Investment*. London: Macmillan.

GLAGOW, M. and H. WILLKE (eds) (1987) *Dezentrale Gesellschaftssteuerung. Probleme der Integration polyzentrischer Gesellschaft*. Pfaffenweiler: Centaurus.

GLIŃSKI, B. (1985) *Zarzadzanie w Gospodarce Socjalistycznej* (Management in the Socialist Economy). Warsaw: Państwowe Wydawnictwo Ekonomiczne.

GLYN, A. and B. SUTCLIFFE (1972) *Capitalism in Crisis*. New York: Random House.

GOLAN, G. (1981) *The Czechoslovak Reform Movement: Communism in Crisis 1962–1968*. New York: Cambridge University Press.

GOLDTHORPE, J.H. (1978) 'The current inflation: towards a sociological account', in F. HIRSCH and J.H. GOLDTHORPE (eds) *The Political Economy of Inflation*. Oxford: Martin Robertson.

GOLDTHORPE, J.H. (1987) 'The end of convergence: corporatism and dualist tendencies in modern Western societies', in J. GOLDTHORPE (ed.) *Order and Conflict in Contemporary Capitalism: Studies in the Political Economy of Western European Nations*. Oxford: Oxford University Press.

GOLDTHORPE, J.H. (1986) 'Employment, class and mobility: a critique of liberal and Marxist theories of long-term change'. Paper presented at the conference on Social Change and Development, Berkeley, 26–8 August 1986.

GOLDTHORPE, J.H. et al. (1980) *Social Mobility and Class Structure in Modern Britain*. Oxford: Clarendon Press.

GOLZIO, K.H. (1985) 'Max Weber on Japan: the role of the government and Buddhist sect', in A.E. BUSS (ed.) *Max Weber in Asian Studies*. Leiden: E.J. Brill.

GORDON, D.M. (1978) 'Up and down the long roller coaster', in *U.S. Capitalism in Crisis*. URPE.

GORDON, D.M. (1988) 'The global economy: new edifice or crumbling foundations?', *New Left Review* 168: 24–64.

GORDON, M.S. and M. TROW (1979) *Youth Education and Unemployment Problems*. The Carnegie Council on Policy Studies in Higher Education.

GÓRSKI, M. and G. JEDRZEJCZAK (1987) *Rówowaga i Stabilność w Gospodarce Socjalistycznej* (Equilibrium and Stability in the Socialist Economy.) Warsaw: Państwowe Wydawnictwo Naukowe.

GOSPODINOV, K. (ed.) (1986) *Social Problems of the Young Generation Today*. Sofia: Institute of Youth Studies.

GRANOVETTER, M. (1984) 'Small is bountiful: labor markets and establishment size', *American Sociological Review* 49(June): 323–34.

GRANOVETTER, M. (1985) 'Economic action and social structure: the problem of embeddedness', *American Journal of Sociology* 91(3): 481–510.

GRANT, W. and W. STREECK (1985) 'Large firms and the representation of business interests in the UK and West German construction industry', in A. CAWSON (ed.) *Organized Interests and the State*. London: SAGE Publications.

GRAS, N.S.B. (1939) *Business and Capitalism: an Introduction to Business History*. New York: F.S. Croft.

GRIFFITH, D. (1924) *What is Socialism?* London.

GROSFEL, I. and A. SMOLAR (1981) 'Economie parallèle en Pologne', *Futuribles* 40.

GROSSMAN, G. (1966) 'Economic reforms: a balance sheet', *Problems of Communism* (November/December): 8–11.

GROU, P. (1983) *La structure financière du capitalisme multinational*. Paris: Presses de la fondation nationale des sciences politiques.

GRUNWALD, J. and K. FLAMM (1985) *The Global Factory*. Washington DC: The Brookings Institution.

GUHA, A.S. (1981) *An Evolutionary View of Economic Growth*. Oxford: Oxford University Press.

HABERMAS, J. (1985) *Die neue Unübersichtlichkeit*. Frankfurt: Suhrkamp.

HAGEN, Everett (1962) *On the Theory of Social Change: How Economic Growth Begins*. Homewood, IL: Dorsey.

HAGGARD, S. and TUN-JEN CHENG (1987) 'State and foreign capital in the East Asian NICs', pp. 84–135 in F.C. DEYO (ed.) *The Political Economy of the New Asian Industrialism*. Ithaca, NJ: Cornell University Press.

HALEVY, Elie (1928) *The Growth of Philosophical Radicalism*. Translated by Mary Morris. New York: Macmillan.

HALL, J.A. (1985) *Powers and Liberties*. London: Penguin Books.

HALSEY, A.H. (1977) 'Towards meritocracy? The case of Britain', in J. KARABEL and A.H. HALSEY (eds) *Power and Ideology in Education*. New York: Oxford University Press.

HALSEY, A.H., A.F. HEATH and J.M. RIDGE (1980) *Origins and Destinations: Family, Class and Education in Modern Britain*. Oxford: Oxford University Press.

HAMMER, H.-J. and J.W. GARTRELL (1986) 'American penetration and Canadian development: a case study of mature dependency', *American Sociological Review* 51(2): 201–13.

HARDEN, G. (1968) 'The Tragedy of the Commons', *Science* 162: 1234–47.

HARRIS, N. (1987) *The End of the Third World: Newly Industrializing Countries and the Decline of an Ideology*. New York: Viking Penguin.

HAWLEY, J.P. (1984) 'Protecting capital against itself: U.S. attempts to regulate the eurocurrency system', *International Organization* 38(1): 131–65.

HAYTER, T. (1971) *Aid as Imperialism*. Harmondsworth: Penguin.

HEATH, A. (1976) *Rational Choice and Social Exchange*. Cambridge: Cambridge University Press.

HEERTJIE, A. and P. BARTHELEMY (1984) *L'économie souterraine*. Paris: Economica.

HEINZE, R. and T. OLK (1982) 'Development of the informal economy. A strategy for solving the crisis of the welfare state', *Futures* (June).

HEISLER, B.S. (1986) 'Immigrant settlement and the structure of emergent immigrant communities in Western Europe', *The Annals* AAPSS, 485(May): 76–86. (Special issue on 'From foreign workers to settlers? Transnational migration and the emergence of new minorities'.)

HELLEINER, G.K. (1973) 'Manufactured exports from less-developed countries and multinational firms', *The Economic Journal* 83: 21–47.

HELLEINER, G.K. (1975) 'Transnational enterprises in the manufacturing sector of the less-developed countries', *World Development* 3(9): 641–50.

HELLEINER, G.K. (1981) *Intra-firm Trade and the Developing Countries*. London: Macmillan.

HENDERSON, J. and M. CASTELLS (eds) (1987) *Global Restructuring and Territorial Development*. London: SAGE Publications.

HENNART, J.-F. (1982) *A Theory of Multinational Enterprise* Ann Arbor: University of Michigan Press.

HENRY, S. (1978) 'The working unemployed. Perspectives on the informal economy and unemployment', *The Sociological Review* 3.

HIDY, R.W. (1949) *The House of Baring in American Trade and*

Finance: English Merchant Bankers at Work 1763–1861. Cambridge, MA: Harvard University Press.

HILL, T.P. (1979) *Profits and Rates of Return*. Paris: OECD.

HINDESS, B. (1987) *Freedom, Equality and the Market. Arguments on Social Policy*. London: Tavistock Publications.

HIRSCH, F. (1976) *Social Limits to Growth*. Cambridge, MA: Harvard University Press.

HIRSCH, F. (1977) *Social Limits of Growth*. London: Routledge and Kegan Paul.

HIRSCHMAN, A.O. (1967) *Development Projects Observed*. Washington DC: The Brookings Institution.

HIRSCHMAN, A.O. (1968) 'The political economy of import-substituting industrialization in Latin America', *The Quarterly Journal of Economics* 82: 2–32.

HIRSCHMAN, A.O. (1987) 'The political economy of Latin American development: seven exercises in retrospection', *Latin American Research Review* 22(3): 7–36.

HIRSCHMEIER, J. and T. YUI (1975) *The Development of Japanese Business 1600–1973*. London: George Allen and Unwin.

HOEL, B. (1982) 'Contemporary clothing sweatshops, Asian female labor and collective organization', in J. WEST (ed.) *Work, Women and the Labor Market*. London: Routledge and Kegan Paul.

HOFFMEYER-ZLOTNIK, J. (1982) 'Community change and invasion: the case of the Turkish guest workers', in J. FRIEDRICH (ed.) *Spatial Disparities and Social Behaviour: A Reader in Urban Research*. Hamburg: Christians Verlag.

HOLMAN, J. (1984) 'Underdevelopment aid: a critique of the International Monetary Fund and the World Bank', *Berkeley Journal of Sociology* 29: 119–52.

HOMANS, George (1974) *Social Behavior: Its Elementary Forms* revised edition. New York: Harcourt, Brace, Jovanovich.

HONG, W. (1979) *Trade, Distortions and Employment Growth in Korea*. Seoul: Korea Development Institute.

HOOD, N. and S. YOUNG (1983) *Multinational Investment Strategies in the British Isles*. London: Her Majesty's Stationery Office.

HORVATH, B. (1982) *The Political Economy of Socialism*. Armonk, NY: M.E. Sharpe.

HORVATH, B., M. MARKOVIC and R. SUPEK (1977) *Self-governing Socialism*. New York: International Arts and Sciences Press.

HOUT, M. (1987) 'Recent changes in occupational mobility of men and women in the United States 1972–1986: opportunity and change'. Paper presented at the ISA Research Committee on Stratification Meetings, Berkeley, 20 August 1987.

HUAN-MING LING, L. (1984) 'East Asian migration to the Middle East: causes, consequences and considerations', *International*

Migration Review 18(1): 19–36.
HUBER, J. (1979) 'Autogestion et économie duale', *Futuribles* 24.
HUDSON, R. and J. LEWIS (eds) (1985) *Uneven Development in Southern Europe: Studies of Accumulation, Class, Migration and the State*. London: Methuen.
HUGON, P., N.L. ABADIE and A. MORICE (1977) *La petite production marchande et l'emploi dans le secteur 'informel'. Le cas africain*. Paris: Université de Paris.
HYMER, S. (1976) *The International Operations of National Firms: a Study in Direct Foreign Investment*. Cambridge, MA: MIT Press.
HYMER, S. (1979) *The Multinational Corporation: a Radical Approach. Papers by Stephen Herbert Hymer*. Cambridge: Cambridge University Press.
ILLICH, I. (1981) *Le travail fantôme*. Paris: Seuil.
ILLICH, I. et al. (1977) *Disabling Professions*. London: Marion Boyars.
ILO (INTERNATIONAL LABOUR OFFICE) (1976) *The Impact of Multinational Enterprises on Employment and Training*. Geneva: ILO.
ILO (1981a) *Employment Effects of Multinational Enterprises in Developing Countries*. Geneva: ILO.
ILO (1981b) *Employment Effects of Multinational Enterprises in Industrialised Countries*. Geneva: ILO.
IMF (INTERNATIONAL MONETARY FUND) (1987) *International Financial Statistics Yearbook* (National Accounts Statistics). Washington DC: IMF.
Informationen über Multinationale Konzerne (various issues). Vienna: Kammer für Arbeiter und Angestellte für Wien.
IWANOWSKA, A. (1982) *Dynamika Systemu Zarzadzania Gospodarka* (Dynamics of the System of Management of the Economy). Warsaw: Ksiażka i Wiedza.
JACKSON, J.A. (ed.) (1969) *Migration: Sociological Studies* 2. Cambridge: Cambridge University Press.
JACOBY, N.H. (1966) *U.S. Aid to Taiwan*. New York: Praeger.
JANOWITZ, M. (1976) *The Social Control of the Welfare State*. New York.
JANSEN, C.J. (1970) 'Migration: a sociological problem', in C.J. JANSEN (ed.) *Readings in Sociology of Migration*. Oxford: Pergamon.
JENCKS, C. and S. BARTLETT et al. (1979) *Who Gets Ahead? The Determinants of Economic Success in America*. New York: Basic Books.
JENCKS, C.S., M. SMITH, H. ACLAND, M.J. BANE, D. COHEN, H. GINTIS, B. HEYNS and S. MICHELSON (1972) *Inequality: A Reassessment of the Effects of Family and Schooling in America*. New York: Basic Books.

JOHNSON, C. (1987) 'Political institutions and economic performance: the government–business relationship in Japan, South Korea and Taiwan', pp. 136–64 in F.C. DEYO (ed.) *The Political Economy of the New Asian Industrialism*. Ithaca, NY: Cornell University Press.

JONES, G. (1984) 'The growth and performance of British multinational firms before 1939: the case of Dunlop', *The Economic History Review* 37: 35–53.

JUNANKER, P. (ed.) (1987) *From School to Unemployment? The Labour Market for Young People*. London: Macmillan.

KAELBLE, H. (1987) *Auf dem Weg zu einer europäischen Gesellschaft. Eine Sozialgeschichte Westeuropas 1880–1980*. Munich: E.H. Beck.

KALECKI, M. (1972) 'Political aspects of full employment', in M. KALECKI *Selected Essays on the Economic Growth of the Socialist and the Mixed Economy*. Cambridge: Cambridge University Press.

KARABEL, J. and A.H. HALSEY (eds) (1978) *Power and Ideology in Education*. New York: Oxford University Press.

KARPIŃSKI, A. (1986) *40 Lat Planowania w Polsce* (40 Years of Planning in Poland). Warsaw: Państwowe Wydawnictwo Ekonomiczne.

KASER, M. (1986) 'The economic imperatives in the Soviet education reform of 1984', *Oxford Review of Education* 12(2): 181–5.

KATSENLIBOIGEN, A. (1977) 'Coloured markets in the Soviet Union', *Soviet Studies* 1.

KAUFMAN, R.R. (1988) *The Politics of Debt in Argentina, Brazil and Mexico: Economic Stabilization in the 1980s*. Berkeley, CA: University of California at Berkeley, Institute of International Studies.

KAUFMAN, R.R. (1990) 'How societies change development models or keep them: reflections on the Latin American experience in the 1930s and the post-war world', in G. GEREFFI and D. WYMAN (eds) *Manufacturing Miracles: Paths of Industrialization in Latin America and East Asia*. Princeton, NJ: Princeton University Press.

KEANE, J. and J. OWENS (1986) *After Full Employment*. London: Hutchinson.

KEELY, C.B. and B. SAKET (1984) 'Jordanian migrant workers in the Arab regions: a case study of consequences for labour supplying countries', *Middle East Journal* 38(4): 685–98.

KEESING, D.B. (1981) 'Exports and policy in Latin American countries', pp. 18–43 in W. BAER and M. GILLIS (eds) *Export Diversification and the New Protectionism*. Champaign, IL: National Bureau of Economic Research.

KENDE, P. and Z. STRMISKA (eds) (1984) *Egalité et inégalités en Europe de l'Est*. Paris: Presses de la Fondation Nationale des Sciences Politiques.

KENEDI, J. (1982) *Faites-le vous-mêmes. L'économie parallèle en Hongrie*. Paris: Maspero.

KERR, C. (1983) *The Future of Industrial Societies*. Cambridge, MA: Harvard University Press.

KERR, C. et al. (1960, 1973) *Industrialism and Industrial Man*. Cambridge, MA: Harvard University Press.

KEYDER, C. and A. AKSU (1986) *External Labor Migration from Turkey and Its Impact*. Report prepared for IDR, Istanbul.

KEYNES, J.M. (1936) *The General Theory of Employment, Interest and Money*. London: Macmillan.

KIM, I. (1981) *The New Urban Immigrants: Korean Immigrants in New York City*. Princeton, NJ: Princeton University Press.

KIM, S. (1982) *Contract Migration in the Republic of Korea* Working Paper 4. Geneva: ILO, International Migration for Employment Project.

KIM, S. (1983) 'Labor migration from Korea to the Middle East: its trends and impact on the Korean Economy'. Paper presented at the conference on Asian Labor Migration to the Middle East. Honolulu: East–West Population Centre.

KINDLEBERGER, C.P. (1978) 'The formation of financial centres', pp. 66–134 in *Economic Response: Comparative Studies in Trade, Finance and Growth*. Cambridge, MA: Harvard University Press. First published 1974.

KINDLEBERGER, C.P. (1984a) *Multinational Excursions*. Cambridge, MA: MIT Press.

KINDLEBERGER, C.P. (1984b) *A Financial History of Western Europe*. London: George Allen and Unwin.

KING, R. (1979) 'Return migration: a review of some case studies from Southern Europe', *Mediterranean Studies* 1(2): 3–30.

KING, R. (1984) 'Emigration, return migration and internal migration', in A. WILLIAMS (ed.) *Southern Europe Transformed*. New York: Harper and Row.

KING, R., J. MORTIMER, A. STRACHAN and A. TRONO (1985) 'Return migration and rural economic change: a South Italian case study', in R. HUDSON and J. LEWIS (eds) *Uneven Development in Southern Europe: Studies of Accumulation Class, Migration and the State*. London: Methuen.

KIRIM, A.S. (1986) 'Transnational corporations and local capital: comparative conduct and performance in the Turkish pharmaceutical industry', *World Development* 14(4): 503–21.

KNICKERBOCKER, F.T. (1973) *Oligopolistic Reaction and the Multinational Enterprise*. Cambridge, MA: Harvard University Press.

KOCKA, J. (1974) 'Organisierter Kapitalismus oder staatsmonopolistischer Kapitalismus. Begriffliche Vorbemerkungen', pp. 19–35 in H.A. WINKLER (ed.) *Organisierter Kapitalismus. Voraussetzungen und Anfänge*. Göttingen: Vandenhoeck und Ruprecht.

KOHL, J. (1983) 'Staatsausgaben', pp. 395–403 in D. NOHLEN (ed.) *Pipers Wörterbuch zur Politik* volume 2. Munich: Piper.

KOHL, J. (1985) *Staatsausgaben in Westeuropa. Analysen zur langfristigen Entwicklung der öffentlichen Ausgaben*. Frankfurt: Campus.

KOLTAY, J. (1986) 'Réforme économique et démocratie industrielle en Hongrie', *Revue d'études comparatives Est–Ouest* 2: 41–53.

KORBONSKI, A. (1975) 'Les aspects politiques des reformes économiques en Europe de l'est', *Revue d'études comparatives Est–Ouest* 1.

KORNAI, J. (1980) *Economics of Shortage*. Amsterdam/New York/Oxford: North Holland.

KORNAI, J. (1984) 'Shortage — fundamental problem of centrally planned economies and Hungarian reform', interview with A. JUTTA-PLETSCH in *Revue d'études comparatives Est–Ouest* 3: 13–14.

KORNAI, J. and X. RICHET (eds) (1986) *La voie hongroise. Analyse et expérimentation économiques*. Paris: Colman Levy.

KORPI, W. (1980) 'Social policy and distributional conflict in the capitalist democracies. A preliminary comparative framework', *West European Politics* 3: 296–316.

KOŹMIŃSKI, A.K. (1976) 'The role of the manager in the socialist economy', in J. BODDEWYN (ed.) *European Industrial Managers: West and East*. New York: International Arts and Sciences Publishers.

KOŹMIŃSKI, A.K. (1982) *Po Wielkim Szoku* (After a Big Shock). Warsaw: Państwowe Wydawnictwo Ekonomiczne.

KOŹMIŃSKI, A.K. (1986) 'Le development économique et la politique industrielle en Pologne. Le défi des années 1990', *Revue d'études comparatives Est–Ouest* 3: 107–17.

KOŹMIŃSKI, A.K., K. MREŁA, M. RAMUS and A. RYCHARD (1982) *Reforma Gospodarcza w Praktyce* (Economic Reform in Practice). Warsaw: TNOiK.

KOŹMIŃSKI, A.K. and K. OBŁOJ (eds) (1983) *Gry o Innowacje* (Innovation Games). Warsaw: Państwowe Wydawnictwo Ekonomiczne.

KOŹMIŃSKI, A.K. and K. OBŁOJ (1984) 'Collaboration de la recherche scientifique et de l'industrie à l'innovation technique', *Revue d'études comparatives Est–Ouest* 2: 89–95.

KRASNER, S.D. (ed.) (1983) *International Regimes*. Ithaca/London: Cornell University Press.

KRITZ, M.M., C.B. KEELY and S.M. TOMASI (eds) (1981) *Global Trends in Migration: Theory and Research on International Population Movements*. New York: Center for Migration Studies.

KRUEGER, A.O. and B. TUNCER (1982) 'An empirical test of the infant industry argument', *The American Economic Review* 72(5): 1142–52.

KUBAT, D. (ed.) (1984) *The Politics of Return: International Return Migration in Europe*. Rome: Centro Studi Emigrazione.

KUBAT, D. and H.-J. HOFFMAN-NOWOTNY (1982) 'International and internal migration: towards a new paradigm', in T. BOTTOMORE, S. NOWAK and M. SOKOLOWSKA (eds) *Sociology: the State of the Art*. Newbury Park, CA: SAGE Publications.

KUCZYŃSKI, W. (1981) *Po Wielkim Skoku* (After a Big Jump). Warsaw: Państwowe Wydawnictwo Ekonomiczne.

KUROWSKI, S. (1956) 'Demokracja i Prawo Wartości' (Democracy and value law). *Kierunki* 17 (19 August).

KUZNETS, S. (1966) *Modern Economic Growth: Rate, Structure and Spread*. New Haven: Yale University Press.

LAGUERRE, M. (1984) *American Odyssey: Haitians in New York*. Ithaca, NY: Cornell University Press.

LALL, S. (1978) 'Transnationals, domestic enterprises and industrial structure in host LCDs: a survey', *Oxford Economic Papers* 30(2): 217–48.

LALL, S. (ed.) (1983) *The New Multinationals: the Spread of Third World Enterprises*. Chichester: Wiley.

LALL, S. and P. STREETEN (1977) *Foreign Investment, Transnationals and Developing Countries*. Boulder, CO: Westview Press.

LANDES, D.S. (1960) 'The Bleichröder Bank: an interim report', pp. 201–20 in *Publications of the Leo Baeck Institute, Year Book V*. London: East and West Library.

LANDES, D.S. (1969) 'The old bank and the new: the financial revolution of the nineteenth century', pp. 112–27 in F. CROUZET, W.H. CHALONER and W.M. STERN (eds) *Essays in European Economic History 1789–1914*. London: Edward Arnold.

LANDES, D.S. (1979) *Bankers and Pashas: International Finance and Economic Imperialism in Egypt*. Cambridge, MA: Harvard University Press. First published 1958.

LANE, D. (1985) *Soviet Economy and Society*. Oxford: Basil Blackwell.

LANE, F.C. (1979) *Profits from Power: Readings in Protection Rent and Violence-controlling Enterprises*. Albany: State University of New York Press.

LANE, J.E. (1985) 'Introduction: public policy or markets? The demarcation problem', in J.E. LANE (ed.) *State and Market*. London: SAGE Publications.

LANGE, O. (1936) 'On the economic theory of socialism', *Review of Economic Studies* IV(1).

LAPPLE, D. (1985) 'Internationalization of capital and the regional problem', in J. WALTON (ed.) *Capital and Labor in the Urbanized World*. London: SAGE Publications.

LAPPLE, D. and P.V. HOOGSTRATEN (1980) 'Remarks on the spatial structure of capitalist development: the case of Netherlands', in J. CARNEY et al., (eds) *Regions in Crisis*. London: Croom Helm.

LAUTER, G.P. (1972) *The Manager and Economic Reform in Hungary*. New York: Praeger.

LAVIGNE, M. (1979) *Les économies socialises — soviétique et européenes*. Paris: Armand Colin.

LAYARD, R. and G. PSACHAROPOULOS (1974) 'The screening hypothesis and the return to education', *Journal of Political Economy* 82(5): 985–98.

LAZO, L.S. et al. (1982) *Contract Migration Policies in the Philippines* Working Paper 3. Geneva: International Migration for Employment Project.

LEE, E.S. (1966) 'A theory of migration', *Demography* 1: 47–57.

LENIN, V.I. (1985) 'Imperialismen som kapitalismens högsta stadium', pp. 402–522 in V.I. LENIN *Valda verk* volume 5. Goteborg: Fram. First published 1917.

LERNER, A.P. (1936/37) 'A note on socialist economics', *Review of Economic Studies* 4(1).

LERNER, A.P. (1938) 'Theory and practice in socialist economics', *Review of Economic Studies* 4.

LEWIS, W.A. (1959) *The Theory of Economic Growth*. London: Allen and Unwin.

LIGHT, I. (1972) *Ethnic Enterprise in America*. Berkeley, CA: University of California Press.

LIGHT, I. (1984) 'Immigrant and ethnic enterprise in North America', *Ethnic and Racial Studies* 7(2): 195–219.

LIM, L.Y.C. and PANG ENG FONG (1982) 'Vertical linkages and multinational enterprises in developing countries', *World Development* 10(7): 585–95.

LIN, CHING-YUAN (1973) *Industrialization in Taiwan 1946–72*. New York: Praeger.

LINDBLUM, C.E. (1977) *Politics and Markets: the World's Political Economic Systems*. New York: Basic Books.

LIPIŃSKI, J. and U. WOJCIECHOWSKA (eds) (1987) *Proces Wdraźania Reformy Gospodarczej* (Process of the Implementation of the Economic Reform). Warsaw: Państwowe Wydawnictwo Ekonomiczne.

LISLE-WILLIAMS, M. (1984a) 'Beyond the market: the survival of family capitalism in the English merchant banks', *British Journal of Sociology* 35(June): 241–71.

LISLE-WILLIAMS, M. (1984b) 'Coordinators and controllers of capital: the social and economic significance of the British merchant banks', *Social Science Information* 23: 95–128.

LISLE-WILLIAMS, M. (1984c) 'Merchant banking dynasties in the English class structure: ownership, solidarity and kinship in the City of London, 1850–1960', *British Journal of Sociology* 35(September): 333–62.

LUHMANN, N. (1984) *Soziale Systeme. Grundriss einer allgemeinen Theorie*. Frankfurt: Suhrkamp.

LU NANQUAN (1986) 'La réforme du système économique soviétique depuis l'arrivée au pouvoir de Gorbachev', *Revue d'études comparatives Est–Ouest* 1: 21–9.

LUTZ, B. (1982) 'Kapitalismus ohne Reservearmee? Zum Zusammenhang von Wirtschaftsentwicklung und Arbeitsmarktsegmentation in der europäischen Nachkriegszeit', pp. 329–47 in G. SCHMIDT et al. (eds) *Materialien zur Industriesoziologie*. (Special volume of *Kölner Zeitschrift für Soziologie und Sozialpsychologie*.)

MACFARLANE, A. (1978) *The Origins of English Individualism*. Oxford: Basil Blackwell.

MADDISON, A. (1987) 'Growth and slowdown in advanced capitalist economies: techniques of quantitative assessment', *Journal of Economic Literature* 25: 649–98.

MAGAZINER, I.C. and R.B. REICH (1982) *Minding America's Business. The Decline and Rise of American Industry*. New York: Vintage/Random House.

MAKLER, H.M., A. MARTINELLI and N.J. SMELSER (1982) 'Introduction', pp. 3–33 in H.M. MAKLER, A. MARTINELLI and N.J. SMELSER (eds) *The New International Economy*. Newbury Park, CA: SAGE Publications.

MALINOWSKI, B. (1922) *Argonauts of the western Pacific*. London: Routledge and Kegan Paul.

MALINOWSKI, R. (1986) *Reforma Gospodarcza — Zagadnienia Administracyjno-Prawne* (Economic Reform — Administrative Law Problems). Warsaw: IOZDiK.

MANASIAN, D. (1987) 'Gorbachev's economic revolution', *International Management* 42(9): 24–30.

MANGALAM, J.J. and H.K. SCHWARTZWELLER (1970) 'Some theoretical guidelines toward a sociology of migration', *International Migration Review* 4: 5–21.

MARCH, J.G. and H.A. SIMON (1959) *Organizations*. New York: John Wiley and Sons.

MARES, D. (1985) 'Explaining choice of development strategies: suggestions from Mexico 1970–1982', *International Organization* 39(4): 667–97.

MARS, G. and R. WARD (1984) 'Ethnic business development in Britain: opportunities and resources', in R. WARD and R. JENKINS (eds) *Ethnic Communities in Business*. Cambridge: Cambridge University Press.

MARSHALL, A. (1872) 'The future of the working classes', reprinted in A.C. PIGOU (ed.) (1925) *Memorials of Alfred Marshall*. London: Macmillan.

MARSHALL, T.H. (1950) *Citizenship and Social Class*. Cambridge: Cambridge University Press.

MARTINELLI, A. (1987) *Economia e sociétá* third edition. Milan: Communitá.

MARX, K. (1913) [1859] *Contribution to the Critique of Political Economy*. Chicago, IL: Kerr.

MARX, K. (1965) *Capital* volume 1. Moscow: Progress Publishers.

MARX, K. and F. ENGELS (1964) [1848] *The Communist Manifesto*. New York: Monthly Review Press.

Materijaly XXVII Siezda KPSS (Materials of the XXVIIth Congress of the CPSU) (1986). Moscow: Politizdat.

MATTELART, A. (1983) *Transnationals and the Third World: the Struggle for Culture*. South Hadley, MA: Bergin & Garvey.

MATTHEWS, R.C.O. (1968) 'Why has Britain had full employment since the war?', *Economic Journal* 78: 555–79.

MAUSS, M. (1954) *The Gift*. Glencoe, IL: The Free Press.

McCLELLAND, David (1961) *The Achieving Society*. Princeton, NJ: van Nostrand.

McCRACKEN, P. et al. (1977) 'Towards full employment and price stability. A report to the OECD by a group of independent experts'. Paris: OECD.

McMICHAEL, P. (1985) 'Britain's hegemony in the nineteenth-century world-economy', pp. 117–50 in P. EVANS, D. RUESCHEMEYER and E. HUBER-STEVENS (eds) *State Versus Markets in the World-Systems*. Newbury Park, CA: SAGE Publications.

MELLER, P. and A. MIZALA (1982) 'US multinationals and Latin American manufacturing employment absorption', *World Development* 10(2): 115–26.

MELOTTI, U. (1977) *Marx and the Third World*. London: Macmillan.

MENDELSOHN, M.S. (1980) *Money on the Move: the Modern International Capital Market*. New York: McGraw-Hill.

MEYER, D.R. (1986) 'The world system of cities: relations between international financial metropolises and South American cities', *Social Forces* 64: 553–81.

MEYER-FEHR, P. (1980) 'Technologische Kontrolle durch multinationale Konzerne und Wirtschaftswachstum', pp. 106–28 in V. BORNSCHIER (ed.) *Multinationale Konzerne, Wirtschaftspolitik und nationale Entwicklung im Weltsystem*. Frankfurt: Campus.

MICHALET, C.-A. (1976) *Le capitalisme mondial*. Paris: Presses Universitaires de France.

MICHALET, C.-A. (1979) 'Etats nations, firmes multinationales et capitalisme mondial' (Nation states, multinational firms and world capitalism), *Sociologie et sociétés* 11(2): 39–57.

MICHALET, C.-A. and R. COHEN (1978) 'Transnational banks and the integration of WCS (world capitalist systems)'. Paper presented at a conference of the International Sociological Association, Uppsala, Sweden.

MICHEL, A. (1983) 'Multinationales et inégalités de classe et de sèxe', *Current Sociology* 31(1): 1–211.

MILLER MARK, J. (1981) *Foreign Workers in Western Europe: an Emerging Political Force*. New York: Praeger.

MILLER MARK, J. (1986) 'Policy ad-hocracy: the paucity of co-ordinated perspectives and policies', p. 485 in *The Annals* AAPSS, May.

MINTZ, B. and M. SCHWARTZ (1985) *The Power Structure of American Business*. Chicago, IL: University of Chicago Press.

MIZRUCHI, M.S. (1982) *The American Corporate Network 1904–1974*. Newbury Park, CA: SAGE Publications.

MODGIL, S. and C. MODGIL (1987) *Arthur Jensen: Consensus and Controversy*. Lewes, Sussex: The Falmer Press.

MOFFIT, M. (1983) *The World's Money: International Banking from Bretton Woods to the Brink of Insolvency*. New York: Simon and Schuster.

MOORE Jr, B. (1966) *The Social Origins of Dictatorship and Democracy*. Boston, MA: Beacon Press.

MORAN, T.H. (1978) 'Multinational corporations and dependency: a dialogue for dependentistas and non-dependentistas', *International Organization* (Special issue on 'Dependence and dependency in the global system') 32: 79–100.

MORAWSKI, W. (ed.) (1983) *Demokracje i Gospodarka* (Democracy and Economy). Warsaw: Warsaw University Press.

MORISHIMA, M. (1976) *The Economic Theory of Modern Society*. Cambridge: Cambridge University Press.

MORISHIMA, M. (1982) *Why has Japan 'Succeeded'?* Cambridge: Cambridge University Press.

MOROKVASIC, M. (1984a) 'Strategies of return of Yugoslavs in France and the Federal Republic of Germany', in D. KUBAT (ed.) *Politics of Return: International Return Migration in Europe*. Rome: Centro Studi Emigrazione.

MOROKVASIC, M. (1984b) 'Editorial introduction', *Current Sociology* 32(2): 16–39. (Special issue on 'Migration in Europe'.)

MOROKVASIC, M., A. PHIZACKLEA and H. RUDOLPH (1986) 'Small firms and minority groups: contradictory trends in the French, German and British clothing industries', *International Sociology* 1(4): 397–419.

MORTON, A.L. (1938) *A People's History of England*. London: Lawrence and Wishart.

MÜLLER, R. and R.D. MORGENSTERN (1974) 'Multinational corporations and balance of payment impacts in LDCs: an econometric analysis of export pricing behaviour', *Kyklos* 27: 304–12.

MYRDAL, G. (1972) *Asian Drama: An Inquiry into the Poverty of Nations* abridged version. New York: Vintage Books.

NAGI, M.H. (1983) 'Asian labor migration to the Middle East: determinants of current trends and future outlook', *Conference on Asian Labor Migration to the Middle East*, East–West Center, Honolulu.

NAGY, T. (1970) 'On the expedient forms of reallocating capital in Hungarian society', *Acta Oeconomica* 5.

NELSON, B.N. (1949) *The Idea of Usury: from Tribal Brotherhood to Universal Otherhood*. Princeton, NJ: Princeton University Press.

NEWFARMER, R.S. (ed.) (1985) *Profits, Progress and Poverty*. Notre Dame, IN: University of Notre Dame Press.

NEWFARMER, R.S. and MARSH (1981) 'Foreign ownership, market structure and industrial performance: Brazil's electrical industry', *Journal of Development Economics* 8: 47–75.

NEWFARMER, R.S. and S. TOPIK (1982) 'Testing dependency theory: a case study of Brazil's electrical industry', in M. TAYLOR and N. THRIFT (eds) *The Geography of Multinationals*. London: Croom Helm.

NICHOLAS, S.J. (1982) 'British multinational investment before 1939', *The Journal of European Economic History* 11(3): 605–30.

NICHOLAS, S.J. (1983) 'Agency contracts, institutional modes and the transition to foreign direct investment by British multinationals before 1939', *Journal of Economic History* 153(3): 675–86.

NIEDERMAYER, O. (1979) *Multinationale Konzerne und Entwicklungsländer*. Königstein: Hain.

NORTH, D.C. (1987) *The Economics of Public Issues*. New York: Harper.

NOVE, A. (1977a) *Economic History of the USSR*. Harmondsworth: Penguin.

NOVE, A. (1977b) *The Soviet Economic System*. London: Allen and Unwin.

NYMAN, S. and A. SILBERSTON (1978) 'The ownership and control of industry', *Oxford Economic Papers* 30: 74–101.

OBERSCHALL, Anthony (1973) *Social Conflict and Social Movements*. Englewood Cliffs, NJ: Prentice Hall.

OCHEL, W. (1982) *Die Entwicklungsländer in der Weltwirtschaft*. Cologne: Bund Verlag.

O'DONNELL, G., P. SCHMITTER and L. WHITEHEAD (1986) *Transitions from Authoritarian Rule: Latin America*. Baltimore, MD: Johns Hopkins University Press.

OECD (ORGANISATION FOR ECONOMIC COOPERATION AND DEVELOPMENT) (1979) *The Impact of Newly Industrializing Countries on Production and Trade in Manufactures*. Paris: OECD.

OECD (1981) *International Investment and Multinational Enterprises: Recent International Direct Investment Trends*. Paris: OECD.

OECD (1987) *Historical Statistics 1960–1985*. Paris: OECD.

OECD (1989) *Economic Outlook*. Paris: OECD.

OFFE, C. (1987) 'Democracy against the welfare state? Structural foundations of neoconservative political opportunities', *Political Theory* 15: 501–37.

O'HANLON, R. (1985) *Caste, Conflict and Ideology*. Cambridge: Cambridge University Press.

OKUN, A.M. (1975) *Equality and Efficiency. The Big Trade Off*. Washington: The Brookings Institution.

OLLE, W. (1983) *Strukturveränderung der internationalen Direktinvestitionen und inländischer Arbeitsmarkt*. Munich: Minerva.

OLSON, M. (1968) *The Logic of Collective Action*. New York: Schocken Books.

OMVELDT, G. (1980) 'Migration in colonial India: the articulation of feudalism and capitalism by the colonial state', *Journal of Peasant Studies* 7(2): 185–212.

ÖNCÜ, A. (1987) 'Turkish migrants returning from Europe: a review of research', *Turkish Studies Association Bulletin* 11(2): 55–64.

ORNSTEIN, M. (1984) 'Interlocking directorates in Canada: intercorporate or class alliance', *Administrative Science Quarterly* 29: 210–31.

ŌTSUKA, H. (1955) A bibliographical introduction to the Japanese version of M. WEBER's *The Protestant Ethic and the Spirit of Capitalism*. Tokyo: Iwanami Library.

PAHL, R. (1984) *Divisions of Labour*. Oxford: Blackwell.

PAHL, R.E. and J.H. DENNETT (1981) 'Industry and employment in the Isle of Sheppey'. Work Strategies Unit Working Paper, University of Kent at Canterbury.

PAINE, S. (1974) *Exporting Workers: The Turkish Case*. Cambridge: Cambridge University Press.

PAJESTKA, J. (ed.) (1986) *Gospodarka w Procesie Reformowania* (Economy in the Process of Reform). Warsaw: Państwowe Wydawnictwo Ekonomiczne.

PAPEDEMETRIOU, D.G. (1983a) 'A retrospective look at Mediterranean labor migration to Europe', in C.F. PINKELE and A. POLIS (eds) *The Contemporary Mediterranean World*. New York: Praeger.

PAPADEMETRIOU, D.G. (1983b) 'Rethinking international migration: a review and a critique', *Comparative Political Studies* 15(4): 469–98.

PAPADEMETRIOU, D.G. (1984) 'Return in the Mediterranean Littoral: Policy Agendas', in D. KUBAT (ed.) *The Politics of Return: International Return Migration in Europe*. Rome: Centro Studi Emigrazione.

PARETO, V. (1935) *The Mind and Society*. New York: Harcourt, Brace, Jovanovich.

PARSONS, T. (1937) *The Structure of Social Action*. New York: McGraw-Hill.

PARSONS, T. (1954) 'The motivation of economic activities', in *Essays in Sociological Theory* revised edition. Glencoe, IL: The Free Press.

PARSONS, T. and N.J. SMELSER (1956) *Economy and Society. A Study in the Integration of Economic and Social Theory*. New York: The Free Press.

PAYER, C. (1974) *The Debt Trap: the International Monetary Fund and the Third World*. New York: Monthly Review Press.

PAYER, C. (1982) *The World Bank: A Critical Analysis*. New York: Monthly Review Press.

PAYNE, J. (1985) 'Changes in the youth labour market, 1974–1981', *Oxford Review of Education* 11(2): 167–79.

PAYNE, J. (1987) 'Does unemployment run in families? Some findings from the General Household Survey', *Sociology* 21(2): 199–214.

PAYNE, J. and C. PAYNE (1985) 'Youth unemployment 1974–1981: the changing importance of age and qualifications', *The Quarterly Journal of Social Affairs* 1(3): 177–92.

PEATTIE, L. (1987) 'An idea in good currency and how it grew: the informal sector', *World Development* 15(7): 851–60.

PEEK, P. and G. STANDING (eds) (1982) *State Policies and Migration: Studies in Latin America an the Caribbean*. London: Croom Helm.

PETRAS, E.M. (1980a) 'Towards a theory of international migration: the new division of labor', in B. LAPORTE (ed.) *Sourcebook on the New Immigration*. New Brunswick, NJ: Transaction.

PETRAS, E.M. (1980b) 'The role of national boundaries in a cross-national labour market', *International Journal of Urban and Regional Studies* 4(2): 157–95.

PETRAS, E.M. (1981) 'The global labour market in the modern world economy', in M. KRIZ et al. (eds) *Global Trends in Migration: Theory and Research on International Population Movements*. New York: Center for Migration Studies.

PFISTER, U. and C. SUTER (1986) 'Verschuldung im Weltsystem: eine systemtheoretische Analyse der internationalen Finanzbeziehungen, Schlussbericht zum Nationalfondsprojekt: Zu Struktur und Wandel des Weltsystems seit 1960'. Zurich: Sociological Institute (mimeo).

PIORE, M. (1979) *Birds of Passage: Migrant Labour and Industrial Societies*. Cambridge: Cambridge University Press.

PIORE, M. (1986) 'The shifting grounds for immigration', in *The Annals* 485(May): 23–33. AAPSS.

PIORE, M. and C. SABEL (1984) *The Second Industrial Divide. Possibilities for Prosperity*. New York: Basic Books.

PLACONE, D., H. ULBRICH and M. WALLACE (1985) 'The crowding out debate: it's over when it's over and it isn't over yet', *Journal of Post-Keynesian Economies* 8: 91–6.

POLANYI, K. (1957) *The Great Transformation*. Boston, MA: Beacon Press. First published 1944.

POLANYI, K. (1971) [1944] *The Great Transformation*. Boston, MA: Beacon Press.

POLANYI, K., C. ARENSBERG and H. PEARSON (1957) *Trade and Market in the Early Empires*. Glencoe, IL: The Free Press.

POMMEREHNE, W. and B. FREY (1981) 'Les modes d'évaluation de l'économie occulte', *Futuribles* 50.

PORTES, A. (1978a) 'Migration and underdevelopment', *Politics and Society* 8(1): 1–48.

PORTES, A. (1978b) 'Towards a structural analysis of illegal (undocumented) migration', *International Migration Review* 12(4): 469–84.

PORTES, A. (1981) 'Modes of structural incorporation and present theories of immigration', in M.M. KRITZ et al. (eds) *Global Trends in Migration*. New York: Center for Migration Studies.

PORTES, A. and R.L. BACH (1984) *Latin Journey, Cuban and Mexican Immigrants in the United States*. Berkeley: University of California Press.

PORTES, A. and S. SASSEN-KOOB (1987) 'Making it underground: comparative material on the informal sector in western market economies', *American Journal of Sociology* 93(1): 30–61.

PORTES, A. and J. WALTON (1981) *Labor, Class and the International System*. New York: Academic Press.

PREOBRAZHENSKY, E. (1927) 'Khoziaistwennoe Rawnowsie v Sistiemie SSSR' (Economic equilibrium in the Soviet system), *Vestnik Kommunisticheskoi Akademii* 22.

PREOBRAZHENSKY, E. (1966) *La nouvelle économique*. Paris: Presses Universitaires de France.

PUHLE, H.-J. (1984) 'Historische Konzepte des entwickelten Industriekapitalismus. "Organisierter Kapitalismus" und "Korporatismus"', *Geschichte und Gesellschaft* 10: 165–84.

RAFFE, D. (ed.) (1984) *Fourteen to Eighteen: The Changing Pattern of Schooling in Scotland*. Aberdeen: Aberdeen University Press.

RANIS, G. (1981) 'Challenges and opportunities posed by Asia's superexporters: implications for manufactured exports from Latin America', pp. 204–26 in W. BAER and M. GILLIS (eds) *Export Diversification and the New Protectionism*. Champaign, IL: National Bureau of Economic Research.

Reforma Gospodarcza: Propozycje, Tendencje, Kierunki Dyskusji (Economic Reform: Proposals, Tendencies, Discussion Trends) (1981). Warsaw: Państwowe Wydawnictwo Ekonomiczne.

REIFFERS, J.-L., A. CARTAPANIS, W. EXPERTON and J.-L. FUGUET (1982) *Transnational Corporations and Endogenous Development: Effects on Culture, Communication, Education and Science and Technology*. Paris: Unesco.

REPSZE, J. (1926) 'Naszi Ekonomiczeskie Problemy' (Our economic problems), *Planowoe Khoziaistwo* 2.

REUBER, G.L. (1973) *Private Foreign Investment in Development*. Oxford: Clarendon Press.

Revue d'études comparatives Est–Ouest (1975). (Special issue on 'Economic reform in Eastern Europe'.)

REX, J., D. JOLY and C. WILPERT (eds) (1987) *Immigrant Associations in Europe*. Aldershot: Gower Publishing.

REYNERI, E. and C. MUGHINI (1984) 'Return migration and sending areas: from the myth of development to the reality of stagnation', in D. KUBET (ed.) *The Politics of Return: International Return Migration in Europe*. Rome: Centro Studi Emigrazione.

ROBERTS, P. (1971) *Alienation and the Soviet Economy. Toward a General Theory of Marxian Alienation. Organizational Principles and the Soviet Economy*. Albuquerque: University of Mexico Press.

ROBERTSON, H.M. (1933) *Aspects of the Rise of Economic Individualism*. Cambridge: Cambridge University Press.

ROBINSON, J. (1948) *The Economics of Imperfect Competition*. London: Macmillan.

ROGERS, R. (ed.) (1985) *Guests Come to Stay: Effects of European Labor Migration on Sending and Receiving Countries*. Boulder, CO: Westview Press.

ROIZEN, J. and M. JEPSON (1985) *Degrees for Jobs: Employer Expectations of Higher Education*. Guildford, Surrey: SRHE and NFER-Nelson.

ROSE, R. (1984) *Understanding Big Government. The Programme Approach*. London: SAGE Publications.

ROSTOW, W.W. (1971) *The Stages of Economic Growth: A Non-communist Manifesto* second edition. London: Cambridge University Press.

ROTHGEB Jr, J.M. (1984) 'Investment penetration in manufacturing and extraction and external public debt in the third world states', *World Development* 12(11/12): 1063–76.

RUGMAN, A.M. (1981) *Inside the Multinationals*. London: Croom Helm.

RYCHARD, A. (1980a) *Reforma Gospodarcza. Socjologiczna Analiza Zwiazków Polityki i Gospodarki* (Economic Reform. Sociological Analysis of the Relationship between Politics and Economy). Wrocław, Warsaw: Ossolineum.

RYCHARD, A. (1980b) 'Politics and economics: the case of Polish economic reform', *International Studies of Management and Organization* 3: 27–39.

SACHS, I. (1981) 'L'économie cachée. Esquisse d'une problématique', *Dossier FIPAD* (Fondation Internationale pour un Autre Développement) 22.

SAHLINS, M. (1972) *Stone Age Economics*. Chicago, IL: Aldine-Atherton.

SAMUELSON, P. (1973) *Economics* ninth edition. Tokyo: McGraw-Hill Kogskusha Ltd.

SASSEN-KOOB, S. (1980) 'Immigrant and minority workers in the organization of the labor process', *The Journal of Ethnic Studies* 8(1): 1–34.

SASSEN-KOOB, S. (1981) 'Towards a conceptualization of immigrant labor', *Social Problems* 29(October): 65–85.

SASSEN-KOOB, S. (1982) 'Recomposition and peripheralization at the core', *Contemporary Marxism* 5(summer): 89–100. (Special issue 'The new nomads: immigration and change in the international division of labor'.)

SASSEN-KOOB, S. (1987) 'Issues of core and periphery: labor migration and global restructuring', in J. HENDERSON and M. CASTELLS (eds) *Global Restructuring and Territorial Development*. London: SAGE Publications.

SAUNDERS, P. and F. KLAU (1985) 'The role of the public sector. Causes and consequences of the growth of government', *OECD Economic Studies* 4.

SCASE, R. and R. GOFFEE (1982) *The Entrepreneurial Middle Class*. London: Croom Helm.

SCHARPF, F.W. (1987) *Sozialdemokratische Krisenpolitik in Westeuropa*. Frankfurt: Campus.

SCHIFF, M. and R. LEWONTIN, R. (1986) *Education and Class: The Irrelevance of IQ Genetic Studies*. Oxford: Oxford University Press.

SCHLUPP, F. (1985) 'Geschichte, Stand und Tendenzen der Diskussion über Multinationale Konzerne', pp. A1–A18 in P.H. METTLER (ed.) *Multinationale Konzerne in der Bundesrepublik Deutschland*. Frankfurt am Maine: Haag & Herchen.

SCHMIDT, G. (1969) 'The economic fundaments of the Renaissance', *International Review of Sociology* 5(1): 21–35.

SCHMIDT, M. (1983) 'The welfare state and the economy in periods of economic crisis: a comparative study of twenty-three OECD nations', *European Journal of Political Research* 11: 1–26.

SCHMITTER, P.C. (1979) 'Modes of interest intermediation and models of societal change in western Europe', pp. 63–94 in P.C. SCHMITTER and G. LEHMBRUCH (eds) *Trends towards Corporate Interest Intermediation*. Newbury Park, CA and London: SAGE Publications.

SCHNEIDER, F. and B.S. FREY (1985) 'Economic and political determinants of foreign direct investment', *World Development* 13(2): 161–75.

SCHULTZ, T.W. (1961) 'Investment in human capital', *American Economic Review*, 51: 1–17.

SCHUMPETER, J. (1934) *The Theory of Economic Development*. Cambridge, MA: Harvard University Press.

SCHUMPETER, J. (1939) *Business Cycles: a Theoretical, Historical and Statistical Analysis of the Capitalist Process*. New York: McGraw-Hill.

SCHUMPETER, J. (1943) *Capitalism, Socialism and Democracy* first edition. London: George Allen and Unwin.

SCHUMPETER, J. (1950) *Capitalism, Socialism and Democracy* second edition. New York: Harper.

SCHUMPETER, J. (1954) *The History of Economic Analysis*. New York: Oxford University Press.

SENGHAAS, D. and U. MENZEL (eds) (1976) *Multinationale Konzerne und Dritte Welt*. Opladen: Westdeutsche Verlag.

SEUROT, F. (1983) *Inflation et emploi dans les pays socialistes*. Paris: Presses Universitaires de France.

SHONFIELD, A. (1965) *Modern Capitalism. The Changing Balance of Public and Private Power*. London: Oxford University Press.

SHOUP, L.H. (1975) 'Shaping the post-war world: the Council on Foreign Relations and United States war aims during World War Two', *Insurgent Sociologist* 5(3): 9–52.

SHOUP, L.H. and MINTER (1977) *Imperial Brain Trust: the Council on Foreign Relations and United States Foreign Policy*. New York: Monthly Review Press.

SIMES, D.K. (1975) 'The Soviet parallel market', *Survey* 21(3): 97.

SIMON, H. (1957) *Models of Man: Social and Rational. Mathematical Essays on Rational Human Behavior in a Social Setting*. New York: Wiley.

SJAASTAD, L.A. (1962) 'The costs and returns of human migration', *The Journal of Political Economy* 70(5): 80–93.

SLATER, D. (1985) 'The state and issues of regional analysis in Latin America', in J. WALTON (ed.) *Capital and Labor in the Urbanized World*. London: SAGE Publications.

SMILGA, I. (1926) 'Piat Let Nepa' (Five years of NEP), *Płanowoe Khoziaistwo* 2.

SMITH, A. (1937) *The Wealth of Nations*. New York: Modern Library.

SMOLAR, A. (1974) 'Utopie et science: l'économie politique dans la vision Marxienne du communisme et pendant l'industrialisation soviétique', *Revue de l'est* 4: 109–10.

SOLINAS, G. (1982) 'Labor market segmentation and workers' careers: the case of the Italian knitwear industry', *Cambridge Journal of Economics* 6: 331–52.

SOOS, K.A. (1985) 'Planification impérative, régulation financière, grandes orientations et compagnes', *Revue d'études comparatives Est–Ouest* 2: 45–61.

SPENGLER, J.J. and G.G. MYERS (1977) 'Migration and socio-economic development: today and yesterday', in A.A. BROWN and

E. NEUBERG (eds) *Internal Migration: A Comparative Perspective*. New York: Academic Press.

SPULBER, N. (1964) *Soviet Strategy for Economic Growth*. Bloomington, IN: Indiana University Press.

STALEY, E. (1935) *War and the Private Investor: a Study of the Relationship of International Politics and International Private Investment*. Chicago, IL: University of Chicago Press.

STALLINGS, B. (1982) 'Euromarkets, third world countries and the international political economy', pp. 193–230 in H. MAKLER, A. MARTINELLI and N.J. SMELSER (eds) *The New International Economy*. Newbury Park, CA: SAGE Publications.

STALLINGS, B. (1990) 'The role of foreign capital in economic development', in G. GEREFFI and D. WYMAN (eds) *Manufacturing Miracles: Paths of Industrialization in Latin America and East Asia*. Princeton, NJ: Princeton University Press.

STERN, F. (1979) *Gold and Iron: Bismarck, Bleichröder and the building of the German Empire*. New York: Vintage. First published 1977.

STIGLER, G.J. (1961) 'The economics of information', *Journal of Political Economy* 69: 213–25.

STIGLITZ, J.E. (1986) *Economics of the Public Sector*. New York: W.W. Norton and Company.

STOKMAN, F.N., R. ZIEGLER and J. SCOTT (eds) (1985) *Networks of Corporate Power: a Comparative Analysis of Ten Countries*. Cambridge: Polity Press.

STRACHEY, J. (1956) *Contemporary Capitalism*. London: Victor Gollancz Ltd.

STREECK, W. and P.C. SCHMITTER (1985) 'Community, market state and associations? The prospective contribution of interest governance to social order', *European Sociological Review* 1: 119–38.

SULLIVAN, G. (1983) 'Uneven development and national income inequality in third world countries: a cross-national study of the effects of external economic dependence', *Sociological Perspectives* 26(2): 201–31.

SUNKEL, O. and P. PAZ (1970) *El subdesarrollo latinoamericano y la teoría del desarrollo*. Mexico D.F.: Siglo Ventiuno.

SVEDBERG, P. (1978) 'The portfolio: direct composition of private foreign investment in 1914 revisited', *Economic Journal* 88: 763–77.

SWEDBERG, R. (1986) 'The doctrine of economic neutrality of the IMF and the World Bank', *Journal of Peace Research* 23(4): 377–90.

SWEDBERG, R. (1987) *Sociologists Look at Banks*. Stockholm: University of Stockholm, Department of Sociology.

Taiwan Statistical Data Book 1987 (1987) Taipei, Taiwan: Council for Economic Planning and Development.

TANZI, V. (ed.) (1982) *The Underground Economy in the United States and Abroad*. Lexington, KY: Lexington Books.

TAWNEY, R.H. (1977) *Religion and the Rise of Capitalism*. London: Pelican Books.

TEICHLER, U. (1984) in AVAKOV, R. et al. *Higher Education and Employment in the USSR and in the Federal Republic of Germany*. Paris: Unesco, International Institute for Educational Planning.

TEICHOVA, A., M. LEVY-LEBOYER and H. NUSSBAUM (eds) (1986) *Multinational Enterprise in Historical Perspective*. Cambridge and Paris: Cambridge University Press and Editions de la Maison de la Sciences de l'Homme.

The Banker (1984) 'Banking tomorrow — communications', October: 73–6.

The Economist (1987a) 'International banking: a game of skill as well', 21 March: 3–70.

The Economist (1987b) 'Euromarkets: now for the lean years', 16 May: 4–34.

THUROW, L.C. (1975) *Generating Inequality: Mechanisms of Distribution in the US Economy*. New York: Basic Books.

THUROW, L.C. (1981) 'Equity, efficiency, social justice and redistribution', pp. 137–50 in OECD *The Welfare State in Crisis*.

TIMBERLAKE, M. and J. KENTOR (1983) 'Economic dependence, overurbanization and economic growth: a study of less developed countries', *Sociological Quarterly* 24(4): 489–508.

TIMBERLAKE, M. and K.R. WILLIAMS (1984) 'Dependence, political exclusion and government repression: some cross-national evidence', *American Sociological Review* 9(1): 141–6.

TITMUSS, R.M. (1958) *Essays on the Welfare State*. London: Allen and Unwin.

TODARO, M.P. (1976) 'International migration in developing countries: a review of the theory', *Evidence, Methodology and Research Priorities*. Geneva: ILO.

TOMAS, P.A. (ed.) (1970) *The Changing Face of Communism in Eastern Europe*. Tucson, AZ: University of Arizona Press.

TOMAS, P.A. (1983) 'Overseas employment in the Philippines: policies and programs'. Paper presented at the conference on Asian Migration to the Middle East. Honolulu: East–West Population Center.

TREVELYAN, G.M. (1944) *English Social History*. London: Pelican.

TROW, M. (1961) 'The second transformation of American secondary education', *International Journal of Comparative Society* 2: 144–66.

TROW, M. (1961) 'Problems in the transition from elite to mass higher education', pp. 55–101 in OECD *Policies for Higher Education*.

TROW, M. (1987) 'Comparative perspectives on higher education policy in UK and US', *Oxford Review of Education* 14(1).

TSAKOK, I. (1982) 'The export of manpower from Pakistan to the Middle East, 1975–1985', *World Development* 10(4): 319–25.

TURNER, B.S. (1986) *Citizenship and Capitalism. The Debate over Reformism*. London: Allen and Unwin.

US News and World Report (1985) 'The air goes out of Asia's business balloon', 16 December: 48–9.

UNGER, K. (1984) 'Occupational profile of returnees in three Greek cities', in D. KUBAT (ed.) *The Politics of Return: International Return Migration in Europe*. Rome: Centro Studi Emigrazione.

UNITED NATIONS (1978) *Transnational Corporations in Development: a Re-examination*. New York: UNCTNC.

UNITED NATIONS (1983) *Transnational Corporations in World Development, 3rd Survey*. New York: UNCTNC.

USEEM, M. (1980) 'Corporations and the corporate elite', *Annual Review of Sociology* 6: 41–77.

USEEM, M. (1984) *The Inner Circle: Large Corporations and the Rise of Business Political Activity in the U.S. and the United Kingdom*. New York: Oxford University Press.

VAN AMERSFOORT, H., P. MUUS and R. PENNINX (1984) 'International migration, the economic crisis and the state: an analysis of Mediterranean migration to western Europe', *Ethnic and Racial Studies* 7(2).

VEBLEN, T. (1953) [1899] *The Theory of the Leisure Class: An Economic Study of Institutions*. New York: New American Library.

VERNON, R. (1971) *Sovereignty at Bay: the Multinational Spread of U.S. Enterprises*. New York/London: Basic Books.

VERNON, R. (1973) *The Economic and Political Consequences of Multinational Enterprise* second edition. Boston, MA: Graduate School of Business Administration, Harvard University.

VERNON, R. (1979) 'The product cycle hypothesis in a new international environment', *Oxford Bulletin of Economics and Statistics* 41(4): 255–67.

VERNON, R. (1985) *Exploring the Global Economy*. Lanham, MD: University Press of America.

VILLARREAL, R. (1983) *La contrarevolución monetarista*. Mexico D.F.: Siglo Ventiuno.

VOGT, W. (1983) 'Warum gibt es Massenarbeitslosigkeit?', *Leviathan* 11: 376–93.

WACHTEL, H. (1980) 'A decade of international debt', *Theory and Society* 9: 504–18.

WADE, R. (1990) 'Industrial policy in East Asia — does it lead or follow the market?', in G. GEREFFI and D. WYMAN (eds) *Manufacturing Miracles: Paths of Industrialization in Latin America and East Asia*. Princeton, NJ: Princeton University Press.

WAGNER, A. (1876) Grundlegung der politischen Oekonomie. Teil I: Grundlagen der Volkswirthschaft. Leipzig: Winter.

WAKAR, A. (ed.) (1965) *Zarys Teorii Gospodarki Socjalistycznej* (An Outline of the Theory of the Socialist Economy). Warsaw: Państwowe Wydawnicto Naukowe.

WAKAR, A. (ed.) (1969) *Teoria Pieniadza w Gospodarce Socjalistycznej* (Theory of Money in the Socialist Economy). Warsaw: Państwowe Wydawnicto Naukowe.

WALDINGER, R. (1984) 'Immigrant enterprise in the New York garment industry', *Social Problems* 32(1): 60–71.

WALDINGER, R. (1985) 'Immigration and industrial change: a case study of the New York apparel industry', in M. TIENDA and G. BORJAS (eds) *Hispanic Workers in the United States Economy*. New York: Academic Books.

WALDINGER, R., R. WARD and H. ALDRICH (1985) 'Trend report: ethnic business and occupational mobility in advanced societies', *Sociology* 19(1): 586–97.

WALLERSTEIN, I. (1974) (1980) *The Modern World-system* volumes I and II. New York: Academic Press.

WALLERSTEIN, I. (1979) *The Capitalist World Economy*. Cambridge: Cambridge University Press.

WALLERSTEIN, I. (1980) *The Modern World System II: Mercantilism and the Consolidation of the European World Economy 1600–1750*. New York: Academic Press.

WALLERSTEIN, I. (1984) *The Politics of the World Economy: the States, the Movements and the Civilizations*. Cambridge: Cambridge University Press.

WALTON, J. (ed.) (1985) *Capital and Labour in the Urbanized World*. Newbury Park, CA: SAGE Publications.

WARD, A. (1975) 'European capitalism's reserve army', *Monthly Review* 27(7): 24–36.

WARREN-PIPER, D. (ed.) (1981) *Is Higher Education Fair?* Papers presented to the 17th annual conference of the Society for Research into Higher Education, Manchester. Guildford, Surrey: SRHE.

WEBER, M. (1920 Vol. I; 1921 Vol. II; 1922 Vol. III) *Gesammelte Aufsätze zur Religionssoziologie*, J.C.B. Mohr (Paul Siebeck).

WEBER, M. (1927) *Wirtschaftsgeschichte, Abriss der universalen Sozial- und Wirtschaftsgeschichte* [1924, Leipzig: *General Economic History*]. Translated by F.H. Knight. New York: The Free Press.

WEBER, M. (1930) *The Protestant Ethic and the Spirit of Capitalism*. London: George Allen and Unwin.

WEBER, M. (1947) *The Theory of Social and Economic Organization*. Translated by A.M. Henderson and Talcott Parsons. New York: Oxford University Press.

WEBER, M. (1956) *Wirtschaft und Gesellschaft, Grundriss der verstehenden Soziologie*, J.C.B. Mohr (P. Siebeck); G. ROTH and C. WITTICH (eds) (1978) *Economy and Society*. University of California Press.

WELLS, L.T., Jr. (1983) *Third World Multinationals: The Rise of Foreign Investment from Developing Countries*. Cambridge, MA: MIT Press.

WERBNER, P. (1984) 'Business on trust: Pakistani entrepreneurship in the Manchester garment trade', in R.WARD and R. JENKINS (eds) *Ethnic Communities in Business*. Cambridge: Cambridge University Press.

WIATR, J.J. (1979) *Przyczynek do Zagadnienia Rozwoju Społecznego w Formacji Socjalistycznej* (Annexe to the Problem of Social Development in Socialist Formation). Warsaw: Ksiażka i Wiedza.

WIENER, M.J. (1981) *English Culture and the Decline of the Industrial Spirit 1850–1980*. Cambridge: Cambridge University Press.

WILES, P. (1982) 'Are there any communist economic cycles?', *ACES Bulletin* 2.

WILKINS, M. (1970) *The Emergence of Multinational Enterprise: American Business Abroad from the Colonial Era to 1914*. Cambridge, MA: Harvard University Press.

WILKINS, M. (1974) *The Maturing of Multinational Enterprise: American Business Abroad from 1914 to 1970*. Cambridge, MA: Harvard University Press.

WILKINSON, F. (ed.) (1981) *The Dynamics of Labor Market Segmentation*. London: Academic Press.

WILLIAMSON, W. (1979) *Education, Social Structure and Development: A Comparative Analysis*. London: Macmillan.

WILLIAMSON, O.E. (1981) 'The modern corporation: origins, evolution, attributes', *Journal of Economic Literature* 19(December): 1537–68.

WILLIS, P. (1977) *Learning to Labour: How Working Class Kids get Working Class Jobs*. London: Saxon House.

WILSON, K.L. and A. PORTES (1980) 'Ethnic enclaves: a comparison of the Cuban and black economies in Miami', *American Journal of Sociology* 88(2): 295–319.

WINDOLF, P. (1985) 'Mass universities for the many: elite universities for the few'. Paper presented to the Anglo-German Conference on Educational Expansion and Partisan Dealignment, Frankfurt 1985.

WOLPE, H. (1972) 'Capitalism and cheap labour power in South Africa', *Economy and Society* 1(4): 425–56.

WOOD, C.H. (1982) 'Equilibrium and historical-structural models of migration', *International Migration Review* 16(2): 299–319.

WOOD, R. (1985) 'The aid regime and international debt: crisis and structural adjustment', *Development and Change* 16: 179–212.

YOUNG, M. (1958) *The Rise of the Meritocracy, 1870–2033*. London: Thames and Hudson.

YOUNG, M.F.D. (1971) *Knowledge and Control*. London: Collier-Macmillan.

YUDELMAN, M. (1976) 'The role of agriculture in integrated rural development projects: the experience of the World Bank', *Sociologia Ruralis* 16(4): 308–25.

ZAFANOLLI, W. (1985) 'Chine: de la transition socialiste à la transition capitaliste', *Revue d'études comparatives Est–Ouest* 4: 5–46.

ZALESKI, E. (1975) 'Reorganisations administrative ou réforme du système', *Revue d'études comparatives Est–Ouest* 1: 51.

ZAPF, W. (1986) 'Development, structure and prospects of the German social state', in R. ROSE and R. SHIRATORI (eds) *The Welfare State. East and West*. New York: Oxford University Press.

ZIELIŃSKI J.G. (1973) *Economic Reforms in Polish Industry*. London: Oxford University Press.

ZIELIŃSKI J.G. (1986) *Rachunek Ekonomiczny w Socjaliźmie* (Economic Calculation in Socialism). Warsaw: Państwowe Wydawnicto Naukowe.

ZOLBERG, A.R. (1981) 'International migrations in political perspective', in M. KRITZ et al. (eds) *Global Trends in Migration: Theory and Research in International Population Movements*. New York: Center for Migration Studies.

ZOLBERG, A.R. (1983) 'Contemporary transnational migrations in historical perspective: patterns and dilemmas', in M.M. KRITZ (ed.) *US Immigration and Refugee Policy*. Lexington, KY: Lexington Books.

ZWASS, A. (1978/79) 'Money, Banking and Credit in the Soviet Union and Eastern Europe', *Eastern European Economics* (fall/winter).

Index